ATLA BIBLIOGRAPHY SERIES
edited by Dr. Kenneth E. Rowe

The Book of Amos

An Annotated Bibliography

Henry O. Thompson

ATLA Bibliographies, No. 42

The Scarecrow Press, Inc.
Lanham, Md., & London
1997

SCARECROW PRESS, INC.

Published in the United States of America
by Scarecrow Press, Inc.
4720 Boston Way
Lanham, Maryland 20706

4 Pleydell Gardens, Folkestone
Kent CT20 2DN, England

British Library Cataloguing in Publication Information Available

Library of Congress Cataloging-in-Publication Data

Thompson, Henry O.
    The book of Amos : an annotated bibliography / Henry O. Thompson.
        p.   cm. — (ATLA bibliography series ; no. 42)
    Includes bibliographical references and indexes.
    ISBN 0-8108-3274-7 (cloth : alk. paper)
    1. Bible. O.T. Amos—Bibliography. I. Title. II. Series
Z7772.C1T46   1997
[(BS1585.2)]
016.224'8—dc21   97-11933

ISBN 0-8108-3274-7 (cloth : alk. paper)

♾™ The paper used in this publication meets the minimum requirements of
American National Standard for Information Sciences—Permanence of
Paper for Printed Library Materials, ANSI Z39.48–1984.
Manufactured in the United States of America.

In Honorem

William & Dorothy

Adams

CONTENTS

SERIES EDITOR'S FOREWORD

The American Theological Library Association has been publishing this bibliography series with Scarecrow Press since 1974. Guidelines for projects and selections for publication are made by the ATLA Publications Section in consultation with the editor. Our goal is to stimulate and encourage the preparation and publication of reliable bibliographies and guides to the literature of religious studies in all of its scope and variety. Compilers are free to define their field, to make their own selections, and to work out internal organization as the unique demands of the subject indicate. We are pleased to publish Henry O. Thompson's *The Book of Amos: An Annotated Bibliography*.

The author studied at Iowa State (BSc), Drew (MDiv, PhD), Syracuse (MSc Education), Jersey City State (MA Educational Psychology), Diploma (School Psychology), post-graduate Rutgers, Newark (psychology). He was a Diplomate, American Institute of Human Relations. He has published 48 books (e.g., *Biblical Archaeology, The Authority of the Bible, World Religions in War and Peace*, an annotated bibliography on Daniel; with Joyce E. Thompson, *Ethics in Nursing*, etc.; edited and co-edited works on world religions, moral development, Africa, Carl Michalson) and several hundred articles and reviews. He was born in Iowa, had two sons (a lawyer in New Jersey; a doctor in Tennessee), had active duty in the U.S. Air Force, served churches in Minnesota and New Jersey, excavated at Shechem, Hesban, the Amman (Jordan) area, and served as director of the American Center for Oriental Research. He lectured on archaeology in Hong Kong, Jordan, and the United States. He taught at Upsala, The University of Amman, Jersey City State College, Oberlin, Eastern,

Colgate-Rochester, Syracuse, New York Theological Seminary, and the School of Nursing/Medical University of South Carolina. Until his death in April 1997, he taught Bible and ministry at the Unification Theological Seminary, and ethics in the School of Nursing, University of Pennsylvania. He and Dr. Joyce E. Thompson have lectured on ethics in Australia, Colombia, Spain, Russia, Kenya, and various U.S. locations. He was a member of the Carl Michalson Society, the Archaeological Institute of America, the American Schools of Oriental Research, the Professors' World Peace Academy, the Faith and History Association, the North Central Conference (United Methodist Church), and was an affiliate of the Eastern Pennsylvania Conference.

PREFACE

This bibliography is one of several on books of the Bible. The general rubric for this work is that it should be representative, with comprehensive coverage of works since World War II and greater selectivity for works from earlier years. Comprehensive is not exhaustive. It usually means these works are available, although a few items might be known but not available. The annotation is selective (basic information, judgments and cross-references as appropriate), especially for foreign language items, but on the whole it should be sufficient. Readers can be of service in several ways. Please notify the author of the appearance of materials after this volume has been published, as it may see a revised edition. You may wish to include corrections; perfection is an ideal dreamed, seldom attained. Finally, if users know the source of unavailable items, this author would appreciate the information. The bibliography is useful for Bible students at any level, and we are all students of the Bible, or we are fooling ourselves. It should of value to laity and professionals and groups interested in the Book of Amos. It is of course a reference work at home in libraries of many kinds.

There are several things this volume is not. As a bibliography, it is not a commentary nor is it the standard introduction to Amos, his life or time, although it includes a brief overview of Amos. Commentaries and introductions do appear as items in the text. Similarly, this is not a history of scholarly interpretation, although such items appear and continued use of the text might give some sense of such history. There are many items on prophecy but the bibliography is on Amos, not prophecy per se.

Within the text, there are items on his visions but the present volume is not on visions per se. Some references seek the meaning of a phrase which involves Amos and were included because the Amos reference seemed significant to be worthy of attention. Some references to Amos may be too minimal to include here. This is a judgment call; one would not expect everyone to agree with the judgment to include or exclude but hopefully the present work is more inclusive than exclusive and will serve most people in a very significant way. There is no comprehensive review of material for children, music, or fiction, although some examples are included. Book reviews are not normally included.

Most items are in English although a number of non-English, mostly European, items are available. The bibliography should be helpful for doctoral work. Dissertations have been listed in a separate appendix. Most are available from University Microfilms (Ann Arbor, MI). Items seen are in the main text, including published dissertations, sometimes in revised form. Many have been summarized in DAI, now available on computer disks, updated periodically.[1] Others have been referenced in the literature and not seen by this author but were included in this list to increase its usefulness. Anyone who knows of other dissertations on Amos is welcome to share this for future editions.

References are listed by author. Where names have several spellings, e.g., Woude or van der Woude, the item is listed with the more normative. The author index has the variants, other authors, editors. Subject and scripture indices will guide the user to specifics. It is useful to know the journals where studies of Amos are found so these are listed in an appendix. Abbreviations and sources for the work are in the front matter.

The titles of biblical books have been abbreviated when they appear in the titles of articles as part of a notation, e.g., Jer 3:1, except where to do so might cause confusion. The notation of biblical references has been made in the same style. Journals are cited by arabic numerals.

A special thank you to all the libraries and librarians who have made this work possible, and to Dr. Kenneth Rowe who has facilitated its appearance.

NOTE

1. Dissertation Abstracts International. Ann Arbor, MI: University Microfilms. DAI appears in units, e.g., Section A, Humanities and Social Sciences, Part 2, Philosophy and Religion. The second half of each monthly volume has key words, e.g., "Amos." North American

dissertations are in the Comprehensive Dissertation Index, e.g., 1988 Supplement vol 4, Social Sciences and Humanities, Part 2, Philosophy and Religion (pp. 559-625). The Dissertation Abstracts Ondiscs has DAI on computer disk. The 1861-June 1980 listings do not have abstracts. Abstracts are included from July 1980.   NB: Several indices list dissertations, e.g., ETL, IZBG, Langevin.

SOURCES

Ackroyd, Peter R., ed. *Bible Bibliography 1967-1973 Old Testament: The Book Lists of the Society for Old Testament Study 1967-1973*. Oxford: Basil Blackwell, 1974. 505 pp.

American Doctoral Dissertations [ADD]. Ann Arbor: University Microfilms International. Earlier titles and publishers vary.

Anderson, George Wishart, ed. *A Decade of Bible Bibliography: The Book Lists of the Society for Old Testament Study 1957-1966*. Oxford: Basil Blackwell, 1967. 706 pp.

Bible Bibliography see Langevin

Bible Bibliography 1967-1973 Old Testament: The Book Lists of the Society for Old Testament Study 1967-1973 ed Peter R. Ackroyd. Oxford: Basil Blackwell, 1974. 505 pp.

Botterweck, G. Johannes and Helmer Ringgren. *Theological Dictionary of the Old Testament*. Grand Rapids: Eerdmans, 1974- [vol. 1, rev, 1979].

The Catholic Periodical and Literature Index [CP&LI]. Haverford, PA: Catholic Library Association, 1940-.

Childs, Brevard S. *Old Testament Books for Pastors & Teachers* Philadelphia: Westminster, 1977. 120 pp. Author index.

Christian Periodical Index [CPI]. Buffalo, NY: Christian Librarians' Fellowship, 1956-. [preface says 1956-60 vol. is 3rd issue]

Danker, F.W. *Multipurpose Tools for Bible Study*, 3rd ed. St Louis: Concordia, 1970.

A Decade of Bible Bibliography: The Book Lists of the Society for Old Testament Study 1957-1966 ed George Wishart Anderson. Oxford: Basil Blackwell, 1967. 706 pp.

Dissertation Abstracts International. Ann Arbor, MI: University Microfilms. Issued in units, e.g., Section A, Humanities and Social Sciences, Part 2, Philosophy and Religion. The second half of each monthly volume has key words, e.g., "Amos." North American dissertations are in the *Comprehensive Dissertation Index*, e.g., 1988 Supplement, vol. 4, Social Sciences and Humanities, Part 2, Philosophy and Religion (pp. 559-625). The Dissertation Abstracts Ondiscs has the DAI on disk, 1861-June 1980, without abstracts; July 80+ with abstracts. NB: Several indices list dissertations, e.g., ETL, IZBG, Langevin.

"Elenchus Bibliographicus Biblicus." part of *Biblica*. Rome: Biblical Institute Press, 1920-1949. replaced by
Elenchus Bibliographicus Biblicus. ibid., 1950-1967. bound separately. replaced by
Elenchus Bibliographicus Biblicus. ibid., 1968-1985. replaced by
Elenchus of Biblica. ibid., 1985-.

"Elenchus Bibliographicus." A number (issue) of *Ephemerides Theologicae Lovanienses* [ETL]. Louvain, Belgium. 1924-.

Fitzmyer, Joseph A. *An Introductory Bibliography for the Study of Scripture*, 3rd ed. Rome: Pontifico Instituto Biblico, 1990. original, Glanzman, G.S. and Fitzmyer. Woodstock Papers No. 5. Westminster: Newman, 1961. xix + 135 pp.

Gorman, G.E. and Lyn Gorman. *Theological and Religious Reference Materials: General Resources and Biblical Studies*, vol. 1. Westport, CT: Greenwood Press, 1984. xvi + 526 pp.

Gottcent, John H. *The Bible as Literature: A Selective Bibliography*. Boston: Hall, 1979. 170 pp.

Hupper, William G., comp. and ed. *An Index to English Periodical Literature on the Old Testament and Ancient Near Eastern Studies.* ATLA Bibliography Series No. 21. London/Metuchen, NJ: ATLA/ Scarecrow Press. 1 (1987), lvi + 516; 2 (1988), xxxviii + 502; 3 (1990), xxxvii + 783; 4 (1990), xlvii + 544; 5 (1992), xliv + 708 pp.; 6 (1994), lii + 728 pp.

Index to Jewish Periodicals [IJP]. Cleveland Heights, OH: JP, 1963-.

Internationale Zeitschriftenschau fur Bibelwissenschaft und Grenzgebiete [IZBG] (International periodical review for biblical studies and related areas). Stuttgart: Katholisches Bibelwerk, 1951ff. Dusseldorf: Patmos, 1986-.

IZBG. *Internationale Zeitschriftenschau fur Bibelwissenschaft und Grenzgebiete*

Kelly, Balmer H. and Donald G. Miller. *Tools for Bible Study.* Richmond: Knox, 1956.

Langevin, Paul-Emile, ed. *Biblical Bibliography.* Quebec: Laval, 1972. Vol. 1 covers 1930-70; vol. 2, 1930-75; vol. 3, 1930-83. Each volume expands the number of journals and works, from an initial 70 Roman Catholic periodicals in French, English, German, Italian, Spanish and Portuguese, plus a number of Catholic works, particularly in French, English and German. The volumes are divided into sections. The first is for introductory material, the second for OT, third for NT, fourth for Christ, the fifth for biblical themes.

McPhail, David, ed. *A Basic Bibliography for Ministers*, 2nd ed. NY: Union Theological Seminary, 1960. 139 pp.

Minor, Mark. *Literary-Critical Approaches to the Bible: An Annotated Bibliography.* West Cornwall, CT: Locust Hill, 1992.

OT - see Ackroyd; Anderson; Botterweck; Childs; OTA.

Old Testament Abstracts. Washington, D.C.: Catholic Biblical Association, Catholic University of America, 1978-.

Religion Index One - Periodicals. Chicago: American Theological Library Association, 1949ff.

Religion Index Two - Multi-Author Works. Ibid., no volume number. The first volume, 1960, is for 10 years so the series starts with 1950.

Religious and Theological Abstracts. Myerstown, PA: RTA, 1958-.

Theological Dictionary of the Old Testament ed G. Johannes Botterweck and Helmer Ringgren. Grand Rapids: Eerdmans, 1974-. [Vol. 1, rev 1979]

van der Wal, Adri. *Amos. A Classified Bibliography* 3rd ed. *Applicatio, Computer Application in Theology* 3rd ed H. Leene and E. Talstra. Amsterdam: Free University, 1986. xv + 283 pp. (original, 1981) lst ed. Dutch; 2nd ed. Eng; works published 1800-1983. The third edition has an additional 500 titles. Items are listed with minimal reference, e.g., "Bic, M. Das Buch Amos. Berlin (1969)." The first unit refers to commentaries on the minor prophets. The second is on Amos in general. The bulk of the references are sequential, verse by verse.

INTRODUCTION

The Hebrew Bible, the Jewish Tanakh or the Christian Old Testament, is historically divided into three sections. The Torah or Pentateuch (five scrolls) is the first five biblical books, traditionally called The Five Books of Moses. The Nabiim, or Prophets in Hebrew, are divided into the Former Prophets (historical books: Joshua, Judges, Samuel and Kings) and Latter Prophets (The Prophets: Isaiah, Jeremiah, Ezekiel and the Twelve). The Kethubim or Writings include the Psalms, Wisdom literature, Daniel, etc. In the Hebrew text, known now most commonly as the Massoretic Text (MT)[1] and dating from the tenth century CE,[2] Amos is with the Twelve, commonly called the Minor Prophets because these works are shorter than the Great (longer books) Prophets of Isaiah, Jeremiah and Ezekiel. Amos comes after Hosea and Joel in many arrangements, so Amos is the third Minor Prophet according to the MT, but second in the LXX (Septuagint, the Greek version of the Tenakh). Historically, Amos is the first of the 12.

History

King David (c 1000-960 BCE) followed King Saul (c 1020-1000), and created an empire which he left to his son Solomon (c 960-922) who kept it more or less intact. The seeds of division were already there, however. Historians disagree on how far back the tribal divisions of the Hebrews really go. The biblical picture is of 12 tribes descended from Jacob, grandson of Abraham. David was king in Hebron, over the tribe of Judah, for seven years. After the death of King Saul's son Ishba'al, leaders of the northern tribes asked David to be their king also. Solomon's son Rehoboam (c 922-915) was readily accepted as king in Judah. However, Solomon had favored Judah and taxed the northerners more heavily. Now the northern tribes wanted tax relief. Rehoboam refused. The north revolted to form the separate kingdom of Israel under the leadership of Jeroboam I (c 922-901), a former labor battalion captain for Solomon. The Davidic dynasty continued in the southern kingdom of Judah but Israel had a series of rulers. The dynasty of Omri (876-842) was destroyed by an army captain named Jehu (c 842-815). The country's fortunes waxed and waned until Jehu's great-grandson Jeroboam II (c 786-746) reestablished military superiority. With this came both the tribute of subjected people and the increased wealth of trade. The new luxury was limited to the upper classes and did not extend to the poor. The latter were exploited even further by powerful and greedy rich people. The rich were generous with the official cult, contributing sacrifices to such shrines as those at Dan and Bethel, established by Jeroboam I as counter attractions to the Temple of Solomon in Jerusalem. The Jehu dynasty was followed by five individual kings. The northern kingdom was destroyed by the Assyrians in 722-721 BCE.

Amos: Man and Book

In his encounter with Amaziah the priest at Bethel, Amos claimed to be a shepherd from Tekoa, and a dresser of sycamore fruit. Tekoa (Khirbet Teku'a) is 20 km south of Jerusalem so we note here he was from the southern kingdom of Judah. While both the south and the north were "Hebrews," whatever that means, he was nationally a "foreigner" in the northern kingdom. When Amaziah told Amos to go home and earn his bread, he presumably meant go back to Judah or even specifically to Tekoa.

Traditionally, Amos has been seen as a poor shepherd. The sycamore tree does not grow in Tekoa but does near the Mediterranean and the Dead Sea. The sycamore fruit is gashed at one stage of its development, allowing it to ripen. The fruit is said to be food for the very poor. However, as a shepherd, Amos calls himself a *noqed*, a term used by King Mesha of Moab (2 Kgs 3:4). Mesha, of course, was not a poor man watching someone else's sheep as a hired hand. He was the owner of large flocks. Some speculate then that Amos owned the sheep he shepherded and thus he was a man of substance. At Ugarit (1400-1200 BCE), the word is used in relation to the flocks of the temple. On this basis, some guess Amos was part of the cult personnel.

He may have seen the injustice and corruption of the northern kingdom when he took the sheep and/or their wool, to market in the north.

Amos also told Amaziah that he, Amos, was not a prophet nor a son of the prophets. This has been interpreted in various ways. One view is that Amos was saying he was not a professional prophet, nor a member of a prophetic guild. Traditionalists and fundamentalists have normally seen the entire book as the words of God given through or even dictated to Amos. A variation on this theme is that God spoke to Amos' heart and mind and he put the divine message into human words. The book, like the Bible as a whole, is the Word of God - in spirit, in essence. But these are not the literal words of God, whether in the Elizabethan English of my beloved King James Version, or Today's English Version. Some claim it was written by Amos' disciples. Others note editorial efforts of the Deuteronomists and others in preserving the prophetic writings. The language of Amos is called classical Hebrew. This suggests the editorial hand to some, while to others it suggests that Amos was something more than a simple peasant shepherd watching sheep. If he were the owner as cited above (*noqed*), he may have had the education of a scribe, or could afford to hire a professional who put it all into classical form. Of course, if God spoke to an ordinary shepherd, the latter might very well write in classical Hebrew.

In the past several hundred years, literary, higher, or source criticism has suggested parts of the book are not really Amos's. At one time, most of the book was "not Amos" with very little going back to the Tekoan. This denial of Amos authorship is especially the case for the "hopeful" material. The non-Amos material may have come from disciples or editors of the text. Others think the hope is not only scattered throughout the text but integrated so it is "original." Some claim that the prophets always had hope, even if it was pretty small or limited on occasion. Theological interpretation is a significant part of the bibliographic entries. That includes a number of sermons cited inter alia.

If some literary critics and deconstructionists are right, we know nothing at all about Amos. There is no empirical evidence outside of his book that he even existed. The deuteronomic history includes a number of prophets such as Nathan, Elijah, et al. Amos is not mentioned. Other explanations are that the deuteronomists edited the prophetic books and simply kept them separate from the history which runs from Deuteronomy to the end of 2 Kings. Thus they did include Amos in their work, but in his own book.

Through the ages and today, he remains a vivid personality. He stood up to count his sheep and at Bethel he stood up to be counted for the

LORD. He spoke out against the king, the high priest, the nobility, the commoners, all who failed to fulfill the covenant, all who violated their relationship with God. He was not only courageous to speak, he was a clever speaker. He chastised the surrounding nations and then Judah and only at last the nation in front of him. While he condemned others for violating the laws of human decency, he condemned his own Hebrew people for violating their special relationship with God. Because they were the chosen people, they had special responsibilities to obey the God who had chosen them. They were thus doubly condemned. He stood the tradition on its head - instead of glorious victory on the Day of the LORD, they would face judgment and doom.

If the words are truly his, and no one has ever proven otherwise, he was brave, clever, innovative, and steeped in the knowledge of Hebrew history and tradition. He was a citizen of the world, well versed in what was going on at least in that area of the earth. If the classical Hebrew was indeed his own language, he was a master of it. He was educated in history, religion and the arts. He had a rich vocabulary, with an extensive range of rhetorical elements, e.g., word play, metaphor. His use of imagery shows a man with keen observation of his world. His visions suggest a spiritual sensitivity to the presence of God, but not such an overwhelming sense that he could not "argue" with God in trying to get the verdict reduced or postponed. This suggests we have here no vicious soul rejoicing in corpses and maimed bodies, but a person concerned for the welfare of his people.

Ultimately one must note, of course, that the Book of Amos is not about Amos. It is about God and the message of God for God's people. Some would say this God is a universal, monotheistic God (who creates the wind, who made Orion) while others are not so sure. Monotheism comes later, they say, with a Jeremiah or the second part of the Book of Isaiah. There may be more agreement about a God who calls his people into covenant relationship and then expects them to live by their own promises. Above all, from the words of Amos, we picture a God of justice for the poor, the downtrodden, the oppressed, the helpless, the widow and orphan. It is a divine demand upon the rich, the powerful, the upper classes, the rulers, the Establishment. The Word fell on deaf ears, then, as now.

People thought they could hide in the dark, but Amos said no - on the darkness of that Day of the LORD, their sin would be known. People claimed Amos must be wrong for they were very religious. But no, they were religious with their lips, with the externals of faith, but not with their hearts. Their hearts were too busy making plans to exploit the poor. Like other prophets, Amos is said to have condemned worship, religious ritual. This may be. Others say that goes too far - it was the external substituted for the heart that was condemned. And this external religion was condemned through the whole of sociey as the rich bribed judges, stole ancestral lands, took the clothes off people's backs, sold poor children into debtor's slavery (many sermons and straight exegesis have compared this scene with the "present"). To all this, Amos proclaimed, "Let justice roll down like waters, and righteousness like an everflowing stream!"

In a later day, Amos was part of the Hebrew prophetic tradition rediscovered by people like Washington Gladden and Walter Rauschenbusch. The social gospel movement was born out of the desperate search to face the injustice of a new age. So today, the cry is repeated by wave after wave of the disinherited, the disenchanted, the poor and oppressed, the minorities of every color and clime.

The Text

The text of Amos in its current and traditional form opens with an editorial giving his name, his home in Tekoa, and the time in terms of the kings of Judah and Israel, "two years before the earthquake."

God speaks from Jerusalem with a voice like a blast of heat that withers vegetation all the way to Mt. Carmel. The pattern of "three transgressions .. and for four" circle around with judgments on Damascus, the Philistines, Tyre, Edom, the Ammonites, Moab, Judah, and then Israel. He touches on the Exodus and Israel's special place, and special punishment. They are so evil, they do not know how to do right. They will be destroyed, with only a tiny remnant surviving. God tried small punishments but people did not return to him. God, or Amos, laments over the coming ruin. But people may still "seek the LORD and live," "seek good, and not evil."

God says he despises feasts, hates the music of their worship. He wants justice. But self-contained people have turned justice into poison.

Chapter 7 begins a series of visions. It opens with a vision of locusts. Amos pleaded with God who turned from this plague. A second vision showed fire destroying the land. Again Amos pleaded and God turned from this plague. A more mysterious vision of a plumb line, perhaps symbolic of a standard of behavior, brings forth no plea from Amos and no turning by God.

The series is interrupted by Amos' encounter with Amaziah the high priest at Bethel. He alerted the king to Amos' conspiracy in saying Jeroboam must die. Amaziah encouraged Amos to run away, go back to Judah to eat (earn?) his bread. Amos answered with the shepherd and sycamore vocations. Since Amos was obviously a prophet, people have puzzled over his answer that he was not a prophet. One interpretation is that he was not a professional prophet. For his efforts, Amaziah and his family are condemned to a horrible destruction.

The visions continue with one of a basket of summer fruit, a play on words, and more condemnation for oppression. In a vision of God standing beside an altar, he calls for a shattering from which none will escape.

A remarkable dialogue with the chosen people shows God's universal power over (and concern for?) others - Ethiopians, Philistines, Syrians and yes, the Israelites. The sinful kingdom will be destroyed. But there is yet hope in Israel for God says that he will "raise up the booth of David." Debate continues on whether this is the dynasty or the city of Jerusalem. Christians often interpret this as a prediction of Jesus. God predicts a future restoration and prosperity, security and no more exile. Presumably the last means no more sin on the part of the chosen people but the text does not say this. These closing hopeful words may be an editorial epilogue as many think, Amos' quoting his visionary Source, or the disciples adding a last word. As noted earlier, the constant doom of the text seems out of tune with hope, but then hope often has the last word.

NOTES

1. The MT, sometimes called the *textus receptus*, the "received text," is really a whole constellation of manuscripts with varying degrees of accuracy. The original texts were consonantal, without vowels. Between 500-1000 CE, the Jewish scholars called Massoretes added symbols called vowel points. At times they disagreed with the written text, *ketib*, and put their own reading, *qere,* in the margin. The autographs, the original texts of biblical books are long gone and unknown. Some say they never existed since the texts, as in Jeremiah, accumulated over time. A number of modern Hebrew Bibles, e.g., the third edition of Kittel's *Biblia Hebraica* and the *Biblia Hebraica Stuttgartensia* are based on the MT

from the Leningrad Museum (Codex Leningradensis, 1008 CE), with comparisons as appropriate to the variant spellings, terms, order, etc. of other manuscripts, e.g., the Dead Sea Scrolls. While the latter are the oldest known copies of the Bible, merely being old does not make them correct, accurate, or original.

2. CE = Common Era. It is often used in place of AD, Latin *Anno Domini*, "in the year of our Lord." The latter is a Christian designation while CE is somewhat preferred by non-Christians. Similarly BCE, "before the Common Era," is used instead of BC, "Before Christ."

REFERENCES

Andersen, Francis I. and David Noel Freedman. *Amos. A New Translation with Introduction and Commentary*. Anchor Bible 24A. Garden City: Doubleday, 1989. xlii + 979 pp.

Fosbroke, Hughell E.W. and Sidney Lovett. "The Book of Amos." 6 (1956), 761-853 in *The Interpreter's Bible* 12 vols ed George Arthur Buttrick. Nashville: Abingdon, 1952-1957. xii + 1144 pp. The KJV and RSV are printed in parallel columns. Fosbroke wrote the "Introduction" (pp. 763-766) and "Exegesis" (pp. 767-853) while Lovett did the "Exposition" (pp. 761-853).

Hammershaimb, Erling. *The Book of Amos. A Commentary*, 3rd ed. NY/Oxford: Schocken/Blackwell, 1970. 148 pp. Tr of *Amos Fortolket* (Danish). Copenhagen, Nyt Nordisk, 1946, 2nd ed, 1958, 3rd ed, 1967. 140 pp.

Hayes, John H. *Amos: The Eighth-Century Prophet - His Times and His Preaching*. Nashville: Abingdon, 1988. 256 pp.

McKeating, Henry. "The Book of Amos." pp. 12-70 in *The Books of Amos, Hosea and Micah*. Cambridge Bible Commentary on the New English Bible ed Peter R. Ackroyd et al. Cambridge: Cambridge University Press, 1971. x + 198 pp.

Stuart, Douglas. "Amos." pp. 63-87 in *Hosea-Jona.* Word Biblical Themes ed David A. Hubbard, et al. Dallas: Word, 1989. x + 121 pp.

Willoughby, Bruce E. "Amos, Book of." Vol 1:203-212 in *The Anchor Bible Dictionary*, 6 vols, ed David Noel Freedman, et al. NY: Doubleday, 1992. 1:lxxviii + 1232.

ABBREVIATIONS

Names of biblical books are abbreviated in articles except where to do so might cause confusion. Journals are cited by arabic numerals.

AD	*Anno Domini*, "The Year of Our Lord," replaced by CE.
ADD	*American Doctoral Dissertations*. Ann Arbor: University Microfilms International. Earlier titles and publishers vary.
AJSL	*American Journal of Semitic Languages*. Chicago. 1884-1942
ANE	Ancient Near East(ern)
ATLA	American Theological Library Association. Chicago. Microfiche project.
BASOR	*Bulletin of the American Schools of Oriental Research*. Baltimore. 1919
BCE	Before the Common Era (the Christian BC, Before Christ)
Bib	*Biblica*. Rome. 1920
BIES	The Bulletin of the Israel Exploration Society (Jerusalem)
BM	*Beth Mikra*. Jerusalem. 1956
BN	*Biblische Notizen*. Bamberg, Germany. 1907, 1977
BS	*Bibliotheca Sacra*. Dallas, TX. 1843
BT	*The Bible Today*. Collegeville, MN. 1962
BTr	*The Bible Translator*. London. 1950
BV	Biblical Viewpoint
BW	Biblical World
BZ	*Biblische Z*. Paderborn, Germany. 1903. ns 1956
BZAW	Beiheft ZAW.
CBQ	*Catholic Biblical Quarterly*. Washington, DC. 1939
CE	Common Era = the Christian A.D.

DAI   Dissertation Abstracts International
Diss   Dissertation

EI   Eretz-Isreal
Eng   English\England
ET   *Expository Times*. Edinburgh. 1889
ETR   *Etudes Theologiques et Religieuses*. Montpellier. 1925
EvT   *Evangelische Theologie*. Munich. 1934
Exp   *The Expositor*. London. 1875

Ger   German/Germany
GTJ   *Grace Theological Journal*. Winona Lake, IN. 1980

Heb   Hebrew(s)
HR   *The Homiletic Review*. NY. 1876-1934
HUCA   *Hebrew Union College Annual*. Cincinnati. 1925

INT   *Interpretation*. Richmond, VA. 1947

J   Journal
JBL   *J of Biblical Literature*. Atlanta, GA. 1881
JETS   *J of the Evangelical Theological Society*. Wheaton, IL. 1957
JNES   *J of Near Eastern Studies*. Chicago. 1942
JSOT   *J for the Study of the Old Testament*. Sheffield, England. 1976
JTS   *J of Theological Studies*. Oxford/London. 1899. ns 1950

KJV   King James Version of the Bible (1611)

LXX   Septuagint, Greek translation of the OT

MT   Masoretic Text

NIV   New International Version
NT   New Testament

OT   Old Testament
OTA   *OT Abstracts*. Washington. 1978
OTE   Old Testament Essays (Pretoria)
OTS   *Oudtestamentische Studien*. Leiden. 1942
OTWSA   Ou Testamentiese Werkgemeenskap in Suid Afrika

PG   *Patrologiae Cursus Completus: Series Graeca*, ed Jacques P.
        Migne, 162 vols (including Index vol by F. Cavellera; Paris,
        1912). Paris: Migne, 1857-1866.
PL   *Patrologiae Cursus Completus: Series Latina*, ed Jacques P.
        Migne, 221 vols (including 4 Index vols, 218-221). Paris:
        Migne, 1844-1864. Supplement ed Adalbert Hamman, 3 vols.
        Paris: Garnier Freres, 1958-1966.
Pol   Polish/Poland

R&E   *Review and Expositor*. Louisville, KY
RB   *Revue Biblique*. Paris. 1889. ns 1890. ns 1904 [reverted back to
        1890]
RGG   *Religion in Geschichte und Gegenwart*, 1st ed, 5 vols, ed
        Hermann Gunkel, et al. Tubingen: Mohr, 1903-1913. 2nd ed, 5
        vols, ed Alfred Bertholet, et al. 1927-1932. 3rd ed, 7 vols, ed
        Kurt Galling, et al., 1957-1965.
RSV   Revised Standard Version

SBL   Society of Biblical Literature
SWJT   *Southwestern J of Theology*. Fort Worth, TX

TE   *Theological Educator*. New Orleans. 1967
TLZ   *Theologische Literaturzeitung*. Leipzig. 1885
TSK   *Theologische Studien und Kritiken*. Hamburg. 1828
TZ   *Theologische Z*. Vienna. 1819. Basel. 1945

UF   Ugarit-Forschungen (Kevelaer/Neukirchen-Vluyn)

VD   *Verbum Domini*. Rome. 1920
VT   *Vetus Testamentum*. Leiden. 1951
VTS   VT Supplement

Z   Zeitschrift
ZAW   *Z fur die Alttestamentliche Wissenschaft*. Berlin/Hawthorne, NY.
        1881

THE BIBLIOGRAPHY

A.

1. Abbott, Walter M., et al., eds. "The Book of Amos." pp. 535-542 in *The Bible Reader: An Interfaith Interpretation with Notes from Catholic, Protestant and Jewish Traditions and references to Art, Literature, History and the Social Problems of Modern Man* by the eds. London/NY: Chapman/Bruce, 1969. xxiv + 995 pp. A general introduction to the volume notes the growth of the Bible as a book of religion which is not authoritative in mathematics, astronomy, etc. Appendices discuss rabbinic tradition, the documentary theory, ANE myths, English translation, history and law. The selections of biblical text presented in the volume were chosen as most important or current in our culture, associated with religious observances and beliefs. A general introduction to the twelve minor prophets includes their universalism, objection to ritual without true faith (God wants love, not sacrifices), judgment, a faithful remnant, symbolic actions as well as words. The introduction to Amos reviews the man, his message of social justice, the day of the Lord and a remnant. The selections are divided under headings which serve as a guide to the content. Selections have a mini-introduction plus exegetical commentary that explains and interprets.

2. Abbott, Walter M. and S. Abramski. "'I Am Not a Prophet Nor a Son of a Prophet.'"pp. 64-68 in *Studies in the Bible Dedicated to the Memory of Umberto Cassuto on the 100th Anniversary of His Birth* ed Samuel E. Loewenstamm. Jerusalem: Magnes, 1987.

3. Abrego de Lacy, Jose Maria. "Profetas del reino de Israel: Amos, Oseas." pp. 47-96 in *Los libros profeticos*. Introduccion al Estudio de la Biblia 4 ed Jose Manuel Sanchez Caro, et al. Estella, Navarra: Editorial Verbo Divino (evd), 1993. 300 pp. Gives the historical background, Amos' (pp. 51-71) activities, his profession, the debate on his prophethood, the book, oracles against the nations and Israel, injustice, the cows of Bashan, the cult, the visions, doxologies, God as the Lord, Israel's election, punishment and restoration, the book's theology, practical applications.

4. Ackermann, Petro Four. "Amos." pp. 247-344 in *Prophetae Minores: Perpetua Annotatione.* Vienna: Volke, 1830. viii + 799 pp. Hebrew text with commentary including NT connections, exegesis, critical notes, comparison of MT, LXX, Vulgate, Syriac and other traditions.

5. Ackroyd, Peter R. "Amos 7:14." *ET* 68, No. 3 (Dec 56), 94. Amos said, "Am I not a prophet? ...the Lord took me..." The second question should follow as a parallel: "Am I not a son of a prophet?" The latter is simply an alternate phrase for prophet and not for cultic prophet.

6. Ackroyd, Peter R. "A Judgment Narrative Between Kings and Chronicles? An Approach to Amos 7:9-17." pp. 71-87 in *Canon and Authority: Essays in Old Testament Religion and Theology* ed George W. Coats and B. O. Long. Philadelphia: Fortress, 1977. xvii + 190 pp. Reprinted, pp. 195-208 in *Studies in the Religious Tradition of the Old Testament.* London: SCM, 1987. xiv + 305 pp. This is the only narrative passage in the Book of Amos. Reviews structure, language, thought, consequences. The negative is an interrogative: "Am I not a prophet?" The narrative serves like other call and conflict narratives to show the authority of the prophetic message, which validates it. There may be a parallel with 1 Kgs 13 and 2 Kgs 23. Perhaps Amos' grave was at Bethel.

7. Ackroyd, Peter R. "Understanding Amos." *Learning for Living* 2, No. 1 (Sep 62), 6-9. Discusses the man (background, identity, activity at Bethel), his message (the Exodus, universalism, absolute allegiance to Yahweh, justice, absolute judgment; seek Yahweh and live). Translates 7:14: Am I not a prophet?

8. Adamo, D.T. "Amos 9:7-8 in an African Perspective." *Orita* (Ibadan, Nigeria) 24, Nos. 1-2 (June-Dec 92), 76-84. Interprets Kushites as Africans. Gives the historical background, critical analysis of the text, its interpretation including earlier studies. Cites western scholars who see the verse as referring to sub-Saharan African slaves but there is nothing in the text to relate Africans to slavery. Amos' concern is the universalism of God. God is the Lord of all nations.

9. Adams, John. "Amos." pp. 26-32 in *The Minor Prophets.* Bible Class Primers ed Principal Salmond. Edinburgh: Clark, 1902. 111 pp. A

general introduction to the book reviews Israel's ideal (political supremacy, attractions of Baal worship, the rise of the Church), Assyria (first and second empires, fall of Samaria) and Hebrew prophecy (prophetic order, nature of their call, character of their calling). The commentary notes the man, his time and his message.

10. Adler, Elizabeth. "Amos Today." *Student World* 57 [Issue No. 224], No. 2 (1964), 105-109. We need a new Amos today but since we do not have one, we might listen to the old as he condemns those who oppress the poor. There are true and false prophets among journalists today. She compares media stories about foreign aid as an example.

11. Aerathedathu, Thomas. "The Social Teaching of Amos." *Indian J of Spirituality* 4, No. 2 (1991), 149.

12. Ahlstrom, G.W. "King Josiah and the *dwd* of Amos 6:10." *J of Semitic Studies* (Manchester) 26, No. 1 (Spr 1981), 7-9. The term means kinsman. The 10 men of the house of death are the 10 dead tribes of the north. This prophecy justified Josiah's actions against the brother people of Samaria (2 Kgs 32:15ff).

13. Albert, Edwin. "Einige Bemerkungen zu Amos." ZAW 33, No. 3 (1913), 265-271. Exegesis of 2:6, 9b, 10-12 (5:25), 8:11-13. Surveys earlier studies.

14. Alexandre, Jean. *Parmentier Roger, Lire et ecrire la Bible. Traduction et transcrition d'Amos.* Dialogue 79f. Paris: Mouvement Paix Jeunes, 1978. 53 pp.

15. Alger, B. "The Theology and Social Ethic of Amos." *Scripture* 17, No. 40 (Oct 65), 109-116. We know little of Amos' personal life but his theology and ethics give depth to his personality. He spoke in a time of prosperity related in corruption and injustice. God is universal. Israel's special place is in the covenant. Amos interceded for Israel but failed and the message was judgment on their sins. Beyond judgment is hope for the future and the renewal of the covenant.

4 The Book of Amos

16. Allen, Leslie C. "Amos, Prophet of Solidarity." *Vox Evangelica* 6 (1969), 42-53. Discusses heavenly council, community, covenant and the happy ending with the terms "my people" and "your God."

17. Alonso Diaz, J. "El Nuevo Tipo de Profecia que Inicia Amos." *Cultura Biblica* (Madrid/Segovia) 23, No. 1 (Jan-Feb 66), 36-42. Reviews the history of prophecy in Israel, Amos as a new type and his reply to Amaziah, the continuation of this type in later prophets.

18. Alonso Diaz, Jose. "Proceso antropomorfizante y desantropomorfizante en la formacin del concepto biblico de Dios." pp. 147-159 in *La idea de Dios en la Biblia* with A. Munoz Alonso, et al. XXVIII Semana Biblica Espanola (Madrid 23-27 Sept 1968). Madrid: Consejo Superior de Investigaciones Cientificas, 1971. Primitive understanding of Yahweh was anthropomorphic but this changed with Amos and Hosea. Amos was revolted at the immorality of the north and told them their rituals would do no good.

19. Alonso Schokel, Luis and Jose Luis Sicre Diaz in collaboration with S. Breton and E. Zurro. "Amos." pp. 951-993 in *Profetas. Introduccion y comentarios. II. Ezequiel. Doce Profetas Minores. Daniel. Baruc. Carta de Jeremias*, 2nd ed. Nueva Biblia Espanol (The New Spanish Bible). Madrid: Ediciones Cristiandad, 1987. iv + 654-1373 pp. (original 1980) The introduction discusses the historical situation (political, social, religious), the man, his message (condemnation and cause), his book (structure, problems), the use of Amos in the NT, and adds a select bibliography. Commentary on the text includes translation, exegesis, comparisons with other OT texts.

20. Alonso Schokel, Luis, and Jose Maria Valverde. "Amos." pp. 59-83 in *Doce Profetas Menores: Oseas, Joel, Amos, Abdias, Miquias. Traduccion, Introducciones, Notas* (The 12 Minor Prophets: Translation, Introduction, Notes). Los Libros Sagrados (The Holy Books). Madrid: Ediciones Cristiandad, 1966. 223 pp. History, theology, critical notes.

21. Alvarez Barredo, Miguel. *Relecturas Deuteronomisticas de Amos, Miqueas y Jeremias*. Publicaciones del Instituto Teologico Franciscano Serie Mayor 10. Murcia, Spain: Editorial Espigas, 1993. 229 pp. Diss. Pontificia Universidad Urbaniana, 1992. The first part

of the study reviews Deuteronomy, its structure, doctrine, central theme. The commentary on Amos (pp. 53-82) includes comparison with Deuteronomy and deuteronomistic editing of Amos.

22. Alvarez Valdes, Ariel. "El enfrentamiento entre profetas y falsos profetas." *Revista Biblica* (Buenos Aires), 53, ns 44, No. 4 (1991), 217-229. A general study of the problem of false prophets including Kings, Amos (pp. 221-223), and Jeremiah. Reviews text, context and interpretations.

23. "Amos." pp. 131-156 in *Liber Duodecim Prophetarum ex interpretatione Sancti Hieronymi cum praefationibus et variis capitulorum seriebus.* Biblia Sacra iuxta Latinam Vulgatam Versionem ad codicum fidem iussu Ioannis Pauli PP. II, cura et studio Monarachum Abbatiae Pontificiae Sancti Hieronymi in urbe Ordinis Sancti Benedicti edita, 17. Rome: Vatican, 1987. xlvii + 291 pp. A critical version of the Latin text and of introductory materials, e.g., Jerome's prologue to the Twelve, to Amos, etc. The introduction gives the background of the Jerome commentaries, compares Jerome, Isidor, liturgies and other sources, discusses the manuscripts available, textual difficulties, name of the collection, problems of individual books. Appendices note orthography, personal and place names.

24. Amsler, Samuel. "Amos." pp. 157-247 in *Osee, Joel, Amos, Abdias, Jonas* by Edmond Jacob, Carl A. Keller and Samuel Amsler. Commentaire de L'Ancien Testament 11a, ed Robert Martin-Achard, et al. Neuchatel: Delachaux & Niestle, 1965. 295 pp. Title page has Jacob, "Osee," Keller, "Joel, Abdias, Jonas," Amsler, "Amos." [2nd ed, Geneva: Labor et Fides, 1982, 293 pp., with a revised bibliography; 3rd ed, 1992, with additional bibliography] Each book has an introduction, a new translation, and a section by section commentary. The introduction reviews the historical background, the man (a cult prophet), his time, his message, his book (text, plan and formation).

25. Amsler, Samuel. "Amos et les droits de l'homme (Etude d'Am 1 et 2)." pp. 181-187 in *De la Torah au Messie. Etudes d'exegese et d'hermeneutique bibliques offertes a Henri Cazelles pour ses 25 annees d'enseignement a l'Institut Catholique de Paris (Octobre*

1979) ed Maurice Carrez, Joseph Dore and Pierre Grelot. Paris: Desclee, 1981. 648 pp. The rights of man include the dignity inherent in members of the human family. This is Amos' concern.

26. Amsler, Samuel. "Amos, prophete de la onzieme heure." TZ (Basel) 21, No. 4 (July-Aug 65), 318-328. General discussion with translation of selected passages and the history of interpretation.

27. Andel, J. van. "Amos." pp. 94-136 in *De Kleine Profeten*, 2nd ed. Kampen: Bos, 1905. ix + 359 pp. (original, Leeuwarden, 1881) The introduction gives the historical background and relationships with other biblical texts. The commentary gives a Dutch translation in small units with interpretation including additional comparisons.

28. Andersen, Francis I. and A. Dean Forbes. *A Synoptic Concordance to Hosea, Amos, Micah.* The Computer Bible 6, ed J. Arthur Baird and David Noel Freedman. Wooster, Ohio: Biblical Research Association, 1972. xxi + 329 pp. The introduction notes the order of the concordance. Nouns were stripped to their stems while verbs were left intact. Parts of speech are ordered appropriate to their grammatical features, e.g., prepositions are alphabetized. The list of pronouns begins with the personal form. There are 12 units in the text, e.g., conjunctions, the article, the relative, etc.

29. Andersen, Francis I. and A. Dean Forbes. *Eight Minor Prophets: A Linguist Concordance.* The Computer Bible 10, ed J. Arthur Baird and David Noel Freedman. Wooster: Biblical Research Associates, 1976. x + 612 pp. The first edition (CB 6, 1972) contained Amos, Hosea and Micah. Here the authors have corrected mistakes, updated their process and added Joel, Obadiah, Nahum, Habakkuk and Zephaniah. There are 32 divisions, e.g. exclamation, article, prepositions, numbers, pronouns, verbs, adverbs, conjunctions, etc.

30. Andersen, Francis I. and David Noel Freedman. *Amos. A New Translation with Introduction and Commentary.* Anchor Bible 24A. Garden City: Doubleday, 1989. xlii + 979 pp. The introduction, pp. 3-149 is a book in itself on contents, reconstruction of Amos' mission, his view of God, etc. The bibliography is 25 pp. They follow the MT rather than scholarly conjecture and attribute most of

the contents to Amos or an editor who worked closely with him. Scholarly attempts to establish later dates fall short of proof.

31. Anderson, Bernhard W. *The Eighth Century Prophets: Amos, Hosea, Isaiah, Micah.* Proclamation Commentaries: The Old Testament Witnesses for Preaching ed Foster R. McCurley. Philadelphia: Fortress, 1978. xvi + 111 pp. The general introduction reviews the importance of the prophets. Amos is included in the discussion in Chs 1-4 in the metaphor of the lion has roared, who can but speak, the shock of the future, repentance and justice. The first includes the historical background and God's plan to punish Israel for sin. The end has come. The only hope is to repent and do justice and since you refuse to do so, "Prepare to meet your God!"

32. Anderson, Bernhard Word. "The Herdsman from Tekoa." pp. 291-301 in *Understanding the Old Testament,* 4th ed. Englewood Cliffs, NJ: Prentice- Hall, 1986. xv + 685 pp. Reprinted, pp. 192-202 in *Perspectives on Old Testament Literature* ed Woodrow Ohlsen. NY: Harcourt Brace Jovanovich, 1978. xiii + 450 pp. Discusses Amos the man and his message (God's sovereignty; the covenant promises and threat of doom). Amos saw his society as sick with sin and called them to repentance. The promise is based on the grace of God.

33. Andersson, C.H. *Commentarius in Amos.* Gotha, 1854.

34. Andinach, Pablo Ruben. "Amos: Memoria y profecia - Analisis estructural y hermeneutica." *Revista Biblica* 45, ns 12, No. 4 (1983), 209-301. Reviews the history of interpretation. Discusses and illustrates the structure.

35. Andreasen, N. "From Vision to Prophecy." *Adventist Review* 159 (28 Jan 82), 4-7.

36. Andrew, Maurice E. "What might 'God punishing' mean in South East Asia (An Interpretation of Amos 3:1-2)." *South East Asia J Theology* (Manila) 23, No. 2 (1982), 116-120. God knows his people and punishes them. We need involvement and response. Andrew quotes Wolff on Amos 3:1-2 who noted Luke 12:48. Andrew agrees and then reverses with, "From whom much is required, much is

given." Andrew's reward mentality may or may not be biblical. In the case at hand, Israel had already been given.

37. Andrews, Mary E. "Hesiod and Amos." *J of Religion* (Chicago) 23, No. 3 (July 43), 194-205. These two conservatives from the 8th century have a word for us today when one third of the nation is ill-fed, ill-clothed, ill-housed. Justice is central among divine commands. Both laid more emphasis on the punishment for injustice than the rewards of justice. They differ in the prophet's role as the personal spokesman for God. Hesiod has a wider range of interests.

38. Annecchino Manni, Marialuisa. "Il prologo del commentario di Giuliano d'Eclano sui profeti Osea, Gioele e Amos." *Annali della Facolta di Lettere e filosofia dell'Univ* (Naples) 28 (1985-1986), 15-21.

39. Arango, Jose Roberto. "Opresion y Profanacion del Santo Nombre de Dios: Estudios del Vocabulario de Am. 2:7b." *RIBLA: Revista de Interpretacion Biblica Latin-Americana* (San Jose, Costa Rica) 11 (1992), 49-63. Discusses Amos' time, person, message, oracles against Israel, the sins of Israel, exegesis on the accusation and the consequences of the accusation. Israel has profaned God's holy name. Arango claims sex with the young woman humiliated her and eliminated the possibility of marriage and family. The father also sinned in perverting his role of parental guide. Amos 2:7b denounces the corruption of the family. Rev, OTA 16 # 2 (June 93).

40. Arieti, James A. "The Vocabulary of Septuagint Amos." JBL 93, No. 3 (Sep 74), 338-347. LXX is vaguer and conveys a broader meaning because a more specialized meaning might be inaccurate where there is no exact corresponding word. Where the meaning is unknown, the context is used. Vocabulary enables us to tell one translator from another.

41. Asen, Bernhard Arthur. "No, Yes and Perhaps in Amos and the Yahwist." VT 43, No. 4 (Oct 93), 433-441. Amos proclaimed the no of God's judgment. Gerhard Pfeifer emphasizes Amos' yes to God's call, God's actions towards Israel and the nations. Amos hoped Israel would seek the Lord and perhaps the Lord would show favor to the

remnant. The Yahwist also says no and yes and perhaps. Both the "perhaps" turn on society's response to justice.

42. Ashbel, Dev. "Notes on the Prophecy of Amos" (Heb). BM 11 [Issue Nos. 25/26], Nos. 1-2 (Nov 65), 103-107. "Does a Bird Fall into a Trap?" "Does a Lion Raise His Voice from His Lair unless He Has Caught Something?"

43. Ashby, Godfrey W. *Theodoret of Cyrrhus as Exegete of the Old Testament.* Grahamstown, South Africa: Rhodes University, 1972. v + 173 pp. Theodoret (393-458 [453? 466?] C.E.), a theologian of the Antiochene school, was bishop of Cyrrus in Osroene Syria (423). Amos, pp. 45, 141. His interpretation is Christological. The emphasis in Amos is the long term goal of punishment - a universal restoration.

44. Ashworth, Richard H. "Oracle to America, through Amos, from God (1992)." p. 15 in *Many Voices: Multicultural Responses to the Minor Prophets* ed Alice Ogden Bellis. Lanham, MD: University Press of America, 1995. xiv + 101 pp. The writers in this book try to apply the minor prophets today. An oracle of judgment against technology, materialism, sexual sin, failure to be a light to the world.

45. Asurmendi, Jesus. *Amos et Osee.* Cahiers Evangile 64. Paris: Cerf, 1988. 59 pp.

46. Atger, Jacques and Francoise Atger. "Le Message d'Amos." *Christianisme Social* (Paris) 74 (1966), 303-312. The authors discuss justice and judgment.

47. Atkinson, E.E. "The Religious Ideas of the Book of Amos." *The Old Testament Student* (New Haven, CT) 8, No. 8 (Ap 1889), 284-290. Gives the historical and immoral background of the times, Amos' idea of God (a moral being), sin, right conduct, covenant (you only have I known), ethical monotheism.

48. Aubert, Alexandre. *Les Experiences Religieuses et Morales du Prophete Amos.* Geneva: Kundig, 1911. 199 pp. The introduction develops the method, object and plan of study while the first part reviews the relationship of God and Israel, earlier conditions, the

political state and the society of Israel in the time of Amos. The second part is a study of Amos - his life, his work, his personality, his relationship with God. God is a God of justice who is master of world history, of heaven and earth. He is alone and unique. Discusses Amos and the cult, the moral experience of Yahweh by Amos, Yahweh's care and Israel's disobedience, the punishment and the Day of Yahweh, hope or eschatology of Amos.

49. Auge, Ramir. *Profetes Menors*. La Biblia, versio dels textos originals i commentari pels monjos de Montserrat 16. Barcelona: Monestir de Monserrat, 1957.

50. Auld, A. Graeme. *Amos*. OT Guides ed. R.N. Whybray. Sheffield: JSOT, 1986. 89 pp. Reviews Amos the person - visionary, prophet - Israel and her neighbors (Amos' oracles against them), literary, social and religious critiques, his message, and various scholarly views. Amos' concern with social justice gives him perennial appeal. He was more than a simple shepherd. He was a *noqed*, a term used for King Mesha of Moab while *rb nqdm*, a term from Ugarit, has been translated "chief of shepherds."

51. Auld, A. Graeme. "Amos and Apocalyptic: Vision, Prophecy, Revelation." pp. 1-14 in *Storia e tradizioni di Israele. Scritti in onore di J. Alberto Soggin* ed Daniele Garrone and Felice Israel. Brescia: Paideia, 1991. xlvii + 310 pp. Suggests prophetic texts may have been touched up by apocalyptic. We may have little or nothing of the prophets except a later view or rendition. Detailed study of Amos 3:7, with reviews of earlier studies, including Soggin who considers it original Amos. Auld analyzes the content in the context of Yahweh's servants the prophets. The verse is an apocalyptic interpolation to claim prophetic status for Amos and his words. It dates from the period of the books of Ezra and Daniel.

52. Azcarraga Servert, Maria Josefa de. "Am," pp. 39-57 in *Minhat Say de Y.S. de Norzi: Profetas Menores (Traduccion y anotacion critica)*. Textos y Estudios "Cardenal Cisneros" 40, ed Federico Perez Castro, et al. Madrid: Instituto de Filologia, Consejo Superior de Investigaciones Cientificas [CSIC], Departmento de Filologia Biblica y de Oriente Antiguo, 1987. lxix + 259 pp. The introduction reviews references to the Mantua, Italy, Rabbi Jedidiah Solomon

Raphael ben Abraham Norzi (1560-1626), including Textos y Estudios 24 (1979) by E. Fernandez Tejero, with an overview of Norzi's study of the Hebrew Bible and his work *Goder Peres*, published as *Minhat Say* (Mantua, 1742-1744; also transliterated as *Minhat Shai*), its publication history, an overview of the present work - translation with critical notes, biblical, talmudic and midrashic references, the masorah, discrepancies with other masoretic lists, manuscripts and other sources. The introduction to the commentary has language (mixture of Hebrew and Aramaic), style, sources, personal characteristics of Norzi. The commentary is concerned with grammar, textual discrepancies, masoretic expressions, exegetical commentary, biblical and talmudic references, punctuation. Azcarraga's critical notes analyze, compare, cite variants, reflect later and present resources. The present volume closes with an extensive bibliography and indices.

B.

53. Bach, Robert. "Amos." Vol. 1 (1956), cols 101-102 in *Evangelisches Kirchenlexikon [EKL]: Kirchlich-theologische Handworterbuch*, 4 vols, 2nd ed, ed Heinz Brunotte, Otto Weber, Robert Frick, et al. Gottingen: Vandenhoeck & Ruprecht, 1956-1961. 1:iv + 1736 cols. Reviews Amos' life and ministry, his visions and concern for social justice. For the 3rd ed, EKL, see Thiel.

54. Bach, Robert. "Erwagungen zu Amos 7:14." pp. 203-216 in *Die Botschaft und die boten. Festschrift fur Hans Walter Wolff zum 70. Geburtstag* ed Joachim Jeremias and Lothar Perlitt. Neukirchen-Vluyn: Neukirchener, 1981. ix + 426 pp. Detailed analysis of the context and what it means to be a prophet.

55. Bach, Robert. "Gottesrecht und weltliches Recht in der Verkundigung des Propheten Amos." pp. 23-34 in *Festschrift fur Gunther Dehn zum 75. Geburtstag am 18. April 1957* ed Wilhelm Schneemelcher. Neukirchen Kreis Moers: Erzeihungsvereins, 1957. 267 pp. Discusses Amos' perspective compared with other biblical and non-biblical sources, and a review of interpretations.

56. Bachar, Shlomo. "Seer - Go Away" (Heb). BM 33, No. 114 (1987-8), 392-396. Amos 7:10-17. Exegesis, noting earlier studies.

57. Bade, Joh. "Der Prophet Amos." pp. 169-176 in *Christologie des Alten Testamentes oder die Messianischen Verheissungen, Weissagungen und Typen, mit besonderer Berucksichtigung ihres organischen Zusammenhanges. Dritter Theil, enthaltend die Weissagungen in den Propheten. Zweite Abtheilung: Die Propheten Jeremias, Ezechiel, Daniel, Osee, Joel, Amos, Michaas, Aggaus, Zacharias, Malachias Nebst den Messianischen Typen.* Munster: Deiters, 1852. v + 336 pp. A commentary on 9:11-15 noting

messianic elements, introductory comments, translation, exegesis, notes on earlier studies.

58. Badia, Leonard F. "Amos: A Model for Pastoral Ministry." BT (Collegeville, MN) 20, No. 3 (May 82), 160-165. Amos' freedom, courage and community mindedness apply today. Badia discusses the historical background, oracles, hope, legacy. Pastors subject to financial pressures may speak ambiguously, muzzled by expediency. The four women martyred in San Salvador had courage like Amos. Today's pastors must know the community. Amos loved people and tried to correct their injustices.

59. Baentsch, D. "Amos." RGG 1 (1909), cols 435-440. 1st ed. Discusses the man, his call, social situation, historical context, his main ideas, concept of God (e.g., the question of monotheism), place in religious history, style and form, the book itself. RGG, 2nd ed (1927), cf Balla; 3rd ed (1957), cf Maag.

60. Bailey, D. Waylon. "Theological Themes in the Prophecy of Amos." TE = *The Theological Educator* (New Orleans, 1967) 52 (Fall 95), 79-85. Amos helps us understand who God is by what He has done. God is sovereign of the earth. Bailey discusses freedom and responsibility, election, sin (breaking the relationship with God), true worship, the nature of prophecy, the Day of the Lord, Messianic hope. There are no specific references to the latter but it comes from the phrase, "the booth of David."

61. Bailey, Joseph G. "Amos: Preacher of Social Reform." BT 19, No. 5 (Sep 81), 306-313. Amos was a small businessman, travelling the country as an entrepreneur, so he saw firsthand the exploitation he condemned. The rich oppressed the poor and were meticulous about the rituals. Amos is not used much in the American Lectionary.

62. Bailey, Moses. "The Formation of the Book of Amos." JBL 56 (1937), ix. A paper given at the SBL and Exegesis 31 Dec 36. Disciples memorized Amos' oracles for several generations before writing them down, e.g., they expanded four oracles against the nations to seven.

63. Balla, Emil. "Amos." pp. 73-92 in *Die Botschaft der Propheten* ed Georg Fohrer. Tubingen: Mohr, 1958. vii + 484 pp. Includes (abbreviated, revised, updated) his *Droh- und Scheltworte*. Discusses the background and message of Amos, an ethical monotheist, and his relationship with cult prophets.

64. Balla, Emil. "Amos." RGG 1 (1927), cols 306-309. 2nd ed, 5 vols. Discusses the man and his call, his significance, the book. RGG, 1st ed (1909), cf Baentsch; 3rd ed (1957), cf Maagioni #914.

65. Balla, Emil. *Die Droh- und Scheltworte des Amos*. Zur Feier des Reformationsfestes und des Ubergangs des Rektorats auf Heinrich Siber. Leipzig: Edelman, 1926. iii + 52 pp. See his *Botschaft*.

66. Ballarini, Luigi. "Amos." Vol 1 (1961), cols 1020-1027 in *Bibliotheca Sanctorum*, 12 volumes. Rome: Istituto Giovanni XXIII of the Pontificia Universita Lateranense, 1961-1970 (including Index). Discusses the man, his time, his message at Bethel, the authenticity of the book.

67. Baltzer, Klaus. "Bild und Wort: Erwagungen zu der Vision des Amos in Am 7:7-9." pp. 11-16 in *Text, Methode und Grammatik: Wolfgang Richter zum 65. Geburtstag* ed Walter Gross, Hubert Irsigler, Theodor Seidl. St. Ottilien: EOS Verlag Erzabtei, 1991. xii + 606 pp. Exegesis with word studies, analysis of earlier interpretations, the culture of Israel, ways of knowing.

68. Banney, A.B. *Amos de Tekoa, Son Epoque et son Livre*. Montauban, 1899.

69. Barackman, Paul F. "Preaching from Amos." INT 13, No. 3 (July 59), 296-315. An outline of the book with its judgments, people's reactions, the prophetic visions. The message echoes across the centuries that we are to know, worship, trust God.

70. Barre, Michael L. "Amos." pp. 209-216 in *The New Jerome Biblical Commentary* ed Raymond S. Brown, Joseph A. Fitzmyer and Roland E. Murphy. Englewood Cliffs, NJ: Prentice-Hall, 1990. xlviii + 1475 pp. (original 1968, see King #784) Reviews the man, his time, message and theology. There are four main themes: judgment, social

justice, cult and the word. Israelites turned a deaf ear to the words of the prophets, which meant a deaf ear to God, so the word will be cut off (Am 8:11-12). The note of hope in Am 9:11-15 is an editorial conclusion.

71. Barre, Michael L. "Amos 1:11 Reconsidered." CBQ (Washington, DC) 47, No. 3 (July 85), 420-427. Reviews the history of exegesis and translates: "Because he pursued his treaty-partner with the sword and utterly destroyed his allies, With his anger raging perpetually and his wrath ever fuming."

72. Barre, Michael L. "The Meaning of *l' 'shybnw* in Amos 1:3 - 2:6." JBL 105, No. 4 (Dec 86), 611-631. There is no consensus on the meaning "I will not." Reviews the suggestions. No emendation is necessary with the translation "I will not let him return" [to me]. Yahweh is cancelling the covenant.

73. Barrett, Michael P.V. "Christ's Kingdom: Good News for Everybody (Amos 9:8-15)." BV (Greenville, SC, 1967) 27, No. 2 (Nov 93), 35-45. Most of what Amos preached was not good news but the revelation of the remnant is and so is the coming kingdom and the reversal of the captivity. In Acts 11:18, James quoted Amos 9:11, 12, to exempt Gentiles from ceremonial requirements. Barrett discusses the variants of James' quote, MT and LXX. The key difference is not the meaning but the application.

74. Barstad, Hans M. "Die Basankuhe in Amos 4:1." VT 25, No. 2a (May 75), 286-297, Discusses the various interpretations of the cows of Bashan. It's the fertility cult and not the ladies.

75. Barstad, Hans M. *The Religious Polemics of Amos: Studies in the Preaching of Am 2:7b-8; 4:1-13; 5:1-27; 6:4-7; 8:14.* VTS 34. Leiden: Brill, 1984. xiv + 244 pp. Diss. Studies in the Religious Polemics... Oslo: Det Teologiske Fakultet, 1982. Reviews scholarly opinions. The book is the message of Amos. While there is moral concern, it is a polemic against the god Baal. Yahwism was as much a fertility cult as Baalism. The prophet's job was to convince people that Yahwism was *the* fertility religion. Amos was a missionary. The study includes reviews of the archaeological data on Bethel, Gilgal,

Dan and Beersheba. Sections include studies on the cow as a fertility symbol in the ANE, the Day of Yahweh, the sacred meal.

76. Bartczek, Gunter. *Prophetie und Vermittlung. Zur literarischen Analyse und theologischen Interpretation der Visionberichte des Amos.* Europaische Hochschulschriften Series 23, Vol 120. Frankfurt am Main: Lang, 1980. 330 pp. Diss. Die Visionsberichte des Amos. Literische Analyse und theologische Interpretation. Wilhelms University (Munster im Westfalen), 1977. An overview of visions in OT prophecy. Amos' visions are described and analyzed by literary, form, redaction, structural, *gattung* (type) criticism and theologically.

77. Barth, Karl. "Gerichtsbotschaft des Propheten Amos." pp. 502-509 in *Die Kirchliche Dogmatik* 4/2. Zollikon/ Zurich: Evangelischer, 1955. Eng tr, pp. 445-452 in *Church Dogmatics* 4/2 *The Doctrine of Reconciliation* Edinburgh: Clark, 1958. 4/2: xv + 867 pp. The Eng tr is in Ch 15 on Jesus Christ, Sec 65 on "The Sloth and Misery of Man," part 2. "The Sloth of Man." Barth discusses man's inhumanity to man. He adds an interlude on Amos, a proprietor who refuses to be in the tradition of Elijah and Elisha. Amos is under direct compulsion to speak an unequivocal message of judgment. The message is one sided and concrete. The sin is the inhumanity of social relations. God's wrath is irrevocable. Compare the oracles against the nations. The sin is not violation of the covenant but their inhumanity. Barth gives the historical background, the social conditions including the fat and greasy wives of the pashas, details of the oppression of the poor, syncretistic worship, the covenant.

78. Barthelemy, Dominique. "Amos." pp. 642-696 in *Critique textelle de l'Ancien Testament: Tome 3. Ezechiel, Daniel et les 12 Prophetes.* Orbis Biblicus et Orientalis 50/3. Fribourg, Switzerland/ Gottingen: Editions Universitaires/Vandenhoeck & Ruprecht, 1992. xxiv + ccxliv + 1150 pp. The introduction, a book in itself, discusses methodologies, ancient manuscripts, MT, Qumran, Jerome, ancient versions, critical apparatus. The Comite pour l'analyse textuelle de l'Ancien Testament hebreu (1970-1979) analyzed thousands of emendations of the MT in the RSV, Jerusalem Bible, Ecumenical Bible, etc. This supports MT and criticizes text criticism. The analysis is a real history of interpretation, on the origin of the

emendation, pro and con, comparative study, a recommended text.

79. Bartina, Sebastian. *The Book of Amos*. Madrid: Paideia, 1968.

80. Bartina, Sebastian. "'Hiendo los higos de los sicomoros' (Amos 7:14)." *Estudios Biblicos* (Madrid) 25, Nos. 3-4 (1966), 349-354. Transliteration, translation. Reviews many translations, earlier studies, identity of the sycamore.

81. Bartina, Sebastian. "'Vivit Potentia Beer-Seba!' (Amos 8:14)." VD (Rome) 34 (1956), 202-210. Linguistic analysis with extensive review of the literature.

82. Barton, John. *Amos's Oracles Against the Nations: A Study of Amos 1:3 - 2:5*. Society for OT Study Monograph Series 6 ed R.E. Clements. Cambridge: Cambridge University, 1980. x + 83. Reviews some of the many scholarly opinions. The Judah oracle is certainly, the Edom oracle almost certainly, and the Tyre oracle very probably, not by Amos. The others are authentic. There is very little hope of dating these. The oracles are not monotheism, cultic, covenant law, but international law. Israel's election means more accountability than others. An appendix reviews international law in the ANE.

83. Barton, John. "History and Rhetoric in the Prophets." pp. 51-64 in *The Bible as Rhetoric: Studies in Biblical Persuasion and Credibility* ed Martin Warner. Warwick Studies in Philosophy and Literature ed David Wood. London/NY: Routledge, 1990. x + 236 pp. There are two themes in the classical prophets: denunciation for sin, and, judgment. These lead in some places to a third: the call to repent. This simple combination is a *tour de force*. The prophets selectively used history to justify God's ways in the world, i.e., to form a coherent theodicy. They were not visionaries but rational interpreters. Their originality was not the future but the theological interpretation of the future as the will of Yahweh. In the ANE, pride and crimes against humanity angered the gods. The latter, perhaps from the wisdom tradition, includes offences against the natural order. The prophets argued on these two bases that the wrath of Yahweh was judging their nation(s). Yahweh is not arbitrary. Amos and Jeremiah are among the examples of this thinking.

84. Basarab, Mircea. "Cartea profetului Amos. Introducere, traducere si comentariu" (The Book of the Prophet Amos. Introduction, translation and commentary). *Studii Teologice* ser 2, Vol 31, Nos. 5-10 (1979), 391-571.

85. Bates, William H. "The Book of Amos." *The Bible Champion* 28 (1922), 362-363.

86. Bauer, L. "Einege Stellen des Alten Testaments. Amos 4:1-3." TSK 100, No. 4 (1927-1928), 437-438. Exegesis.

87. Bauer-Kayatz, Christa. "Exegetische Informationen uber Eschata, Fortschritt und gesellschaftliches Engagement in der Sicht des Alttestamentlers." pp. 89-118 in *Eschatologie und geschichtliche Zukunft* ed Geog Scherer, et al. Thesen und Argumente 5 (Katholischen Akademie die Wolfsburg). Essen: Fredebeul & Koenen, 1972. 221 pp. Notes the developing concern from 1905-1969. Amos is an example.

88. Baumann, Eberhard. "*shub shboth*. Eine exegetische untersuchung." ZAW 47, No. 1 (1929), 17-44. Word study, history of interpretation, use of the term in Amos and elsewhere.

89. Baumann, Eberhard. *Der Aufbau der Amosreden*. BZAW 7. Giessen: Ricker (Topelmann), 1903. x + 69 pp. Literature review, literary criticism, metrical structure of text.

90. Baumann, Eberhard. "Eine Einzelheit." ZAW 64, ns 23, No. 1 (1952), 62. Amos 7:14. Notes various views, Amos as a cult prophet.

91. Baumann, F. and K. Naef. *Amos. Eine Botschaft aus Alter Zeit fur uns Monderne Menschen*. Zurich: Gotthelf, 1962. 111 pp.

92. Baumgartner, Mia J. "A Revision of Amos 5:21-6:7 (1992)." pp. 16-17 in *Many Voices: Multicultural Responses to the Minor Prophets* ed Alice Ogden Bellis. Lanham, MD: University Press of America, 1995. xiv + 101 pp. The writers in this book try to apply the minor prophets today. This revision is an oracle of judgment against

shallow entertainment, Euro-centric hymns, money, defense, Silicon Valley, etc.

93. Baumgartner, Walter. "Amos 3:3-8." ZAW 33, No. 1 (1913), 78-80. Notes the history of interpretation, gives the Hebrew text rearranged, plus commentary.

94. Baumgartner, Walter. "Kennen Amos und Hosea eine Heilseschatologie?" *Schweizerische Theologische Z* (Zurich) 30 (1913), No. 1:30-42; No. 2:95-124; No. 3:152-170. Diss. Zurich, 1913. Bibliography, review of earlier studies, historical background, commentary, comparative textual analysis.

95. Baur, Gustav A.L. (1816-1889). *Der Prophet Amos erklart.* Giessen: Ricker, 1847. x + 453 pp. The introduction (162 pp.) reviews the historic interpretations, Amos' background and personality, the historical situation, his writing and the composition of the book. The German translation is followed by a verse by verse commentary.

96. Baxter, J. Sidlow. "The Prophet Amos." pp. 125-144 in *Explore the Book: A Basic and Broadly Interpretive Course of Bible Study from Genesis to Revelation.* Vol. 4: Ezekiel to Malachi by Baxter. Grand Rapids: Zondervan, 1966. 4:269 pp. The 1960 original is in 6 volumes. The 1966 version is the 6 printed together, keeping separate pagination. The presentation is in lessons, with the NT Book of Revelation as Lesson No. 147. Amos is covered in Lesson 90. Directions for reading, inspirational thought, an outline of the text and questions for discussion. The latter may be grouped, e.g., questions on Amos are together at the end. Book 3, Lessons 69-70 (pp. 197-214) are a general introduction to the prophets, and prophecy. The lesson includes the background of the man, characteristics of the book, an outline, the theme of judgment.

97. Beach, Eleanor Ferris. "The Samaria Ivories, *Marzeah*, and Biblical Text." *Biblical Archaeology* 56, No. 2 (June 93), 94-104. Amos 6:4-7 says those who lie on beds of ivory will be the first to go into exile. The *marzeah* (revelry) will pass away. Beach interprets the carved ivories found in archaeological excavations as inlays for furniture. This is shown in Assyrian reliefs. She puts these together with the text to relate the Assyrian scenes and other data to make the *marzeah*

a feast memorializing the dead. It may have involved sacred sexual intercourse. The beds of Amos are part of a ceremonial setting. The latter may have been in the house of *marzeah*, Jer 16:5-9. Beach gives a detailed study of the ivories. Amos 6:9-10 refers to 10 men, perhaps a *minyan* for the observance of the *marzeah*. The adaptation of *marzeah* imagery may have helped conceptualize a role for Yahweh beyond death, a relationship of divine and deceased.

98. Beaucamp, Evode. "Amos." pp. 1-18 in *Prophetic Interpretation in the History of Man*. Staten Island, NY: Alba House, 1970. xix + 230 pp. Tr "Amos." pp. 27-47 in *Sous la Main de Dieu. I. Le Prophetisme et l'Election d'Israel*. Paris: Fleurus, 1956. 286 pp. The shepherd came from Tekoa, south of Bethlehem in the time of Jeroboam II, 783-743 BCE. It was a time of great prosperity but he condemned the corruption and pronounced judgment on the nations including Israel. There is only one way open to Israel. "Seek God and you shall live!"

99. Beaucamp, Evode. "Amos 1-2. Le pesha' d'Israel et celui des Nations" (Amos 1-2. A commentary on Israel and the nations). *Science et Esprit* 21, No. 3 (1969), 435-441. Tr, reprinted, pp. 325-330 in *Atualidades Biblicas. Miscelanea em memoria de Frei Joao Jose Pedreira de Castro, O.F.M.* (Biblical Currents: Miscellanea in memory of Brother John Joseph Pedreira de Castro, Franciscan). Sob os auspicios da Liga de Estudios Biblicos (Done under the auspices of the League of Biblical Studies). Obra coletiva de colaboracao international organizada por Joaquim Salvador (Collected work of international collaboration organized by Joaquim Salvador), ed Frei Simao Voigt and Frei Frederico Vier. Petropolis, Brazil: Vozes, 1971. 655 pp. Here the author is called Paul-Evode. Discusses earlier studies, the case of Israel and that of the nations, the literary genre, the nature of the commentary and its double context, the affirmation of the authority of Yahweh the King.

100. Beaucamp, Evode. "Lecture nouvelle des livres d'Amos et d'Osee: A propos d'une 'nouvelle' traduction." *Laval Theologique Philosophique* 28 (1972), 185-192. Amos and Hosea in the ecumenical translation of the Bible. Paris: Cerf, 1969. 116 pp.

101. Bechar, Schlomo. "Seer, go, flee" (Heb). BM 33, No. 3 [Issue No. 114] (1988), 392-396. Amos 7:10-17. Discusses Amos and Amaziah.

102. Bechmann, Ulrike. "Amos - das Wichtigste auf den Punkt gebracht." *Katechetische Blatter* (Munich) 115 (1990), 387-390.

103. Beck, Eleonore. "Amos - Fur das Recht des Menschen." pp. 43-72 in *Gottes Traum: Eine menschliche Welt. Hosea - Amos - Micha.* Stuttgarter Kleiner Kommentar Altes Testament 14, ed Gabriele Miller and Franz Josef Stendebach. Stuttgart: Katholisches Bibelwerk, 1972. 95 pp. Reviews the background of Amos, earliest of the Yahweh prophets. The commentary is in sections.

104. Becker, Joachim. "Amos 8:4-7 (25. Sonntag des Jahres)." Vol. 3 (1971), 61-74 in *Die alttestamentlichen Lesungen der Sonn- und Festtage Auslegung und Verkundigung* ed Josef Schreiner. Schriftleitung Erich Zenger. 20. Sonntag des Jahres bis Christkonig Lesejahr C. Vol. 3. in den Verlagen Echter Katholisches Bibelwerk. Wurzberg: Echter, 1971. 169 pp. Discusses the text and the situation, theological implications (the prophet as social critic) and suggested outlines for preaching.

105. Beecher, Willis J. "The Doctrine of the Day of Jehovah in Obadiah and Amos." HR (NY) 19, No. 2 (Feb 1890), 157-160. Obadiah dates from the time of Amaziah, 2 Kgs 14:7. Edom was punished. Obadiah was influenced by Joel a few years earlier. Amos is about 35 years later. Gives the historical background.

106. Beecher, Willis J. "The Historical Situation in Joel and Obadiah." JBL 8, No. 1 (June 1888), 14-40. Reviews the historical background for both books, compares them to Amos, discusses locusts, human invaders, the Edomites. An objective reader can see that Obadiah and Amos quote Joel, not the other way.

107. Beecher, Willis J. "The Jehovah Hymn in Amos." HR 18, No. 1 (July 1889), 62-65. Notes fragments of a hymn, e.g., Amos 4:13. Some call this as a gloss. Beecher says Amos is preaching, throwing in a fragment of a well-known hymn and continuing.

108. Beecher, Willis J. "Some Instances of Quotations." HR 51, No. 1 (Jan '06), 49-51. Amos 1:2//Joel 3:16 (4:16). Amos 9:13//Joel 3:18 (4:18) In Joel, the passage runs smoothly. In Amos, quotes appear in different parts. Amos quoted from Joel.

109. Beek, Martinus Adrianus. *Amos. Een Inleiding tot het Verstaan der Profeten van het Oude Testament.* "Uit de Wijngaard des Heeren" ed H. Faber and J.M. van Veen. Lochem: N.V. Uitgeversmaatschappij "De Tijdstroom," 1947. 55 pp. Discusses the historical background, prophecy, Amos' visions, the day of the Lord, oracles of the restoration, the false service of God, etc.

110. Beek, Martinus Adrianus. "The Religious Background of Amos 2:6-8." OTS (Leiden) 5 (1948), 132-141. [annual, ed P.A.H. de Boer. Leiden: Brill.] The judgment in the oracles against the nations is an offence against international law. Judah and Israel are reproached for sins in their own community. For the judgment on Israel, pay special attention to the identity of the poor with the *saddik.* The rich man is impious by virtue of his riches.

111. Beek, Martinus Adrianus. "The Visions of Amos." pp. 148-150 in *A Journey Through the Old Testament.* NY: Harper & Brothers, 1959. 254 pp. (original Dutch, 1953) Amos left his work to be a prophet. The visions are strange but the threat of doom in prosperity is stranger. Amos is neither a scientific predictor nor a political genius. But he knew godlessness spells doom.

112. Beeley, Ray. *Amos. Introduction and Commentary.* London: Banner of Truth Trust, 1970. 117 pp. Reviews the man, his situation, his message, the doctrine (God, the failure of man, religious failure). God created the universe. Transcendent, omniscient He chose the Hebrews and demands social righteousness while rejecting empty formal religion. Human failure includes the selfish luxury of the upper classes, the insatiable greed of the merchants, the covetous landowners and the perversion of justice. Religious failure includes prostitution, drunken orgies, a blind sense of security. There are no drunken orgies in Amos but Hosea indicates they were common at court.

113. Begg, Christopher. "The non-mention of Amos, Hosea and Micah in the Deuteronomistic history." BN (Munich) 32 (1986), 41-53. If there was a deuteronomic editing of these books, the lack of reference in the history is not from ignorance, nor for lack of importance. Some of their words could have been objectionable. Begg's discussion includes only the portions of the books widely accepted as authentic. The prophets were concerned with justice while the deuteronomic history is on the cult. Hosea condemns the house of Jehu while the history approves of Jehu and even has God approve of Jehu. The history condemns other dynasties but not Jehu's. Amos' condemnation of Jeroboam II is thus out of line also. Micah predicted the fall of Jerusalem but Hezekiah reformed the cult. The history gives little more than passing attention to Hezekiah, perhaps to leave the bulk of reform to Josiah. Thus Micah's prediction would detract from Hezekiah's reform and seem to contradict it, giving it more attention than the deuteronomist wanted.

114. Bell, H.I. and H. Thompson. "A Greek-Coptic Glossary to Hosea and Amos." *J of Egyptian Archaeology* 11 (1925), 241-246. Four plates. Also published separately. Describes the fragments of papyri, dated 300 BCE or earlier. Transcription of the inscriptions with detailed exegetical notes. Suggests the original was probably for the private use of a scholar rather than liturgics, teaching, etc.

115. Bell, Robert D. "National Judgments (Amos 1-2)." BV 27, No. 2 (Nov 93), 3-7. These chapters provide an excellent basis for strong preaching on God's judgment against the nations for their evil. Bell considers the principles rather than the externals, e.g., God's revelation, the sin of cruelty, punishment by destruction of the population.

116. Bell, Robert D. "The Theology of Amos." BV 27, No. 2 (Nov 93), 47-54. Studies the structure of the book and its theological themes - God, sin, judgment. Sections and themes are tabulated for ease of reference.

117. Bellas, Basileios M. "The Prophet Amos" (Greek). Vol 1 (1957), 149-170 in *Threskeutikai Prosopikotetes tes Palaias Diathekes*, 2nd

ed, 5 vols. Athens: np, 1957. 1:367 + 4 pls. original, Athens: Aster, 1947-1950. A commentary.

118. Bellett, J.G. "Amos." pp. 28-30 in *The Minor Prophets*. London: Allan, 1870. 126 pp. The theme is judgement for Jew and Gentile alike. We are to live by *every* word of God.

119. Bellis, Alice Ogden. "The Book of Amos." pp. 1-2 in *Many Voices: Multicultural Responses to the Minor Prophets* ed Bellis. Lanham, MD: University Press of America, 1995. xiv + 101 pp. The writers in this book try to apply the minor prophets today. Bellis' introduction gives historical, compositional and theological background, and application.

120. Bennett, F.W. *Devotional Studies in Amos*. Grand Rapids: Baker, 1966.

121. Benson, Alphonsus. "'From the Mouth of the Lion.' TheMessianism of Amos." CBQ 19, No. 2 (Ap 57), 199-212. Judgement and disaster but punishment is not total. There is hope for the future. Reviews scholarly opinions and notes the terms prosperity, peace and justice as traditional prophetic images to describe the wonders of the Messianic age. The restored kingdom will be perpetual with no more punishment.

122. Bentzen, Aage (1894-1953). "Amos." Vol 2 (1952), 139-143 in *Introduction to the Old Testament*, 2 vols, 2nd ed. Copenhagen: Gad, 1952. 2:300 (original, 1948-1949) A 32 page addition includes the additions (with an index) to vols 1-2. Vol 1 is on text, canon, literary forms. Discusses the man, historical background, contents, composition (compiler, perhaps related to the liturgy pattern), authenticity and integrity (much debate). Describes several opinions and bibliography.

123. Bentzen, Aage. "The Ritual Background of Amos 1:2-2:16." OTS 8 (1950), 85-99. [annual, ed P.A.H. de Boer. Leiden: Brill, 1950. ix + 322 pp.] Reviews the history of interpretation. Comparisons do not automatically mean direct borrowing. Compares the Egyptian Execration Texts - curses on enemies - to Hebrew prophetic oracles against foreign nations. Amos was opposed to the cult.

124. Benze, C. Theodore. "The Prophet Amos and His Times." *Lutheran Church Review* (Philadelphia) 37, No. 2 (Ap 1918), 111-133. Summarizes the history, the religious situation, the geography, Amos' earlier life, his message. The latter is judgment but hope for the future.

125. Berg, Werner. *Die sogenannte Hymnenfragmente im Amosbuch.* Europaische Hochschulschriften, Series 23, Theology 45. Bern/Frankfurt am Main: Herbert Lang/Peter Lang, 1974. vii + 356 pp. Diss. Ludwig-Maximilians-Universitat, 1974. Amos 4:13, 5:8(9), 9:5-6, and the history of interpretation. Reviews textual and literary criticism, oral tradition, form and *gattung*, redaction and composition criticism, with several excursi, e.g., "Yahweh . . . is his name."

126. Bernard, Michel. "Amos. Exegetical Study." *Ministry* 5 (1965), 66-69, 118-120. 6 (1966), 21-23, 98-105, 158-162. 7 (1967), 178-183. 8 (1968), 77-82, 185-190. 9 (1969), 22-26.

127. Berquist, Jon L. "Dangerous Waters of Justice and Righteousness: Amos 5:18-27." *Biblical Theology Bulletin* 23, No. 2 (Sum 93), 54-63. Review of earlier studies. The Justice and Righteousness are God's own activity to purge Israel for its failure to provide Justice and Righteousness for all people.

128. Berridge, John M. "Jeremia und die Prophetie des Amos." TZ 35 (1979), 321-341. Amos pronounced judgement on the northern kingdom. Jeremiah applied Amos's message to the southern kingdom.

129. Berridge, John M. "Zur Intention der Botschaft des Propheten Amos. Exegetische Uberlegungen zu Amos 5." *Theologische Z* 32, No. 6 (Nov-Dec 76), 321-340. Exegesis with extensive notes on earlier studies.

130. Bertholet, Alfred. "Zu Amos 1:2." pp. 1-12 in *Theologische Festschrift G. Nathanael Bonwetsch zu seinem siebzigsten Geburtstag (17. Februar 1918)*. Leipzig: Deichert, 1918. iii + 154 pp. Commentary, noting alternate views, comparative background.

131. Betteridge, Walter R. "The Attitude of Amos and Hosea toward the Monarchy." BW 20, No. 5 (Nov '02), 361-369, No. 6 (Dec '02), 457-464. Notes the two views of the monarchy, pro and con. Discusses Amos in No. 5 and Hosea in No. 6. Amos saw the monarchy (Davidic dynasty) as necessary to continue Jehovah's kingdom. Israel will be destroyed.

132. Bewer, Julius A. "Amos and Hosea." pp. 89-102 in *The Literature of the Old Testament*, 3rd ed, rev Emil G. Kraeling. The Records of Civilization: Sources and Studies 5 ed Jacques Barzun, et al. NY: Columbia University Press, 1962. xvi + 496 pp. (original 1922) Reviews the historical background, Amos' message of destruction, God's concern for others and not just Israel, a future restoration. The final hope may have been added later.

133. Bewer, Julius A. "Amos." pp. 469-489 in *The Prophets in the King James Version with Introduction and Critical Notes*. NY: Harper & Brothers, 1955. viii + 663 pp. Originally published in fascicles, e.g., "Amos." pp. 15-35 in *The Book of the Twelve Prophets. Vol. 1. Amos, Hosea and Micah*. Harper's Annotated Bible 1. NY: Harper & Brothers, 1949. 79 pp. Annotated KJV. The general introduction notes the beauty of the KJV and special characteristics such as the use of LORD for the name of God. There is an essay on the historical background of the eighth century prophets and another on the prophets and their writings. We do not have the original editions of prophetic books but later versions preserved by their disciples. The later elements, valuable in their own right, can be determined by literary criticism. The introduction to each book has an outline of the book and historical background. The introduction to Amos summarizes his time, work, continuing significance. The notes give more background, identifications, etc. as relevant.

134. Bewer, Julius A. "Critical Notes on Amos 2:7 and 8:4." AJSL (Chicago) 19, No. 2 (Jan '03), 116-117. Notes earlier studies which were wrong. The LXX misunderstood 2:7 which should be tr: "Who trample to the dust of the earth and oppress the poorest of all." The second is like it: "Ye who crush altogether the needy, and oppress the poor of the land."

135. Bewer, Julius A. "Note on Amos 2:7a." JBL 28, No. 2 (1909), 200-202. Suggests "Who long for bribes and oppress the poor in the gate." The LXX had the same Hebrew text as MT and the corruption in this text preceded both.

136. Beyer, Douglas. "Preaching from Amos." SWJT (Fort Worth) 38, No. 1 (Fall 95), 36-42. A series of eight sermons, e.g., "God's Word Seen and Heard" including locusts, plumb line, ripe fruit.

137. Beyerlin, Walter. *Bleilot, Brecheisen Oder Was Sonst? Revision einer Amos-Vision*. Orbis Biblicus et Orientalis 81 ed. Othmar Keel et al. Freiburg, Schwitzerland, and Gottingen: Universitatsverlag and Vandenhoeck & Ruprecht, 1988. 61 pp. Amos 7:7-9 has four examples of 'anak which is not found elsewhere in the OT. Most people think it is the lead plummet of the plumb line but Beyerlin says it means tin.

138. Beyerlin, Walter. *Reflexe der Amosvisionen im Jeremiabuch*. Orbis Biblicus et Orientalis 93 ed Othmar Keel et al. Freiburg, Switzerland/Gottingen: Universitatsverlag/ Vandenhoeck & Ruprecht, 1989. 119 pp. A review of visions in Jeremiah and a comparison with Amos' visions, e.g., Amos 9:4b and Jer 21:10a.

139. Bic, Milos. *Das Buch Amos*. Berlin: Evangelische Verlagsanstalt, 1969. 208 pp. The introduction outlines the book, reviews problems, e.g., Amos' personality. The commentary is by small units.

140. Bic, Milos. "Der Prophet Amos - ein Haepatoskopos." VT 1, No. 4 (Oct 51), 293-296. Reviews interpretations, including *noqed* as a sacral person, i.e., King Mesha was high priest, with implications for Amos' vocation.

141. Biguzzi, Giancarlo. "L'elezione di Israele e dei popoli in Amos." pp. 265-278 in *La Salvezza Oggi*. Pontificia Universitas Urbaniana Studia Urbaniana 34. Rome: Urbaniana University Press, 1989. 609 pp. Discusses the history, the oracles, the election, responsibility, contra the exodus, contra the election.

142. Billeb, Hermann. *Die wichtigsten Satze der neueren alttestamentlichen Kritik vom Standpunkte der Propheten Amos und Hosea aus betrachtet.* Halle a.S.: Anton, 1893. ii + 136 pp. After a general introduction, the two prophets are compared to Job, Joel, Obadiah, Deuteronomy, the Priestly code, etc.

143. Bishop, Eric F.F. "Amos: The Highlands of Tekoa." pp. 173-182 in *Prophets of Palestine: The Local Background to the Preparation of the Way.* London: Lutterworth, 1962. 280 pp. A general introduction notes the continuity of life in Palestine - drought, flood, locusts, but also handicrafts, rituals (e.g., Samaritans), language, etc. Bishop describes the flora and fauna, customs and culture, topography and history noted in Amos and modern continuities, e.g., international relations with surrounding peoples, the common attitude of fatalism, summer figs, shepherds.

144. Bjorndalen, Anders Jorgen. "Erwagungen zur Zukunft des Amazja und Israels nach der Uberlieferung Amos 7:10-17." pp. 236-251 in *Werden und Wirken des Alten Testaments: Festschrift fur Claus Westermann zum 70. Geburtstag* ed Rainer Albertz, Hans-Peter Muller, Hans Walter Wolff and Walther Zimmerli. Gottingen/Neukirchen-Vluyn: Vandenhoeck & Ruprecht/Neukirchener, 1980. 481 pp. Surveys interpretations and discusses particularly Israel, Amaziah and the reader.

145. Bjorndalen, Anders Jorgen. "Jahwe in den Zukunftsaussagendes Amos." pp. 181-202 in *Die Botschaft und die Boten. Festschrift fur Hans Walter Wolff zum 70. Geburtstag* ed Jorg Jeremias and Lothar Perlitt. Neukirchen: Neukirchener, 1981. ix + 426 pp. Detailed analysis of verses, and of Yahweh as lord and person.

146. Bjorndalen, Anders Jorgen. *Untersuchungen zur allegorischen Rede der Propehten Amos und Jesaja.* BZAW 165, ed Otto Kaiser. Berlin/NY: de Gruyter, 1986. xi + 398 pp. Diss. Oslo, 1982. The introduction (pp. 1-132) discusses metaphor, allegory (wider application than usual) and simile. There is a detailed study of Amos 2:9 and 5:2 (pp. 134-174). Rev, Richard J. Coggins, ET 98, No. 12 (Sep 87), 363-364.

147. Bjorndalen, Anders Jorgen. "Zu den Zeitstufen der Zitatformel... *kh 'mr* im Botenverkehr." *ZAW* 86, No. 4 (1974), 393-403. A study of the messenger speech, the formula for quoting direct speech. Compares various usages including Amos 7:11, where the sender and person quoted are not the same, an unusual situation.

148. Blaquart, Jean-Luc. "Parole de Dieu et Prophetes d'Amos a Ezechiel." pp. 15-30 in *L'Ancienne Testament Approches et Lectures: Des Procedures de Travail a la Theologie* presented by Antoine Vanel. Le Point Theologique 24. Paris: Beauchesne, 1977. 209 pp. Discusses the theological and textual problems of the Word of God, the origins of the concept, the expression of faith, variant phrases, different usages, e.g., promise and fulfillment, the experience of the prophets. There are several functions for the Word, e.g., social, cultic. Theologically, it serves the prophets' reflection on their mission, the Deuteronomic reflection on history and mediates the sacred. A chart shows the various usages for Amos, Ezekiel and other prophets.

149. Bleeker, L.H.K. "Amos." pp. 5-123 in *De kleine Propheten. 1. Hosea, Amos*, 3 vols, by Bleeker and G. Smit. Text en Uitleg, ed F.M.Th. Bohl and A. van Veldhuizen. Gronigen: Wolters, 1932. 248 pp. Introduction, translation, commentary. The introduction gives an overview of Amos, comparison with other biblical materials, etc.

150. Blenkinsopp, Joseph. "Amos." pp. 86-96 in *A History of Prophecy in Israel*. Philadelphia: Westminster, 1983. 287 pp. The book reviews the history of prophecy in the Bible and the ANE, with additional background for individual prophets. The new international scene may be why the biblical material turns from stories about a prophet to quoting his words, which are directed to the whole people. His words, including his visions and his arrest for sedition, were preserved by his disciples and edited by the deuteronomic school. The elements of hope are exilic and postexilic but his basic message remains: a society that neglects social justice does not deserve to survive.

151. Block, David M. Samuel Terrien's *The Elusive Presence* as reflected in the Day of the Lord in Amos, Joel, and Zephaniah.

Diss. Southwestern Baptist Theological Seminary, 1990. 234 pp. DAI 52-A (July 91), 189. Terrien, *The Elusive Presence: The Heart of Biblical Theology*. San Francisco: Harper & Row, 1978. Block compares the "Presence" with the day of the Lord. Analyzes the latter in the three prophets. The elusive presence may be a bridge to the NT.

152. Blok, Hanna. "Geografie bij Amos" (Amos and Geography). *Amsterdamse Cahiers voor exegese en Bijbelse theologie* (Kampen) 6 (1985), 91-110. Dutch with Eng summary. An annual ed Karel A. Deurloo, et al. Kampen: Kok, 1985. 198 pp. In translating Amos, should one translate geographical names literally? He is not locating places but expressing a meaning, e.g., in 1:5 he refers to the Beqa Valley between the Lebanon and Antilebanon mountains as the Valley of Evil and strengthens that with the name Bet Eden, House of Lust. Eden is the faraway Bit Adini but that is not important. When Amos names a place, do not translate. When he uses a double meaning, translate for the sake of those who do not know Hebrew. Blok reviews all the names in Amos, checking for double meanings.

153. Blum, E. "Amos in Jerusalem: Beobachtungen zu Am 6:1-7." *Henoch* 16 (1994), 23-47. Several verses reflect a leaders' gathering in Jerusalem, 711-705. These verses are a commentary which reapplies to Jerusalem Amos' words against Samaria. Rev, OTA 18 (June 95), 348-349, # 1024.

154. Boecker, Hans J. "Uberlegungen zur Kultpolemik der vorexilischen Propheten." pp. 169-180 in *Die Botschaft und die Boten. Festschrift fur Hans Walter Wolff zum 70. Geburtstag* ed Jorg Jeremias and Lothar Perlitt. Neukirchen: Neukirchener, 1981. ix + 426 pp. Literature review and discussion of Amos 7:14 and related texts on the prophetic polemic against the cult.

155. Boehmer, Julius. "Ad Amos 3:1-2." *Teologisk Tidsskrift* (Copenhagen) Series 4, Vol 9 (1928), 96-98. Exegesis.

156. Boehmer, Julius. "Amos Nach Gedankengang und Grundgedanken." *Nieuwe Theologische Studien* (Wageningen) 10 (1927), 1-7. A detailed outline of the text, arranged by themes.

157. Boehmer, Julius. "Die Eigenart der prophetischen Heilspredigt des Amos." TSK 76 (1903), 35-47. A general introduction, noting background and earlier studies.

158. Boehmer, Julius. "Die Grundstelle von Amos." *Nieuwe Theologische Studien* 10 (1927), 82-83. Exegesis of Amos 3:1-2.

159. Bogaard, L. van den. "Amos in de Groot Nieuws Bijbel: Functioneel-Equivalent Vertaald?" *Amsterdamse Cahiers voor Exegese en Bijbelse Theologie* 6 (1985), 111-143. Exegesis of the whole book, focusing on functional equivalents.

160. Bohl, F.M.Th. "Amos." pp. 21-22 in *Het Oude Testament.* Bijbelsch-Kerkelijk Woordenboek, I, ed A. van Veldhuizen, et al. Gronigen/The Hague: Wolters, 1919. vii + 332 pp. A general statement about the meaning of the name, the prophet, date, message, analysis/outline of the text, bibliography.

161. Bohlen, Reinhold. "Zur Sozialkritik des Propheten Amos." *Trierer Theologische Z* 95 (1986), 282-301. Analysis of 2:6-8 and 8:4-7 show Amos had no restoration program. He spoke for God and not the oppressed. Rev, OTA 10 (1987), 177.

162. Boice, James Montgomery. "Amos." pp. 131-186 in *The Minor Prophets: An Expositional Commentary. Vol. I. Hosea - Jonah.* Ministry Resources Library. Grand Rapids: Zondervan, 1983. 261 pp. The volume includes Hosea, Joel, Amos, Obadiah and Jonah. In his general introduction, Boice notes that in preaching about the minor prophets, he found them powerful, speaking to present sin and calling for present action. They highlight God's sovereignty - he's in charge of history. God is holy; sin is an offense calling for judgment. God loves. Liberal scholars see love as incompatible with justice so they leave out the love. But he sends judgment because he loves. Boice spread his preaching out over 10 years. The church has not paid much attention to Amos. People are guilty of the sins he condemned. Millions live in poverty and starvation while the rich get richer. Amaziah the priest thought Amos was in it for the money too. Boice notes that he too has been warned that if he "wants to get ahead," he must do so and so. The book of Amos has three lessons. God is righteous. God is not satisfied with

formalism in religion. We need to accept Amos' challenge to do good.

163. Bonnardiere, Anna Marie La. "Livre D'Amos." pp. 23-24 in *Les Douze Petits Prophetes*. Biblia Augustiniania A.T. 3. Paris: Etudes Augustiniennes, 1963. 55 pp. The introduction discusses Augustine's use of the Minor Prophets, including the NT, with an emphasis on Christology. Each of the 12 books is presented in table lists with references for that book in the writings of Augustine. Notes give additional data.

164. Bonora, Antonio. *Amos. Il Profeta della Giustizia.* Leggere Oggi la Bibbia, Antico Testamento (Bible Study for Today 1; OT 24) 1.24, ed Luigi Della Torre, Mario Masini, Antonio Bonora. Brescia: Queriniana, 1979. 78 pp.

165. Bonora, Antonio. "Amos difensore del diritto e della guistizia." pp. 69-90 in *Testimonium Christi: Scritti in onore de Jacques Dupont* with Maria Grazia Angelini, et al. Brescia: Paideia, 1985. The social critic of today is interested in Amos' concern for justice but this was not political ideology. Amos' concern was the will of God.

166. Booij, Peter J. "Translation Problems in the Amos Doxologies" (Dutch). pp. 90-97, 193 in *Beginnen bij de Letter Beth: Opstellen over het Bijbels Hebreeuws en de Hebreeuwse Bijbel voor Dr Aleida G. van Daalen, leesmoeder in Amsterdam* ed Karel A. Deurloo and F.J. Hoogewoud. Kampen: Kok, 1985. 205 pp. Gives a transcription and translation of the doxologies with detailed exegesis and commentary. The English summary notes the background of this study of the doxologies is the translation by members of the Societas Hebraica Amstelodamensis. It considers difficult words and phrases, differences between Hebrew and Dutch syntax, stylistic effects in Hebrew and Dutch.

167. Boone, Tony. "Oracle in the Style of Amos (1993)." p. 11 in *Many Voices: Multicultural Responses to the Minor Prophets* ed Alice Ogden Bellis. Lanham, MD: University Press of America, 1995. xiv + 101 pp. The writers in this book try to apply the minor prophets today. Boone gives an oracle of judgment against affirmative action that does not act.

168. Borger, Rykle. "Amos 5:26, Apostelgeschichte 7,43 und Surpu II,180." ZAW 100, No. 1 (1988), 70-81. The Shurpu reading *Sag-kud Kajamanu* is actually *Sag-kud Nita* (Sagkud = Ninurta; Kajamanu = Kewan = Saturn). This reading can no longer be used to confirm the reading "Sakkut" in Amos 5:26. The reading, Sakkut, can not be confirmed or denied and should be listed as hypothetical.

169. Boschi, B. "La Tradizione dell'esodo nei primi profeti (Amos, Osea, I Isaia, Michea)." *Rivista Biblica* (Italy) 16 (1968), 129-142.

170. Bose, H.M. du. "The Oldest Written Prophecy." HR 108, No. 1 (1934), 61-63. A sermon on Amos 1:2, noting decline, challenge and redemption, the prophet's call, the need for repentance.

171. Bosman, H.L. "Does Disaster Strike Only When the Lord Sends It? Prophetic Eschatology and the Origin of Evil in Amos 3:6." OTE (Pretoria) 1, No. 2 (1988), 21-30. The verse is eschatological. Amos was not interested in the ultimate source of evil (a mystery) but Yahweh as the source of judgment in the form of natural disasters. Other nations will be judged. The new element is Amos' expectation that Israel will also be judged.

172. Bosshard, Everett. "Septuagint Codices V, 62, and 147 in the Book of Amos." JBL 58, No. 4 (1939), 331-347. There was no uniform Greek version before Aquila, Theodotion and Symmachus. Codex V is a later recension in the same family as 62 and 147. Scholars debate with some saying the Lucianic family and others saying no. Bosshard discusses the characteristics of the Lucian tradition, Montgomery's application of this to the study of Daniel, and Bosshard's application to the study of Amos (pp. 337-347) concluding Codices 62 and 147 represent the Parent Text of Lucian.

173. Botterweck, G. Johannes. "Amos." vol 1 (1957), cols 1295-1296 in *Lexikon fur Theologie und Kirche*, 2nd ed, 14 vols, ed Josef Hofer and Karl Rahner. Freiburg: Herder, 1957-1968. 4:49 pp. + 1272 cols. Reviews the name, historical background, syncretism, false worship, the message of doom.

174. Botterweck, G. Johannes. "Zur Authentizitat des Buches Amos." BZ (Freiburg im Breisgau) 2, No. 2 (1958), 179-189. Reviews the history of interpretation, analyzes the meter of selected passages. Amos' message is in no way abrogated.

175. Botterweck, G. Johannes. "'Sie verkaufen den Unschuldigen um Geld.' Zur sozialen Kritik des Propheten Amos." *Bibel und Leben* (Dusseldorf) 12, No. 4 (1971), 215-231. Studies the social criticism of the prophet Amos, historical and sociological background, the law, morality, and wisdom traditions, the faith of the prophets.

176. Bouwman, Gisbert. *Des Julian von Aeclanum Kommentar zu den Propheten Osee, Joel und Amos. Ein Beitrag zur Geschichte der Exegese.* Analecta Biblica Investigationes Scientificae in Res Biblicas 9. Rome: Pontifical Biblical Institute, 1958. xx + 154 pp. + 2 pls. Part of the history of exegesis. Julian (380-455) of Eclanum (southern Italy) was a Pelagian. Bouwman provides a context by reviewing Julian's polemic and exegetical (Job, Minor Prophets, Song of Solomon) works and those which are doubtful.

177. Bouwman, Gisbert. "Juliani Aeclanensis commentarius in prophetas minores tres: Osee, Joel und Amos." VD 36 (1958), 284-291. A summary of the defense of his thesis. Compares the exegetical methods of Jerome, Theodore of Mopsuestia, et al. Julian translated Theodore's *Commentary on the Psalms*.

178. Bouzon, Emanuel. "Amos 7:12-15 (15. Sonntag des Jahres)." Vol. 3 (1970), 56-64 in *Die alttestamentlichen Lesungen der Sonn- und Festtage Auslegung und Verkundigung* ed Josef Schreiner. Schriftleitung Erich Zenger. 10. Sonntag des Jahres bis Christkonig Lesejahr B. Vol. 3. in den Verlagen Echter Katholisches Bibelwerk. Wurzberg: Echter, 1970. 251 pp. Discusses the text and the situation, theological implications and suggested outlines for preaching.

179. Bovati, Pietro and Roland Meynet. *Le Livre du Prophete Amos.* Rhetorique Biblique 2 ed Bovati and Meynet. Paris: Cerf, 1994. 443 pp. The volume is condensed in paperback as *La Fin d'Israel: Paroles d'Amos.* Lire la Bible 101. Paris: Cerf, 1994. 238 pp. The

introduction reviews the history of interpretation and the concept
of rhetorical analysis on which this commentary is based.

180. Bowman, G. *Das Julian von Aeclanum Kommentar zu den
Propheten Osee, Joel und Amos*. Ein Beitrag zur Geschichte der
Exegese. Rome, 1958.

181. Box, G.H. "Amos 2:6 and 8:6." ET 12, No. 8 (May '01), 377-378.
The reference is to bribery. The shoe was a symbol of possession.

182. Box, G.H. and W.O.E. Oesterley. "Amos 6:9 and 10." ET 12, No.
5 (Feb '01), 235-236. Compares MT and LXX and the doublets in
each. Vss 9-10 are Amos and not an editor.

183. Boyle, Marjorie O'Rourke. "The Covenant Lawsuit of the Prophet
Amos: 3:1-4:13." VT 21, No. 3 (July 71), 338-362. Notes the
history of interpretation on covenant in the prophets and
specifically in Amos. Most scholars just accept the conclusions of
others without further thought. She discusses exceptions, e.g.,
Amos as a liturgy of covenant renewal. Analyzes the lawsuit in
Amos. It's also used in Micah, Isaiah and Jeremiah.

184. Bracke, John M. "*Shub shebuth*: A Reappraisal." ZAW 97, No. 2
(1985), 233-244. The phrase refers to restoration through God's
reversal of his judgment. Reviews earlier studies and OT usage of
the phrase including Amos 9:14-15 where it reverses all the earlier
threats.

185. Braithwaite, Edward E. "Is the Book of Amos Post-Exilic?" BS
(Oberlin, OH) 59, No. 234 (Ap '02), 366-374. No. A review of Day
and Chapin in AJSL, the arguments pro and con.

186. Braithwaite, Edward E. "Why Did Amos Predict the Captivity?" BS
59, No. 233 (Jan '02), 192-197. God told him. Reviews various
scholarly opinions, the historical background, the religious situation
in the time of Amos.

187. Brandt, Theodor. "Amos." pp. 10-13 in *Von Amos bis Daniel*. Witten: Luther Verlag, 1953. 63 pp. Reviews the background and message.

188. Brandt, Theodor. *Die Botschaft des Amos*. Leipzig: Madchen-Bibel-Kreises, 1931. 78 pp.

189. Brandt, Theodor. *Das Zeugnis des Amos und Hosea*, 2nd ed. Bad Salzuflen: MBK (Missions- und Bibel-Kunde), 1948. 80 pp. Reviews the historical background of the two prophets. For Hosea, he notes the power of love, the new covenant, the Syro-Ephraimite war, the role of Jacob.

190. Braslabi/Braslavi, Joseph. "Amos - Noqed, Boqer and Boles Shikmim" (Heb). BM 12 [Issue No. 31], No. 3 (July 67), 87-101.

191. Braslabi, Joseph. "Does a Lion Roar in the Forest When He Has No Prey?" (Heb). BM 12 [Issue No. 30], No. 2 (Mar 67), 12-16.

192. Braslabi, Joseph. "Jer 16:5 and Amos 6:7" (Heb). BM 17 [Issue No. 48], No. 1 (Oct-Dec 71), 5-16. A study of the marzeach.

193. Braslabi, Joseph. "The Lions of the Wilderness of Tekoa in the Book of Amos" (Heb). BM 13 [Issue No. 32], No. 1 (Oct 67), 56-64. A general review including earlier studies.

194. Bratisiotis/Mpratsiotes, Pan.I. "'Amos." 2 (1963), 447-449 in *Threskeutike kai Ethike Enkyklopaideia*. Athens: Martinos, 1963. xiv + 1246 cols. A general review.

195. Braun, Michael A. "James' Use of Amos at the Jerusalem Council: Steps Toward a Possible Solution of the Textual and Theological Problems." JETS 20, No. 2 (June 77), 113-121. There are glaring textual discrepancies between the MT of Amos 9:11-12 and Acts 15. Reviews problems and opinions, e.g., pronominal suffixes disagree in number and gender. The LXX may have a different Hebrew *vorlage*. James used Amos to convince and unite the assembly. How? Both Jews and Gentiles seek the Lord. The "remnant" is an important concept here. James preserves the

distinction while he pleads for the inclusion of the Gentiles in the fellowship.

196. Breisch, Francis. "The God We Hate to Live With." *His* (Downers Grove, IL) 30, No. 3 (Dec 69), 16-18. Amos told people the more they worshipped, the more they sinned. Discusses calamities and God's call to greatness.

197. Breisch, Francis. "No Shoes for the Poor." *His* 30, No. 2 (Nov 69), 7-9. Amos 1-2. God's judgment is on us today - on American society, on the Church. Amos calls us to repent.

198. Breisch, Francis. "Price of Prophetic Speech." *His* 30, No. 4 (Jan 70), 28-30. We need Amos today. He spoke with conviction but not in his own name. We need to be personally involved and must shed godly tears.

199. Breisch, Francis. "When God is Silent." *His* 30, No. 5 (Feb 70), 15-16, 21. Amos 8:1. Our society is much like Amos' society. He cried out against the active abuse of people. Will we work for God's standard of justice?

200. Bright, John. "Amos." pp. 27-29 in *Dictionary of the Bible* ed James Hastings, rev Frederick C. Grant and Harold Henry Rowley. NY: Scribner's, 1963. xxi + 1059 pp. Discusses Amos the man, his time, contents and theology of the book. The message is terrifyingly simple: repent or you are doomed. Amos did not promote a new doctrine. His preaching was based on the covenant. People had violated the covenant. The Day of Yahweh will be a day of judgment.

201. Bright, John. "A New View of Amos." Int 25, No. 3 (July 71), 355-358. A review essay of Wolff (BK, 1969).

202. Brillet, Gaston. "Amos." pp. 17-63 in *Amos et Osee*. Temoins de Dieu [Witnesses of God] 3. Paris: Cerf, 1944. 108 pp. The series title is cited in secondary literature but does not appear in the text actually seen. A general introduction gives the historical background. The introduction to Amos gives specifics and reviews

Amos the man, his vocation, his message. There is a chapter on Amos as a witness of God and of conscience.

203. Brin, Gershon. "The Visions in the Book of Amos (7:1-8:3): Studies in Structure and Ideas" (Heb). 2:275-290 in *Isac [sic] Leo Seeligman Volume: Essays on the Bible and the Ancient World*, 3 vols, ed Alexander Rofe and Yair Zakovitch. Jerusalem: Rubinstein, 1982. Vol 2:v + 275 - 572. Discusses the literary genre, structure of the text, earlier opinions and comparative textual studies.

204. Briscoe, D. Stuart. "Hearing What God Has to Say: Amos." pp. 43-56 in *Taking God Seriously: Major Lessons from the Minor Prophets*. Waco, TX: Word, 1986. 190 pp. The primary purpose of the OT prophets was not predicting or foretelling. Prophecy is not a crystal ball to see into the future. The prophets relayed the word of God to their contemporaries. One piece of this was future but much was for the here and now of the people. [Someone suggested they were "forthtellers."] Amos confronted Amaziah the priest who should have been ministering the Word to the people. Instead he told Amos to leave. Amos continued to speak and speaks to us now. But people then refused to listen. People today are in church in body, but in spirit? God's response was to despise their assemblies, their music. God has spoken. Have you been listening?

205. Bronznick, Norman M. "More on *hlk 'l*." VT 35, No. 1 (1985), 98-99. Translates Amos 2:7 "sexual intercourse" as does the Targum of Jonathan. Cites other scholars, the Akkadian, other examples in the Bible.

206. Brooke, G.J. "The Amos-Numbers Midrash (CD 7:13b-8:1a) and Messianic Expectation." ZAW 92, No. 3 (1980), 397-404. Earlier versions of the Damascus Documents referred to one Messiah. In later recensions, the Zechariah material was removed and replaced by the Amos-Numbers material supporting two Messiahs, in line with the rest of Qumran material.

207. Brown, S. Lawrence. "Amos: The Man and His Message." *The Interpreter* (London) 3, No. 3 (Ap '07), 296-304. Tells the story. Amos was a new type of prophet, neither ecstatic nor for hire.

Amos was a layman, trained in the hard school of nature. The pious Jew saw the hand of God in everything. Amos wrote in pure classical Hebrew, with a wide range of knowledge, winning the attention of his audience with a remarkable skill. He was not a socialist for he had no new social scheme. He was simply a preacher of righteousness, disgusted with Israel's sins (Brown describes), appealing to the universal conscience of mankind. With Amos, we move from monolatry to monotheism. God is God of the whole world.

208. Brown, Walter E. "Amos 5:26: A Challenge to Reading and Interpretation." TE 52 (Fall 95), 69-78. The verse has been translated in many ways. Brown examines key terms, e.g., are the nouns common or are they proper names? The latter is most probable though the evidence is ambiguous. The verse is probably a parody of popular religion, proclaiming the real God over the people of Israel.

209. Browning, Jo Ann. "Oracle in the Style of Amos (1990)." p. 14 in *Many Voices: Multicultural Responses to the Minor Prophets* ed Alice Ogden Bellis. Lanham, MD: University Press of America, 1995. xiv + 101 pp. The writers in this book try to apply the minor prophets today. Browning gives an oracle of judgment against South Africa.

210. Brueggemann, Walter. "Amos 4:4-13 and Israel's Covenant Worship." VT 15, No. 1 (Jan 65), 1-15. The passage opens with "prepare to meet your God." This is not a gloss but the opening for covenant making. The preparation is an act of sanctification in holy war. The curses are part of the covenant. The whole is a liturgy of covenant renewal.

211. Brueggemann, Walter. "Amos' Intercessary Formula." VT 19, No. 4 (Oct 69), 385-399. The conventional interpretation of Amos as a preacher of Judgment is under challenge. Now he is placed in a context of covenant worship or wisdom teaching. The judgment of 7:2, 5, stands but now it's in a context of covenant liturgy and lawsuit. Discusses Israel as small, the form of the intercession, Amos as covenant mediator. Ch 9:11-15 may not be a gloss but the central kerygma.

212. Bruin, Cebus Cornelis de, ed. "Prophetia Amos." pp. 292-299 in *Het Oude Testament. Derde Stuk. Jesaja - II Maccabeen.* Verzameling van Middlenederlandse Bijbelteksten Grote Reeks Afdeling I: Het Oude Testament. Corpus Sacrae Scripturae Neerlandicai Mediiaevi Series Maior Tomus I: Vetus Testament Pars Tertia. Leiden: Brill, 1978. 3:x + 408 pp. Translation plus annotation and critical notes.

213. Brunet, Gilbert. "La vision de l'etain. Reinterpetation d'Amos 7:7-9." VT 16, No. 4 (Oct 66), 387-395. Discusses the history of interpretation.

214. Bruno, Arvid. "Amos." pp. 53-77 in *Das Buch der Zwolf: Eine rhythmische und textkritische Untersuchung.* Stockholm: Almqvist & Wiksell, 1957. 234 pp. A translation with the text presented in poetic form in strophes, etc. There is also further discussion on the strophes and charts showing the proportions among the minor prophets (pp. 189-196) and critical notes (Amos pp. 208-212).

215. Bruns, H. *Sie Waren Gottes Mund. Die Botschaft der Zwolf Kleinen Propheten.* Gladbeck, 1956.

216. Bruston, Edouard. "Messages prophetiques: I. Le message d'Amos." ETR (Montpellier) 7 (1932), 158-172. Gives historical and religious background, Amos's call, the structure of the text, the visions, comparisons with other texts and studies.

217. Brzegowy, T. "The oldest description of the prophetic call." (Pol). pp. 112-124 in *Serutamini Scripturas. Ksiega pamiatkowa S. Lacha.* Cracow, 1980. Amos 7:10-17.

218. Buber, Martin and Franz Rosenzweig. "Amos." pp. 631-653 in *Bucher der Kundung*, rev. Cologne: Hegner, 1958. 778 pp. Original, Die Schrift XIII. Das Buch Zwolf. Berlin: Lambert Schneider, 1934. German paraphrase of the biblical text, without notes.

219. Buck, Fidel. "Amos." pp. 185-241 in *La Sagrada Escritura, texto y comentario. Antiguo Testamento 6. Daniel y Profetas menores* (The Sacred Scripture, Text and Commentary. Old Testament 6.

Daniel and the minor prophets), collaborators Jose Alonso Diaz and Buck. Biblioteca de autores cristianos 323, ed. Juan Leal, et al. Madrid: Editorial Catolica, 1971. xxxii + 608 pp. Spanish text with section by section commentary. The general introduction to the minor prophets includes bibliography. The introduction to Amos includes a review of his life, his ministry, the authenticity of the book, major doctrines, special studies and commentaries.

220. Buck, Harry M. "Amos." pp. 183-197 in *People of the Lord: The History, Scriptures, and Faith of Ancient Israel*. NY: Macmillan, 1966. xvii + 653 pp. Discusses the history, Amos' call, the confrontation with Amaziah, the visions, Israelite religion, universalism, the added note of hope.

221. Budde, Karl Ferdinand Reinhardt (1850-1935). "Amos 1:2." ZAW 30, No. 1 (1910), 37-41. Exegesis. Notes earlier studies.

222. Budde, Karl. "Amos." Vol. 1:530-33 in *The Jewish Encyclopedia*, 12 vols, ed Isadore Singer, Cyrus Adler, et al. NY: KTAV, n.d. (original 1901). His date of birth and death are unknown. He was from Tekoa. He did not need fees for prophesying because he was well to do, a sheep herder and dresser of sycamore trees, not found in Tekoa but in the Shephalah, the hill country leading to Philistia. He was the first writing prophet. Cheyne thinks he wrote in Jerusalem and left his work with disciples there. He had an uncompromisingly moral conception of the universe. This did not preclude forgiveness if there was genuine repentance so the hopeful verses are not spurious. There are later additions such as 7:10-17 which report his expulsion from the northern kingdom in the third person. Other vss such as the doxologies - 4:13, 5:8, 9:56 - have also been called additions.

223. Budde, Karl. "Eine folgenschwere Redaktion des Zwolfprophetenbuchs." ZAW 39, No. 2 (1921), 218-229. The study draws examples from several of the Twelve, including Amos. Contributes to understanding the collection as a whole.

224. Budde, Karl. "Zur Geschichte des Buches Amos." pp. 63-77 in *Studien zur semitischen Philologie und Religionsgeschichte: [Festschrift fur] Julius Wellhausen zum siebzigsten Geburtstag am*

17. Mai 1914 ed Karl Marti. BZAW 27. Giessen: Topelmann, 1914. xi + 388 pp. Notes the history of interpretation, the question of Amos' status in Tekoa in relation to the prophetic tradition and the cult at Bethel. The prophet-editor who compiled his works left the goodness of the Lord for the Messiah Himself who shall come to restore the Golden Age. The Prophets of Israel were never shaken in this belief that the Messiah would be called David's Son. A chronological chart suggests Amos was born c 805 and died c 747 BCE.

225. Bushey, Stanley Lewis. "Theology of Amos." BV 14, No. 4 (Ap 80), 62-67. Summarizes Amos' concept of God as just, universal.

226. Byargeon, Rick W. "The Doxologies of Amos: A Study of Their Structure and Theology." TE 52 (Fall 95), 47-56. Amos has two genres: oracles and visions. Interspersed at significant junctures are three doxologies. Byargeon examines the structure of Amos' prophecy, repetition as a structural key to Amos' prophecy, the structural significance of the doxologies. God is the Creator who controls all of creation. He will judge and right the wrongs of the world.

C.

227. Cadman, S. Parkes. "Amos." pp. 28-35 in *The Prophets of Israel*. NY: Macmillan, 1933. xi + 197 pp. Amos lived in a time of prosperity which was undermined by pagan rites. Amos, an obscure peasant, brooded long and darkly over the obscenities that degraded the Northern Kingdom. He told the people at Bethel that God would destroy them. They thought that was sheer insanity so Amaziah the priest told him to go home to Judah and prophecy. Amos said Amaziah's wife would be a prostitute in the city, his sons and daughters and he himself would die in an unclean land. There was still hope but God required righteousness - hate evil and love good - seek me and live. Amos returned to his sheep and sycamores.

228. Caiger, Stephen L. "Amos." pp. 76-97 in *Lives of the Prophets: A Thousand Years of Hebrew Prophecy Reviewed in Its Historical Context*. London: SPCK, 1954. 333 pp. (original, 1936; rev, 1948) Amos and Hosea inaugurated the epoch of the "Writing Prophets." Caiger discusses the childhood of Amos, the latter's call, Amos at Beth-el, his expulsion from Bethel. The prophet-editor who compiled his works left the "goodness of the Lord" because the Messiah Himself shall come to restore the Golden Age. The Prophets of Israel were never shaken in this belief that the Messiah would be called David's Son. A chronological chart suggests Amos was born c 805 and died c 747 BCE.

229. Calkins, Raymond. "Amos." pp. 13-30 in *The Modern Message of the Minor Prophets*. NY: Harper & Brothers, 1947. ix + 205 pp. The title, "Minor Prophets," is from St. Augustine, because they are short compared to the "Major" prophets. Hebrew literature calls them "The Book of the Twelve." In English Bibles, they come at the end of the Old Testament but we do not know why. Their collection and arrangement is also "wrapped in obscurity." We can

assume we have only a remnant of what they said. We also have
more than what they said because later editors added to the material
to form the present texts. They all spoke in evil days but they all
had hope. Amos is the first literary prophet. Amos was not a
prophet but an original spiritual genius. As a sheepherder, he
probably traded wool in the Bethel and Samaria markets, a day's
journey from Tekoa. He met men of many lands and learned from
them. He saw sin - the rotten social order beneath apparent
prosperity - and he saw the inevitable judgment. After preaching at
Bethel, he went home and wrote his book. He was a writer of
consummate skill. The book is an authentic record of his preaching.
He taught that righteousness is a universal principle, God is
universal righteousness, only righteousness can satisfy him (not
sacrifices) and unrighteousness will be punished in Israel like
anywhere else.

230. Calvin, John. "The Commentaries of John Calvin on the Prophet
Amos." Vol 2: 145-413 in *Commentaries on the Twelve Minor
Prophets*, 5 vols, tr John Owen. Grand Rapids, MI: Eerdmans,
1950. 530 pp. (reprint from 1849 ed). Reprinted in various editions,
e.g., Banner of Truth, 1986. Owen's preface notes the lectures were
extemporaneous. Some who heard them took notes, which were
later corrected by Calvin. The publication is of these corrected
notes. The introduction to Amos notes the historical background,
Amos' origin in the tribe of Judah but his preaching to the Ten
Tribes. The commentary is in lectures (Nos. 49-69) with
interpretations, closing with a prayer. The text is given in English
and Latin. The volume closes with a translation of Calvin's version
of the three prophets. Amos is pp. 469-484. A second appendix
provides additional notes on Amos (pp. 510-513).

231. Campbell, Antony F. *The Study Companion to Old Testament
Literature: An Approach to the Writings of Pre-Exilic and Exilic
Israel*. Old Testament Studies 2. Wilmington, DE: Glazier, 1989.
viii + 504 pp. Reviews the Pentateuch, deuteronomic history, the
pre-exilic prophets, Jonah and Job. Campbell considers the
prophetic books as literary works, and the prophetic censure of,
threat to, and hope for Israel, plus a chapter on the theology of the
pre-exilic prophets. Amos is cited extensively for these categories.

232. Campbell, Edward F. "Archaeological Reflections on Amos's Targets." pp. 32-52 in *Scripture and Other Artifacts: Essays on the Bible and Archaeology in Honor of Philip J. King* ed Michael D. Coogan, et al. Louisville, KY: Westminster/John Knox, 1994. xxvii + 452 pp. House 1727 at Shechem is examined in detail as an example of the wealthy against whom Amos preached.

233. Camroux, Martin. "Let Justice Roll." ET 105, No. 8 (May 94), 244-245. Amos 7:10-15. Gives the historical background, Amos' response to injustice, God's concern today, opposition to racism, concern for the homeless.

234. Canney, Maurice A. "Amos." pp. 547-554 in *A Commentary on the Bible* ed Arthur S. Peake. NY/London: Nelson/Jack, 1920. xxiii + 1014 pp. Amos is the first of the writing prophets though we do not know if he wrote the book himself or dictated it. This was probably done after he preached at Bethel and returned to Tekoa. Later editing rearranged materials but left the original intact though some passages are probably later, e.g., 9:9-15. Elaborate reconstructions have been attempted but the result is probably very different from Amos. He had a passionate love for justice and a hatred for oppression and senseless luxury. His religion was far in advance of his own day, and ours.

235. Carbone, Sandro Paolo and Giovanni Rizzi. *Il Libro di Amos: Lettura ebraica, greca e aramaica.* EDB: Edizioni Dehoniane Bologna. Bologna: Dehoniane, 1993. 176 pp. The introduction discusses comparisons of the three sources - history, style, etc. The text of Amos is given in three parallel columns from the MT, LXX and Targum with detailed exegetical and comparative notes.

236. Carlsen, Bodil Hjerrild. "Amos in Judeo-Persian." pp. 73-112 in *Orientalia J[acques] Duchesne-Guillemin emerito oblata.* Acta Iranica 23. Hommages et Opera Minora 9. Leiden: Brill, 1984. 542 pp. + lxiv pp. of plates. A study of the Amos portion of MS 101 in H. Zotenberg, *Catalogue des Manuscrits Hebreaux et Samaritains de la Bibliotheque Imperiale.* Paris, 1866. The manuscript contains the 12 minor prophets and Lamentations. The Amos portion is a bad translation based on MT but uses occasional LXX readings. It

is annotated in the margin by a later hand. Carlsen gives a transliteration, critical notes and plates.

237. Carlson, Agge. "Profeten Amos och Davidsriket." *Religion och Bibel* (Lund) 25 (1966), 57-78. Notes many earlier studies, compares Amos with other texts, e.g., Samuel, translates pericope, including 9:11-15 (God will raise the booth of David) with commentary.

238. Carny, Pin'has. "Amos 4:13 - A Doxology?" (Heb). pp. 143-151. *HaZvi Israel: Studies in Bible Dedicated to the Memory of Israel and Zvi Broide* ed Jacob Licht and Gershon Brin. Tel Aviv: Tel Aviv University, School of Jewish Studies, 1976. 168 pp. Exegesis, discussion, review of scholarly opinions.

239. Carny, Pin'has. "Doxologies - A Scientific Myth." *Hebrew Studies* (Louisville, KY) 18 (1977), 149-159. Amos 4:13 is usually considered a doxology. Carny says no. It is the prophecy of destruction of vs 12. Detailed exegesis and review of earlier studies.

240. Carrier, A.S. "The *Hapax Legomena* of the Minor Prophets." *Hebraica* 5, Nos. 2-3 (Jan-Ap 1889), 131-136. Amos pp. 135-136. Exegesis.

241. Carroll, Robert P. "Amos." pp. 19-21 in *A Dictionary of Biblical Interpretation* ed Richard J. Coggins and J.L. Houlden. London/Philadelphia: SCM/Trinity, 1990. xvi + 751 pp. Notes the continuing influence of Amos (limited), including application in liberation theology because of Amos' concern for social justice. Amos' encounter with Amaziah and his denial of his identity as a prophet raises the question of prophecy. His switch from total doom to salvation is a later addition. The editorial history of Amos has been a major scholarly concern. Carroll notes several theories and continuing concerns, e.g., Amos' ethics.

242. Carroll R.[sic], Mark Daniel. *Contexts for Amos: Prophetic Poetics in Latin American Perspective.* JSOT Supplement 132, ed David J.A. Clines and Philip R. Davies. Sheffield, England: JSOT, 1992. 362 pp. Diss. University of Sheffield, 1990. An alternative

approach to Latin American liberation theologians. A sociological study, including the puritans who condemned Catholic England, and modern sociologists who apply their concepts to today, e.g., Geertz, Berger, MacIntyre, Hauerwas, et al. Compares Latin American morality with Israelite morality, the moral authority of the Bible, a poetic reading of Amos with a discussion of the social construction of reality in Amos, and applying Amos in a modern context. The poetic reading is more fruitful than the myriad of sociological reconstructions of so much recent scholarship. There are two appendices, one on tradition and history in Amos (e.g., cult, covenant, wisdom, historical background) and one on textual method in Latin American liberation theology (survey of Miranda, Tamez, Andrinach, Croatto).

243. Carroll R.[sic], Mark Daniel. "The Prophetic Text and the Literature of Dissent in Latin America: Amos, Garcia Marquez, and Cabrera Infante Dismantle Militarism." *Biblical Interpretation* 4, No. 1 (Feb 96), 76-100. Compares Amos and the Latin American novels of dissent, especially the Colombian Marques and the Cuban Infante. Literary strategies can show the pretense and cruelty. Amos ridicules and condemns militarism through literary technique. He echoes many concerns today. He not only can be read this way but helps the people of God confront the harsh realities of life. It is God, not Amos, who destroys militarism. Israel's reality is a lie. But beyond that, there is another reality - of security and abundance (Amos 9:11-15). There is hope.

244. Cartledge, Samuel A. "The Book of Amos." pp. 113-116 in *A Conservative Introduction to the Old Testament.* Grand Rapids, MI: Zondervan, 1943. 238 pp. A general introduction to the prophets reviews Hebrew terms, prediction, disciples, false prophets, revelation. The name means burden or burden bearer. Reviews Amos' life, the date, socio-economic situation, the contents of the book, literary unity, the debate over the hopeful future.

245. Casalis, Georges. "Du Texte au Sermon 12: Amos 8." ETR 46, No. 2 (1971), 113-124. Exegesis, structural analysis, commentary, interpretation.

246. Caspari, Wilhelm (1814-1892). "Amos." pp. 49-54 in *Die
      israelitischen Propheten*. Wissenschaft und Bildung 122. Leipzig:
      Quelle & Meyer, 1914. 156 pp. The volume has a general
      introduction to prophecy, style, true and false prophets,
      apocalyptic. This is followed by a review of individual prophets,
      followed by a section on writing (symbolic language, relationship
      to the Pentateuch and especially deuteronomic tradition,
      anonymous prophecies, etc.) and one on "The Spirit" (inspiration,
      tendencies to universalism, etc.). The unit on Amos discusses
      personal history, his visions, historical context, the relationship
      between God and Israel, the judgment, etc.

247. Caspari, Wilhelm. "Erwarten Amos und Hosea den Messias?" *Neue
      Kirchlich Z* (Erlangen/Leipzig) 41, No. 12 (1930), 812-824.
      Discusses the general problem, the issue of eschatology, translation
      difficulties, and some alternate opinions.

248. Caspari, Wilhelm. "Wer hat die Ausspruche des Propheten Amos
      gesammelt?" *Neue Kirchlich Z* 25, No. 9 (1914), 701-715. Notes
      earlier studies, critical problems, exegetical concerns, commentary.

249. Cate, Robert L. "Amos." pp. 297-307 in *An Introduction to the Old
      Testament and Its Study*. Nashville, TN: Broadman, 1987. 539 pp.
      A general introduction to the eighth century prophets gives the
      historical background. The discussion of Amos includes the date
      ("most scholars date Amos's ministry about 765 BC"), his nature
      and character ("a master of oratory"), content with detailed outlines,
      message. God's judgment was redemptive. "Even when we
      experience the wrath of God, we are still inside His love."

250. Cathcart, Kevin J. "Amos." pp. 75-96 in *The Targum of the Minor
      Prophets Translated, with a Critical Introduction, Apparatus, and
      Notes* by Cathcart and Robert P. Gordon. The Aramaic Bible 14, ed
      Martin McNamara, et al. Wilmington, DE: Glazier, 1989. xvi + 259
      pp. Cathcart did Hosea to Micah and Gordon did Nahum to
      Malachi. A Targum is a translation [or paraphrase] of a biblical
      book into Aramaic. The Targum for the Minor Prophets is part of
      the Targum Jonathan (Jonathan ben Uzziel, a pupil of Hillel the
      elder) to the Prophets. The general introduction includes

translational characteristics, theology (the *Shekinah*, resurrection, nationalism, etc.), life setting (stronger links to the synagogue than to the home), text and versions (MT, LXX, Syriac, Vulgate, etc.), language (Palestinian but edited in Babylonia; Old Aramaic - Nabataean, Palmyrene, Qumran - rather than new Aramaic), dating (after 70 CE), manuscripts. The latter section is a brief discussion of the six manuscripts and three printed editions used by Alexander Sperber. The authors use Sperber's accurate translation but not his critical apparatus which has frequent errors. Each of the prophets is translated with annotation. Variations from MT, LXX and other sources are noted.

251. Cathcart, Kevin J. "*Ro'sh*, 'Poison,' in Amos 9:1." VT 44, No. 3 (July 94), 393-396. Notes numerous studies. Horst was right. The meaning "poison" parallels snake in vs 3, Jer 8:17.

252. Cazelles, Henri. "Amos." Vol 1 (1948), cols 485-486 in *Catholicisme hier Aujourd'hui Demain* ed G. Jacquemet et al. Paris: Letouzey et Ane, 1948+. 1:x + 1528 cols. Discusses the man, the book, the historical background, the nature of God.

253. Cazelles, Henri. "L'Arriere-Plan historique d'Amos 1:9-10." Vol. 1:71-76 in Division A, *The Proceedings of the Sixth World Jewish Congress of Jewish Studies held at The Hebrew University of Jerusalem 13-19 August 1973 under the auspices of The Israel Academy of Sciences and Humanities* ed Avigdor Shinan. Jerusalem: World Union of Jewish Studies, 1977. vii + 427 (Eng) + vii + 221 (Heb) Some of the oracles against the nations in Amos 1-2 are contested as unauthentic for literary reasons. Cazelles discusses the oracle against Tyre with a review of earlier interpretations.

254. Ceresko, Anthony R. "Janus Parallelism in Amos's 'Oracles Against the Nations'." JBL 113, No. 3 (Fall 94), 484-493. Amos 1:3-2:16. Discusses the problems of interpretation and many earlier suggestions. Ceresko thinks *l' 'sybnw* both looks back (hiphil of *swb*) and forward (hiphil of *nsb*), in what C.H. Gordon called Janus parallelism. One word has two or more meanings.

255. Ceuppens, F. *De Kleine Profeten. Het Oude Testament.* Bruges: de Brouwer, 1924.

256. Chaine, Joseph. "Amos." pp. 42-49 in *Introduction a la Lecture des Prophetes.* Etudes Bibliques. Paris: Gabalda, 1946. 274 pp + 10 pls, map, chronological table. This is called "Neuvieme Edition Revue." The preface is dated 1932. A general introduction with historical background.

257. Chambers, Talbot W. "The Literary Character of Amos." *The Old Testament Student* 3, No. 1 (Sep 1883), pp. 2-6. Some past interpreters have thought Amos was a crude clod without education. His style actually shows refined rhetoric with a fine sense of words and arrangement, with effective use of illustration and language.

258. Chancellor, William E. "The Literary Study of the Bible: Its Methods and Purposes Illustrated in a Criticism of the Book of Amos." *The Old Testament Student* 8, No. 1 (Sep 1888), 10-19. General discussion of the value of literary study of the Bible, with Amos as a prime example. Describes historical background, Amos' mission, his role as a prophet, the significance of Amos and the continuing relevance of the book today. Notes the coming of the Messiah and God's word in the Bible.

259. Chavez, Moises. *Modelo de oratoria. Obra basada en el analisis estilistico del texto hebreo del libro de Amos* (Models of oratory. Basic works in the stylistic analysis of the Hebrew text of the Book of Amos). Miami, FL: Editorial Caribe, 1979. 144 pp. In the first part, Chavez discusses the man and his message, his book, his theology, the relationship of prophecy and judgment. In the second part, he describes models of communication, e.g., proclamation, judicial process, visions, the homily, and, figures of speech. The latter include metaphors, hyperbole, cliches, symbols, etc. Amos also used alliteration, rhyme, anagrams and other approaches. An appendix gives Chavez' translation of Amos while a second appendix discusses Martin Luther King, Jr.'s sermon, "I Have a Dream."

260. Cherian, C.M. "The Message of Amos the Pioneer Prophet." *Clergy Monthly* 22 (1958), 81-91.

261. Cheyne, Thomas Kelly (1841-1915). "Amos." vol 1 (1899), cols 147-158 in *Encyclopedia Biblica: A Critical Dictionary of the Literary, Political and Religious History of the Bible*, 4 vols, ed Cheyne and J. Sutherland Black. NY: Macmillan, 1899-1903. Discusses Amos' prophetic activity, home, preparation (life experiences), date, circumstances, analysis (the content comes from a variety of sources, including post-exilic insertions), Amos's style, originality, pessimism, idea of God, denunciations, significance (great moral truths).

262. Cheyne, Thomas Kelly. "Notes on Obscure Passages in the Prophets." Exp 5th ser, 5, No. 1 (Jan 1897), 41-51. Amos 5:26. Amos does not accuse the Israelites of worshipping foreign gods anywhere else. The verse is editorial interpretation. Amos 9:7-15, pp. 44-47, is also.

263. Cheyne, T.K. "The Witness of Amos to David as a Psalmist (Amos 6:5)." ET 9, No. 7 (Ap 1898), 334. Exegesis, restoration. Amos is not a witness to David as a psalmist.

264. Childs, Brevard S. "Amos." pp. 395-410 in *Introduction to the Old Testament as Scripture*. Philadelphia: Fortress, 1979. 688 pp. Extensive Bibliography. Discusses historical critical problems, the canonical shape of Amos (multiple layers, superscription, Israel and the nations, visions, hymns, ch 9), theology and interpretation. The book says the "living God calls his people into obedient worship which is tested by the standard of God's justice and righteousness (5:24)."

265. Chisholm, Robert B., Jr. "Amos." pp. 69-108 in *Interpreting the Minor Prophets* by Chisholm. Grand Rapids: Academie Books (Zondervan), 1990. 317 pp. A general introduction gives historical background, discusses structure and style (inclusio, chiasmus, the judgment speech, the woe oracle, etc), stylistic devices (imagery, wordplay, irony, allusion), theology (sin, judgment, salvation), eschatology and history, prophetic telescoping (near and far events in the same context). On the latter point, we must carefully

distinguish the fulfilled from the eschaton. Amos wrote the book. He may have edited it later and modified some speeches, e.g., the reference to Zion in 6:1. The book is in three sections: 1-2, 3-6, 7-9. The Lord, Creator and Ruler of the universe, would come as a mighty warrior to judge the nations and would punish Israel in particular for breach of covenant - oppressive economics, empty religious formalism, arrogant self-confidence. But God will not abandon Israel forever. He would preserve a remnant to form the basis of a purified community and never again remove Israel from its land.

266. Chisholm, Robert B., Jr. "'For Three Sins . . . Even for Four': The Numerical Sayings in Amos." BS 147, No. 586 (Ap-June 90), 188-197. This is a rhetorical pattern: x/x + 1. Amos altered it for Israel (10 + 4) to emphasize her guilt as surpassing her neighbors.

267. Chouraqui, Andre. "'Amos." pp. 77-115 in *La Bible. Douze Inspires 1. Hoshea', Yoel, 'Amos, 'Ovadyah, Yona, Mikha.* Paris: Desclee De Brouwer, 1976. 175 pp. Chouraqui's new translation into French. A general introduction describes the translation of *La Bible.* The introduction to Amos notes the historical background, his concern with justice and the irresistible nature of his mission. The text is not annotated.

268. Christensen, Duane L. "Amos and the Transformation of the War Oracle." pp. 17-73 in *Transformations of the War Oracles in Old Testament Prophecy: Studies in the Oracles Against the Nations.* Harvard Dissertations in Religion 3, ed Caroline Bynum and George Rupp. Missoula, MT: Scholars Press, 1975. xii + 305 pp. A general introduction reviews the tradition of the oracles against the nations (OAN). The unit on Amos goes back to the Exodus, with pp. 57-73 focused on Amos 1-2. Amos took the war oracle against another nation and transformed it into a judgment speech against Israel. The study includes transliteration and translation of the texts with notes and commentary.

269. Christensen, Duane L. "The Prosodic Structure of Amos 1-2." *Harvard Theological Review* 67, No. 4 (Oct 74), 427-436. There is no *a priori* reason for making the poetry banal and monotonous.

Analyzes the oracles with transliterations and translation. The first six oracles (except Judah) are in three pairs.

270. Christenson, Sonja E. "Oracle in the Style of Amos (1992)." pp. 5-6 in *Many Voices: Multicultural Responses to the Minor Prophets* ed Alice Ogden Bellis. Lanham, MD: University Press of America, 1995. xiv + 101 pp. The writers in this book try to apply the minor prophets today. An oracle of judgment against the church and comfortable church-goers.

271. Churn, Serenus T. "Amos of the 1960s." *J of Religious Thought* 25, No. 1 (Spr-Sum 1968-1969), 79-82. A paraphrase of Amos in the days of Lyndon B. Johnson 192 years after the signing of the Declaration of Independence and 1968 years after the coming of the Messiah. The oracles are against Russia, Red China, Cuba, Viet Nam, the United States. Amos is a migrant worker from the Eastern Shore of Maryland. He is reported to Johnson by the Committee on Un-American Activities.

272. Ciric, Iwan. "Zu Amos 5:6 und 7." BZ 8 (1910), 133-134. Exegesis.

273. Clarke, Adam (1762-1832). "Amos." pp. 669-692 in *The Holy Bible Containing the Old and New Testaments with A Commentary and Critical Notes. The Old Testament. Vol 4. Isaiah to Malachi.* NY: Abingdon-Cokesbury, 1950. 860 pp. original, 1810 (whole commentary, 1798-1825), with numerous reprintings, e.g., 1827, 1977, 1985. A 1985 edition is part of BPC = *The Bethany Parallel Commentary of the Old Testament.* Minneapolis: Bethany House, viii + 1983 pp. The material is printed in parallel columns with the commentaries of Matthew Henry, and Jamieson/Fausset/Brown. BPC, cols 1853-1872 for Amos. The general introduction to Amos gives historical background. Sub-headings in the text correlate the book with many dates in other areas of the Mediterranean as well as traditional dates for the Bible. Each chapter has a mini-introduction. The text has footnoted cross references. The commentary contains exegesis, exposition, homiletic material.

274. Clements, Ronald E. "Amos and the Beginnings of Written Prophecy." pp. 27-44 in *Prophecy and Covenant.* Studies in Biblical Theology 43, ed C.F.D. Moule, et al. London/ Naperville,

IL.: SCM/Allenson, 1965. 135 pp. Amos is part of a long tradition, the highlight rather than the beginning of prophecy. Amos is not claiming a new authority for his words. Preaching judgment was not new but this was not cleansing. It was the end of the covenant. Note the curses of the covenant. However, there will be a new beginning, Amos 9:11-12.

275. Clements, Ronald E. "Amos and the Politics of Israel." pp. 49-64 in *Storia e tradizioni di Israele. Scritti in onore di J. Alberto Soggin* ed Daniele Garrone and Felice Israel. Brescia: Paideia, 1991. xlvii + 310 pp. Reprinted, pp. 23-34 in *Old Testament Prophecy: From Oracles to Canon*. Louisville, KY: Westminster/John Knox Press, 1996. x + 278 pp. The introduction surveys the interpretation of OT prophecy from 1965-1995. The text reviews prophet, king, messiah, Isaiah, Jeremiah, Ezekiel, apocalyptic, the canon. Amos is part of the first unit. Israel has no future. What does this mean? The answer is the vision of the plumb bob - or better, wall of tin. The section, Amos 7:7-17, was added later to support Amos as a true prophet. There are 3 levels each noting the end of Israel: vss 7-8, the oldest, have Yahweh's violence but this action can be revoked if people repent; vs 9, added after 745, "fulfills" Amos' prophecy on the overthrow of the Jehu dynasty; vss 10-17, reflect 722-701 BCE. The editors were trying to show how Amos' words came true.

276. Clements, Ronald E. *When God's Patience Runs Out: The Truth of Amos for Today*. Living Word Series. Nottingham: Inter-Varsity, 1988. 192 pp.

277. Clines, David J.A. "Metacommentating Amos." pp. 142-160 in *Of Prophets' Visions and the Wisdom of Sages: Essays in Honour of R. Norman Whybray on His Seventieth Birthday* ed Heather A. McKay and David J.A. Clines. JSOT Supplement 163. Sheffield: JSOT, 1993. 335 pp. A critical reflection on what commentators claim to do and what they actually do. Most commentators join in with Amos' condemnation of wealthy women, but Judith Sanderson also notes his failure to be concerned with women among the poor. Clines reviews the commentators and the social critique of Amos, the religious ideology of Amos including true and false prophets,

and aspects of Amos' message. Clines notes many commentators are not objective but read into the text their own biases.

278. Coffman, J.B. *Minor Prophets: Joel, Amos and Jonah.* Vol 1. Abilene, TX: Abilene Christian University Press, 1984.

279. Cohen, Gary G. "Amos." pp. 81-172 in *Hosea and Amos* by H. Ronald Vandermey and Cohen. Everyman's Bible Commentary. Chicago: Moody, 1981. 172 pp. Both northern and southern kingdoms were rising in prosperity and falling in morals. Amos' yelling seemed like the chatter of a *Chasid*, a holy man out of tune with modern mores. The land was one of ironclad military strength, new homes and luxurious food. But beneath it all was idolatry. The land was doomed. Amos' cry in the night was her last chance to repent. The commentary notes that nations and ingrates and God's own people are judged by God. Suffering should cause repentance but ceremonies, confidence and chasing the preaching will not help the unrepentant. In the end, however, God will restore.

280. Cohen, Simon. "Amos." Vol 1:280-82 in *The Universal Jewish Encyclopedia*, 10 Vol, ed Isaac Landman, et al. NY: KTAV, 1969. (original 1939) A migratory worker (sycamores do not grow in Tekoa) active c 760 BCE. Israel enjoyed outward prosperity but behind the facade there was injustice. Amos' demands for justice met a religion based on a bargain relationship - God chose them so they offer sacrifices. Amos had a universal view of God, an ethical monotheism. Chosenness meant responsibility rather than favor. God cannot be bribed. His literary style is remarkably fine with poetic, incisive, well chosen words.

281. Cohen, Simon. "Amos *Was* a Navi." HUCA (Cincinnati) 32 (1961), 175-178. Except for 7:14, Amos talks like a prophet and claims to have the word of God. Both Amos and Amaziah describe Amos' activities as prophesying. The LXX translates that he was not a prophet when God called him. Most commentators claim Amos was saying he was not a professional prophet. Amos actually said to Amaziah, "No! I am indeed a Navi (prophet), but not a Ben Navi (professional prophet)." Just ignore the masoretic punctuation. The latter did not arise until centuries later. Navi now has a new

meaning, one who speaks for God, not a professional soothsayer nor a cultic servant.

282. Cohen, Simon. "The Political Background of the Words of Amos." HUCA 36 (1965), 153-160. Earlier prophets spoke to the king and predicted doom for the royal family. Amos and successors spoke to the people and predicted doom and later hope for the entire nation. From Amos on, God is a universal Being. The reign of Jeroboam is often seen as one of prosperity but Amos implies a defensive war is being fought against Ammon and Syria. The armies of the latter have broken through the borders.

283. Cohon, Beryl D. "Amos." pp. 23-37 in *The Prophets: Their Personalities and Teachings*. NY: Scribner's, 1939. xiii + 232 pp. (reprint, 1960) A general introduction reviews the characteristics of the prophets (divine compulsion, a critic of the social order, predictions, solitary men of God), true prophets vs mad enthusiasts (professional, false prophets), idolatry (Baalim, Asherah, Moloch, et al.). The discussion of Amos describes his appearance at Beth-El and confrontation with Amaziah, Amos' background in Tekoa, his oracles against the nations, his visions, the greatness and weakness of Amos. The two sides of the latter are uncompromising justice. His justice is the moral order of the universe but it is not backed by mercy.

284. Cole, R. Dennis. "The Visions of Amos 7-9." TE 52 (Fall 95), 57-68. A commentary on each vision, all of which have a message of destruction and hope.

285. Coleman, Robert O. "Amos." pp. 61-62 in *Wycliffe Bible Encyclopedia* ed Charles F. Pfeiffer, et al. Chicago: Moody, 1975. xxii + 982 pp.

286. Collins, John J. "Behold I make all things new: Eschatology in the Biblical Tradition." *Chicago Studies* 24, No. 2 (Aug 85), 193-207. Amos 8:2. Amos was the first to proclaim the end, the Day of the Lord. Discusses the Combat Myth, the New Creation, Daniel, Christianity, the Book of Revelation, the Apocalypse now, the language of hope (consolation of the oppressed).

287. Collins, John J. "History and Tradition in the Prophet Amos." *Irish Theological Quarterly* (Maynooth) 41 (Ap 74), 120-133. Reprinted, pp. 121-133 in *The Bible in its Literary Milieu: Contemporary Essays* ed Vincent L. Tollers and John R. Maier. Grand Rapids, MI: Eerdmans, 1979. ix + 447 pp. All are agreed on the historical mind of the biblical writers but history means many different things. The consensus for the OT has been challenged by George Fohrer and his student Jochen Vallmer. Compares Bultmann and Cullmann for the NT. The question is real event vs the faith of the community. The issue is whether Yahweh removes the possibility of decision and dooms people to total destruction. Amos preaches unqualified doom. Salvation is the gift of Yahweh but it is given on condition of Israel's obedience. Collins discusses the conditional nature of the election and the continuity in the Bible. No one can depend on a past tradition for salvation.

288. Condamin, Albert. "Amos 1:2-3:8. Authenticite et Structure Poetique." *Recherches de Science Religieuse* (Paris) 20, No. 2 (1930), 298-311. Discusses authenticity and poetic structure. Gives a new translation with critical notes.

289. Condamin, Albert. "Les chants lyriques des prophetes." RB 10 (1901), 352-376. Discusses the thought, symmetry, prelude, inclusion, movement to conclusion for selections from Amos and Isaiah. The Amos (pp. 353-363) section has translation into French with critical notes.

290. Condamin, Albert. "Le pretendu 'fil a plomb' de la vision d'Amos." RB 9, No. 4 (1900), 586-594. Reviews what he calls the chaos of the commentaries. The symbol refers to war, the ruin and chastisement of the people.

291. Coninck, Lucas de. *Iuliani Aeclanensis: Expositio Libri Iob, Tractatus Prophetarum Osee, Iohel et Amos*. Corpus Christianorum Series Latina 88. Turnhold: Brepols, 1977. xxxiv + 432 pp. The introduction gives an overview of Julian's writings, noting their sequence and context, in part while he was exiled (see Julian) for supporting Pelagius. The commentary on the three prophets was written after 431 CE. Pelagianism is not completely absent but is not imposed. The work is admirable for its historical and messianic

interpretation, its original and judicious exegesis. The Tractatus is pp. 111-329, with a preface noting the Rufinius connection. Amos is pp. 260-329, the Latin text of Amos, commentary and critical apparatus.

292. Cook, Henry. "Amos: Justice and Judgment." pp. 35-45 in *The Prophets of the Bible: The Canonical Prophets - Who They Were and What They Said.* London: Student Christian Movement, 1935. 215 pp. The general introduction reviews prediction, inspiration, the literature and message of prophecy, Christ and prophecy. The prophets did predict but this is not the vital element of their ministry. Their real power was to help us feel the presence of the living God. God is personal, transcendent, alone and supreme. We do not proof-text as much any more but the prophets were part of God's revelation which culminated in Christ. The volume is in three parts: pre-exilic, exilic, post-exilic. Each part has an introduction. The first gives the historical background from Jeroboam II to the destruction of Jerusalem. The history is further developed for Amos, with his message of justice and judgment. While the latter was for social iniquity, he was not a reformer but spoke for a righteous God.

293. Cooper, Alan. "The Absurdity of Amos 6:12a." JBL 107, No. 4 (Dec 88), 725-727. Eliezer de Beaugency suggested horses and oxen are metaphors for Israel's army. They will be crushed by the crag (*sela'*). Cooper emends to, "Does a wild ox plow in the Valley?" The Valley is the Beqa' of Lebanon. The northern limits of the kingdom of Jeroboam are Sela. The stronghold of Edom is the southern limits. It's a riddle which is a play on words. While Israel's forces ran on the crag and plowed the valley, they could only do so with God's power. Now that is reversed - God will raise an enemy to conquer from border to border.

294. Coote, Robert B. "Amos 1:11 *rhmyw*." JBL 90, No. 2 (June 71), 206-208. Notes earlier studies and problems. The legal interpretation *is* correct. It's a covenant term reflected in ANE usage.

295. Coote, Robert B. *Amos Among the Prophets: Composition and Theology.* Philadelphia: Fortress, 1981. v + 138 pp. The book

developed in three stages. Stage A, the oracles of doom, was by the prophet. Stage B was by a Jerusalem scribe after the death of Josiah while Stage C and the final form of the book was in the exilic period. Amos' message is single and basic: the powerful elite have oppressed the powerless. The elite will be destroyed. In B, the Israelites are warned that God is angry and they must repent. In Stage C, it's all over. The nations will be destroyed but God's people will be restored. God's justice is a common theme in all three stages. The ending is compared with Jonah who was angry at God's mercy.

296. Coote, Robert B. *Amos Among the Prophets: Composition and Theology*. Philadelphia: Fortress, 1981. v + 138 pp. For ministers and seminary students. "I remain in doubt whether God should ever pardon a person for writing a book about a book." Prophecy comes in spurts and we normally use it that way but considering longer sections or even the whole book can help us understand the short sections. Amos was written by more than one author at more than one time. The book of Amos had three stages: Amos, the final editor and in between (there may have been several editions in between but here they are treated as one). Stage A was written by someone before 722 BCE, the B or Bethel stage came between Hezekiah and Josiah while C belongs to the 6th century. Stage A condemns, B offers a choice, C promises restitution. The three reflect life as a task we have failed, life as a task, life as a gift. The translation is Coote's.

297. Coote, Robert B. "Ripe Words for Preaching: Connotative Diction in Amos." *Pacific Theological Review* (San Anselmo) 8 (Sum 76), 13-19. Connotative refers to multiple meanings while denotative refers to single meanings. Modern advertising frequently shows the former in word plays, as does Amos (gives examples) and Hebrew poetry. Amos used oblique and direct types, associations of words that sound alike, conceptual types, ambiguous types. He used irony, integration, the dramatic. While he announces God's judgment (denotative), he also pronounces God's hope (connotative).

298. Copass, Benjamin Andrew. *Amos*. Nashville: Broadman, 1939. 99 pp. Covers Amos, his time, his message, doctrine of God, doctrine of man, doctrine of salvation, results of his preaching, relevance

today. Will preachers today trust and live and preach as Amos did?

299. Copass, Benjamin Andrew. "Amos as a Preacher." SWJT 5, No. 2
     (Ap '21), 59-67. Historical background, exegesis, exposition,
     homiletics.

300. Coppens, Joseph. *Les douze petits Prophetes. Breviaire du
     Prophetisme.* Bruges/Louvain: Desclee de Brouwer/Publications
     Universitaires, 1950.

301. Cornet, P. Bertrand. "Une 'crux': Amos 7:7-9: 'anak = Belier."
     Etudes Franciscaines (Paris) 2, No. 4 (Feb 51), 61-83. Literature
     review, exegesis, comparative study.

302. Cornick, David. "Amos's legacy to us." ET 98, No. 11 (Aug 87),
     342-344. A sermon. Applies Amos to today, e.g., the wealthy have
     mansions and gourmet cooking. The poor are trampled. The legal
     system is a travesty. The religious establishment is a sham. He
     leaves us uncomfortable with large questions like "what place does
     God have in my life".

303. Cornill, Carl Heinrich (1854-1920). "Amos." *Open Court*
     (Chicago) 9, No. 400 (25 Ap 1895), 4473-4475. In 760,
     worshippers at the Autumn Festival were joyous. Damascus was
     defeated, prosperity was high. They were interrupted by a plain
     looking man with a funeral dirge. Amaziah tried to stop him but
     Amaziah was condemned. God demands justice and Israel lacks
     justice. The end is at hand. Through Amos, the God of Israel
     becomes the God of the entire world and this religion becomes
     universal.

304. Cornill, Carl Heinrich. "Amos." pp. 37-46 in *The Prophets of Israel*
     by Cornill. Chicago: Open Court, 1894. 11th ed, Open Court, 1917.
     xv + 194 pp. Ancient Israelite worship was a rejoicing in God.
     Restoring the relationship of man to God was an utterly strange
     idea. The prophets saw in the drunken debaucheries remnants of
     Canaanite paganism. In 760, people celebrated a new prosperity.
     God was on their side. Amos brought a different, astonishing
     message predicting their destruction and then went back to his
     sheep and sycamores. But he wrote down his prophecies. He

incorporated the moral law. God is a God of Justice. The fall of Israel is the triumph of truth and justice over sin and deception. Amos' view is monotheism with God in power in heaven and earth.

305. Cornill, Carl Heinrich. "Das Targum zu den Propheten." ZAW 7, No. 2 (1887), 177-202. Amos pp. 196-197. Transcription of the Hebrew.

306. Coulot, Claude. "Propositions pour une structuration du livre d'Amos au niveau redactionnel." *Revue de Sciences Religieuses* 51, Nos. 2-3 (Ap-July 77), 169-186. Reviews recent studies of structure and concludes two units, 1-6, and 7-9, each with sub-sections. Rev, OTA 1 (1978), 57.

307. Cox, Dermott. "Inspired Radicals. The Prophets of the Eighth Century." *Studium Biblicum Franciscanum Liber Annuus* (Jerusalem) 25 (1975), 90-103. These prophets (Micah, Amos, Hosea, Isaiah) smashed the traditions of their people, that all was guaranteed to them by God: election, monarchy, independence. The covenant is for mission, not privilege. Notes Amos on God's concern with Ethiopians and Philistines, punishment for Israelites, punishment for Tyre for violating the covenant. The covenant raised the whole life of the people to the level of the sacred. Amos saw social injustice as violation of the covenant.

308. Cox, Samuel. "*The Harvest Cart*; or, the Oracle of Amos against Israel." Exp 2nd ser, 8, No. 5 (Nov 1884), 321-338. Amos 2:6-16. Detailed discussion of the sins of Israel, the appeal of God, His mercies and the transgressions of men. Compares these open, gross sins of greed, injustice, hypocrisy, to our sins today.

309. Craghan, John F. "How Do the Readings Speak to You?" *Today's Parish* (Mystic, CT) 21, No. 6 (Oct 89), 27-28. Discusses the poor and Amos' concern.

310. Craghan, John F. "The Prophet Amos in Recent Literature." *Biblical Theology Bulletin* 2, No. 3 (Oct 72), 242-261. Surveys recent Amos studies on composition, vocation, the cult, wisdom, history.

311. Craghan, John F. "Traditions and Techniques in the Prophet Amos." BT 14, Issue No. 60 (Ap 72), 782-786. Amos challenged the status quo. His message was based on the Exodus and the covenant. The Day of the Lord is coming with destruction. He drew on the traditions of the Law, wisdom, the funeral dirge. Compares the execration texts of Egypt.

312. Craigie, Peter C. "Amos." pp. 120-194 in *Twelve Prophets. Vol. 1. Joel, Amos, Obadiah, and Jonah.* The Daily Study Bible (Old Testament) ed John C.L. Gibson. Philadelphia: Westminster, 1984. vi + 239 pp. This series parallels William Barclay's series on the NT, in hopes of doing the same for the OT - making it come alive for the Christian believer in the 20th century. The purpose, like Barclay's, is to present modern scholarship to the reader, but primarily to enable men and women to know Jesus Christ. He was raised on the OT which continues as the Jewish Bible. The general introduction notes the division into major (Isaiah, etc.) and minor (Amos, etc) prophets goes back to Augustine's *City of God.* The Jewish canon called the minor prophets, the "Book of the Twelve Prophets." It was a single "book" or scroll containing all twelve. They range in date from 750 - 400 BCE. The commentary is arranged in small units suitable for daily study. The text of the RSV is reprinted, the story retold with comment, including context and application to people today. The introduction to Amos contrasts him with Hosea (the two should be studied together), Amos' background and his message. The social evils in Israel were compounded by the hypocritical veneer of religion used to cover the injustice. Craigie notes the "cows of Bashan" refer to a breed of cattle famous for their fatness and beef.

313. Craigie, Peter C. "The Book of Amos." pp. 180-183 in *The Old Testament: Its Background, Growth, & Content.* Nashville: Abingdon, 1986. 351 pp. Gives personal and historical background. Compares Amos and Hosea. Summarizes Amos. Notes problems in the history of composition and preservation. Amos' objections to injustice, poverty, pride, corruption makes the book one for all seasons.

314. Craigie, P.C. "Amos the *noqed* in the Light of Ugaritic." *Studies in Religion/Sciences Religieuses* (Waterloo, Ontario) 11 (1982),

29-33. At Ugarit, *nqdm* were part of the royal establishment. These sheep managers were not simple shepherds. While one might have reported to a high priest, there is no evidence they were in a sacral office so this does not show Amos was a temple servant. However, he was no ordinary shepherd.

315. Cramer, Karl. *Amos. Versuch einer theologischen Interpretation.* Beitrage zur Wissenschaft vom Alten und Neuen Testament 51 (third series, No. 15), ed Rudolf Kittel. Stuttgart: Kohlhammer, 1930. iv + 216 pp. A commentary including alternate interpretations, Amos' call, the prophet and people, the Torah, the doxologies, God as Lord, the Day of the Lord, Amos as revolutionary, demagogue, reformer, his politics, etc.

316. Crawford, Angus. "Joel, Obadiah, and Amos." *The Virginia Seminary Magazine* 3 (1889-1890), 161-170.

317. Crenshaw, James Lee. "Amos and the Theophanic Tradition." ZAW 80, No. 2 (1968), 203-215. Reviews scholarly opinion on Amos' use of liturgical language and the possibility he was a cult prophet. Others suggest the wisdom tradition as his background. This paper says theophany. Cites passages of authentic and of uncertain authorship. Amos in fact reverses the liturgical tradition. He used cultic language to make contact with the people. The theophanic tradition may be a bridge between Amos' experience and wisdom.

318. Crenshaw, James L. *Hymnic Affirmation of Divine Justice: The Doxologies of Amos and Related Texts in the Old Testament.* SBL Dissertation Series 24. Missoula: Scholars Press, 1975. xii + 178 pp. Diss. Jimmy Lee Crenshaw, The Doxologies of Amos: A Form-Critical Study in the History of the Text of Amos. Vanderbilt University, 1964. v + 256 pp. DAI 25, No. 9 (Dec 66), 5415. The history of interpretation, a strophic arrangement and translation of the doxologies, the reason for inserting the doxologies, Amos' use of cultic materials, the life setting of the doxologies and the exposition. Amos used doxologies in a completely different sense than the popular meaning. His are doxologies of judgment.

319.   Crenshaw, James L. "The Influence of the Wise on Amos." *ZAW*
        79, No. 1 (1967), 42-52. Reviews the history of interpretation in
        terms of style (rhetoric, numerical pairs, parables, terms) and
        theology (astronomy, lack of concern for idolatry, moralistic
        conception of salvation, Israel and the nations, attack on luxurious
        living, the end of Israel, Isaiah's kinship to Amos). Amos was
        dependent on the wisdom tradition but it may have been in relation
        to wisdom rooted in experience. The language may also have come
        through the theophanic tradition. He was not an *official* functionary
        of the cult but the language of the cult had a stronger influence than
        wisdom.

320.   Crenshaw, James L. "A Liturgy of Wasted Opportunity (Amos
        4:6-12; Isaiah 9:7-10, 4, 5:25-29)." *Semitics* (Pretoria) 1 (1970),
        27-37. A study of concluding refrains shows possibilities for
        studying all the refrains. The purpose of these refrains is a defense
        of God's treatment of his people and an urge to repent, lest God's
        chastisements should be wasted effort.

321.   Crenshaw, James Lee. "*w'dorek 'al-bamote 'ares.*" CBQ 34, No. 1
        (Jan 72), 39-53. Amos 4:13 is an example of the metaphorical
        rather than mythological use of the phrase. God created the
        mountains, the wind, the storm. He will destroy Israel.
        Ugaritic/Canaanite influence is strong throughout. [In NT studies,
        Rudolph Bultmann "demythologized" the Bible. The Hebrews
        "demythologized" their ANE sources.]

322.   Cripps, Richard Seymour. *A Commentary on the Book of Amos.*
        Limited Classical Reprint Library. Minneapolis: Klock & Klock,
        1981. xlii + 362 pp. Reprint of *A Critical and Exegetical
        Commentary on the Book of Amos. The Text of the Revised Version
        Edited with Introduction, Notes & Excursuses*, 2nd ed. London:
        SPCK, 1955. xlii + 365 pp. (original, 1929. xviii + 365 pp.).
        Reprinted, 1960, 1969. The preface, pp. xvii-xxxix, to the second
        edition reviews intervening events, e.g., the excavation of Samaria.
        The introduction (pp. 1-110) summarizes the history of Israel up to
        Amos, the social, moral and religious life at the time, Amos the
        person, date, prophecy in Israel, Amos and the new order of
        prophecy, his teaching (social righteousness), the principles of
        Hebrew poetry, eschatology, literary problems, the phrase, "Thus

saith Jehovah," the visions, political fulfillment, later influence of the book. In addition to the detailed exegesis, the text and commentary are followed by excursi which examine the divine names in the text, Jehovah's relation to Israel, and sacrifice. Cripps doubts that Israel was dominated by eschatological thought before the exile. The book is probably not an entire unity.

323. Crocetti, Giuseppe. "'Cercate me e Vivrete.' La Ricerca di Dio in Amos." pp. 89-105 in *Quaerere Deum* ed Giuseppe Danieli. Atti Della XXV Settimana Biblica Associazione Biblica Italiana ed Antonio Bonora, et al. Brescia: Paideia, 1980. 478 pp. Amos 5:4 says, "Seek me and live but do not seek Bethel." Vss 14-15 have "seek and not evil". Reviews earlier studies, the problem, context, composition, unity of the text, origins. It is a sublime message.

324. Crocker, Piers T. "History and Archaeology in the Oracles of Amos." *Buried History* (Melbourne) 23, No. 1 (Mar 87), 7-15. Discusses the oracles against the nations with historical and archaeological notes on Damascus, Gaza, threshing sledges etc.

325. Crook, Margaret B. "Did Amos and Micah know Isaiah 9:1-7 and 11:1-9." JBL 70 (1951), xiii. Yes. The Isaiah verses took shape in the ninth century. A paper read at the Society's meeting, 28 Dec 50, at Union Theological Seminary, NY.

326. Crook, Margaret B. "Did Amos and Micah know Isaiah 9:1-7 and 11:1-9." JBL 73, No. 3 (Sep 54), 144-151. They seem to reverse Isaiah. The latter two passages are liturgies for the coronation and enthronement of King Jehoash of Judah in 837. Presumably the substance of the Isaiah passages was common property.

327. Cross, Frank Leslie and Elizabeth A. Livingstone, et al. "Amos, Book of." pp. 45-46 in *The Oxford Dictionary of the Christian Church*, 2nd ed. London: Oxford University Press, 1974. xxxi + 1518 pp. (original, 1957) The first of the canonical prophets. Discusses the man and his message, the Day of the Lord as one of justice, God as Lord of Nature and nations. The later may not be explicit monotheism but comes close. Bibliography.

328. Crusemann, Frank. "Kritik an Amos im deuteronomistischen
      Geschichtswerk: Erwagungen zu 2. Konige 14:27." pp.
      57-63 in *Probleme biblischer Theologie (Gerhard von Rad zum 70.*
      Geburtstag) ed Hans Walter Wolff. Munich: Kaiser, 1971. 690 pp.
      Survey of interpretations of the role of the deuteronomist in the
      editing of the prophets.

329. Crusemann, Frank. *Studien zur Formgeschichte von Hymnus und*
      Danklied in Israel. Wissenschaftliche Monographien zum Alten
      und Neuen Testament 32 ed Gunther Bornkamm and Gerhard von
      Rad, et al. Neukirchen-Vluyn: Neukirchener, 1969. Diss. Johannes
      Gutenberg-Universitat Mainz, 1968. ix + 348 pp. His general
      discussion focuses on the psalms but includes the Amos
      doxologies, pp. 97-106. Crusemann notes numerous earlier studies,
      gives translations and analysis.

330. Curtis, Edward L. "Some Features of Old Testament Prophecy
      Illustrated by the Book of Amos." *The Old Testament Student* 6,
      No. 5 (Jan 1887), 136-139. Discusses the oracles against the
      nations. The nations were held accountable. How much more so,
      his people Israel. The prophets as humans had normal human
      insights into conditions around them. Amos obviously was not
      uninformed. The prophets objected to external religion - ceremony
      without internal heart. Compares other prophets on these points,
      and Jesus' concern for the weightier matters of the law.

331. Cyril of Alexandria. "Commentarius in Amos prophetam." Opera
      Omnia 4. PG 71 (1859), cols 407-582. Latin and Greek in parallel
      columns. A brief introduction reviews the situation. The text has
      verse by verse and small units with commentary and critical notes.

D.

332. Dahl, Johann Christian Weilhelm. *Amos neu ubersetzt und erlautert*. Gottingen: Vandenhoeck und Ruprecht, 1975. xii + 267 pp. Reviews the life of Amos, contents of the book, the character of the oracles, comparisons of ancient versions (Aquila and other Greek versions, Vulgate, Syriac, etc.) and earlier commentaries, the historical background. Gives a translation of the entire text of Amos, followed by exegesis, exposition and commentary.

333. Dahmen, Ulrich. "Zur Text- und Literarkritik von Am 6:6a." BN 31 (1986), 7-10. Compares scholarly opinion on LXX and MT, and finds the LXX closer to the original. An example is this verse which is part of the unit of vss 1-7.

334. Dahood, Mitchell J. "Amos 6:8 *meta'eb*." Bib 59, No. 2 (1978), 265-266. There are two words here: *mt* means "surely, indeed" from the dialect of Zenjirli while *'b* means "foe" by analogy with Ugaritic. The vs reads "Truly, the foe am I of Jacob's arrogance."

335. Dahood, Mitchell J. "Can One Plow without Oxen? (Amos 6:12): A Study of *ba-* and *'al*." pp. 13-23 in *The Bible World: Essays in Honor of Cyrus H. Gordon* ed Gary Rendsburg, et al. NY: KTAV, 1980. xiii + 321 pp. The terms have variable meanings, determined by the context. Translating *ba* as "without," "from," as comparative, etc., *'al* as comparative, as agency, etc. clarifies the meaning in this text and many others.

336. Dahood, Mitchell J. "To pawn one's cloak." Bib 42, No. 3 (1961), 359-366. Discusses the tomb of Apollophanes at Marisa (Mareshah) and the Greek inscription (200-150 BCE) which says the writer has "your cloak in pledge." This is a semitism drawing on a Canaanite custom. Dahood gives exegesis, comparisons, biblical background.

337. Daiches, Samuel. "Amos 3:3-8." ET 26, No. 5 (Feb '15), 237. The sense of the passage is cause - effect. The cause is the command of God. The prophesying of the prophet is the effect of a cause.

338. Daiches, Samuel. "Amos 6:2." ET 26, No. 12 (Sep '15), 562-563. Gives a history of interpretation and his own which settles everything. Vs 2 continues vs 1. He tells the nobility to go see the estates in other places and note their own prosperity.

339. Daiches, Samuel. "Amos 6:5." ET 26, No. 11 (Aug '15), 521-522. Reviews the history of interpretations. The harpist divided his fingers and guided them over the strings.

340. Daniel, Jerry L. "At Ease in a Place of Action: Amos 6:1-7." *Restoration Quarterly* 34, No. 3 (1992), 170-172. Discusses Zion - not so much where it was as what it was. While God rested in Zion, it was a place of action. Amos said those at ease in Zion were too comfortable. At ease is good as a blessing from God, not as an escape from duty. Work precedes rest.

341. Danell, Gustaf Adolf. "Var Amos verkligen en nabi?" (Swedish) *Svensk Exegetisk Arsbok* 16 (1951), 7-20.

342. Danell, Gustaf Adolf. "Amos." pp. 110-136 in *Studies in the Name Israel in the Old Testament*. Uppsala: Appelbergs Boktryckeriaktiebolag, 1946. 334 pp. The name refers variously to the whole people, the kingdom of David, the northern kingdom after Solomon. Amos uses the name, Israel, 30 times. Normally he means the northern kingdom, which is doomed. Israel's main sin is worshipping the god Bethel instead of Yahweh.

343. Dangl, Oskar. "Comparison of Different OT Methodologies." pp. 151-180 in *Bible et Informatique* (Bible and Computer: Interpretation, Hermeneutics, Expertise. Proceedings of the Third International Colloquium). Travaux de Linguistique Quantitative 49 ed Charles Muller. Paris/Geneva: Champion/Slatkine, 1992. 661 pp. The conference was sponsored by the Association Internationale Bible et Informatique (AIBI). The spine gives the title underlined. The title page has AIBI. Dangl uses Amos 3:9-15 as an example. Gives Hebrew and translations. His integration

model combines Richter's system of grammar while Schweizer looks for elocution units.

344. Danson, J.M. "Amos." ET 11, No. 10 (July 1900), 442-446. Reviews the man, his times, his call, his message. God is concerned with moral conduct.

345. Davidson, A.B. "The Prophet Amos. I. Jehovah, God of Israel." Exp 3rd ser, 5, No. 3 (1887), 161-179. Discusses the man, his times, his message, including his universal view of God, the sin of nations and judgment. Amos is first of all a theologian, then a moralist. His concern is with the person of God and his relationship with Israel.

346. Davidson, A.B. "The Prophet Amos. II. The People of Israel." Exp 3rd ser, 6, No. 33 (1887), 161-173. Discusses the character of the people, their worship, their syncretism. They were unable to hear the message of Amos.

347. Davies, Gwynne Henton. "Amos - The Prophet of Re-Union." ET 92, No. 7 (Ap 81), 196-199. A review of interpretation since T.H. Robinson. The book is by Amos, calling for unity of the northern and southern kingdoms - in Jerusalem.

348. Davies, Philip R. "*Bytdwd* and *Swkt Dwyd*: A Comparison." JSOT 65 (Dec 94), 23-24. The latter term is in Amos 9:11. Compares the Tel Dan stele. It refers to a building, now needing repairs.

349. Davis, L.D. "Herald of God's Justice." BT 33, No. 5 (Sep 95), 294-297. Reviews Amos and his world, his call, international justice (oracles against the nations), the sins of Israel, perversion of worship, the Day of Yahweh. The last is a day of death instead of great nationalistic victory. [HOT 9 May 96, WTS]

350. Day, Edward and W. Chapin. "Is the Book of Amos Post-Exilic?" AJSL 18, No. 2 (Jan '02), 65-93. The book is a unity, "considerably subsequent to the exile." Notes many opinions and the relevant data.

351. Day, Thomas Franklin. "Amos 5:21." BW 12, No. 5 (May 1899),
340. "I will take no delight" literally means "I will not smell." "The
imagery is the sacrificial meal of the god and his worshippers. The
god's portion was the "sweet smoke." God's refusal was his refusal
to be a guest. The fellowship was broken.

352. Day, Thomas Franklin. "The Moral Range of the Prophet Amos."
The Bible Student 4, No. 3 (Sep '01), 148-154. Describes a
speculative personal biography for Amos, and discusses his concept
of God - an ethical deity, universal in power. The heathen are
invited to come and see the crimes committed by God's people, and
the punishment for these sins. Amos spoke against the ritualism of
his day. His words remain true for our time.

353. Deane, W.J. and J. Edgar Henry, et al., *Amos*, new ed. The Pulpit
Commentary ed H.D.M. Spence and Joseph S. Exell. London/NY:
Funk & Wagnalls, 1913. vii + 196 + iii pp. Bound with Obadiah,
Jonah, Micah, each with its own pagination. Reprinted as vol. 14,
Amos to Malachi, Grand Rapids: Eerdmans, 1950, 1963. Deane
wrote the exposition and Henry the homiletics with homilies by
various authors. The introduction [unsigned; title page may indicate
F.W. Farrar] reviews the man and his time and his general
character. The exposition here is more like exegesis - detailed study
of the text - while the homiletic is, like exposition - expansion on
the text, comparative study, etc. But the two approaches overlap.
The last three pages are a homiletical index.

354. Dearman, John Andrew. "Amos." pp. 18-34 in *Property Rights in
the Eighth-Century Prophets: The Conflict and Its Background.*
SBL Dissertation Series 106 ed J.J.M. Roberts and Charles Talbert.
Atlanta, GA: Scholars Press, 1988. x + 171 pp. Diss. Emory
University, 1981. 312 pp. DAI 42, No. 5 (Nov 81), 2172. After a
review of scholarly opinions, Dearman analyzes sections of Amos,
noting many earlier studies. Amos condemns the nations for
violations of the moral order. His accusations against Israel are
based on the misuse of land and settled existence - infractions of
property and personal rights. Selling the righteous is debt slavery.
The sandals are a symbol of property rights. Their property is being
misappropriated. Amos himself has traditionally been seen as poor.

But if he is a noqed, he may be of the property class. However, Yahweh called him to prophesy to the nation.

355. Deden, Dirk. "Amos." cols. 64-65 in *Bibel-Lexikon* (HBL), 2nd ed, ed Herbert Haag. Zurich/Cologne: Benziger verlag Einsiedeln, 1968. xix pp + 1964 cols. original, 1951. French ed, Paris: Brepols, 1960; 1952-1955. This Lexikon is the German edition of *Bijbelsch Woordenboek* (Biblical word book). Roermond: Roman & Zonen, 1941. Discusses the name, place in the canon, historical background, his claim he was not a prophet, his visions. Bibliography.

356. Deden, Dirk. "Amos (Buch)." cols. 65-66 in *Bibel-Lexikon* (HBL), 2nd ed, ed Herbert Haag. Zurich/Cologne: Benziger verlag Einsiedeln, 1968. xix pp + 1964 cols. original, 1951. French ed, Paris: Brepols, 1960; 1952-1955. This Lexikon is the German edition of *Bijbelsch Woordenboek* (Biblical word book). Roermond: Roman & Zonen, 1941. Outlines the content, discusses the historical background, the unity of the text, theology including the Day of Yahweh. Bibliography.

357. Deden, Dirk. "Amos." pp. 115-166 in *De kleine Profeten uit de grondtekst vertaald en uitgelegd*. De Boeken van het Oude Testament 12 ed A. van den Born, et al. Roermond: Roman, 1953. 400 pp. The introduction considers the person, the book, theology, style. Bibliography. The biblical text is annotated with exegesis and commentary.

358. Deden, D. "Amos en Osee." p. 55 in *De Messiaase Profetieen*. Bijbelse Monographieen ed Jos. Keulers. Roermond/Maaseik: Roman & Zonen, 1947. 160 pp. Commentary as part of the general discussion of messianism in the OT.

359. Deere, Derward William. "The Book of Amos." pp. 75-99 in *The Twelve Speak (Volume I). A Translation of the Books of Obadiah, Joel, Jonah, Amos, Hosea and Micah with Exegetical and Interpretative Footnotes and an Introductory Section on Prophecy*, 2 vols. NY: American Press, 1958-1961. 1:164 pp. The general introduction reviews terms for prophet, the prophetic mission and message. An introduction in vol 2 summarizes each of the Twelve.

The text is a new translation with annotation. An appendix gives a chronology from 931-400 BCE.

360. Deissler, Alfons. "Amos." pp. 89-136 in *Zwolf Propheten. 1. Hosea, Joel, Amos*, 2nd (unchanged) ed, 3 vols, by Deissler. Die Neue Echter Bibel: Kommentar Alten Testament mit der Einheitsubersetzung (The new Echter Bible: A Commentary on the OT with the ecumenical translation) 4, ed Josef G. Ploger and Josef Schreiner. Wurzburg: Echter, 1985. 1:136 (original 1981) Based on the ecumenical translation Einheitsubersetzung. Sirach 49:10 and the Greek tradition refer to the 12 prophets. The Vulgate has Minor Prophets, not referring to quality but to length. The introduction to Amos discusses the man, his time and book. The book is third among the 12 prophets though its origin is first in time.

361. Deissler, Alfons. "Die Propheten Amos und Hosea als 'Wegweiser' fur das Gottesvolk." pp. 43-57 in *Die alttestamentliche Botschaft als Wegweisung: Festschrift fur Heinz Reinelt* ed Josef Zmijewski. Stuttgart: Katholisches Bibelwerk, 1990. 451 pp. Discusses Amos as a social critic and a cult critic, with judgment on the people, the capital, the aristocracy, idolatry.

362. Delcor, Mathias. "Amos." Vol. 8, No. 1:175-238 in *Les Petits Prophetes* by Alfons Deissler and Mathias Delcor (Joel, Amos, Jonah, Habakkuk, Nahum, Zechariah). La Sainte Bible 8 ed Louis Pirot and Albert Clamer. Paris: Letouzey & Ane, 1961. No. 1:668. Fascicle 1 (1961), 1-292, has the general introduction, Hosea, Joel, Amos, Obadiah, Jonah. The general introduction discusses who is a prophet, the origins of prophecy, prophecy in and outside of Israel, cult prophets, the canon including the origin and transmission of the text of the Twelve, the variety of literary genre in the prophetic books, the importance of the Twelve. The introduction to Amos describes him, his book, his message. The commentary gives the Latin and French translation with extensive annotation including exegesis, exposition, comparative analysis of other texts, earlier studies. Words in italics indicate a modification from the MT. Vol 8, No. 2 (1951), 1-239, is on Maccabees by M. Grandclaudon.

363. Dell, Katharine J. "The Misuse of Forms in Amos." VT 45, No. 1 (Jan 95), 45-61. Notes Fohrer's criticism of forms, and distinguishes between the reuse of forms and the misuse of forms. Prophets did the latter to give new content and contradict the original form. Amos is an example. Amos's message is distinctive in both content and the use of forms.

364. Deltombe, Francois. "Amos 1." *Bible et Terre Sainte* No. 164 (Sep-Oct 74), 24. Gives the plan for the series, notes on the text.

365. Deltombe, Francois. "Amos 2." *Bible et Terre Sainte* No. 165 (Nov 74), 24. Amos is the first prophet whose tradition is preserved in writing. Historical background, notes on the text, his relationship to tradition.

366. Dempster, Stephen G. "Amos 3: Apologia of a Prophet." *Baptist Review of Theology* (Gormley, Ontario) 5 (1995), 35-91. A unity with chiasm. Notes the importance of ch 3 for today.

367. Dempster, Stephen G. "The Lord Is His Name: A Study of the Distribution of the Names and Titles of God in the Book of Amos." RB 98, No. 2 (Ap 91), 170-189. The names are carefully arranged to emphasize Yahweh as the God of Hosts and vice versa. The theme of the book is identification and invocation of the deity. The names are relative to the structure of the book, the study of the doxologies (not extraneous), the theurgic function of the Divine name, and the dating of the book (early). [Author's summary.]

368. Denio, F.B. "The Interpretation of Amos 5:25, 26." *The Old Testament Student* 5, No. 8 (1886), 335-337. Discusses the historical background, exegesis.

369. Dentzer, J.M. "Aux origins de l'iconographie du banquet couche." *Revue Archeologique* (Paris) ns 2 (1971), 215-258. Amos 6:4-7 (pp. 226-229) Literature review and discussion.

370. Derousseaux, L. "Acheter le malheureux pour un peu d'argent" (Am 8). *Assemblees du Seigneur* 56 (1974), 56-61.

371. Desnoyers, Louis. "Le prophete Amos." RB 26, Nos. 1&2 (Jan & Ap '17), 218-246. Discusses the man and his doctrine, with translation of selected passages.

372. Devescovi, Urbasno. "Camminare sulle alture." *Rivista Biblica* 9 (1969), 235-242.

373. Dhorme, Edouard. "Amos." Vol 2 (1959), xcvii-c, 736-761 in *La Bible de la Pleiade L'Ancien Testament*, 2 vols, ed Dhorme. Paris: Libraire Gallimard, 1956-1959. clxxxix + 1971 pp. Also called: Bibliotheque de la Pleiade. The first section is part of a general introduction on prophets, prophecy, the literature, with an overview of Amos, including historical background and of the book. The text is an annotated French translation with translation and notes by Dhorme.

374. Dicou, Bert. *Edom, Israel's Brother and Antagonist: The Role of Edom in Biblical Prophecy and Story*. JSOT Supplement Series 169 ed David J.A. Clines, et al. Sheffield: JSOT, 1994. 227 pp. Analyzes the Edomite connection, Obadiah compared with Joel, Amos, Jer 49:7-22, Ezekiel, the historical relationship of Judah and Edom, and the origin of Edom's role. The author of Obadiah copied and refashioned Jeremiah's oracle against Edom. Both Joel and Amos were used in Obadiah and there was some reverse influence, i.e., the editor(s) of the Twelve wrote the closings of all three books.

375. Diebner, Brend Jorg. "Berufe und Berufung des Amos (Am 1:1 und 7:14f)." *Deilheimar Blatter zum Alten Testament und seiner Rezeption in der Alten Kirche* = DBAT (Heidelberg) 23 (1986), 97-120.

376. Diebner, Brend Jorg. "'Sozialgeschichtliche Auslegun' des Alten Testaments als Erbe der 'Offenbarungs-Archaeologie'." *Deilheimar Blatter zum Alten Testament und seiner Rezeption in der Alten Kirche* = DBAT (Heidelberg) 24 (1987), 127-145.

377. Dietrich, Manfried and Oswald Loretz. "BS, TBS, Hebr. SBS (Am 5:11) Sowie Ug. TSY und SBS." UF (Kevelaer/Neukirchen-Vluyn)

10 (1978), 434-435. Comparative analysis noting many earlier studies.

378. Dietrich, Walter. "JHWH, Israel und die Volker beim Propheten Amos (Yahweh, Israel, and the Nations according to the Prophet Amos." TZ 48, Nos. 3&4 (1992), 315-328. A close study of Amos' oracles against the nations, including Israel and Judah. God's people will survive but their army and officials will not.

379. Diez Macho, A. and J.A.G. Larraya. "El Ms. 4083f.9 de la Biblioteca Nacional y Universitaria de Estrasburgo. (Fragmento de Amos 1:8-3:7, en Hebreo y Targum Babilonicos)." *Estudios Biblicos* 19, No. 1 (1960), 91-95. Describes the fragment and transliterates the text with critical notes.

380. DiGangi, Mariano. "Amos: The Unjust Society." pp. 34-44 in *Twelve Prophetic Voices*. Wheaton, IL: Victor (SP Publications), 1985. 167 pp. The prologue says we are witnessing the collapse of a civilization - relativism, materialism, greed, boredom, violence, vice. It is time to examine our standards in the light of an absolute standard. The prophets are part of the revelation though they spoke in their own style in their own situation. When interpreting sacred writings, we need truth, not the imposition of personal biases. There is a dynamic relationship between eschatology, the evangelical and ethics. The prophets both foretold and told forth. They herald the advent of the Messiah. Christ comes to liberate his people. For a keeper of sheep, Amos knew a lot of theology. He confronted the priest Amaziah and condemned Israel's adulterated worship. He denounced sin, pronounced sentence and announced salvation. The fulfillment is in Christianity.

381. Dijkema/Dykema, F. "Le fond des propheties d'Amos." OTS 2 (1943), 18-34. The table of contents spells the name Dykema.

382. Dijkstra, M. "Gelijkenissen in Amos." *Nederlands Theologisch Tijdschift* (Gravenhage) 48, No. 3 (July 94), 177-190, 230 (Eng summary). Compares metaphors, similes and full-fledged parables in the OT with the parables of Jesus, and discusses these forms in Amos.

383. Dillistone, F.W., et al. "Amos." pp. 109-110 in *Westminster Introductions to the Books of the Bible*. Philadelphia: Westminster Press, 1948. 224 pp. Notes the religious struggle against Baalism in both the north and the south, Amos's proclamation of judgment, the historical background, the Day of the Lord.

384. Dines, Jennifer. "Reading the Book of Amos." *Scripture Bulletin* 16, No. 2 (Sum 86), 26-32. "Reading" means the total experience, not just a search for facts. One can read to determine the literary genre, form, role in the canon, key issues. Gives a "tour of the text," discusses judgment (condemned for, and not condemned for), stages in the formation of the text, taking the whole book and not just some part, application.

385. Dion, Paul E. "Le message moral du prophete Amos s'inspirait-il du 'Droit de l'Alliance'?" *Science et Esprit* 27, No. 1 (Jan-Ap 75), 5-34. Reviews earlier studies, discusses the oracles against the nations, Israel, luxury, ritualism, the comparison of judgment and righteousness, the rejection of the prophetic message.

386. Dobbie, Robert. "Amos 5:25." *Transactions of the Glasgow University Oriental Society* 17 (1957-1958), 62-64. Published, 1959. Exegesis. Compares other texts, discusses the use of negative questions with positive answers and related issues. The verse does not warrant belief in sacrifice in the desert period.

387. Doller, Johannes. "Vom 'Uberschussigen' bei Amos." *Studien und Mitteilungen aus dem Benedictiner- und Cistercienser-orden* 28, No. 2 (1907), 413-415. Exegesis. Discusses earlier studies, the oracles against the nations, the significance of Nos. 3-4.

388. Doorly, William J. *Prophet of Justice: Understanding the Book of Amos*. NY: Paulist, 1989. iv + 92 pp. Cf Preaching from the Book of Amos to address problems of economic injustice. Diss. Lancaster Theological Seminary, 1987. 141 pp. DA 48, No. 4 (Oct 87), 948-A. For the general reader. Reviews the way scholars divide the book in parts. Doorly follows Coote and a sociological approach. There are three layers in the history of the book. In the first (by Amos), the poor suffer from oppression by the wealthy. In the Deuteronomic second layer, there is a chance for repentance. In the

third, written after the exile in Babylon, the elite are part of the oppressed. God is the single author of the book. Doorly applies Amos' teaching today against modern discrimination.

389. Dorsey, David A. "Literary Architecture and Aural Structuring Techniques in Amos." Bib 73, No. 3 (1992), 305-330. Notes previous studies and interpretations, closely structured units, e.g., sevenfold groupings. A great deal of deliberate and well-conceived structural design was involved in the final formation of the book. Many structuring techniques aid the listening audience.

390. Douglas, Benjamin. "Amos." pp. 41-53 in *A Translation of the Minor Prophets With an Occasional Brief Note Introduced.* NY: Revell, 1896. ii + 115 pp. Amos prophesied c 810-75 BCE. "In that day" the Millennial Kingdom will be set up.

391. Drinkard, Joel F. "Thus Says the Lord." R&E (Louisville, KY) 92, No. 2 (Spr 95), 219-233. A modern paraphrase naming the Soviet Union, Iran, Iraq, China, Cuba, Libya, Great Britain, the United States.

392. Driver, Godfrey Rolles. "Amos 7:14." ET 67, No. 3 (Dec 55), 91-92. No useful purpose can be served by repeating the numerous explanations for this verse. He never said he was not a prophet. The Hebrew interrogative negative has positive force. Gives many examples. This is also found in cognate languages. In effect, Amos asked, "Do you suppose I am not a prophet because I am a laborer? God has called and sent me."

393. Driver, Godfrey R. "Difficult Words in the Hebrew Prophets." pp. 52-72 in *Studies in Old Testament Prophecy, Presented to Professor Theodore H. Robinson by the Society for Old Testament Study on His Sixty-fifth Birthday, August 9th, 1946* ed Harold Henry Rowley. Edinburgh: Clark, 1950. xi + 206 pp. [reprinted, 1957]. One of the difficult words is in Amos 3:12 (pp. 69-70). He replaces "silken cushions" with "frame" of a bed.

394. Driver, Godfrey Rolles. "A Hebrew Burial Custom." ZAW 66, ns 25, No. 3 (1954), 314-315. Cremation was an idolatrous practice so Amos 6:10 does not mean this. It means one who anoints with resin

and refers to anointing the dead with spices. The tragedy is not
burning the body but that the old bury the young.

395. Driver, Godfrey R. "Hebrew Notes on Prophets and Proverbs." JTS
(Oxford/London) 41, No. 2 (Ap 40), 162-175. Exegesis and notes
on earlier studies. Several items (pp. 171-172) are from Amos.

396. Driver, Godfrey Rolles. "Linguistic and Textual Problems: Minor
Prophets: II. Amos." JTS 39, No. 3 (July 38), 260-273. Study of
selected terms in Amos (pp. 260-264) with exegesis, review of
earlier studies.

397. Driver, Godfrey Rolles. "Two Astronomical Passages in the Old
Testaments." JTS ns 4, No. 2 (Oct 53), 208-212. Amos 5:8-9 opens
with Pleiades and Orion. The last two lines have been translated
several ways. Driver suggests Taurus, Capella (goat), and
Vindemiatrix (Vintager).

398. Driver, Godfrey Rolles. "Waw Explicative in Amos 7:14." ET 68,
No. 10 (July 57), 302. The waw explicative does not have the force
of Amos' negative turned into a positive.

399. Driver, Samuel Rolles (1846-1914), ed. *The Books of Joel and
Amos*. The Cambridge Bible for Schools and Colleges ed A.F.
Kirkpatrick. Cambridge: Cambridge University, 1897. Rev, with
H.C.O. Lanchester, 1915. 243 pp. Amos is on pp. 93-239. Reviews
the man, contents, teachings, literary aspects. He was one of a
settlement of herdsmen at Tekoa who raised a special breed of
stunted sheep prized for their wool. The simple countryman (p. 94)
lived in the atmosphere of the desert, insensitive, unemotional,
unmoved by his message of doom. [The text says nothing about a
settlement, stunted sheep, simple countryman, atmosphere, degree
of Amos' sensitivity.] He was no rustic (p. 103) but a man of
impressive language. The prophetic style is fully matured. He
knows history. The book has three parts: introduction; discourses
disillusioning the Israelites; visions, with 9:11-15 as an epilogue
(the dynasty of David will be reinstated). There is prosperity but the
rich lived in self-indulgence while the poor lived in misery. God
knows only Israel and therefore "will visit upon you all your
iniquities." There is no more favoritism than for Ethiopians. God

demands honesty, justice, purity but Israel is deficient in morality. Privilege brings responsibility. Ritual is no substitute for obeying God. Authorship has been questioned but Smith says this is not an issue of authenticity. The detailed exegesis is still useful today.

400. Driver, Samuel Rolles. "Amos." pp. 313-318 in *An Introduction to the Literature of the Old Testament.* Gloucester, MA: Peter Smith, 1972. xxv + xi + 577 pp. original, 1891. A brief introduction gives Amos' background, the political situation, and divides the book into three parts, with commentary on each. Amos has been called rustic but his language is pure, his style classical and refined.

401. Dubis, Kevin M. The Use of Amos 9:11-12 in Acts 15. MTh. Calvin Theological Seminary, 1989. Micropublished by Theological Research Exchange Network. Portland, Oregon. 1990. 114 pp. Reviews the literature, defends the authenticity of Amos, exegesis, notes as metaphorical reference to the Davidic kingdom. In Acts, James used the Amos text as a model for the Church.

402. Duff, Archibald. "Isaiah and Zion, or, the Development of Thought in Isaiah. A Study in the History of Hebrew Religion." *The Andover Review* (Boston) 9 (1888), No. 52 (Ap), 426-431; No. 53 (May), 528-547. The first article includes: I. Amos and Hosea: Their Sanctuary Faith, pp. 427-431, as part of the developing theme of Zion. Amos is discussed on pp. 427-429. Zion is not the sanctuary of safety. Amos said seek good and live. The sinner will die by the sword. Amos has the naive mind of the godly Hebrew. He proclaimed the stern righteousness of Jahweh.

403. Duhm, Bernhard. "Anmerkungen zu den zwolf kleinen Propheten." ZAW 31 (1911), No. 1:1-43, No. 2:81-110, No. 3:161-204. Amos is unit I, pp. 1-18. A general study with critical notes, exegesis and commentary. The series = *Anmerkungen zu den Zwolf Propheten.* Giessen: Topelmann, 1911.

404. Duhm, Bernhard. "Amos und seine Schrift." pp. 89-98 in *Israels Propheten,* 2nd ed. Lebensfragen 26 ed Hienrich Weinel. Tubingen: Mohr (Paul Siebeck), 1922. viii + 484 pp. (original, 1916) Discusses various texts in historical context with comparison

to the traditions, opposition from Amaziah, Amos' claim he was not a prophet, his visions, etc.

405. Duhm, Bernhard. "Amos." pp. 28-30, 53-80 in *The Twelve Prophets: A Version in the various Poetical Measures of the Original Writings* tr Archibald Duff. London: Black, 1912. viii + 263 pp. Tr of *Die zwolf Propheten, in den Versmassen der Urschrift ubersetzt.* Tubingen, 1910. The book has a general discussion of prophecy, the Book of the Twelve, the nature of prophecy, the form of oracles, and introductions to the individual prophets. The major unit is a translation with notes. Three kinds of type - bold, italics, small italics - are used to distinguish original prophetic utterances, additions by editors and still later additions. The introduction to Amos (c 750 BCE) notes the man (from Tekoa; not a prophet) and his message. Amos proclaimed evil cannot be turned away. He is the prophet of wrath. He speaks plainly but handles his language with a master's skill.

406. Duhm, Bernhard. "Der Prophet Amos." pp. 109-126 in *Die Theologie der Propheten als Grundlage fur die innere Entwicklungsgeschichte der israelitischen Religion.* Bonn: Marcus, 1875. viii + 324 pp. Gives the background, the religious situation, the idea of Amos in context. Discusses the wrath of God and the judgment.

407. Dumbrell, William J. "Amos." pp. 168 in *Covenant and Creation: An Old Testament Covenantal Theology*; Exeter, Devon: Paternoster Press, 1984. Paperback, NY: Nelson, 1985. 218 pp. The American version is subtitled: A Theology of Old Testament Covenants. Discusses Amos in the unit on the new covenant, biblical eschatology and the effect of the exile, and at several other points in the text. The term *berit* appears in Amos 1:11 but it may refer here to a treaty between Solomon and Tyre rather than the relationship of God and Israel. He presupposes the covenant throughout. He does use the covenant terms *yad'*, *torah*, *pesha'*, *hoq*, etc.

408. Dumeste, M.L. *La spiritualite des prophetes d'Israel.* Sources de Spiritualite 5. Paris: Alsatia, 1962. 96 pp. Studies of Amos, Hosea, Isaiah.

409. Dumeste, M.L. "La spiritualite des prophetes d'Israel (Le message du prophete Amos)." *La Vie Spirituelle* 74 (1946), 834-852; 75 (1946), 424-437.

410. Dupont, Jacques. "Je rebatirai la cabane de David qui est tombee" (Acts 15:16 = Amos 9:11) pp. 19-32 in *Glaube und Eschatologie: Festschrift fur Werner Georg Kummel zum 80. Geburtstag* ed Erich Grasser and Otto Merk. Tubingen: Mohr, 1985. vi + 356 pp. Compares these and related materials, e.g., Dan 11:14 (LXX), 4Q 174,1,10-13, Targum, Luke 1:27,32,69; 2:4,11, etc.

411. Durr, Lorenz. "Altorientalisches Recht bei den Propheten Amos und Hosea." BZ 23, No. 1 (1935), 150-157. Reviews current scholarship, Sumerian and Akkadian tradition. Compares Hammurabi and other codes with references in Amos and Hosea.

412. Duster, Friedrich. "Beitrage zur Erklarung des Propheten Amos." TSK 22, No. 4 (1849), 869-914. A response to Baur's *Prophet Amos*, 1847, discussion of the comparison of Amos and Joel, Amos' relation to the kingdom, the critical exegetical approach and difficulties.

E.

413. Earle, Neil. "Amos: Upholding the Covenant." *The Plain Truth* 60, No. 1 (Jan 95), 20-21. Prophets were forthtellers as well as foretellers. Upholding the covenant was one of their tasks. Gives historical background for Amos. His preaching was rooted in the traditions of his people. The covenant revolved around brotherly love - how people should treat one another (Amos' timeless lesson). The rich exploited the poor. Through Amos, God condemned their behavior. To understand the prophets, we need to understand the audience. He called Israel back to the covenant, to focus on God.

414. Eberhard, Kenneth. "The Prophet Amos: No Man to Mince Words." *The Liguorian* 55, No. 4 (Ap 67), 46-50. Gives the historical and economic background. The rich were indifferent to the poor. Justice was perverted. Discusses the confrontation with Amaziah, the covenant, the relevance of Amos today. Wherever people are exploited, wherever people lack concern for others, the covenant is violated. Because of the election, God is more demanding of his people. Worship is nothing without a sincere heart.

415. Ebo, D.J.I. "Another Look at Amos' Visions." *Africa Theological J* 18, No. 1 (1989), 17-27. Notes a variety of earlier views. Claims editors put the visions in the present order with hope followed by total doom. But why should Amos then go on to intercede? He was not just a prophet of doom. The visions should be 8:1-2; 7:1-3, 4-6; 7:7-8f; 9:1f. This makes the intercession reasonable, gives meaning to the lack of intercession in the last three. The judgment is unstoppable but there is hope on the other side.

416. Ebo, D.J.I. "O that Jacob would survive": A study of hope in the book of Amos. Diss. University of Nigeria, 1985. Abstract in *African J of Bible* 1, No. 2 (Oct 86), 186. Ebo agrees with the

majority of scholars on the doom in Amos, but does not think the
hope is secondary. Amos' hope looks beyond judgment. The
remnant motif is Amos' and his exhortations look beyond
judgment. His visions show selective judgment. The undiluted hope
oracle is Amos' word.

417. Edel, Reiner-Friedemann. "Amos." Vol 1 (1968), 46-62 in
     *Hebraisch-Deutsche Praparation zu den "Kleine Propheten" I
     (Hosea bis Jona)*, 2 vols, by Edel. Marburg: Edel, 1968-1972. 1:71
     pp. Vol 1, 3rd ed. The Hebrew is from Kittel (21st ed, Stuttgart,
     1943) with reference to Kohler-Baumgartner (Leiden, 1955, 1958)
     and Gesenius-Buhl (21st ed). Hebrew words are translated into
     German with grammatical analysis, including Hebrew roots. The
     text is printed in lines with parenthesis, and is difficult to follow,
     contrast to vol 2 with words in columns and analysis in footnotes.

418. Edghill, Ernest Arthur and G.A. Cooke. *The Book of Amos*, 2nd ed.
     Westminster Commentaries ed Walter Lock. London: Methuen,
     1926. xxvi + 119 pp. (original, 1914) Cooke edited and introduced
     the work. He reviews the historical background, Amos as a prophet,
     the nature of the book and his literary influence. His prophecy
     came as a result of a direct call which differs from others. His
     teaching came from the tradition with an emphasis on God's moral
     standards. There are parallels between Amos' words and other
     prophets - Hosea, Jeremiah, Ezekiel, Joel, Zechariah and Haggai.
     The full text and exegesis is followed by Amos' words retranslated
     and rearranged according to visions and voices, addresses,
     proclamations of woe, externals, peoples, princes and palaces, and
     fragments. The hope at the end was added by a later prophet.

419. Eggebrecht, Gottfried. "Die Literature." pp. 186-212 in *Das Alte
     Testament und seine Botschaft: Geschichte - Literatur - Theologie*,
     2nd ed, by Hans-Jurgen Zobel and Karl-Martin Beyse. Berlin:
     Evangelische Verlagsanstalt, 1984. 372 pp. (original, 1981) Ch 2
     is on the divided kingdom with a section on the pre-exilic prophets.
     The introduction discusses prophecy, its origins (including outside
     of Israel) and development, e.g., groups (bands) of prophets, the
     classical prophets. The general discussion includes the prophetic
     call, self-understanding, message, social criticism, false prophets,
     the cult, the message of salvation, the covenant and their use of the

early traditions. Eggebrecht discusses the role of the deuteronomic editors - the redaction history, pp. 202-205, for Amos, Isaiah and Jeremiah. Koehn discusses the basic faith and the interpretations of the individual prophets, Amos (pp. 176-177), Hosea, Isaiah, Micah and Jeremiah. The message is discussed by Scholl, pp. 146-154.

420. Ehrlich, Arnold Bogumil (1848-1919). "Amos." 3:401-418 in *The Bible According to Its Literal Meaning. 3. The Prophets* (Heb: Mikra ki-Pheschuto), 3 vols, by Ehrlich. The Library of Biblical Studies ed Harry M. Orlinsky. NY: KTAV, 1969. 3:vi + 519 pp. (original 1898 [one version is Berlin: Poppelauer, 1901]) In his introduction, Orlinsky notes many idiosyncratic interpretations.

421. Ehrlich, Arnold Bogumil. "Amos." Vol 5:227-256 in *Randglossen zur hebraischen Bibel: Textkritisches, Sprachliches und Sachliches. Funfter Band. Ezekiel und die kleinen Propheten*. Hildesheim: Ohms, 1968. ii + 363 pp. (original, Leipzig, 1912) Hebrew word studies, commentary.

422. Eichrodt, Walther. "Die Vollmacht Amos: Zu einer Schwierigen Stelle im Amosbuch." pp. 124-131 in *Beitrag zur alttestamentlichen Theologie. Festschrift fur Walther Zimmerli sum 70. Geburtstag* ed Herbert Donner, et al. Gottingen: Vandenhoeck & Ruprecht, 1977. 580 pp. Notes the publication of commentaries by Wolff and Rudolph, discusses Amos 3:3-8 in comparison with other verses, Mt 16:2-4 and Luke 12:54-56, and the high priest at Bethel.

423. Eiselen, Frederick Carl. "Amos." pp. 191-285 in *Commentary on The Old Testament. Vol. 9. The Minor Prophets*. NY/Cincinnati: Eaton & Mains/Jennings & Graham, 1907. 741 pp. A general commentary for the average reader. Each book has an extensive introduction including historical background, literary analysis and outline. The commentary has copious notes on the KJV text. Amos was the first of the literary prophets. He was shepherd but able to hire an assistant while he took his wool to market. A commoner, he was free of dogma. In contrast to professionals, he was one of those who "Into politics they bring facts, but into religion they bring vision." We know nothing of his later life but Jerome and Eusebius said there was a tomb of Amos at Tekoa. His language is pure, his

sentences smoothly constructed. He has literary power. He was an uncompromising monotheist. The masses had a wrong understanding of the nature of God, but Amos was a reformer. He did not start a new religion. The book is a unity though there is a possibility of later insertions but the arguments for these are inconclusive. That includes the element of hope in Amos.

424. Eiselen, Frederick Carl. "Amos." pp. 35-51 in *Prophecy and the Prophets in Their Historical Relations.* NY: Methodist Book, 1909. 331 pp. Gives the historical (Jeroboam II) and socio-religious (prosperity/luxury; violence/oppression; government attitudes) background, biography, date, message and teachings. The latter included denunciation of luxury, judgment coming, and hope in the future for a remnant. His concept of God included personality, omnipotence, righteousness, mercy. The permanent lessons included justice, privilege implies responsibility, worship is an insult without obedience to God's commands.

425. Eiselen, Frederick Carl. "Amos." 2:404-430 in *The Prophetic Books of the Old Testament: Their Origin, Contents, and Significance.* Biblical Introduction Series. NY: Methodist Book Concern, 1923. Vol 1:314; 2:315-628. Discusses the name and place in the canon, contents and outline, debated passages, historical context, the man and his teachings. The latter objects to moral corruption and calls for social righteousness. God is a Person who created the world. His presence is not limited to Israel. He is righteous. Only rarely does Amos say God is merciful. Israel is supposed to reflect the divine character but it has not. A righteous God must execute justice.

426. Eissfeldt, Otto (1887-1973). "Amos." pp. 395-401 in *The Old Testament: An Introduction including the Apocrypha and Pseudepigrapha, and also the works of similar type from Qumran, The History of the Formation of the Old Testament.* NY and Evanston: Harper & Row, 1965. xxiv + 861 pp. Tr Peter R. Ackroyd from the third German edition (Tubingen: Mohr, 1964) Discusses the prophet (a great poet) and his time, different elements in the book, his share in the book and secondary additions (few). He was an independent cattle owner. After he finished his mission, he may have returned to his profession.

427. Eissfeldt, Otto. "Amos und Jona in volkstumlicher Uberlieferung."
     pp. 9-13 in . . . *und fragten nach Jesus. Festschrift fur Ernst
     Barnikol zum 70 Geburtstag.* Berlin: Evangelische Verlagsanstalt,
     1964. Reprinted, pp. 137-142 in *Kleine Schriften* 4 ed Rudolf
     Sellheim and Fritz Maass. Tubingen: Mohr, 1968. viii + 304 pp.

428. Eitan, Israel. "Biblical Studies." HUCA 14 (1939), 1-22. Sec II is
     on "Stray Notes to Minor Prophets," pp. 5-6. Exegesis for Amos
     1:5,8.

429. Elhorst, Hendrick Jan. "Amos 6:5." ZAW 35, No. 1 (1915), 62-63.
     Emendation of the text, contra Lohmann.

430. Elhorst, Hendrick Jan. *De Profetie van Amos.* Leiden: Brill, 1900.
     vii + 172 pp. The first part of the book gives an overview and
     discusses the integrity of the book and its author. The second part
     of the book is a transcript of the Hebrew and Dutch translation on
     opposite pages, followed by exegesis.

431. Elliger, Karl. "Amos." pp. 1015-1028 in *Biblia Hebraica
     Stuttgartensia* ed Elliger and W. Rudolph, et al. Stuttgart: Deutsche
     Bibelstiftung, 1967-1977. lvii + 1574. The Twelve are pp. 991-
     1086. Liber XII Prophetarum was issued as fascicle 10. Stuttgart:
     Wurttemergische Bibelanstalt, 1970. x + 96 pp. A revised edition
     of Kittel's *Biblia Hebraica,* the Hebrew text with critical apparatus
     plus the Masora.

432. Elliott, Charles. "The Words of Amos." *The Old Testament Student*
     5, No. 1 (Sep 1885), 13-17. Exegesis and commentary. Boqer in
     7:14 and Noqed in 1:1 are not the usual word, Ro'eh, for shepherd.
     Historical background, literary analysis, frequent references to the
     Pentateuch, judgment for violating God's law. The final fulfillment
     - raising up the tabernacle of David - is in Christ.

433. Ellis, Robert R. "Are There Any Cows of Bashan on Seminary
     Hill?" SWJT 38, No. 1 (Fall 95), 44-48. A sermon on Amos 4:1-3,
     including modern application.

434. Ellison, Henry L. "Amos." pp. 128-134 in *The Old Testament
     Prophets: Studies in the Hebrew Prophets,* 3rd ed. Grand Rapids:

Zondervan, 1966. 160 pp. (original 1952; 8th printing, 1979) In general, the prophet is not a predictor but one who speaks for God. In general, they were unpopular. The problem of unfulfilled prophecy remains a problem. Some extend the final fulfillment to the millennium. Others see them as simply unfulfilled. Some see them as suspended, i.e., they will be fulfilled in the future. Amos' prophecy (8:8; 9:5) of the earthquake was fulfilled (1:1) by one of the worst in Palestinian history. We know little of Amos' spiritual history but his prophecy shows the influence of the desert - no half-tones, no fine distinctions between right and wrong. It seems reasonable that his prophecy was given at the three day New Year festival at Bethel. Amos talked to the rich and accused them of sin - violations of the ordinary decencies of life, fraud, inhumanity. Their problem was religious. They had a false idea of God. The final blessings, 9:11-15, are commonly thought to be written by someone else. Ellison thinks Amos added it when he wrote down his message for posterity.

435. Ellison, Henry L. "Amos." pp. 62-69 in *The Prophets of Israel from Ahijah to Hosea*. Grand Rapids: Eerdmans, 1969. 176 pp. A reference to a plague in Amos 4:10 may be reflected in Assyrian inscriptions from 765 BCE. Amos probably did not condemn superfluity as such but in contrast to those who are in need. The luxurious living of rich women was made possible by oppression [presumably this would be true of rich men as well]. Religion had taken the place of humble and active faith and obedience to God.

436. Engnell, Ivan. "Amos." Vol 1 (1948), cols 59-61 in *Svenskt Bibliskt Uppslagsverk*, 2 vols, ed Engnell, Anton Fridrichsen, Bo Reicke. Gavle: Skolforlaget, 1948-1952. viii + 1294 cols.; 2:viii + 1696 cols. 2nd ed, ed Engnell, et al. Stockholm: Nordiska Uppslabocher, 1962-1963. An overview of Amos' home, life, background, faith, preaching in the north, his attitude toward the cult at Bethel.

437. Engnell, Ivan. "Amos' bok." Vol 1 (1948), cols 61-63 in *Svenskt Bibliskt Uppslagsverk*, 2 vols, ed Engnell, Anton Fridrichsen, Bo Reicke. Gavle: Skolforlaget, 1948-1952. viii + 1294 cols.; 2:viii + 1696 cols. 2nd ed, ed Engnell, et al. Stockholm: Nordiska Uppslabocher, 1962-1963. Notes the historical context, the oracles against the nations, the visions, messianic and liturgical elements.

438. Enman, Fred M. "Law as Ministry: A Perspective from the Judeo-Christian Tradition." *Catholic Lawyer* 35, No. 1 (1993), 97-107. Ministry is any act which communicates the love of God to a human being. The love of the actor may also be included in the activity but the key factor is the love of God. Amos is the most eloquent spokesperson for social justice. His critique of Israel has passed the test of time. Efforts to establish and maintain just laws is a ministry. Amos condemned those in a position of power to provide justice but failed to do so. Judges have sold their judgment for money. Ex 23:6-8 and Dt 16:19-20 are clear. "You will not pervert justice or take a bribe." Amos attacked the elite, the rich, corrupt business practices.

439. Erlandsson, Seth. "Amos 5:25-27, ett [sic] crux interpretum." SEA (Lund) 33 (1968), 76-82. Word study and exegesis in relation to the context.

440. Escobar, Donoso S. "Social Justice in the Book of Amos." R&E 92, No. 2 (Spr 95), 169-174. Discusses anomie, social justice vs God's justice, notes earlier studies.

441. Eslinger, Lyle. "The Education of Amos." *Hebrew Annual Review* (Columbus, Ohio) 11 (1987), 35-58. Scholars frequently emend or re-order the visions of Amos but they follow a pattern. Amos begins as an intercessor for Israel but then Amaziah tells Amos to go home and Amos becomes the prosecutor.

442. Estalayo-Alonso, Victor. "Amos, un extranjero indeseable." *Estudios Teologicos* (Guatemala) 6, No. 11 (Jan-June 79), 115-180. Discussion of Amos 7:10-17, the role of Amaziah, the festivals, the role of politics, historical background, the return, the actual figure and message of Amos.

443. Evans, Mary. "Amos." pp. 52-72 in *Prophets of the Lord.* London: Paternoster, 1992. 267 pp. A general introduction reviews the prophets, prophetic literature, historical background, non-writing prophets. This is the first of four sections of the text (eighth century, up to Exile, Exile and after). At the end of each of the four, are questions for discussion, and bibliography. At the beginning of each of the last three is historical background. The study of Amos

includes an outline, the man, the book (written much later), the message, application today. A section called "tasters" has translations and commentary of selected passages. The message is that God is Lord of creation and nations and calls all to justice instead of the injustice of their commerce, self-indulgence and idolatry. Application today includes God as still caring, our own honesty and care instead of self-indulgence, and political involvement to ensure justice in society.

444. Evans-Hamilton, Melbalenia. "An Oracle to the People of the United States of America (1993)." pp. 3-4 in *Many Voices: Multicultural Responses to the Minor Prophets* ed Alice Ogden Bellis. Lanham, MD: University Press of America, 1995. xiv + 101 pp. The writers in this book try to apply the minor prophets today. Oracles of judgment against China, Iraq, West Africa, South Africa, Israel, the USA.

445. Everson, A. Joseph. "The Days of Yahweh." JBL 93, No. 3 (Sep 74), 329-337. A general study of the Day of Yahweh with reference to Amos and other sources. The phrase occurs 16 times in prophetic literature in seven prophetic collections - Isaiah, Ezekiel, Joel, Amos, Obadiah, Zephaniah, Malachi. A variation appears in Zech 14:1. There are also related phrases, e.g., Lam 2:1, 21, and similar concepts, e.g., the day of Jezreel, Hosea 1:11, the day of trouble Nahum 1:7.

446. Everson, A. Joseph. "The Quality of Life in Prophetic Vision." pp. 209-220 in *That They May Live: Theological Reflections on the Quality of Life* ed George Devine. Staten Island, NY: Alba House, 1972. viii + 306 pp. Focuses on Amos and Isaiah, e.g., Assyria (an instrument of judgement rather than an enemy), the Day of the Lord, concern for the poor as a world wide phenomenon.

447. Ewald, Georg Heinrich August von. "'Amos." Vol I (1875), 143-210 in *Commentary on the Prophets of the Old Testament. Vol. I. Yoel, 'Amos, Hosea and "Zakharyah,"* Ch. 9-11, 5 vols. Theological Translation Fund Library 9. London: Williams and Norgate, 1875-81. viii + 334 pp. Tr of *Die Propheten des Alten Bundes*, 2nd ed. Gottingen, 1867-68. A general introduction considers the prophet in general, the prophets of the OT, prophets as writers, the canon.

The introduction notes Amos as a simple, plain man, the historical background (political, cultic), God as righteous, the contents, divisions and style of the book. The commentary includes translation, exposition, exegesis.

448. Exell, Joseph Samuel (1849-1909). "Amos." Vol 10:ix + 107 in *The Biblical Illustrator*, 23 vols. Grand Rapids: Baker, 1988. In the new printing, Amos is bound with Daniel and the minor prophets, with separate pagination. The subtitle of the original series is "The Biblical Illustrator, or, Anecdotes, Similes, Emblems, Illustrations, Expository, Scientific, Geographical, Historical, and Homiletic Gathered from a wide range of home & foreign literature, on the verses of the Bible." Other printings have included Hosea - Micah as The Minor Prophets, Vol I. The introduction discusses the man (a simple shepherd, not the owner of flocks), the message (condemnation of Bethel, doom by the Assyrians, the inflexible righteousness of God), date and historical background in the time of Jeroboam II, outline of the book, Amos' ethics, the OT prophet as one who speaks for God. The commentary itself is verse by verse, phrase by phrase, noting homiletical concerns and citing earlier commentators.

449. Eybers, I.H. "Was Amos a Prophet?" *Theologia Evangelica* (Pretoria) 7, No. 1 (Ap 74), 3-21. Not until the Lord called him. Extensive review of the literature. Analyzes the name, historical background, message (God's universal rule, condemnation of the wealthy, condemnation of the wrong way God is worshipped).

F.

450. Fabian, Norbert. *Protest Gegen Ausbeuter: Amos' Sozialkritische Ansatze in der Alttestamentlichen Prophetie. Ein Werkbuch fur Religionsunterricht, Gemeinschaftskunde und Gemeindearbeit.* Pfeiffer Werkbucher 118. Munich: Pfeiffer, 1973. 136 pp. Diss. Sozialkritische Ansatze in der alttestamentlichen Prophetie, dargestellt am Propheten Amos. Versuch einer praxisbezogenen Aufarbeitung. Munster i.W., 1973. The introduction reviews the theme, global lessons of religious instruction, political theology, teaching prophetic social criticism in the schools, Isaiah, Jeremiah, et al., in relation to Amos. For Amos, Fabian discusses the prophet and his time, Amaziah, the Deuteronomic history, the emancipation of women, social unrest in Israel, criticism of the cult as social criticism, utopia, whether Amos was a revolutionary, the theology of revolution. Discussion points are noted throughout, as is the perspective of ancient and modern writers.

451. Fang, Chih-jung M. "Universalism and the Prophet Amos" (Japanese). *Collectanea Theologica Universitats Fujen* 5, No. 20 (1974), 165-171.

452. Farmer, George. "Note on the Emendation of Amos 2:13 (A.V.) proposed in Q.S., 1912, p. 102." *Palestine Exploration Fund Quarterly Statement* (London) 44 (1912), 159. Suggests ox cart instead of threshing sledge.

453. Farr, Georges. "The Language of Amos: Popular or Cultic?" VT 16, No. 3 (July 66), 312-324. Communication has been a problem for a long time. Amos and other prophets used language familiar to the hearers, blending liturgical and not-liturgical. This includes the doxologies.

454. Farrar, Frederick W. "Amos." pp. 35-68 in *The Minor Prophets*.
      Men of the Bible 14. NY: Randolph, 1890. viii + 245 pp.
      The first
      four chapters discuss the characteristics of Hebrew prophecy (seer,
      prediction,   proclamation   of   righteousness,   Messianic
      announcements, not ecstatic, hopeful), the writings of the prophets,
      their chronological order and the prophets as spiritual teachers. An
      appendix lists verses on the Messiah. The Amos material is in two
      chapters, one the man and his times including his return to Tekoa,
      the other on his message including the last words of hope. The land
      will be one kingdom under a descendent of David. Most of the
      prophecy has not been fulfilled physically but abundantly
      spiritually in the Christian dispensation.

455. Farrar, Frederick W. "The Minor Prophets. I. Amos." Exp 6th ser,
      Vol 5, No. 2 (Feb '02), 82-85. Discusses the historical and
      geographical background, the confrontation with Amaziah, the
      visions, the NT connection. The rabbis said Amos reduced the 613
      commands of Mosaic law to one: Seek me and live. The unit is part
      of a larger study on the Minor Prophets, No. 2 (Feb '02), 81-92; No.
      4 (Ap '02), 271-286.

456. Fausset, Andrew R. (1821-1910). "Amos." Vol 4:527-564 in *A
      Commentary Critical, Experimental, and Practical on the Old and
      New Testament. Vol. IV. Jeremiah to Malachi* by A.R. Fausset.
      Entire commentary by Robert Jamieson, A.R. Fausset and David
      Brown. Philadelphia: Lippincott, 1866. iii + 728 pp. Rev, Grand
      Rapids: Eerdmans, 1935. Rev, Amos, pp. 789-802 in Jamieson,
      Fausset, Brown, *Commentary Practical and Explanatory on the
      Whole Bible*. Grand Rapids, MI: Zondervan, 1961. 1591 pp. The
      introduction provides historical background, his name, message,
      style, quotations in the NT and later writers. A detailed
      commentary including words, phrases, verses, with exegesis, MT,
      numerous cross references with other biblical texts.

457. Feigon, Gershon J. *Yemenite Targum Manuscript to the Twelve
      Minor Prophets*. San Diego, CA: Bureau of Jewish Education,
      1971. 55 pp. Diss. Yeshiva University, 1946. Gives a general
      introduction to Targumim. The Yemenite manuscript (No. 27 of
      Enellow Memorial Collection, Jewish Theological Seminary) has
      400 deviations, half known from other sources. The handwriting

dates 16th century, with both the Hebrew and Targum. Gives a description of the manuscript using references from the Twelve to illustrate the variations. Lists omissions and additions.

458.   Feinberg, Charles L. "Amos: The Righteousness of God." pp. 86-124 in *The Minor Prophets*. Chicago: Moody, 1976. 360 pp. (original, 5 volumes: NY: American Board of Missions to the Jews, 1948, 1951, 1952, including *Joel, Amos and Obadiah*, 1948.) The nations, including Judah and Israel, are condemned and will be punished but in the end, David's dynasty will be restored in the Messiah.

459.   Felsenthal, Bernhard. "Zur Bibel und Grammatik. 2. Zur Eklarung von Amos 6:10." pp. 133-137 in *Semitic Studies in Memory of Rev. Dr. Alexander Kohut* ed George Alexander Kohut (1874-1933). Berlin: Calvary, 1897. xxxv + 615 pp. Exegesis.

460.   Fendler, Marlene. "Zur Sozialkritik des Amos. Versuch einer wirtschafts- und sozialgeschichtlichen Interpretation alttestamentlicher Texte." EvT (Munich) 33, No. 1 (Jan-Feb 73), 32-53. Surveys the historical and social situation, family, corruption, kingdom, luxury, community structure and Amos' critique of it.

461.   Fensham, F. Charles. "Common Trends in Curses of the Near Eastern Treaties and *kudurru*-Inscriptions Compared with Maledictions of Amos and Isaiah." ZAW 75, No. 2 (1963), 155-175. The prophets borrowed from the curses of the vassal treaties. Curses against foreign nations similar to those against disobedient Israel. Notes common terms, numerous parallels in the curses themselves. The magical element is missing in Hebrew where Yahweh is the focal point. There is room to change the curse into a blessing.

462.   Fenton, Terry L. "Ugaritica - Biblica." UF 1 (1969), 65-70. Amos 5:11 (pp. 65-66), is translated on the basis of the Ugaritic: "Therefor, because of your despoiling the child of the poor." This translation is supported by the Talmud.

463. Ferriol, S.L. de. *El Yahve de Amos.* Trabajos Monograficos 3.
      Buenos Aires: Universidad de Buenos Aires, 1987.

464. Feuillet, Andre. "L'universalisme et l'alliance dans la religion
      d'Amos." *Bible et Vie Chretienne* (Paris) 17 (Mar-May 57), 17-29.
      Discusses the historical background, the history of interpretation,
      and the translation of selected passages.

465. Fey, Reinhard. *Amos and Jesaja: Abhangigkeit und
      Eigenstandigkeit des Jesaja.* Wissenschaftliche Monographien zum
      Alten und Neuen Testament 12 ed Gunther Bornkamm and Gerhard
      von Rad. Neukirchen-Vluyn: Neukirchener, 1963. 159 pp. Diss.
      Georg-August-Universitat (Gottingen), 1961. Reviews the basic
      ideas of Amos' preaching, pp. 24-56. Isaiah knew about one-third
      of Amos, probably from an early edition of the prophet. Isaiah did
      not copy Amos but advanced his ideas. Rev, ABB-513.

466. Fillion, Louis-Claude (1843-1927). "La Prophetie D'Amos." Vol.
      6 (1921), 407-442 in *La Sainte Bible (Texte Latin et Traduction
      Francaise) Commentee d'Apres la Vulgate et les Textes Originaux
      a l'Usage des Seminaires et du Clerge,* 5th ed. Paris: Letouzey et
      Ane, 1921. 912 pp. The introduction discusses the prophet, his
      time, the divisions of the book, his style. The commentary has the
      French and Latin translations in parallel columns, followed by
      exposition. The text is illustrated throughout with photographs and
      drawings.

467. Finley, Thomas John. "An Evangelical Response to the Preaching
      of Amos." JETS 28, No. 4 (Dec 85), 411-420. Evangelicals should
      know what the Bible teaches about social morality. Reviews the
      preaching of Amos, including social justice and future restoration.
      Amos described the poor as innocent, needy, the have-nots or
      helpless, suffering. This violates the covenant. Finley notes
      descriptions of oppression, and the demand for a response of
      holiness, justice, mercy. This response must come first from the
      individual, the church, and then business, government, etc.

468. Finley, Thomas John. "Amos." pp. 105-338 in *Joel, Amos,
      Obadiah.* The Wycliffe Exegetical Commentary ed Kenneth
      Barker, et al. Chicago: Moody, 1990. xxiii + 417 pp. The

introduction gives the historical background (date, political and religious situation), literary context (composition, language, style, message, outline, flow of the argument), contemporary application. The argument is that Israel has sinned; God will punish the sin; there will be a restoration. Amos condemned injustice and insincere worship, issues that are here today. The commentary gives translation, exegesis, exposition, compares other translations, earlier studies including debates on translation, interpretation. Additional notes consider special issues, e.g., the meaning of *nqd* - herdsman, chief herdsman, etc. Amos as a whole is divided into nine sections. There are excursi on hymnic passages and on social justice. The figure of God as judge predominates in Amos but mercy is present also.

469.   Finley, Thomas John. "The Waw-Consecutive with 'Imperfect' in Biblical Hebrew: Theoretical Studies and Its Use in Amos." pp. 241-262 in *Tradition and Testament: Essays in Honor of Charles Lee Feinberg* ed John S. Feinberg and Paul D. Feinberg. Chicago: Moody, 1981. xxiv + 325 pp. Reviews the use of verb forms and applies this to Amos. The verb designations of imperfect and perfect are a misleading mixture of form and function. One should use prefix conjugation and suffix conjugation. The study includes comparative semitics, structural analysis, and the synchronic analysis of Amos.

470.   Fischer, J. "In Welcher Schrift Lag das Buch Amos den LXX vor?" *Theologische Quartalschrift* (Tubingen) 106, No. 2 (1925), 308-335. Discusses the content and compares the LXX and MT.

471.   Fischer, T. "Einige neue Beobachtungen zur LXX des Buches Amos." *Anglican Theological Review* (Evanston, IL, 1918) 6, No. 3 (Dec 23), 245-247. Exegesis of selected passages comparing MT and LXX.

472.   Fishbane, Michael. "Additional Remarks on *rhmyw* (Amos 1:11)." JBL 91, No. 3 (Sep 72), 391-393. Expands on his treaty thesis, using a functional approach.

473. Fishbane, M. "The Treaty Background of Amos 1:11 and Related
      Matters." JBL 89, No. 3 (Sep 70), 313-318. Translates allies/friends
      rather than pity. The term is a covenant or treaty term.

474. Flanagan, Neal M. "The Book of Amos." pp. 3-27 in *The Books of
      Amos, Hosea, Micah: Introduction and Commentary*. Old
      Testament Reading Guide 15. Collegeville, MN: Liturgical Press,
      1966. 81 pp. The introduction describes Amos' life and
      background, summarizes his message (doom with a remnant
      saved), notes the book is poetry with later additions. The
      commentary uses the Confraternity of Christian Doctrine
      translation. The discussion gives numerous cross references to other
      biblical texts. Appendices list passages of the prophets used in the
      Mass and in the Breviary, and, review aids and discussion topics.

475. Flanders, Henry Jackson, Robert Wilson Crapps, David Anthony
      Smith. *People of the Covenant: An Introduction to the Old
      Testament*, 3rd ed. NY: Ronald, 1988. xiii + 498 pp. (original,
      1963) Gives historical background, review of content, central
      theme (doom, God of the nations), election and service, death of a
      nation, destruction, a little hope.

476. Flanders, Henry Jackson, Jr. and Bruce C. Cresson. *Introduction to
      the Bible*. NY: Ronald, 1973. xvi + 558 pp. In a unit on the
      Assyrian crisis, the authors give the historical background (victory,
      prosperity, corruption) and an outline of Amos with his unheeded
      message of doom.

477. Fleischer, Gunther. *Von Menschenverkaufern, Baschankuhen und
      Rechtsverkehrern. Die Sozialkritik des Amosbuches in historisch-
      kritischer, sozialgeschichtlicher und archaologischer Perspektive*.
      Athenaums Monografien Theologie. Bonner Biblische Beitrage 74
      ed Frank-Lothar Hossfeld and Helmut Merklein. Frankfurt am
      Main: Athenaum, 1989. xiv + 486 pp. Diss. Bonn: Katholisch
      Theologischen Fakultat, 1988. The introduction reviews the social
      critique of the prophets. The review includes data from archaeology
      discussed in more detail as part of the background of Amos in ch
      4, and specifically for the finds at Tell el-Far'a [North] in ch 5. The
      finds do not demonstrate peasant poverty. Ch 2 discusses Amos in
      broad sections while ch 3 addresses specific details. Poverty came

from population growth and partition of land (inheritance). There is an extensive bibliography, pp. 424-469.

478. Flocken, Louis M. "Physical Evil: Its Sources and Office According to Amos." *The Old and New Testament Student* (Hartford, CT) 12, No. 1 (Jan 1891), 28-33. People choose moral evil and God follows with physical evil to get people to repent.

479. Florival, Ephrem. "Le jour du judgment (Amos 9:7-15)." *Bible et Vie Chretienne* 8 (Dec 54-Feb 55), 61-75. Exegesis and commentary.

480. Fohrer, Georg. "Amos, Amosbuch." cols. 52-54 in *Calwer Bibellexikon*, 5th editing, 2nd ed, ed Karl Gutbrod, et al. Stuttgart: Calwer, 1967. x pp. + 1480 columns. (5 Bearbeitung, cols 52-54, 1961, copyright 1959. vi pp + 1444 cols) Discusses the name, the background, the message.

481. Fohrer, Georg. "Amos." pp. 430-438 in *Introduction to the Old Testament.* NY: Abingdon, 1968. 540 pp. Tr from the 1965 German edition, itself a revision of Ernst Sellin, *Introduction to the Old Testament*, original, 1910, with 7 editions plus two revised by Leonhard Rost. A general introduction to the prophets discusses prophecy in the ANE, prophetic preaching, compilation and transmission of the books. Reviews Amos' life, profession, date, collected sayings, growth of the book, message. He says no to Israel's social conduct and lays the base for a universal theology. Amos calls for repentance. In the tension between Yahweh's wrath and grace, maybe Yahweh will deliver them.

482. Fohrer, Georg. "Amos." pp. 22-55 in *Die Propheten des Alten Testaments.* Vol. 1. *Die Propheten des 8. Jahrhunderts.* Gutersloh: Gutersloher Verlagshaus/Gerd Mohn, 1974. 176 pp. A general introduction discusses methods, OT prophecy, the message of the pre-exilic prophets, the historical background of the 8th century BCE. The Amos chapter reviews the prophet, his book, his message - Israel a people like other people, preaching against sin, the possibility of salvation.

483. Fohrer, Georg. "Der Tag JHWHs." EI 16 (1982), 43*-50*. (pages in non-Hebrew languages have an asterisk) Fohrer discusses the phrase in general and in specific texts including Amos 5:18-20, etc.

484. Foresti, Fabrizio. "Funzione semantica dei brani participali di Amos: 4:13; 5:8s; 9:5s." Bib 62, No. 2 (1981), 169-184. These hymns are background for a new genre of literature - apocalyptic.

485. Fosbroke, Hughell E.W. and Sidney Lovett. "The Book of Amos." 6 (1956), 761-853 in The Interpreter's Bible, 12 vols, ed George Arthur Buttrick. Nashville: Abingdon, 1952-1957. xii + 1144 pp. The KJV and RSV are printed in parallel columns. Fosbroke wrote the "Introduction" (pp. 763-766) and "Exegesis" (pp. 767-853) while Lovett did the "Exposition" (pp. 761-853). The former reviews the political and religious background of Amos, his call and ministry in the northern kingdom, his message of doom, Yahweh as the Lord of nature, history and righteousness and gives an outline of the contents. The permanent value of Amos is in the pervading sense of the transcendent power and majesty of the living God who is involved in the human struggle with his standard of justice. Lovett discusses a new patriotism and the politics of time and eternity.

486. Foulkes, Francis. God's Message to the Nation: A Study Guide to Amos. Achimota, Ghana: Africa Christian Press, 1977. 151 pp.

487. Francisco, Clyde Taylor. "Amos." pp. 141-149 in Introducing the Old Testament rev. Nashville, TN: Broadman, 1977. 315 pp. (original, 1950) An introduction to the prophets discusses the Hebrew concept of prophet. The true prophets spoke for God. Describes the life and call of Amos, his message, historical background. Provides a detailed outline of the book. Amos' opening sermon is in classical Hebrew, marked by the skill of a master orator. The "Essence of True Religion" in 5:1-27 sets the direction of subsequent prophecy. His message includes the idea that religion and social morality are inseparable.

488. Francisco, Clyde T. "Expository Outline of the Prophecy of Amos." R&E 63, No. 4 (Fall 66), 427-428. A detailed outline of the text.

489. Francisco, Clyde T. "Teaching Amos in the Churches." R&E 63, No. 4 (Fall 66), 413-425. Discusses the development of prophecy, varieties of sin, the perils of privilege, unheeded chastisement, the praise of God, the essence of true religion, at ease in Zion, impending judgment. A mini-commentary.

490. Fransen, Irenee. "Cahier de Bible. La moisson du Seigneur: Le livre d'Amos." *Bible et Vie Chretienne* 32 (Mar-Ap 60), 27-36. Discusses the prophet, his language, his time, exegesis including the cause of evil, the harvest, the death of the nation.

491. Frederick, P.W.H. "The Book of Amos." pp. 816-828 in *Old Testament Commentary* ed Herbert C. Alleman and Elmer E. Flack. Philadelphia: Muhlenberg, 1948. vii + 893 pp. The introduction discusses the man and his time, the authenticity (almost never questioned) and divisions of the book.

492. Freedman, David Noel. "But Did King David Invent Musical Instruments?" *Bible Review* 1, No. 2 (Sum 85), 48-51. No. Amos 6:5 is usually translated, "like David invent instruments of music." Freedman translates "improvise on music."

493. Freedman, David Noel. "Confrontations in the Book of Amos." *The Princeton Seminary Bulletin* ns 11, No. 3 (1990), 240-252. Some claim the meeting between Amos and the priest Amaziah is intrusive in Amos 7, between the 3rd and 4th visions. But it is intentionally there in relation to the meeting between Amos and God. The visions (7:1-8:3) are intentionally reversed in chiasm as is the content, e.g., visions 1 & 2 go with the message of Amos 5-6, while visions 3 & 4 go with the message of Amos 1-4. Presumably the editor thought this arrangement made the point better. The priest takes his orders from the king while Amos takes his orders from God.

494. Freedman, David Noel. "Headings in the Eighth Century Prophets." *Andrews University Seminary Studies* (Berrien Springs, MI) 25, No. 1 (Spr 87), 9-26. Includes Isaiah, Hosea, Amos, Micah. Discusses the structure (experience, chronology), orthography (minor prophets are late), compilation. The occasion for the last was in

Hezekiah's time, in celebration for the deliverance of the city. The work was done with the sponsorship of King Hezekiah himself.

495. Freedman, David Noel. "Who Asks (or Tells) God to Repent." BR 1, No. 4 (Wint [Dec] 85), 56-59. In Amos 7:6, God repents. Amos and Moses are the only two prophets to get God to repent. Freedman reviews the divine repentance in other places.

496. Freedman, David Noel and Francis I. Andersen. "Harmon in Amos 4:3." BASOR 198 (Ap 70), 41. Albright identified Ugaritic *hrnm*, the home of Dan'el, with Hermel near Kadesh on the Orontes. The location fits the picture of exile in Amos, "beyond Damascus."

497. Freedman, David Noel and Andrew Welch. "Amos's Earthquake and Israelite Prophecy." pp. 188-198 in *Scripture and Other Artifacts: Essays on the Bible and Archaeology in Honor of Philip J. King* ed Michael D. Coogan, et al. Louisville, KY: Westminster/John Knox, 1994. xxvii + 452 pp. Surveys earthquake data and theory as background for Amos. Earthquakes were associated with theophanies. The note on the earthquake in Amos 1:1 is unique in prophetic records. People did not always believe the prophets, especially when their predictions were delayed. The earthquake legitimated Amos who had no other credentials.

498. Freehoff, Solomon B. "Some Text Rearrangements in the Minor Prophets." *Jewish Quarterly Review* (Philadelphia) 32, No. 3 (Jan 42), 303-308. Critique of this form of textual criticism, with examples drawn from several of the Twelve, including Amos.

499. Freeman, Hobert E. "Amos." pp. 184-190 in *An Introduction to the Old Testament Prophets*. Chicago: Moody, 1968. 384 pp. The first half of the book is on OT prophetism - origin, development, function, prophetic consciousness, revelation, inspiration, true and false prophets, the language of prophecy, messianic prophecy, the end of OT prophecy and prophecy in the NT. The review of Amos includes the nature of the book, the date, the prophet, historical background, problems. Amos wrote the whole book. It is cited in the NT by Stephen and James. Concludes with a detailed outline.

500. Frey, Hellmuth. *Das Buch des Ringens Gottes um seine Kirche:
     Der Prophet Amos.* Die Botschaft des Alten Testament 23/1.
     Stuttgart: Calwer, 1958. 202 pp. 2nd ed 1965. The introduction
     reviews the self revelation of God, the mission of Amos, etc. The
     commentary is in four parts relating to God's judgment but with the
     goal of salvation.

501. Frey, Ruth E. "Oracle Against the Nations (1992)." pp. 12-13 in
     Many Voices: Multicultural Responses to the Minor Prophets ed
     Alice Ogden Bellis. Lanham, MD: University Press of America,
     1995. xiv + 101 pp. The writers in this book try to apply the minor
     prophets today. Oracles of judgment against Iraq, Libya, Haiti,
     South Africa, the United States.

502. Fritz, Volkmar. "Amosbuch, Amos-Schule und historischer Amos."
     pp. 29-43 in *Prophet und Prophetenbuch: Festschrift fur Otto
     Kaiser zum 65 Geburtstag* ed Volkmar Fritz, et al. BZAW 185.
     Berlin/NY: de Gruyter, 1989. v + 284 pp. Reviews some of the
     many interpretations.

503. Fritz, Volkmar. "Die Fremdvolkerspruche des Amos." VT 37, No.
     1 (Jan 87), 26-38. Amos 1:3-5. The oracles against the nations is a
     literary construct by the editors to teach that God treats the sinful
     nations of the world in the same way He treats Israel and Judah.

504. Fuhs, Hans F. "Amos 1:1. Erwagungen zur Tradition und
     Redaktion des Amosbuches." pp. 271-289 in *Bausteine Biblischer
     Theologie, Festschrift fur G. Johannes Botterweck zum 60.
     Geburtstag dargebracht von seinen Schulern* ed Heinz-Josef Fabry.
     Bonner Biblische Beitrage 50, ed Botterweck and Heinrich
     Zimmermann. Bonn: Hanstein, 1977. v + 369 pp. Detailed study of
     the verse, phrase by phrase, review of various interpretations.

G.

505. Gaebelein, Arno Clemens (1861-1954). "Amos." Vol 5 (n.d.), 117-139 in *The Annotated Bible: The Holy Scriptures Analysed and Annotated. Vol V. Daniel to Malachi*, 9 vols, by Gaebelein. NY: "Our Hope," 1913-1924. 5:i + 333 pp. Vol 4 is 1921. The introduction discusses the historical background, the style (elegant composition), the message (judgment). The book is in three sections. The commentary expands on the message. After the judgment, the kingdom will be restored to God's people and Jesus Christ will be on the throne of David.

506. Galil, J. "An Ancient Technique for Ripening Sycamore Fruit in East-Mediterranean Countries." *Economic Botany* (NY Botanical Gardens) 22, No. 2 (Ap 68), 178-190. Amos is called a gatherer or dresser of sycamores, fruit of the poor. Galil gives an illustrated history of the tree, which originated in Africa, tools, fruit before and after cutting. The economic importance of it has declined in recent years. The type now growing in Israel does not need to be pierced or slashed. One species has a wasp that lays its eggs in the flower and develops in the fruit, so some have thought the dressing or cutting was to let the wasps out. But this is not so. The cutting releases ethylene which causes the fruit to swell four times and ripen. One gets the same effect from slashing one fruit or all of them, and today by spraying with a dilute solution of phytohormones which saves all the labor.

507. Garbini, Giovanni. "La 'Deportazione di Salomone' (Amos 1:6-11)." pp. 89-98 in *Storia e tradizioni di Israele. Scritti in onore di J. Alberto Soggin* ed Daniele Garrone and Felice Israel. Brescia: Paideia, 1991. xlvii + 310 pp. Notes earlier studies, compares versions, e.g., MT, LXX, Vulgate, etc., of the oracles against Gaza, Tyre, Edom. Gaza and Tyre delivered to Judah an Israelite king named Solomon.

508. Garcia Cordero, Maximiliano. "Amos." pp. 1142-1178 in *Biblica Comentada. Texto de la Nacar-Colunga. 3. Libros Profeticos*, 2nd edition. Biblioteca de Autores Cristianos [BAC]. Madrid: BAC, 1967. viii + 1348 pp. A general introduction to the prophets covers their number, the history, origin of the movement (from God but also theoretically, e.g., sociological), vocation and mission, revelation (heightened faculties, visions, conscience, ecstasy), predictions, theology (God, universal history, the Messiah, individualism), justice, false prophets, chronological table, bibliography (Catholic and non-Catholic). The introduction to Amos includes the life of the prophet, history, divisions and structure of the book (outline, authenticity, texts and versions, literary style), theology (monotheism, the election of Israel, idolatry, external religious ritual, social justice), bibliography (Catholic and non-Catholic). The commentary has the Spanish translation of the text plus commentary, divided by small units with indicative headings.

509. Garcia de la Fuente, O. "La Busqueda de Dios Segun el Profeta Amos." *Augustinianum* (Rome) 12, No. 2 (1972), 257-276. Reviews the history of interpretation with exegetical study.

510. Garcia-Treto, Francisco O. "A Reader-Response Approach to Prophetic Conflict: The Case of Amos 7:10-17." pp. 114-124 in *The New Literary Criticism and the Hebrew Bible* ed J. Cheryl Exum and David J.A. Clines. JSOT Supplement 143 ed Clines and Philip R. Davies. Sheffield: JSOT, 1993. 276 pp. The author emphasizes his background as poor and powerless, concerned with the performative rather than logic. He reads the story as power games. Amaziah represents institutional power; he does not refer to God. The priest emphasizes Amos is a foreigner and a political threat. Amos responds by agreeing with Amaziah, putting him on, then showing how Amaziah is attacking God, not Amos.

511. Garland, D. David. *Amos*. Bible Study Commentary Series. Grand Rapids: Lamplighter Books (Zondervan), 1966. 96 pp. The 1973 printing is titled, *Amos: A Study Guide*. Study Guide Series. Grand Rapids: Zondervan, 1973, with no reference to Lamplighter. The introduction reviews the personal history of Amos, his date, occupation, historical background, the man himself, summary of

his message (God will punish the guilty). The commentary is concerned with the great themes of the book. Each chapter has questions or suggestions for further study.

512. Garrett, Duane A. "The Structure of Amos as a Testimony to its Integrity." JETS 27, No. 3 (Sep 84), 275-276. Chiasmus and parallelism show the unity.

513. Gaster, Theodor Herzl. "Amos." pp. 648-651 in *Myth, Legend, and Custom in the Old Testament: A Comparative Study with Chapters from Sir James G. Frazer's "Folklore in the Old Testament"*[London: Macmillan, 1918]. NY: Harper & Row, 1969. lv + 899 pp. Study of comparative material, e.g., seek the Lord reflects the pagan search for the vanished spirit of vegetation.

514. Gaster, Theodor H. "An Ancient Hymn in the Prophecies of Amos." *Journal of the Manchester Egyptian and Oriental Society* 19 (1935), 23-26. It is a Hymn of Creation, to Yahweh Sebaoth, Lord of Hosts. Its single motif is universalism because he is the creator and agent of all natural forces. Gives Hebrew text, translation and exegetical notes for 4:13, 5:8, 9:6.

515. Gautier, Lucien. "Amos." I:480-489 *Introduction a L'Ancien Testament*, 2nd ed, 2 vols. Lausanne: Bridel, 1914. Biography and historical background plus commentary on the text.

516. Gehman, Henry S. "Amos." p. 39 in *The New Westminster Dictionary of the Bible*. Philadelphia: Westminster Press, 1970. xi + 1027 + 4 pp. + 16 maps. Based on the Davis Bible Dictionary (1898-1924). Reviews the meaning of the name, personal background, his knowledge of places and history, his boldness in speaking against the sins of the king and people, his religion (monotheism), his pure Hebrew style, use of imagery.

517. Gehman, Henry S. "Amos, The Book of." pp. 39-40 in *The New Westminster Dictionary of the Bible*. Philadelphia: Westminster Press, 1970. xi + 1027 + 4 pp. + 16 maps. Based on the Davis Bible Dictionary (1898-1924). Outlines the book with historical background, theology, judgment, final hope. The permanent lessons from the book include permanent truths, justice among people as

the divine will, privilege and responsibility, elaborate worship an insult to God if people are not trying to live up to his requirements.

518. Gehman, Henry S. "Philological Notes on Two Hebrew Words." *JBL* 58, No. 1 (1939), vi. Proceedings of the 74th meeting of the SBLE 28 Dec 38 at Union Theological Seminary, NYC. Amos 3:5, *moqesh*, means "snare."

519. Geldenhuys, J.N., et al., eds. "Amos." pp. 1950-1971 in *Die Bybel met Verklarende Aantekeninge. Deel II. Job tot Maleagi.* Kaapstad: Protestantse Uitgewers (Edms.) BPK, 1958. Vol. 2:ii + 1011-2062. An introductory note discusses the book (with an outline), the prophet, historical background. The biblical text is given in Afrikaans with annotation, exegesis, comparative notes.

520. Gelin, Albert (1902-1960). "Amos." pp. 271-276 in *Introduction to the Old Testament* ed Andre Robert and Andre Feuillet. NY: Desclee, 1970. tr (with updated bibliography added) from the 2nd French ed., *Introduction a la Bible. Vol. I: Ancien Testament.* Tournai, Belgium: Desclee. (original 1957-59) A general introduction gives an overview of the prophets - history, psychology (ecstatics?, experience), literary, significance (religious, political, social, Christ). Reviews the historical background of Amos, his life, book and message. Amos preached at Samaria and Gilgal as well as Bethel. His message focused on God's justice but a complete change of heart could save the nation. The prophets were not revolutionaries trying to overthrow the government. They defended the moral law, loved the poor.

521. Gelin, A. "Amos." vol 1 (1953), cols 141-142. *Dictionnaire de Theologie Catholique, Tables Generales* ed Bernard Loth and Albert Michel. Paris: Letouzey, 1953. 1:vi pp + 2032 cols. An endnote after cols 2031-2032 gives 1959 as the printing date. Gelin updates the bibliography, reviews recent views, the Day of Yahweh, Amos' background, his sympathy for the poor, early Christian views of Amos.

522. Gelston, A. "Amos." pp. 24-36 in *Dodekapropheton.* pp. xxxi + 100 in *The Old Testament in Syriac According to the Peshitta Version*, Part 3, fascicle 4, ed on behalf of the International

Organization for the Study of the Old Testament by The Peshitta Institute. Leiden: Brill, 1980. xxxi + 100 pp. The Part includes Sprey, Th. "Daniel - Bel - Draco." pp. xx + 48 (separate pagination). In addition to the collated text and critical apparatus, there is an overview of the manuscripts available and studied.

523. Gelston, A. *The Peshitta of the Twelve Prophets.* Oxford: Clarendon, 1987. xxiv + 208 pp. A general study of the Peshitta, includes additional bibliography from "Dodekapropheton."

524. Gemser, B. "Amos in Sy Dadikse Omgewing en Bedryf." *Hervormde Teologiese Studies* 1, No. 2 (1944), 49-58.

525. Gemser, B. "Die Godsgetuienis van Amos." *Hervormde Teologiese Studies* 1 (1943-4), 9-21.

526. Gese, Hartmut. "Amos 8:4-8: Der kosmische Frevel handlerischer Habgier." pp. 59-72 in *Prophet und Prophetenbuch: Festschrift fur Otto Kaiser zum 65 Geburtstag* ed Volkmar Fritz, et al. BZAW 185. Berlin/NY: de Gruyter, 1989. v + 284 pp. Reviews the various interpretations.

527. Gese, H. "Die hebraischen Bibelhandschriften zum Dodekapropheton nach der Variantensammlung des Kennicott." ZAW 69, No. 1 (1957), 55-69. A study in textual criticism and the history of interpretation including a review of the Kennicott manuscript in the light of the Dead Sea Scroll data. Variants in Amos are part of the comparative study.

528. Gese, Hartmut. "Kleine Beitrage zum Verstandnis des Amos buches." VT 12, No. 4 (Oct 62), 417-438. A series of studies on selected passages with exegesis, commentary, earlier investigation.

529. Gese, Hartmut. "Komposition bei Amos." pp. 74-95 in *Congress Volume: Vienna, 1980* ed John Adne Emerton. VTS 32 ed Emerton, et al. Leiden: Brill, 1981. vii + 483 pp. Reprinted, pp. 94-115 in *Alttestamentliche Studien* by Gese. Tubingen: Mohr, 1991. viii + 307 pp. Reviews various interpretions.

530. Gese, Hartmut. "Das Problem von Amos 9:7." pp. 33-38 in *Textgemass: Aufsatze und Beitrage zur Hermeneutik des Alten Testament. Festschrift fur Ernst Wurthwein zum 70. Geburtstag* ed A.H.J. Gunneweg and Otto Kaiser. Gottingen: Vandenhoeck & Ruprecht, 1979. 208 pp. Reprinted, pp. 116-121 in *Alttestamentliche Studien* by Gese. Tubingen: Mohr, 1991. viii + 307 pp. An exegetical study. Reviews earlier opinions.

531. Gevirtz, Stanley. "A New Look at an Old Crux: Amos 5:26." JBL 87, No. 3 (Sep 68), 267-276. Reviews earlier studies and suggests the Israelites were worshipping foreign gods. The punishment will be exile.

532. Geyer, John B. "Mythology and culture in the oracles against the nations." VT 36, No. 2 (1986), 129-145. Amos 1-2 is lacking in mythological reference.

533. Gigot, F.E. "Amos." Vol. 1:435-437 in *The Catholic Encyclopedia*, 15 vols (plus index), ed Charles G. Herbermann, et al. NY: Encyclopedia Press, 1907-1914. Reviews the life and times of Amos and analyzes the book. He was a herdsman of Thecua, 12 miles south of Jerusalem. There is no sufficient ground for the view of most Jewish interpreters that Amos was a wealthy man. Man has a natural tendency to be satisfied with the mechanical performance of religious duties. Amos delivered a stern rebuke and announced their ruin and captivity. The book is in three parts. Amos 1-2 contains oracles against the nations. Amos 3-4 expands on the sins of heartless luxury and external religion. Amos 7-9:8b has visions of judgment. The book concludes with God's promise of restoration. Amos 9:8c-15. The fine style is not incongruent with the life of a shepherd. Oratory was based on shrewd observation and memory. It is true that Amos argues in a concrete manner but his book has truths which can never become obsolete.

534. Gilead, Chaim. "Amos - from the Herdsmen in Tekoa" (Heb, Eng summary) BM 18 [Issue No. 54], No. 3 (Ap-June 73), 375-381, 426-427. Amos was not a permanent resident of Tekoa nor an owner of property. At the end of the grazing period, he did seasonal labor in the Shephalah. As a worker, he experienced the abuse of

the lower classes by the upper classes and saw the corrupt life of the rich.

535. Giles, Terry. "*Dal* and *'ebyon*: The Poor and the Needy in the Book of Amos." *The Baptist Review of Theology* (Gormley, Ontario) 1 (1991), 12-20. Technical terms for Amos' attack on economic abuse.

536. Giles, Terry. "The Dual Occurrence of *qum* in the Book of Amos." *Irish Biblical Studies* 12, No. 3 (June 90), 106-116. The labels poetry and prose are not clearly distinct in Hebrew. Repetition is a common literary device. The word in Amos 5:2; 7:2, 5; 9:11 reflects a salvation theme. It is a sign of hope, the theme of restitution, spread through his message. Cognates appear 10 times in Amos.

537. Giles, Terry. "An Introductory Investigation of Amos by Means of the Model of the Voluntary Social Movement." pp. 135-153 in *Proceedings, Eastern Great Lakes & Midwest Biblical Societies* 8 ed P. Redditt. Georgetown, KY: EGL & MBS, 1988. v + 211 pp. Annual meeting, Cleveland, Ap '88. Some think the prophets were cult officials. They knew priests and language. Others disagree. Giles compares cult and voluntary social movements. The latter has an ideology stated in moral terms. Amos used cultic language but gave it an ironic twist to mean the opposite of the normal. He represents an emerging ideology expressed in moral terms. The salvation oracles, Amos' concern for the poor, etc. are part of an emerging counter-movement to the social movement of the cult.

538. Giles, Terry. "A Note on the Vocation of Amos in 7:14." JBL 111, No. 4 (Wint 92), 690-693. Reviews opinions and discusses two poorly defined categories of people (oppressed and oppressors). The first are the producers - laborers and growers. Amos identifies with these. The statement is not concerned with his economic status as such.

539. Gill, John. "Amos." Vol 2 (1976), 477-515 in *An Exposition of The Books of the Prophets of the Old Testament: In Which It is Attempted to Give an Account of the Several Books, and the Writers of Them; A Summary of Each Chapter; and The Genuine Sense of*

every Verse; and, Throughout the Whole, The Original Text and Various Versions are Inspected and Compared; Interpreters of the Best Note, Both Jewish and Christian, Consulted; and The Prophecies Shewn Chiefly to Belong to the Times of the Gospel, and a Great Number of Them Yet to Come, 2 vols. London: Mathews and Leigh, 1810. 2:iii + 789. Reprinted [several times, e.g.], Streamwood, IL: Primitive Baptist Library, 1976. The introduction summarizes traditions about Amos, his life and death. His authenticity is not in doubt because he is quoted by later writers. The commentary includes extensive references to classical, rabbinic and historical sources, ancient versions, geography, legends and stories related to the text and current interpretations, as well as cross references to biblical texts.

540. Gillingham, Sue. "'Who Makes the Morning Darkness': God and Creation in the Book of Amos." *Scottish J of Theology* 45, No. 2 (1992), 165-184. Cf her "'Der die Morgenrote zur Finsternis macht': Gott und Schopfung im Amosbuch." EvT 53, No. 2 (1993), 109-123. Notes earlier studies, comparative analogies in other books, discusses God and the natural order in Amos, God and natural law, implications of God's relationship with the natural world and God's justice for all nations. The doxologies praise Yahweh's creative power by contradiction. God uses chaos to bring order, e.g., judgment for sin followed by re-creation. This has the ring of truth even today.

541. Ginat, Lippa. "The Order of Amos's Prophecies Against the Nations" (Heb). BM 34 [Issue 118], No. 3 (1989), 250-254. Amos' oracles were independent. The present arrangement is artificial, based on language. Cf. OTA 13 (1990), 288.

542. Ginsberg, H.L. "Notes on the Minor Prophets." EI 3 (1954), 83-83 (Heb), IV (Eng). This is the M.D.U. Cassuto (1883-1951) volume. In Hebrew, the author is H.A. Ginsberg. Amos 2:7, 8:4. Exegesis.

543. Ginzberg, Louis. "Amos: In Rabbinical Literature." Vol. 1:533 in *The Jewish Encyclopedia,* 12 vols, ed Isidore Singer, Cyrus Adler, et al. NY: KTAV, n.d. (original 1901) According to the rabbis, Amos was a stutterer. He was one of the eight princes of Micah 5:5. King Uzziah hit with a glowing iron and killed him. However,

pseudo-Epiphanean writings say he was killed by Amaziah the priest of Bethel.

544. Gitay, Yehoshua. "Amos." *The Encyclopedia of Religion* 1 (1987), 240-243. The first classical prophet whose words are preserved in writing. Previous works, Samuel and Kings, refer to prophets. Amos' time two years before the earthquake has been dated to 760 BCE by earthquake evidence at Hazor. Prosperity created social tensions with the exploitation of the lower classes. Religious practices mirrored the injustice. The cult served as religious protection for the elite. Amos attacked all this. He was a *noqed*, a "shepherd," a term also used for King Mesha of Moab. In Ugaritic, the term is parallel to priest. The book has a well developed style, continuing a well-developed tradition of oratory. He was a great poet and master of language. Current scholarship suggests a long history of editing.

545. Gitay, Yehoshua. "A Study of Amos's Art of Speech: A Rhetorical Analysis of Amos 3:1-15." CBQ 42, No. 3 (July 80), 293-309. The passage is a rhetorical unity with reasonable argument, witnesses and ethical appeal. Gitay discusses methods of audience appeal such as the rhetorical question.

546. Givati, Meir. "The Shabbat of the Prophet Amos" (Heb, with Eng summary). BM 22 [Issue No. 69], No. 2 (Jan-Mar 77), 194-198, 278-279. Contra Benjamin Halevi in BM 21 [Issue No. 66], No. 3 (Ap-June 76), Amos was talking about the traditional sabbath which was not a trading day. The Torah was in full effect, with no work and the commanded rest.

547. Gjerde, Ole Overland. "Profeten Amos." pp. 62-72 in *Skrift og skole: Festskrift til Oddmund Hjelde pa 60-arsdagen 15. mars 1970* with Hjelde, H. Ludin Jansen, et al. Oslo: Land og Kirke, 1970. 175 pp. Discusses the history of interpretation, e.g., Rowley's "Was Amos a nabi?"

548. Glanzman, George S. "Two Notes: Am 3:15 and Os 11:8-9." CBQ 23, No. 2 (Ap 61), 227-233. Amos 3:9-4:3 has a series of oracles which were probably separated but are linked by the theme of the

fall of Samaria. Amos 3:15 has been translated many or great houses. Glanzman translates "houses of the important."

549. Gluck, J.J. "Nagid-Shepherd." *VT* 13, No. 2 (1963), 144-150. The words *nagid* and *noqed* both mean shepherd. The first became an attribute for the ruler and then a title. The term was common in ANE languages. The interchange of g and q presents difficulties. Applied to the ruler, the word carried older connotations of the good shepherd.

550. Gluck, J.J. "Three Notes on the Book of Amos." pp. 115-121 in *Studies on the Book of Amos: Papers Read at 8th Meeting of Die Ou Testamentiese Werkgemeenskap in Suid-Afrika Held at Pretoria University 1965* ed A.H. van Zyl. OTWSA 7-8 (1964-1965). Potchefstroom: Pro Rege - Pers Beperk, 1965. pp. 113-169 pp. Bound with *Studies on the Book of Hosea*, the 7th Congress of the OTWSA, 111 pp., with continuous pagination for a total of 169 pp. Translates 5:9, "He who brings spoilation upon the mighty." In 5:16, *'ikkar* may mean grave digger rather than farmer. In 7:14b, Amos eats, sustains himself on, sycamore fruit.

551. Goliath, August C. "Die Aktualiteit van die profetiese prediking in die boek Amos." *Theologia Evangelica* 17, No. 3 (Sep 84), 57-58. A summary of his Master's thesis under the direction of F.E. Deist. A study of Amos' hermeneutics.

552. Good, Edwin M. "Amos." (notes on) pp. 948-957 in *The Oxford Study Bible, Revised English Bible with the Apocrypha*, 2nd ed, ed M. Jack Suggs, et al. NY: Oxford University Press, 1992. xxviii + 199* + 1597 + 14 maps + 7 (index) pp. (original 1976) The REB is a revision of the New English Bible. Amos speaks with a severity not exceeded in the stern denunciations of other prophets. There is a small hope Israel will repent, but some see this hope as added later. Some also think the doxologies are later additions.

553. Good, Robert M. "The Just War in Ancient Israel." *JBL* 104, No. 3 (Sep 85), 385-400. A review of the jural view of war in Amos 1:3-5, etc.

554. Gordis, Robert. "Amos, Edom and Israel - An Unrecognized
      Source for Edomite History." pp. 109-32 in *Essays on the Occasion
      of the Seventieth Anniversary of the Dropsie University (1909-
      1979)* ed Abraham I. Katsh and Leon Nemoy. Philadelphia:
      Dropsie University, 1979. xvi + 462 pp. Reviews the history of
      interpretation and the history of the relationship of Edom and Israel
      [and Judah], and Amos 1:11-12. A number of theories have
      developed over the last. Gordis notes the lack of evidence for these.
      Discusses the context of Amos as a whole. Amos 8-9 come after his
      expulsion from Bethel. The references to Judah in the first
      collection are negative but in the later collection the references are
      positive. The consistency in structure argues for the authenticity of
      all sections. The Phoenicians and the Philistines sold slaves to
      Edom. It is usually assumed that Amos does not identify the slaves.
      The slaves are usually identified as Israelites. This is most unlikely.
      Amos loved his people but was concerned with humanity. By
      reading the text as lamed accusative and infinitive with lamed,
      Gordis identifies the slaves as Edomites. The slaves may have been
      captured by Amaziah. Edom may have had a civil war which paved
      the way for capture by Amaziah. Amos' oracles against the nations
      is probably his first prophetic address.

555. Gordis, Robert. "The Composition and Structure of Amos." JBL 59,
      No. 1 (1940), vii. A paper read at the Society's 75th meeting, 27
      Dec 39 at Union Theological Seminary, NYC. Published, *Harvard
      Theological Review* 33 (1940), 239-251. Reprinted, pp. 217-229 in
      Poets, Prophets, and Sages: Essays in Biblical Interpretation by
      Gordis. Bloomington: Indiana University Press, 1971. x + 436 pp.
      Reviews the various interpretations, especially 7:10-17. Scholars
      agree it's out of place but disagree on where it should go. Amos 1-
      7:9 was delivered before the encounter at Bethel; chs 8-9
      afterwards; 7:10-17 was added to the first part before the last.

556. Gordis, Robert. "Studies in the Book of Amos." pp. 201-264 in
      American Academy for Jewish Research Jubilee Volume ed S.A.
      Baron and J.E. Barzilay. Proceedings of the American Academy for
      Jewish Research 46-47. NY: American Academy for Jewish
      Research, 1980. Word studies, exegesis, commentary, noting earlier
      work. Discusses sacrifice, irony, selling the needy, doxologies, four
      visions.

557.   Gordon, Alexander R. "Amos the Prophet of Justice." pp. 35-60 in
        The Prophets of the Old Testament, 2nd ed. London: Hodder and
        Stoughton, 1919. original, 1916. 364 pp. Gives the historical
        background - prosperity under Jeroboam II brought corruption. The
        Church was the mere creature of the State. Religion too prospered,
        but it was subverted. A poor man named Amos called for justice.
        His vivid language reflects his desert life. Gordon describes Amos'
        visions in which Amos prayed for Israel but God had spoken and
        the message was disaster - judgment on the nations and on Israel.
        Moral responsibility moved from local to universal. Excerpts from
        the text with critical notes.

558.   Gordon, Dane R. "The Prophet Amos." pp. 165-174 in *Old
        Testament in Its Cultural, Historical and Religious Context*.
        Lanham, MD: University Press of America, 1994. viii + 330 pp.
        original, Englewood, NJ: Prentice-Hall, 1985. A general
        introduction to the OT, the section has discussion questions at the
        end. Gordon describes the political background, the problem with
        formal and empty religion, social injustice, judgment, development
        in the concept of God, the call to seek good and not evil, hope for
        the future.

559.   Gosse, Bernard. "Le recueil d'oracles contre les nations du livre
        d'Amos et l' 'histoire deuteronomique'." VT 38, No. 1 (Jan 88),
        22-40. The oracles against Damascus, Gaza, Ammon, Moab and
        Israel are from "an ancient edition" but they were edited by the
        Deuteronomic redactors. Oracles against Judah, Tyre and Edom are
        attributed to the latter school.

560.   Gottlieb, Hans. "Amos und Jerusalem." VT 17, No. 4 (Oct 67),
        430-463. Surveys earlier studies, compares Hosea and Samaria,
        Amos and Bethel, Isaiah and Jerusalem, and Amos' relationship to
        the cult.

561.   Gottlieb, Hans. "Amos og Kulten." *Dansk Teologisk Tidsskrift* 30,
        No. 2 (1967), 65-101. Discusses Amos and the cult with a review
        of the history of interpretation.

562.   Gottwald, Norman Karol. "Amos." pp. 353-358 in *The Hebrew
        Bible: A Socio-Literary Introduction*. Philadelphia: Fortress, 1985.

xxx + 702 pp. Notes different genres, possible composition of the book, God speaking compared to Amos speaking, critical approaches, a conditional covenant, the murderous oppression of the poor. Amos was a carpetbagger who was sent back home. His words were preserved by impressed followers.

563. Gottwald, Norman Karol. "Amos." pp. 281-291 in *A Light to the Nations: An Introduction to the Old Testament*. NY: Harper & Row, 1959. xxiv + 615 pp. Discusses Amos' personal and historical background, structure of the book, oracles against the nations, justice and practical monotheism, his significance in the tradition.

564. Graf, Karl Heinrich. "Uber Amos 5:26." *Archiv fur Wissenschaftliche Erforschung des Alten Testaments* (Halle) 2 (1870), 93-96. Exegesis and commentary.

565. Graudin, Arthur F. "Fourth Sunday After the Epiphany: Amos 8:11-12, January 29, 1984." *Concordia J* 9, No. 6 (Nov 83), 243. Homiletics with outline, cross references to the NT.

566. Greenfield, Jonas C. "The 'Marzeach' as a Social Institution." pp. 451-455 in *Wirtschaft und Gesellschaft im alten Vorderasien* ed J. Harmatta and G. Komoroczy. Acta Antiqua Academiae Scientiarum Hungaricae 22, Nos. 1-4 (1974). Budapest: Akademiai Kiado, 1976. 44 Socialist Cuneiformist papers from a conference in Budapest, 23-25 Ap 74. Amos 6:4-7. The marzeach is known from the fourteenth century BCE to the third century CE, at Ugarit, Samaria, Jerusalem, etc. It is thiasos dedicated to a particular god with memorial rites celebrated by eating and drinking. It involves a social group, a wealthy group, of limited membership, which owned fields and vineyards. It had state sanction. At Ugarit, the king gave a marzeach a house in perpetuity. Amos threatens the destruction of the marzeach for conspicuous consumption.

567. Gregoriew, Dale I. "Amos in 1975. A Hermeneutical Study of Amos 5." *Princeton Seminary Bulletin* 68, No. 2 (Aut 75), 90-93. Presented in newspaper style, e.g., Amos appeared uninvited in several churches.

568. Gressman, Hugo. "Amos." pp. 322-356 in *Die alteste Geschichtsschreibung und Prophetie Israels (von Samuel bis Amos und Hosea) ubersetzt, erklart und mit Einleitungen versehen.* Die Schriften des Alten Testaments in Auswahl neu ubersetzt und fur die Gegenwart, Part 2, vol 1 ed Gressman, et al. Gottingen: Vandenhoeck & Ruprecht, 1910. xviii + 388 pp. 2nd ed, 1921. Discusses the prophets in the total context of biblical and political history, and each prophet in the specifics of their personal experience and historic background. Gives the text in chronological order with commentary and critical notes.

569. Grether, Herbert G. "Some Problems of Equivalence in Amos 1:3." BTr (London, England) 22, No. 3 (July 71), 116-117. Discusses how to translate this verse in a meaningful way in modern idiom.

570. Grintz, Josef M. "Because They Exiled a Whole Exile to Deliver to Edom" (Heb). BM 13 [Issue No. 32], No. 1 (Oct 67), 24-26. Reprinted, (Heb), pp. 354-356 in *Mosa'e Doroth.* Tel Aviv: Tel Aviv University, 1969. Amos 1:6.

571. Grosch, Heinz. *Der Prophet Amos.* Handbucherei fur den Religionsunterricht 6. Gutersloh: Mohn, 1969. 88 pp. The general introduction includes a review of prophecy in Israel plus the life and times of Amos. The exegesis is selective - Amos and Amaziah (7:10-17), preaching (6:1-8), the worship of false gods (5:21-27), the visions (7:1-9). The closing chapters review the continuing influence of Amos, including Jesus and Christianity.

572. Grossouw, Willem. *The Coptic Versions of the Minor Prophets. A Contribution to the Study of the Septuagint.* Monumenta Biblica et Ecclesiastica 3. Rome: Pontifical Biblical Institute, 1938. ix + 126 pp. Describes the Coptic texts (Achmimic, Sahidic, Bohairic, Fayyumic) for the minor prophets, the recensions of the LXX (Hexapla, Lucianic, Catenae, Hesychian, etc.), the character of the different Coptic traditions including mutual relationships. The Coptic texts are collated with the Greek tradition for each of the Twelve, noting words and phrases and which mss show which forms. Amos is pp. 32-41.

573. Guillaume, A. "Amos 3:12." *Palestine Exploration Fund Quarterly Statement* 79, No. 1 (Jan-Ap 47), 42-44. Exegesis with a review of interpretations, comparing RSV with MT, LXX, etc.

574. Gunneweg, Antonius H.J. "Erwagungen zu Amos 7:14." *Z fur Theologie und Kirche* 57, No. 1 (1960), 1-16. Reprinted, pp. 9-24 in *A.H.J. Gunneweg: Sola Scriptura. Beitrag zu Exegese und Hermenuetik des Alten Testaments Zum 60. Geburtstag*, essays by Gunneweg, ed Peter Hoffken. Gottingen: Vandenhoeck & Ruprecht, 1983. 253 pp. Surveys recent scholarship, discusses the verse including the question of translating, "I am no prophet" or "I was not prophet." We do not know if Amaziah opposed cult prophets, or just this one named Amos.

575. Gunning, Johannes Hermanus (1829-1905). "Een nieuwe Amos." *Theologische Studien* (Utrecht) 18 (1900), 193-225. An extensive review of Hendrick Jan Elhorst. *De Profetie van Amos*. Leiden: Brill, 1900. Gunning includes his own exegesis, commentary, comparative study, review of scholarly opinion.

576. Gunning, Johannes Hermanus. *De Godspraken van Amos vertaald en verklaard*. Leiden, 1885. xi + 200 pp. Dutch translation and commentary.

577. Guthe, Hermann. "Der Prophet Amos." Vol. 2:30-47 in *Die Heilige Schrift des Alten Testament*, 4th ed., ed Emil Friedrich Kautzsch and Alfred Bertholet. Tubingen: Mohr, 1923. iv + 864 pp. (original, 1884). Includes a general introduction with historical background, and a commentary with German translation, critical notes, exegesis.

578. Gutzke, Manford George. "Amos." pp. 35-50 in *Plain Talk on the Minor Prophets*. Grand Rapids, MI: Zondervan, 1980. 140 pp. Devotional.

579. Gwynn, R.M. *The Book of Amos*. Cambridge: Cambridge University Press, 1927. 55 pp.

H.

580. Haag, Ernst. "Das Schweigen Gottes. Ein Wort des Propheten Amos (Am 8:11s)." *Bibel und Leben* 10 (1969), 157-164. Gives a German translation, discusses the problem of the silence of God, the Word of Yahweh, hunger for the word of Yahweh.

581. Haag, Herbert. "Amos (Buch)." cols. 65-66 in *Bibel-Lexikon* (HBL) ed Haag, et al. Zurich/Cologne: Benziger verlag Einsiedeln, 1951. xiii pp + 1784 cols. 2nd ed, 1968. French ed, Paris: Brepols, 1960; 1952-1955. Reviews the content, the date and historical background. Bibliography.

582. Hailey, Homer. "Amos." pp. 81-126 in *A Commentary on the Minor Prophets* by Hailey. Grand Rapids, MI: Baker, 1972. 428 pp. A general introduction gives an overview of prophecy (more forth-telling then fore-telling), including the pre-literary prophets and the major prophets. A chart shows eight scholarly views on the chronology of the literary prophets. The introduction reviews the man (shepherd), dated (760-750), background (the luxury loving rich oppressing the poor; political and religious corruption), the message (doom), God (absolute, righteous), people (judgment coming). Hailey gives a complete outline of the book and then a complete commentary in attractive, easy to read paragraph style.

583. Halevi, Benjamin. "When will the New Moon be Gone?" (Heb). BM 21 [Issue No. 66], No. 3 (Ap-June 76), 333-346, 493 (Eng summary). Amos 8:5. Usually interpreted as strict observance of the holiday while hoping it will soon be over so they can get back to business. Halevi translates "will pass" as "will come." Amos is relevant for his own time and many other verses can be understood from this. The sabbath and festivals were times for selling, e.g., sacrifices and gifts for pledges, and thus cheating and enriching.

The merchants were wishing for the holidays to come to increase their business.

584.   Halevy, Joseph. "Recherches bibliques - Le Livre d'Amos." *Revue Semitique* 11 (1903), No. 1:1-31; No. 2:97-121; No. 3:193-209; No. 4:289-300; 12 (1904), No. 1:1-18. Translation and commentary. The last unit consists of general remarks including comparison with the Torah and other biblical traditions.

585.   Hall, Kevin. "Listen Up People! The Lion Has Roared: A Study of Amos 1-2." SWJT 38, No. 1 (Fall 95), 11-19. Reviews the context, including lions, of the prophecy and its significance for today.

586.   Halpern, Emanuel. "Amos Cap. 9." pp. 23-32 in *Haim M.I. Gevaryahu Memorial Volume*. Jerusalem: World Jewish Bible Center, 1990. The English-French-German section (iv + 145 pp.) is ed Joshua J. Adler. The Hebrew section (iii + 154 pp.) is ed Ben Zion Luria. Halpern gives an exegetical study (in German) of the Hebrew of Amos 9:7-28 with extended commentary on vss 7-10.

587.   Hamilton, Edith. "Amos: Humanity versus Form." pp. 69-86 in *Spokesmen for God: The Great Teachers of the Old Testament*. NY: Norton, 1949. 259 pp. (original, 1936, *The Prophets of Israel*) In the 8th century BCE, form had replaced substance and the spirit was gone. There is nothing resembling the OT prophets in all the literature of the world. They lived in a grown up world with no marvelous happenings while the whole world was dark with magic. "With Amos magical doings ended for the Old Testament." [Not true but an interesting thought.] Amaziah told Amos to go home and earn his bread but Amos responded with hear the word of the Lord. They personified outward show and inward religion. For the first time on record, ritual and righteousness confronted each other. Here are the two highways of religion: worship as an end in itself, and worship as a means to do away with evil. So Jesus said sell and give to the poor, and the Sabbath was made for man, not man for the Sabbath.

588.   Hammershaimb, Erling. *The Book of Amos. A Commentary*, 3rd ed. NY/Oxford: Schocken/Blackwell, 1970. 148 pp. Tr of *Amos Fortolket* (Danish). Copenhagen, Nyt Nordisk, 1946, 2nd ed, 1958,

3rd ed, 1967. 140 pp. The English text is corrected and updated. A complete commentary on Amos. We cannot say whether the shepherd from Tekoa owned the sheep or worked for someone else, or whether he was born in Tekoa. His work may have included travelling to northern towns. He seemed to know the situation. The book is not arranged on a systematic plan. Most of the book goes back to Amos including the promises at the end. The text is one of the best preserved and with only a little textual corruption.

589. Handley, T. "Teaching Amos." *Learning for Living* 2, No. 1 (Sep 62), 9-12. Notes God's call in creation and to individuals, his demands, his warnings, his promises. This five-point pattern is found in all the great prophets. In Amos we find an absolute refutation of easygoing optimism and the pernicious effect of irresponsible living.

590. Hanson, Henry W.A. "The Prophet Amos." *The Lutheran Quarterly* (Gettysburg, PA) 40, No. 1 (Jan 1910), 34-64. Discusses the book, the age, contemporary conditions (historical background), the man (no father's name given), his job, psychological development (inwardness, source of preaching, message, visions).

591. Happel, Otto. "Amos 2:6-16 in Urgestalt." BZ 3 (1905), 355-367. Discussion with translation, analysis of the strophes.

592. Haran, Menahem. "Amos, Book of Amos" (Heb). *Ensiqlopediya Miqra'it* (Jerusalem) 6 (1971), 271-287. Also transliterated *Entsiklopedyah mikra'it* = Encyclopaedia Biblica Institutum Bialik et Museum antiquitatum judaicarum (Jerusalem), 9 vols. 1950-1988. Introduction, commentary, extensive bibliography.

593. Haran, Menahem. "Amos." vol. 2:cols 879-889 in *Encyclopaedia Judaica*, 16 vols, ed Cecil Roth and Geoffrey Wigoder. Jerusalem: Keter, 1971. Amos is the first of the Latter Prophets and to some the first writing prophet. Reviews his life, personality and message, the book, the four divisions of prophecy (against the nations, 1:2-2:6; reproofs, 2:7-5:27; visions, 7:1-8:3, 9:1-6; comfort, 9:7-15).

594. Haran, Menahem. "Observations on the Historical Background of Amos 1:2- 2:6." *Israel Exploration J* 18, No. 4 (1968), 201-207. = *Yedi'ot* (Heb) 30 (1966), 56-69. The Philistines and Tyre are juxtaposed. Both are accused of the same sin, taking whole groups of Israelites into exile and delivering them up to Edom. Joel has Tyre and Sidon and all the regions of Philistia selling the people of Judah to the Greeks. The two areas were naturally linked. Thus the reference to Tyre is not a late addition to Amos. Edom was not a slave trade center. It probably did not have commercial ties with Tyre. Haran emends Edom to Aram, i.e., the slaves were sold to Damascus.

595. Haran, Menahem. "The Period of Amos' Prophecies" (Heb). pp. 268-347 in *Ages and Institutions in the Bible*. Tel Aviv: Am Oved, 1972.

596. Haran, Menahem. "The Rise and Decline of the Empire of Jeroboam ben Joash." VT 17, No. 3 (July 67), 266-297. Tr "The Rise and Fall of the Empire of Jeroboam II" (Heb). *Zion* 31 (1966-1967), 18-38. Reviews the data for the rise, the historical background for Amos 1:2-2:6, the subjugation of Damascus and Hamath, Israel's continuing control of Syria after the death of Jeroboam. The third king, Menahem, sacked Tipsah on the banks of the Euphrates. In the same time frame, Uzziah controlled central Syria. This presupposes a peaceful, covenant relationship between Israel and Judah.

597. Hardmeier, Christof. "Alttestamentliche Exegese und linguistische Erzahlforschung: Grundfragen der Erzahltextinterpretation am Beispiel von Amos 7:10-17." *Wort und Dienst* (Bielefeld) ns 18 (1985), 49-71. This is the Jahrbuch der Kirchlichen Hochschule Bethel ed Han Peter Stahli. Tr "Old Testament exegesis and linguistic narrative research." *Poetics* 15 (1986), 89-109. Notes the context of OT texts and sketches historical-exegetical narrative analysis. The question is: "How is the background reflected in the text?" An example is given in a study of Amos 7:10-17. Hardmeier applies empirical linguistic narrative research to his exegetical narrative analysis. This shows Amos is the hero and he is still relevant to our time. But the Amaziahs have not died out and are working with the same means.

598. Harenbergi, Joannis Christophori. *Amos Propheta Expositus Interprettione Nova Latina.* Lugduni Batavorum: Le Mair and van Hoogeveen, 1763. xxviii + 579 pp. A commentary. The introduction gives an overview of the book, the theology of Amos, etc. Several appendices discuss the relationship of Amos to the NT, etc.

599. Harper, William Rainey. "Amos." pp. c-cxl, clxiv-clxxxv, 1-200 in *A Critical and Exegetical Commentary on the Books of Amos and Hosea.* International Critical Commentary 23, ed Samuel Rolles Driver, et al. Edinburgh: Clark, 1973. clxxxv + 424 pp. (original, 1905) The introduction reviews the personal life, message and ministry of Amos and the literary form of the book and, along with Hosea, the poetical form, language and style, text and versions, and the literature on these prophets. The detailed commentary remains a valuable exegetical study.

600. Harper, William Rainey. "Constructive Studies in the Prophetic Element of the Old Testament. VIII. The Prophetic Message of Amos." BW 24, No. 6 (Dec '04), 448-461. Harper reviews the personal life of Amos, his life circumstances, occupation, call from God, message, popular religion, teachings (God is sovereign, omnipotent, has unlimited power, wants justice and morality more than ritual), antecedents in earlier Hebraic thought, his ministry (developed in stages), the efficacy of his ministry. Bibliography.

601. Harper, William Rainey. "Literary Qualities." pp. 189-192 in *Perspectives on Old Testament Literature* ed Woodrow Ohlsen. NY: Harcourt Brace Jovanovich, 1978. xiii + 450 pp. Reprinted from *A Critical and Exegetical Commentary.* Notes the general structure, orderliness, imagery. A chart shows the parts of Amos, the original verses, secondary sources, a precis of content.

602. Harper, William Rainey. "The Structure of the Text of the Book of Amos." pp. 129-164 in *Semitic Languages and Literature, Biblical and Patristic Greek, Comparative Religion.* The Decennial Publications 5. Chicago: University of Chicago Press, 1904. The entire text, in Hebrew and English, printed in strophic structure noting later additions. Justification for modifications are in the ICC.

The general scheme is in the *Biblical World*. Notes indicate comparisons of MT, LXX, Vulgate, Peshitto, Targum.

603. Harper, William Rainey. "Suggestions Concerning the Original Text and Structure of Amos 1:3-2:5." *American J of Theology* (Chicago) 1, No. 1 (Jan 1897), 140-145. Structural analysis using strophic structure to restore the text. Compares the various judgments. Edom, Judah and Tyre sections were added later.

604. Harper, William Rainey. *The Utterances of Amos Arranged Strophically* Chicago: 1900. Reprinted from BW 12, Nos. 2-5 (Aug-Nov 1898), 86-89; 179-182; 251-256; 333-338. 2nd ed, Edinburgh: Clark, 1901. Translation with critical notes.

605. Harrelson, Walter. "Amos." pp. 339-356 in *Interpreting the Old Testament*. NY: Holt, Rinehart and Winston, 1964. xi + 529 pp. Notes historical background, differences from Hosea, focus on social and cultural conditions but not baalism. Outlines the text and gives a detailed analysis of the contents. Amos is the first prophet to threaten the total annihilation of the covenant people. God is not bound to a faithless people. Israel will be just and obedient or gone.

606. Harrison, Roland Kenneth (1920-1993). "Amos." pp. 625-637 in *Evangelical Commentary on the Bible* ed Walter A. Elwell. Grand Rapids: Baker, 1989. ix + 1229 pp. The introduction reviews the historical background, the development of immorality and corruption, the predicted doom but with a small bit of hope, and gives an outline. The commentary is on small units of text.

607. Harrison, Roland Kenneth. "Amos." Vol. 1:143-150 in *The Zondervan Pictorial Encyclopedia of the Bible*, 5 vols, ed Merrill C. Tenney, et al. Grand Rapids: Zondervan, 1975. 1:xxxii + 1056. Reviews the historical background, authorship, unity, date, origin, purpose, canonicity, content and theology. He preached in a time of prosperity c 760 BCE. He denounced the immorality of his day but the message of doom included hope in 9:8-17. God is the creator of the world who controls nature and nations. Amos does not mention the covenant directly but it is clearly fundamental to his estimate of the relationship between God and Israel. Rituals are

no substitute for morality. He called for repentance and a return to God.

608. Harrison, Roland Kenneth. "The Book of Amos." pp. 883-897 in *Introduction to the Old Testament*. Grand Rapids: Eerdmans, 1969. xvi + 1325 pp. Amos eked out a meager living as a sheep raiser. The *Ficus sycomorus L.*, sometimes called the fig-mulberry, grows in western Judah. Its fruit was mainly for the poor. The vitality and rhetorical force of the oracles are not inconsistent with this poor background. Amos prophesied c 750 BCE. The Bethel address in Amos 7 is the chief source of information on internal conditions in the northern kingdom. The prophecy is in three parts: 1:1-2:16 (oracles against the nations); 3:1-6:14 (oracles against Israel); 7:1-9:15 (the coming judgment). The apocalyptic Amos 9:11-15 promising restoration is common to other prophets also. Harrison reviews the theories on the composition of the book and doubts Amos incorporated hymns. The biographical information and Amos 8:4-7 were interpolated. The Davidic line alone was legitimate. Theologically, God is the lord of creation. While Hosea stressed divine love, Amos stressed divine righteousness.

609. Hartung, Kaspar. *Der Prophet Amos, nach dem Grundtext erklart*. Biblische Studien III/4, ed O. Bardenhewer. Freiburg im Breisgau: Herder, 1898. vii + 169 pp. The introduction discusses the historical situation, the prophet's personal background, the relationship of the book to other OT writings, the content and form, the themes of the book. The commentary includes translation, exegesis, comparisons of MT/LXX and other portions of Scripture, with some notes on earlier studies.

610. Hasel, Gerhard F. "The alleged 'no' of Amos and Amos' eschatology." *Andrews University Seminary Studies* 29, No. 1 (Spr 91), 3-18. Eschatology is the end of the present order, within history or at the end of history. Amos says the end has come for Israel. Some say then, the elements of hope for the future were added by an editor. Hasel discusses the day of the Lord, the remnant, future hope. The day is eschatological and will be the end of national Israel but the remnant by grace will continue. God will restore the fallen booth of David in eschatological reunion.

611. Hasel, Gerhard F. "'New Moon and Sabbath' in Eighth Century Israelite Prophetic Writings (Isaiah 1:13; Hos 2:13; Amos 8:5)." pp. 37-64 in *"Wunschat Jerusalem Frieden."* *Collected Communications to the XIIth Congress of the International Organization for the Study of the Old Testament. Jerusalem 1986* ed Matthias Augustin and Klaus Dietrich Schunck. Beitrage zur Erforschung des Alten Testaments und des Antiken Judentums 13. Frankfurt am Main: Lang, 1988. ix + 480 pp. Reviews the terminology in the biblical contexts, Babylonia, etc. Each culture developed its own tradition. In the prophets, the Sabbath is a 7th day of rest.

612. Hasel, Gerhard F. *Understanding the Book of Amos: Basic Issues in Current Interpretations.* Grand Rapids, MI: Baker, 1991. 171 pp. The bibliography is 66 pp. Amos has 9 chapters, 146 vss, 2,042 words. Reviews the history of modern scholarship, focuses on major issues. Over 60 commentaries on Amos have appeared in the last three decades. Van der Wal has 1800 items in his bibliography while Hasel has 800, 350 of which are not in Wal. We are in the midst of a paradigm change, e.g., Shalom Paul and others note the closing oracles are by Amos. The foci include Amos' professions, his nature as a prophet, his origin (Judah or Israel?), oracles against the nations, his intellectual background (cult, wisdom, theophany, covenant, a wise farmer), doxologies, social criticism, future hope. Amos believed in a future reunion. He was an eschatological prophet.

613. Hastings, Edward, ed. "The Book of Amos." pp. 57-85 in *The Speakers Bible. Vol. 6. The Minor Prophets.* Grand Rapids: Baker, 1971. 255 pp. Reprint, bound with Mt 1-8 (254 pp., separate pagination). Original, Aberdeen: "The Speaker's Bible" Office, 1930. 255 pp. J.A. Selbie reviews the man, the history, the contents of the book and its permanent value. The text draws on multiple authors for homiletic material - exposition - for verses and sections of the text. An index provides a complete listing of sources.

614. Hatch, Hugh Ross. *Amos.* An American Commentary on the Old Testament: Minor Prophets, Vol 1. Philadelphia: American Baptist Publication Society, 1935. 56 pp. Copy bound with Hosea - Micah, each with separate pagination. The introduction notes personal

history (name, home, occupation, education, call, style, character, death), date, integrity of the book, NT quotations from Amos, historical background, a new era of prophecy (morality and spiritual truth), theology (God is just and universal, chosen people, day of the Lord), the relationship of Amos and the Pentateuch. Gives an outline and bibliography. The biblical text is printed in two versions with commentary and exegesis.

615. Hauan, Michael James. "The Background and Meaning of Amos 5:17b." *Harvard Theological Review* 79 (1986), 337-348. This is a covenant ritual rather than a general judgment or a reference to the Exodus "passover." The reversal of the covenant from promise to doom may originate with Amos.

616. Haupt, Paul. "Heb. *galut solema*, A Peaceful Colony." JBL 35, No. 3&4 (1916), 288-292. Amos 1:6-12 was added in the Maccabean period. Gives transcription of the Hebrew, translation, notes and exegesis.

617. Haupt, Paul. "Was Amos a Sheepman?," JBL 35, Nos. 3&4 (1916), 280-287. No. He was a puncturer of sycamore fruit. He was an Israelite, who was expelled from the northern kingdom and became a gardner.

618. Hauret, Charles. "Amos." pp. 7-126 in *Amos et Osee*. Verbum Salutis Ancient Testament 5 ed Mathias Delcor. Paris: Beauchesne, 1970. 282 pp. The commentary is in five parts: introduction (reviews the historical background), prophecies against the nations, against Israel, the visions, the epilogue.

619. Hauret, Charles. "La Vocation d'un Prophete (Amos 7:12-15). *Assemblees du Seigneur* 46 (1974), 30-35.

620. Hausmann, Jutta. "Amos." pp. 184-187 in *Israels Rest: Studien zum Selbstverstandnis der nachexilischen Gemeinde*. Beitrage zur Wissenschaft vom Alten und Neuen Testament 7, ed Siegfried Herrmann and Karl Heinrich Rengstorf. Stuttgart: Kohlhammer, 1987. ix + 301 pp. Diss. Friedrich-Alexander-Universitat (Erlangen-Nurnberg), 1986/1987. Reviews the idea of the remnant in postexilic literature such as Chronicles, Ezra and Nehemiah, in

the exilic period (Ezekiel, Jeremiah) and in the pre-exilic. The closing chapters relate the concept to the Messiah, Zion, theocracy, eschatology, the cult, universalism and particularism. Detailed discussion of Amos 5:14-15, various interpretations.

621.   Hayes, John H. *Amos: The Eighth-Century Prophet - His Times and His Preaching*. Nashville: Abingdon, 1988. 256 pp. A new translation with challenges to all existing scholarship. Amos preached for only a day or a few, in a time of political unrest and economic decline. He never proclaimed the total destruction of the people. He was neither a cultic nor a wisdom prophet. The book is Amos's, written by himself or a member of his audience. Additions to the text are minimal. There is no evidence of or for disciples.

622.   Hayes, John H. "Amos's Oracles Against the Nations." R&E 92, No. 2 (Spr 95), 153-167. Discusses the genre, structure, relationship among the parts, commentary on each one, historical background. The crimes were probably of recent memory. They were wrong in themselves and condemned as such.

623.   Heicksen, H. "Tekoa: Historical and Cultural Profile." JETS 13, No. 2 (Spr 70), 81-89. A general review of the site with bibliography and later references. Tekoa may mean "oil." It was famous for its olives. Its honey was proverbial. Amos had to work hard to make a living there. He was later murdered by King Amaziah. His tomb is associated with a Byzantine church, "The Propheteum of Amos." Pilgrims visited his tomb from the fourth to the fourteenth centuries. Habakkuk and Isaiah are also associated with Tekoa and there was a tomb of Jonah there.

624.   Helberg, J.L. "Disillusionment on the Day of Yahweh with Special Reference to the Land (Amos 5)." OTE 1, No. 2 (1988), 31-45. The Day will be one of judgment because of Israel's social injustice. The salvation of Amos 9:11-15 comes from disillusionment, and is made possible by the grace of God.

625.   Henderson, Ebenezer (1784-1858). "Amos." pp. 125-183 in *The Twelve Minor Prophets Translated from the Original Hebrew with a Critical and Exegetical Commentary* by Henderson. Grand Rapids, MI: Baker, 1980. xii + 463 pp. (original 1845, rev 1858)

The 12 prophets are first noted by Sirach (Ecclus 49:10), the same term as in the Talmudic tract Baba Bathra. Jerome says the Book of the Twelve Prophets is the eighth in prophetic books. Melito uses the same terms. Stephen refers to the book of the prophets (Acts 7:42) in quoting Amos 5:25-27. Jewish tradition says they were collected by the Great Sanhedrin (Ezra to Simon the Just) while many say Nehemiah completed the collection (2 Macc 2:13). In the commentary each book and each chapter has an introduction in addition to copious notes drawing on Hebrew, Arabic, Syriac, Ethiopic, Greek, etc. Amos was a shepherd brought up in poverty (7:14) who became a prophet, without intervening circumstances for more favorable mental culture. God told him to go from Judah to Israel, where he denounced the idolatry immorality of every description. Ch 7:10-13 suggests his ministry was at Bethel but we do not know whether he left there or what happened to him.

626.   Hengstenberg, Ernest Wilhelm (1802-1869). "The Prophet Amos." pp. 256-291 in *Christology of the Old Testament*, 2 vols. McLean, VA: MacDonald, 1976. iv + 1396 (continuous pagination) pp. (original, Eng tr, 1854-1857, 3 vols in 4; Ger 1829, 3 vols) Reprinted in various editions, e.g., Grand Rapids, MI: Kregal, 1970, reprint of 1847 abridged (by T.K. Arnold) edition. A general introduction describes Amos, the historical and religious situation. Selected texts have their own introduction of history and purpose followed by translation, exegesis, commentary and exposition, comparative textual study, drawing on several languages and versions, noting earlier studies of the text from church fathers, rabbinics and more recent scholars.

627.   Henry, Matthew (1662-1714). "An Exposition, with Practical Observations, of the Prophecy of Amos." 4 (1712), 1224-1269 in *Matthew Henry's Commentary on the Whole Bible. IV. Isaiah to Malachi*, 6 vols. McLean, VA: MacDonald, n.d. Reprint. 4:xii + 1506. Each chapter has a short note including an outline, followed by a portion of text, then detailed commentary. The introduction describes Amos, alternate interpretations, his challenge to Amaziah and the people of Israel to repent.

628.   Hernando, E. "Pueblo de Dios y Convivencia Humana (Amos - Oseas)." *Lumen Vitor* 24 (1975), 385-411.

629. Herntrich, Volkmar. *Amos, der Prophet Gottes*. Wege in die Bibel 5. Gottingen: Vandenhoeck & Ruprecht, 1941. 86 pp.

630. Herntrich, Volkmar. "Das Berufsbewusstsein des Amos." *Christentum und Wissenschaft* 9 (1933), 161-176.

631. Herrmann, Siegfried. "Amos." pp. 118-126 in *Die prophetischen Heilserwartungen im Alten Testament: Ursprung und Gestaltwandel*. Beitrage zur Wissenschaft vom Alten und Neuen Testament Funfte Folge 5 (whole series, 85), ed Karl Heinrich Rengstorf and Leonhard Rost. Stuttgart: Kohlhammer, 1965. viii + 325 pp. Discusses the formation of the salvation theme in the ANE, in the OT, and in the prophets, with an extensive review of the history of interpretation. Amos is discussed in terms of justice, the day of the Lord and other motifs.

632. Herrmann, W. "Jahwes Triumph uber Mot." UF 11 (1979), 371-377. Yahweh took over the functions of Canaanite gods at least on earth. With Amos 9:2, this extends to Sheol. Rev, OTA 4 (1981), 54.

633. Hertz, Joseph Herman. *The Pentateuch and Haftorahs: Hebrew Text, English Translation and Commentary*. London: Soncino, 1937. xi + 990 pp. (original Eng, 5 vols, 1936) Second edition, 1967, xi + 1067 pp., includes festivals and fast days. Amos 2:6-3:8 (Haftorah Vayyeshev) is introduced with historical background, man's inhumanity to man, Israel's responsibility. Amos 3:2 is the most famous "therefore" in history. Because of Israel's chosenness, God demands higher standards. The text is given in Hebrew and English, with annotation.

634. Heschel, Abraham J. "Amos." pp. 27-38 in *The Prophets*. NY and Evanston: Harper & Row, 1962. xix + 518 pp. Reprinted, Harper Torchbook, vol I (1969), xv + 235 pp, with this essay. Vol II (1975), xix + 287 pp. Reviews Amos and his time (Assyria weak, Israel prosperous, the poor oppressed), the anger of God (Israel's injustice), God's mighty voice (in contrast to "Most of us who care for the world bewail God's dreadful silence"), a redeemer pained by his people's failure, iconoclasm. The last notes that Israel is chosen not for privilege but to seek the good. God repents, not because

people are innocent, but because they are small. Compassion prevails over justice. Amos has compassion for man and sympathy for God.

635. Hesse, Franz. "Amos 5:4-6, 14f." ZAW 68, ns 27, Nos. 1-3 (1956), 1-17. Surveys earlier work, outlines the contents, exegesis.

636. Hesselberg, Heinrich. "Amos." pp. 85-126 in *Die Zwolf Kleinen Propheten Ausgelegt*. Koenigsberg: Unzer, 1838. iv + 306 pp. A general introduction reviews the Twelve prophets as a whole, a comparison to other prophets and texts, a summary of the teaching of each of the Twelve. The introduction to Amos gives the historical background and a summary of the oracles against the nations. The German translation of the complete text is followed by exegesis and commentary, grammatical and geographical notes, comparative textual studies.

637. Heyns, Dalene. "In the face of chaos: Border-existence as context for understanding Amos." OTE 6, No. 1 (1992), 72-89. Tekoa was on the border of the wilderness. This is a metaphor for Israel's situation. Amos' metaphors reflects this border existence, in history but also from nature. The border is a symbol of crisis. He uses images of destruction, e.g., lion, and for order, e.g., agriculture.

638. Heyns, Dalene. "A Social Historical Perspective on Amos's Prophecies Against Israel." OTE ns 3, No. 3 (1990), 303-316. Amos' economic interests as a sheep breeder depended on just rule in Israel. He preached in the north because of these interests as well as Yahweh's call.

639. Heyns, Dalene. "Teologie in beeld. Oor die visioene van Amos." *Ned Geref Teologiese Tydskrif* (Stellenbosch/Kaapstad, S. Africa) 36, No. 2 (June 95), 139-150. A general discussion of theology and Amos' visions.

640. Heyns, M. Amos - Advocate for Freedom and Justice; A Socio-historical Investigation. Diss. Unisa (Pretoria), 1989. OTE 2, No. 3 (1989), 108. The summary says this is a practical exercise in biblical historiography. Takes the text seriously in contrast to those who say we can know only the writer, not Amos. Discusses the

agricultural context of the man Amos, using archaeology to fill out the picture. The theoretical model allows for the autonomy of faith in the supernatural.

641.   Hicks, R. Lansing. Introduction and Notes to "The Book of Amos." pp. 1107-1117 in *The Oxford Annotated Bible: The Holy Bible, Revised Standard Version containing the Old and New Testaments* ed Herbert G. May and Bruce M. Metzger. NY: Oxford University Press, 1962. xxiv + 1544 pp. + 12 maps with 7 pp. index. Bound with *The Apocrypha* ed Bruce M. Metzger. 1965. xxi + 298 pp. + 2 maps with 2 pp. index. Under Jeroboam II (786-746 BCE), people considered their peace and prosperity the Lord's special favor, deserved for their extravagant support of the official shrines. Amos denounced Israel and her neighbors for relying on the military and for injustice, immorality, shallow piety. "His personal confrontation of the priest Amaziah (7:10-17) remains one of the unforgettable scenes in Hebrew poetry." He was expelled from Bethel and probably returned home to write down the book we have, in three parts: oracles against the neighbors, against Israel, visions of the coming doom.

642.   Hicks, R. Lansing/Walter Brueggemann. "Amos." pp. 1170-1182 in *The New Oxford Annotated Bible with the Apocryphal/Deuterocanonical Books, New Revised Standard Version* ed Bruce M. Metzger and Roland E. Murphy. NY: Oxford University Press, 1991. xxxvi + 1237 (OT) xv + 364 (Apocrypha) + x + 432 (NT) + 14 maps & pp index. Text with notes.

643.   Highfield, H. "Gleanings from the Septuagint." ET 38, No. 1 (Oct 26), 44-45. Exegesis, comparative study. His third gleaning is Amos 6:1 (p. 45). The LXX has "make light of Zion" and "mountain of Samaria." Exegetes should check the LXX before emending the MT.

644.   Hillers, Delbert R. "Amos 7:4 and Ancient Parallels." CBQ 26, No. 2 (Ap 64), 221-225. There are over a dozen proposed emendations. As the text stands, it could read "...was calling for a legal contest involving fire." No such contest is known in the ANE. Max Krenkel proposed an emendation in 1866 (ZAW 14), "he was summoning a rain of fire..." The prophet's vision was of the conflict

of Yahweh with the primordial monster of the deep, with his weapon of lightning or supernatural fire. The text thus requires no change in the consonantal text. The corruption comes from a misdivision of the text.

645. Hillers, Delbert R. "Palmyrene Aramaic Inscriptions and the Old Testament, especially Amos 2:8." *Z fur Assyriologie* 8, No. 1 (1995), 55-62. Gives the larger context for Palmyrene Aramaic, notes earlier studies and describes how this language helps explain OT elements. Amos 2:8 refers to the wine of the treasury. Sacred banquets called *marzeah* were held at the expense of the treasury with the best wine.

646. Hirota, K. *An Interpretation of Amos 5:18-20.* Tokyo: St Paul's/Rikkyo University, 1978. 135 pp.

647. Hirscht, Arthur. "Textkritische Untersuchungen uber das Buch Amos." *Z fur wissenschaftliche Theologie* 44, No. 1 (1901), 11-73. Textual criticism and exegesis, the LXX and other Greek versions (Aquila, Symmachus, Theodotion), Targum, Syriac, Vulgate with commentary on selected verses from Chs 1-8 with critical notes.

648. Hirth, Volkmar. "Der Dienst fremder Gotter als Gericht Jahwes." BN No. 45 (1988), 40-41. Amos 5:18-27. Exegesis, literary analysis, source criticism, literature review.

649. Hitzig, Ferdinand. "Amos." pp. 103-150 in *Die zwolf kleinen Propheten erklart*, 4th ed, with Heinrich Steiner. Kurzgefasstes Exegetisches Handbuch 1. Leipzig: Hirzel, 1881. x + 433 pp. (original, 1838) The introduction discusses the historical background, place in the canon, the day of Yahweh, contents, where Amos preached. The exegesis draws on MT, LXX and other ancient versions with comparative studies.

650. Hobbs, T.R. "Amos 3:1b and 2:10." ZAW 81, No. 3 (1969), 384-387. The verses are not deuteronomic. Deuteronomy used the Exodus tradition but the use of Exodus is not specifically deuteronomic.

651. Hoenig, Sidney B. and Samuel H. Rosenberg. "Amos." pp. 116-120 in *A Guide to the Prophets*. NY: Bloch, 1942. xv + 191 pp. The authors give personal and historical background, contents, comments. The book has Amos' original compositions but it was edited and re-arranged. The three independent unified parts show God is Lord of all nations and will judge all people. Israel is chosen and has additional responsibility. The chapter closes with suggestions for further study, the haftorah readings and time of synagogue recital.

652. Hoepers, Matthaeus. *Der neue Bund bei den Propheten. Ein Beitrag zur Ideengeschichte der messianischen Erwartung.* Freiburger Theologische Studien 39, ed Arthur Allgeier and Engelbert Krebs. Freiburg im Breisgau: Herder, 1933. xv + 142 pp. Hoepers gives a general overview of the old covenant, i.e., the covenant with the Fathers, the people of God, God - king, Davidic covenant, etc. He traces the idea of the new covenant through the prophets (Amos, pp. 39-42) with a review of scholarly references and comparisons with other texts, summarizes the concept and finds its fulfillment in the NT.

653. Hoffken, Peter. "Eine Bemerkung zum 'Haus Hasaels' in Amos 1:4" (An observation on "house of Hazael" in Amos 1:4). ZAW 94, No. 3 (1982), 413-415. The term designates the territorial state.

654. Hoffmann, Georg. "Versuch zu Amos." ZAW 3 (1883), No. 1:87-126, No. 2:279-280. Exegesis with comparative analysis noting LXX, Syriac, etc.

655. Hoffmann, Hans Werner. "Form - Funktion - Intention." ZAW 82, No. 3 (1970), 341-346. The three terms relate to exegetical problems including distinction between the later function and the intent of the author. Amos 5:1-3 is used as an example.

656. Hoffmann, Hans Werner. "Zur Echtheitsfrage von Amos 9:9f." ZAW 82, No. 1 (1970), 121-122. (Eng summary) In 9:10, *yisra'el* is not added after *'ammi*. This argues against the authenticity of Amos 9:9-10.

657. Hoffmann, Yair. "The Day of the Lord as a Concept and a Term in the Prophetic Literature." ZAW 93, No. 1 (1981), 37-50. Amos 5:18-20

658. Hoffmann, Yair. "Did Amos Regard Himself as a *nabi*?" VT 27, No. 2 (Ap 77), 209-212. Refutes Zevit. Amos was ambiguous about his own identity.

659. Hoffmann, Yair. "A North Israelite Typological Myth and a Judaean Historical Tradition: The Exodus in Hosea and Amos." VT 39, No. 2 (Ap 89), 169-182. Reprinted, "Exodus in Hosea and Amos" (Portuguese) *Revista Biblica Brasileira* 8, No. 4 (1991), 241-255. Hosea and Amos are representatives of Israel and Judah. The Exodus is constitutive for Israel but Judah rejects this pretension. The OT is a Judean collection. The exodus is a northern myth. It is mentioned in Hos 2:15 (Heb 17), 12:9(10), 13(14), 13:4 and hinted at in 11:1, 8:13, 9:3, 11:5. Its theological importance formed the background for Hosea's typological use of it. The exodus is in Amos 2:10-11, 3:1, 9:7. Each reference is part of a polemic. Amos' audience thought the exodus was theologically important but Amos rejected this. After the fall of Samaria, pre-Deuteronomic northern traditions penetrated Judah. It was only then that the exodus myth established itself in Judea, when it no longer threatened the Judean competitor, the royal Davidic myth.

660. Hogg, Hope W. "The Starting-Point of the Religious Message of Amos." I:325-327 in *Transactions of the Third International Congress for the History of Religions* ed P.S. Allen and J. de M. Johnson. Oxford: Clarendon, 1908. xl + 327 pp. What is it that is, or is not turned back? Assyria. God will not turn Assyria back because of the triple and quadruple sin of his people.

661. Holladay, William L. "Amos 6:1Bb: A Suggested Solution." VT 22, No. 1 (Jan 72), 107-110. Surveys earlier opinions on the last colon which raises the question of who comes to whom? Discusses context and possible emendations. Translates "The pick of the first (fruits) of the nations, the cream of the crop of the house of Israel."

662. Holladay, William L. "Once More, *'anak* = 'Tin,' Amos 7:7-8." VT 20, No. 4 (Oct 70), 492-494. It's a wall of tin (Assyrian) and not a plumb-bob.

663. Holland, Martin. "Der Prophet Amos." pp. 85-231 in *Die Propheten Joel, Amos und Obadja*. Wuppertaler Studienbibel Reihe: Altes Testament ed Gerhard Maier and Adolf Pohl. Wuppertal: Brockhaus, 1991. 259 pp. The introduction discusses Amos' home, person, proclamation, book and its arrangement. The commentary gives a German translation, critical notes and commentary. Discusses the oracles against the nations, the Day of the Lord, the people and the law, hunger and thirst for God and the splendor of the future.

664. Holwerda, Benne. "Da exegese van Amos 3:3-8." pp. 31-47 in . . . *Begonnen hebbende van Mozes* . . . Terneuzen: Littooij, 1953. 118 pp. (original article, 1947; published as a separate work, Kampen: Kok, 1948. 20 pp.) Detailed exegesis with analysis of various interpretations.

665. Hommel, Fritz. "The God Ashima of Hamath." ET 23, No. 1 (Nov '11), 93. Amos 8:14. Exegesis. Ashmat of Samaria is a god, not the "sin" of Samaria.

666. Honeycutt, Roy Lee, Jr. *Amos and his Message: An Expository Commentary*. Nashville: Broadman, 1963. x + 182 pp. A commentary mostly chapter by chapter. The introduction gives an overview of the man and his message. The message of hope may be a later editor but it represents the purpose of God.

667. Honeycutt, Roy L. "Amos and Contemporary Issues." R&E 63, No. 4 (Fall 66), 441-457. Discusses the nature and character of the biblical revelation, man in community, the priority of reformation, grace and judgment (life on the edge between them). Revelation is both changing and changeless. We need Amos' emphasis on the social reality of man, our responsibility toward one another.

668. Honeycutt, Roy L. "The Lion has Roared! An Expository Outline of the Book of Amos." SWJT 9, No. 1 (Fall 66), 27-35. Detailed outline of the text in interpretive form.

669. Hoonacker, Albin van. "Amos." pp. 190-284 in *Les douze petits Prophetes, traduits et commentes*. Etudes Bibliques. Paris: Gabalda, 1908. xxiii + 761 pp. The general introduction discusses the Book of the Twelve as a whole, adds bibliography and chronological table. The introduction to Amos reviews the man, his time, his predictions, the character of the literature, the state of the text, its divisions. The commentary has a French translation and exegesis with a review of the history of interpretation, comparison with biblical and extra-biblical sources, MT, Vulgate, Arabic and other versions.

670. Hoonacker, Albin van. "Notes d'exegese sur quelques passages difficiles d'Amos." RB 14 (ns 2), No. 2 (Ap '05), 163-187. Exegesis and commentary on selected passage.

671. Hoonacker, Albin van. "Le sens de la protestation d'Amos 7:14-15." ETL 18 (1941), 65-67. Discusses various meanings of what Amos meant in saying he was not a prophet, in his protest to Amaziah.

672. Hope, Edward R. "Problems of Interpretation in Amos 3:4." BTr 42, No. 2 (Ap 91), 201-205. Lions are quiet while hunting. They do not live in dens. They growl while eating only when several are eating on the same carcass. Lions growl, i.e., to warn others away, when they have caught something. He translates growl, snarl, hiding place. The structure of Amos 3:3-8 is harmony, warning, disaster, confusion, disaster, warning, harmony.

673. Horst, Friedrich. "Die Doxologien in Amosbuch." ZAW 47, No. 1 (1929), 45-54. Reprinted, pp. 155-166 in *Gottes Recht: Gesammelte Studien zum Recht im Alten Testament. Aus Anlass der Vollendung seines 65. Lebensjahres* ed Hans Walter Wolff. Theologische Bucherei 12. Munich: Kaiser, 1961. 344 pp. A study of the doxologies with a review of the history of interpretation. The doxologies promote the majesty of God.

674. Horton, Robert Forsman (1855-1934). "Amos." pp. 114-177 in *The Minor Prophets Hosea, Joel, Amos, Obadiah, Jonah, and Micah* ed Horton. The Century Bible ed Walter F. Adeney. Edinburgh: T.C. & E.C. Jack, 1904. vii + 274 pp. A general introduction reviews the

Book of the Twelve, mentioned in Sirach, its relationship with
other prophets and internal relationships of the Twelve, the
traditional and critical (textual and source) approaches to the text,
Horton's use of both and many earlier studies, and a chronology.
The introduction to Amos gives the immediate historical
background, the general teaching of the book, questions of
authenticity (most of it is unquestioned as an autograph) and many
earlier studies. For Amos, national privilege carried no immunity
from punishment, and ceremonial religion has no power over the
Most High. Gives a synopsis of the content. The commentary uses
the Revised Version with annotation - critical notes, exegesis,
commentary. Amos' claim to not be a prophet means he is not a
professional prophet.

675.   Hottel, W.S. *Hosea - Malachi*. Cleveland: Union Gospel Press, n.d.

676.   House, Paul R. "Amos and Literary Criticism." R&E 92, No. 2 (Spr
       95), 175-187. A general review of earlier opinions, noting a shift to
       the received text. Looks at the structure, plot and characteristics of
       the book.

677.   House, Paul R. *The Unity of the Twelve*. JSOT Supplement 97, ed
       David J.A. Clines and Philip R. Davies. Bible and Literature Series
       27, ed David M. Gunn, et al. Sheffield, England: Almond, 1990.
       262 pp. Jewish and Christian scholars have puzzled for centuries
       over the arrangement of the twelve minor prophets with guesses
       about date, length, etc. House reviews the various interpretations.
       House claims the minor prophets are arranged as a unified literary
       work. The structure of the Twelve is based on Covenant and
       Cosmic sin (Hosea, Joel, Amos, Obadiah, Jonah, Micah),
       punishment (Nahum, Habakkuk, Zephaniah) and restoration
       (Haggai, Zechariah, Malachi). Hosea and Joel represent the
       "downward trek." Amos to Micah are complications in the plot.
       Nahum and Habakkuk are the crisis point in the Twelve. Zephaniah
       is climax and falling action. Resolution comes with the last 3. The
       implied author is a post-exilic member of the remnant who
       acknowledges the sin but sees hope in the restoration.

678.   Houston, David. "Amos, Revealer of the Law of Ethical Conduct."
       pp. 111-125 in *The Achievement of Israel: A Study in Revelation*

applied to Life. London: Clarke, 1923. 256 pp. Gives historical background. Amos teaches that the nations will be judged, not because they do not worship Israel's God, but because they have broken the laws of universal humanity. God is one and humanity is one. Israel is judged for its heartlessness. Notes the relevancy of Amos for his own day.

679. Houtsma, M.Th. "Boekbeoordeelingen." H.J. Elhort, *De Profetie van Amos.* Leiden: Brill, 1900. *Theologisch Tijdschrift* (Leiden) 34, No. 4 (1900), 429-437. A book review with Houtsma's own exegesis and interpretation of Amos.

680. Howard, George. "Revision Toward the Hebrew in the Septuagint Text of Amos." EI 16 (1982), 125-133. This is the Harry M. Orlinsky Volume. Studies the variations in LXX and later Greek translations compared to the MT of Amos. There are 270 variant readings unsupported by other uncials, groups, recensions - 153 against MT, 40 or 41 favor MT, 73 are neutral, 3 are ambiguous. Thus the majority do not favor a tendency to revise the Greek toward MT.

681. Howard, George. "Some Notes on the Septuagint of Amos." VT 20, No. 1 (Jan 70), 108-112. Amos 8:12-9:10 is a separate unit. Sec A was by one translator while Sec B was by another. Refuted by Muraoka, VT 20, No. 4 (Oct 70), 496-500.

682. Howard, James Kier. "Amos." pp. 892-913 in *The International Bible Commentary with the New International Version*, rev, ed F.F. Bruce, et al. London/ Grand Rapids: Marshall Pickering/Zondervan, 1986. xv + 1629 pp. (original, 1979) Reviews the life and times and message of Amos. The historical background is military and economic prosperity. The prophet was probably not an ordinary shepherd but an owner and culturally sophisticated. His mastery of the pure Hebrew style was never surpassed. He probably visited Israel's markets and knew corruption and injustice firsthand. There is evidence for an earthquake at Hazor dated c 760 BCE. This may be the one in Amos 1:1.

683. Howard, James Kier. "Amos." pp. 949-971 in *The New Layman's Bible Commentary in One Volume* ed George Cecil Douglas Howley, et al. Grand Rapids, MI: Zondervan, 1979. 1712 pp. Surveys the historical background, Amos' vocation and faith, his message (condemnation of the whole of society). Gives detailed outline. The commentary is on small units of text. The whole land is corrupt and will be punished but God will not totally destroy everything. In due time he will restore the land and raise the booth of David.

684. Howard, James Kier. *Amos Among the Prophets*. The New Minister's Handbook Series. Grand Rapids/London: Baker/Pickering & Inglis, 1967. viii + 120 pp. The London edition is titled: *Among the Prophets*. The introduction reviews the prophetic tradition, the historical situation, critical considerations. The prophets were servants of God. They spoke to the crisis of the nation. In the process, they made predictions about the nations. Sometimes these had further fulfillment later, e.g., in Christ. The commentary is in small units. Amos' denial he was a prophet is repudiating connection with the official prophetic movement.

685. Howie, Carl G. "Expressly for Our Time: The Theology of Amos." INT 13, No. 3 (July 59), 273-285. Amos' words "Seek the Lord and live" remain valid for today as does his call to let justice roll down as waters. The God of nature and the God of history speaks again to the 20th century.

686. Howington, N.P. "Toward an Ethical Understanding of Amos." R&E 63, No. 4 (Fall 66), 405-412. For the Hebrews, morality and religion were bound up together. Discusses economic, political, social, religious morality and Amos' contribution to these, his conditional judgment, hope in God. "Amos' most significant contribution is his strong ethical monotheism."

687. Hubbard, David Allan. "Amos." pp.87-245 in *Joel & Amos: An Introduction and Commentary*. The Tyndale OT Commentaries ed D.J. Wiseman. Downers Grove, IL: InterVarsity Press, 1989. 245 pp. Reviews Amos' personal history (a man of substance), the book's place in the canon (logically following Hosea and Joel), the date (760-755 BCE), the book's unity (a closely crafted, artfully

stylized composition, but the inspiration of Scripture allows for editorial activity as part of the process) and the message. The latter is that Yahweh rejects Israel's social and religious practices. God judges all of life. Hubbard quotes approvingly Hanson's words that the cult has been prostituted into the king's sanctuary, pushing Yahweh aside. A generation sensitive to injustice has adopted Amos's social heart-cry as a credo and he has become *the* prophet of our age.

688. Huey, F.B., Jr. "The Ethical Teaching of Amos, Its Content and Relevance." SWJT 9, No. 1 (Fall 66), 57-67. Morality and religion are inseparable. Discusses the sins of Israel, the relevance of Amos then and now. Israel did not have a social conscience. The Church throughout history has tended to identify itself with the status quo. Those who condone or encourage social injustice have missed the true spirit of what it means to be a disciple of Jesus.

689. Huffmon, Herbert Bardwell. "The Social Role of Amos' Message." pp. 109-116 in *The Quest for the Kingdom of God: Studies in Honor of George E. Mendenhall* ed Herbert B. Huffmon, et al. Winona Lake, IN: Eisenbrauns, 1983. viii + 316 pp. Amos addressed the faithful--in their own eyes. After Jeroboam II restored the borders, new people and new prosperity brought a sharp contrast between urban elite and village poor - a contrast not emphasized by Hosea. Amos spoke to the elite. He said the end is coming. His message was ideological, not practical. It was a challenge to reintegrate the old values with the new circumstances.

690. Humbert, Paul. "*bolam shqmim* Amos 7:14." *Orientalistische Literaturzeitung* 20, No. 10 (Oct '17), cols 296-298. Exegesis, comparing LXX, Syriac, MT, Targum, modern and ancient sources.

691. Humbert, Paul. "Un heraut de la justice." *Revue de Theologie et de Philosophie* (Lausanne) ns 5 (1917), 5-35. A general discussion with translation of selected passages.

692. Humbert, Paul. "Quelques Aspects de la Religion d'Amos." *Revue de Theologie et de Philosophie* ns 17, No. 73 (1929), 241-255. Reviews concepts of God, the Day of the Lord, Amos' concern with justice.

693. Hunter, A. Vanlier. *Seek the Lord! A Study of the Meaning and Function of the Exhortation in Amos, Hosea, Isaiah, Micah, and Zephaniah.* Baltimore: St. Mary's Seminary & University, 1982. xix + 324 pp. Diss. Basel: University of Basel, 1981. A study of the true intention of prophecy. Was it to pronounce inevitable disaster, or, was it a call for repentance to avoid it? Surveys the history of research, the Deuteronomic interpretation as a call to repent to avoid disaster. The discussion of Amos (pp. 56-123) includes translation and exegesis of parts of ch 5, and 4:12, with commentary, form criticism and review of earlier opinions. Amos pronounced inevitable disaster.

694. Hunter, John E. "No One Will Get Away With Anything/Amos." pp. 28-36 in *Major Truths from the Minor Prophets.* Grand Rapids, MI: Zondervan, 1977. 128 pp. Compares self-inflicted suffering by Hindus seeking forgiveness, with Amos' judgment, e.g., those who lie on beds of ivory. Discusses visions, judgment, future restoration.

695. Huxoll, H. "Der Prophet Amos und seine Botschaft." *Evangelist* 83 (1932), 7-10.

696. Hyatt, James Philip. "Amos." pp. 617-625 in *Peake's Commentary on the Bible* ed Matthew Black and Harold Henry Rowley. London: Nelson, 1962. xv + 1126 + 4 (map index) + 16 (maps) pp. The introduction surveys Amos' life, times, message and text. The latter is well preserved with only a small amount of secondary material. Israel will be punished. The Day of Yahweh will bring defeat. Seek the Lord, establish justice, and Yahweh may be merciful.

697. Hyatt, James Philip. "The Book of Amos." INT 3, No. 3 (July 49), 338-348. Notes Amos as poet as well as prophet, speaker rather than writer, additions to the text, historical situation, Amos the man, his message (Day of the Lord, doom, but a remnant will be saved), the nature of God (justice for all), relevance today. We do not have slavery but we do have social injustice with courts giving one kind of justice to the poor and another to the rich. Privilege means responsibility; those who forget this will be punished.

698. Hyatt, James Philip. "The Translation and Meaning of Amos 5:23-24." ZAW 68, ns 27, Nos. 1-3 (1956), 17-24. Exegesis, including comparison with other OT books and internally with Amos. The pericope is integral to the text. The verbal form expresses purpose. Justice and righteousness (salvation) come from God but throughout the text, the response is to establish justice. People are to seek the Lord and live. This is a conditioned promise.

I.

699. Inman, V. Kerry. *Prophets of Doom in an Age of Optimism: A Textbook on Amos, Hosea & Joel* by Inman. 134 pp. Philadelphia: Great Commission Publications, 1981. The introduction notes that in studying the books of the OT, we must always focus on the person of Jesus Christ. Review the prophet's credentials - an Israelite like Moses through whom God will speak and what he speaks will happen. Reviews the history, social and religious scene. Several maps and figures are helpful. Each chapter has questions for review and questions for discussion. Discusses (pp. 23-62) Amos' sermons, visions, message of judgment, restoration and fulfillment. The message is applied to America today. People have turned from God, polluted the land, live dishonestly, neglect the poor. Inman cautions that we should try to understand the vision in the way it was intended. Look for meaning in the scriptures themselves and be careful not to find meaning where there is none. Amos predicted the coming of Christ.

700. Ironsides, Henry A. "Notes on Amos." pp. 140-185 in *Notes on the Minor Prophets*. NY: Loizeaux Brothers, Bible Truth Depot, 1928. 464 pp. Chapter by chapter commentary. Amos's biography is significant. God prepares people for the work he wants them to do. We read of no hesitation on Amos' part in response to his call. In his preaching, judgment is the theme but it prepares for glory.

701. Irwin, Clarke H. "Amos." pp. 322-324 in *The Universal Bible Commentary/The International Bible Commentary*. London/Philadelphia: Religious Tract Society, Winston, 1928. 572 pp. The American version is 575 pp. with the addition of a preface by S. Parkes Cadman. The general preface gives a history of the notes reaching back to the first paragraphed Bible of John Reeves (1802) and the Annotated Paragraph Bible (1838), revised several times up to 1894, reprinted 1923, and the basis of Irwin's notes. The

Introduction to Amos summarizes his denunciation of the evils of his time, his five visions, judgment and promises of Divine restoration. The detailed notes of the commentary translate, give explanations, exegesis, earlier studies.

702. Irwin, William A. "The Thinking of Amos." AJSL 49, No. 2 (Jan 33), 102-114. The book has many separate and independent units, some mere scraps. The frequent effort to find some deep lying unity is futile. Amos was not a great thinker. His mental habits were the simplest and his intellectual furnishing meager. This is not to belittle Amos. He had great and true emotions, noble conduct, great courage. He had moral stamina and fiber. Do not try to read back into the situation our own current values.

703. Isaacs, Albert A. "The Difficulties of Scripture. Amos 9:11,12." The Everlasting Nation (London) 2 (1890), 459-461.

704. Isbell, Charles D. "Another Look at Amos 5:26." JBL 97, No. 1 (Mar 78), 97-99. Utilizing the LXX, Isbell translates, "You will take up the tabernacle of Milcom, The star of your god [which is] Kiyun, Your images which you have made for yourselves." Milcom will be exiled and unable to help the Hebrews.

705. Isbell, Charles D. "A Note on Amos 1:1." JNES 36, No. 3 (July 77), 213-214. Relates the MT and LXX. The latter can be translated, "The sayings of Amos which were (current) among the Noqdim from Tekoa." This shows a connection with the wisdom tradition.

J.

706. Jack, J.W. "Recent Biblical Archaeology." ET 53, No. 12 (Sep 42), 367-370. The archaeology includes pools, cisterns, altars, Kue, leprosy, the pit. On p. 370, he discusses Amos 1:1, the herdsman. The word means sheepmaster in Ras Shamra texts and in the Mesha inscription.

707. Jackson, Jared J. "Amos 5:13 Contextually Understood." ZAW 98, No. 3 (Aut 86), 434-435. The verse is usually translated, "he who is prudent will keep silent in . . . an evil time." It means "he who is prosperous will lament . . . a time of disaster" for oppressing the poor. It is part of Amos' original announcement and not a later addition.

708. Jackson, Jared J. "Amos and His Environment." *Proceedings: Eastern Great Lakes and Midwest Biblical Societies* 5 (1985), 81-86. A study of the names of material objects cited in the book.

709. Jacobs, Paul F. "'Cows of Bashan' - A Note on the Interpretation of Amos 4:1." JBL 104, No. 1 (Mar 85), 109-110. When Amos said the women of Samaria were fat cows, he may have been using a cultic term. They called themselves that, as consorts of the bull, Ba'al. Inscriptions found at Kuntillet 'Ajrud refer to Yahweh and his Asherah. A drawing under one inscription on a pottery jar shows two figures with bovine features, i.e., Yahweh is the bull and his consort a cow.

710. Jaeggli, J. Randolph. "Prosperous People Ignore Impending Judgment (Amos 6)." BV 27, No. 2 (Nov 93), 23-28. They trusted their national defense, abandoned themselves to sensual enjoyment, forbade spiritual influence, exalted their own accomplishments. Politicians have not changed.

711. James, Fleming. "Amos." pp. 211-228 in *Personalities of the Old Testament*. NY: Scribners, 1939. xvi + 632 pp. Discusses the text (on the whole, the genuine words of Amos), historical background, Amos' call and preaching at Bethel (judgment, monotheism, care for all nations, justice not sacrifice, etc.), lack of specific future, the shock of judgment but the attraction of justice, purity, truth.

712. Janssen, H. "Amos of Amasja." *Schrift* 52 (Aug 77), 132-137.

713. Janssen, H. *Voorliefde en Verantwoordelijkheid - Een Eksegetiese Studie Over Amos 3:1-2 en 9:7*. Utrecht: Theological Institute, 1975.

714. Jarvis, F. Washington. "Amos and Hosea." pp. 150-166 in *Prophets, Poets, Priests and Kings*. NY: Seabury, 1974. xii + 292 pp. Selected passages from Amos (pp. 150-158) with commentary on Amos' message.

715. Jellicoe, Sidney. "The Prophets and the Cultus." ET 60, No. 9 (June 49), 256-258. They were not opposed. Amos is an example. He does not condemn sacrifice as such but Israel's disloyalty and abuse of the practice. The prophets did not all think alike. Jeremiah and Micah seem to object to the sacrificial system as such.

716. Jenkins, Sara. *Amos Prophet of Justice*. Heroes of God Series. NY: Association Press, 1956. 127 pp. Describes Amos' journey to Bethel, the problem of false prophets, his cry for justice, the fickle crowd and the end of his mission. Told as a story, embellished with detail but ending with the note that our modern concepts of the goodness of God and his justice come from Amos.

717. Jensen, J.K.R. *Amos og Hosea*. Copenhagen, 1914.

718. Jepsen, Alfred. "Amos: Gottes harte Gerchtigkeit." pp. 69-98 in *Das Zwolfprophetenbuch ubersetzt und ausgelegt*. Bibelhilfe fur die Gemeinde ed Erich Stange, et al. Leipzig/Hamburg: Schlossmanns, 1937. 200 pp. A general introduction gives an overview of the history of Israel and the 12 prophets. The introduction to Amos discusses the historical situation in the ANE and in Israel. The

commentary rearranges the units of the text with German translation followed by discussion.

719. Jeremias, Jorg. "Amos 3-6: From the Oral Word to the Text." pp. 217-229 in *Canon, Theology, and Old Testament Interpretation: Essays in Honor of Brevard S. Childs* ed Gene M. Tucker, et al. Philadelphia: Fortress, 1988. xix + 347 pp. Tr and rev from, "Amos 3-6. Beobachtungen zur Entstehungsgeschichte eines Prophetenbuches." ZAW 100, Supplement (1988), 123-138. Amos 3-6 went through at least two editions or even three. The deuteronomic verses may mean four editions. The doxologies and atonement liturgy presuppose the Fall of Jerusalem (587 BCE). The words of Amos (Amos 1:1) were compiled by his followers, e.g., 4:4-5 are a condensation of the prophet's words. Every presentation of a prophet's oral preaching rests on a reconstruction. The oral was for a particular people, place and time. The written version is not intended to be a literal transmission of the original but expands the circle to a larger audience. In doing so, originally independent oracles are joined together to present the message in a more comprehensive fashion. The effect was to sharpen Amos' accusations and extend them to all Israel, calling people to a new beginning. Modern exegesis must deal with the text as it is, but this includes trying to understand its origins in earlier forms, written and oral. Each stage backwards is successively more difficult to determine.

720. Jeremias, Jorg. "Amos 8:4-7: ein Kommentar zu 2:6f." pp. 205-220 in *Text, Methode und Grammatik: Wolfgang Richter zum 65. Geburtstag* ed Walter Gross, et al. St. Ottilien: EOS Verlag Erzabtei, 1991. xii + 606 pp. Analyzes the texts with selected Hebrew transcription, translation and review of earlier views.

721. Jeremias, Jorg. "Jakob im Amosbuch." pp. 139-154 in *Der Vater Israels. Beitrage zur Theologie der Patriarchenuberlieferungen im Alten Testament: Festschrift fur Josef Scharbert zum 70. Geburtstag* ed Manfred Jorg with the cooperation of Augustin R. Muller. Stuttgart: Katholisches Bibelwerk, 1989. 461 pp. Discusses the little Jacob, the house of Jacob, etc. in relationship to the house of Israel, the house of Isaac, and the traditions of the patriarchs.

722. Jeremias, Jorg. "Tod und Leben in Amos 5:1-17." pp. 134-152 in *Der Weg zum Menschen: Zur philosophischen und theologischen Anthropologie fur Alfons Deissler* ed Rudolf Mosis and Lothar Ruppert. Freiburg im Breisgau: Herder, 1989. x + 344 pp. Analyzes the passage and the central theme of death; reviews various interpretations.

723. Jeremias, Jorg. "Das unzugangliche Heiligtum. Zur letzten Vision des Amos (Am 9:1-4)." pp. 155-167 in *Konsequente Traditionsgeschichte: Festschrift fur Klaus Baltzer zum 65.* Geburtstag ed Rudiger Bartelmus, et al. Orbis Biblicus et Orientalis 126 ed Othmar Keel, et al. Freiburg, Switzerland/Gottingen: Universitatsverlag/Vandenhoeck & Ruprecht, 1993. v + 401 pp. Analytical study with exegesis, comparative textual review, discussion of earlier views.

724. Jeremias, Jorg. "Volkerspruche und Visionsberichte im Amosbuch." pp. 82-97 in *Prophet und Prophetenbuch: Festschrift fur Otto Kaiser zum 65 Geburtstag* ed Volkmar Fritz, et al. BZAW 185. Berlin/NY: de Gruyter, 1989. v + 284 pp. Reviews the various interpretations.

725. Jeremias, Jorg. "'Zwei Jahre vor dem Erdbeben.' (Am 1:1)." pp. 15-31 in *Altes Testament Forschung und Wirkung: Festschrift fur Henning Graf Reventlow* ed Peter Mommer and Winfried Thiel. Bern: Peter Lang, 1994. xii + 407 pp. Literature review, historical background, literary context, word studies.

726. Jerome, Saint (Eusebius Sophronius Hieronymus, 340-420 CE). "Commentariorum in Amos Prophetam." PL 25 (1865), cols 1037-1150. This is vol 6 of Jerome's works. Introduction, translation in Latin with notes. Jerome's (347-420) Roman name was Sophronius Eusebius Hieronymus. He was born to Christian parents on the border of Dalmatia. He was not baptized until 366 in Rome where he was educated. He travelled in the East and spent several years as a hermit in the Syrian desert where he began learning Hebrew. He lived in Bethlehem from 386-420, where he and/or his patroness Paula founded a convent for women and a monastery for men, where he did most of his writing. He translated and revised various

portions of Scripture. He made his famous Vulgate Latin translations (389-405 CE), based on the Hebrew text.

727. Jerome. "Commentariorum in Amos Prophetam." pp. 211-348 *S. Hieronymi Presbyteri Opera. Pars I. Opera Exegetica 6. Commentarii in Prophetas Minores.* Corpus Christianorum Series Latina 76 ed M. Adriaen. Turnholt: Brepols, 1969. xii + 524 pp. This volume includes Hosea, Joel, Amos, Obadiah, Jonah and Micah. Latin text with critical apparatus.

728. Jerome, "Praefatio S. Hieronymi in Duodecim Prophetas: Incipit Liber Amos Prophetae." PL 28 (1865), cols 1089-1098. This is vol 9 of Jerome's works. A short introduction and Latin translation with notes.

729. Jimenez Gomez, Humberto. "La critica social en el profeta Amos." *Cuestiones Teologicas Medellin* (Colombia) 10th year, No. 27 (1983), 1-14. Reviews the historical background, the situation in Israel in the time of Amos, the predictions of Amos. He was concerned with justice and the poor.

730. John, E.C. "Righteousness in the Prophets." *The Indian J of Theology* (Calcutta) 26, No. 3 (July-Sep 77), 132-142. Amos, pp. 132-136, is a major example. Discusses crushing the poor, exterminating the humble, violence. The accused are the leading men and women.

731. Johnson, Rick. "Prepare to Meet the Lion: The Message of Amos." SWJT 38, No. 1 (Fall 95), 20-29. Amos' words fell on Israel like a lion attacking its prey. Notes the rebellion, injustice, worthless worship, future hope. Does the lion still roar? Yes.

732. Johnson, Sherman Elbridge. *The Septuagint Translators of Amos.* Chicago: University of Chicago Libraries, 1938. ii + 24 pp. Diss. University of Chicago, 1936. Thackeray distinguished two translators - "a" and "b" of Ezekiel. Translator "a" did the minor prophets. Others have different perspectives. The evidence is conflicting. The Amos translator rendered the hif'il as a compound verb 71 times. Amos is intermediate between a true translation and systematic representation. There are disagreements among the three

groups: Amos 1-4, 5-6, 7-9. This could suggest different translators. Johnson finds chs 5-6 by a different translator but one who belonged to the "school" of translators who did the rest.

733. Jones, Barry Alan. *The Formation of the Book of the Twelve: A Study in Text and Canon*. SBL Dissertation Series 149 ed Michael V. Fox and Pheme Perkins. Atlanta, GA: Scholars Press, 1995. xii + 266 pp. Diss. Duke University, 1994. 392 pp. DAI-A 55, No. 7 (Jan 95), 2002. Gives a general overview of the Book of the Twelve. Compares MT, LXX and DSS to three different forms of the text. Discusses Amos and the evidence of the LXX (pp. 170-213). Amos 9:12 is analyzed at great length to show the LXX had a Hebrew vorlage different from the MT. Amos is part of the literary unity of the Twelve (pp. 191-199, 203-212). Hosea, Amos and Micah may have been the first collection of prophesies, with literary, thematic and chronological facets. Jones also compares the three with Joel and Obadiah.

734. Jordan, W.G. "Amos the Man and the Book in the Light of Recent Criticism." *Biblical World* 17, No. 4 (Ap '01), 265-271. Discusses the value of Amos which remains. To call a verse secondary does not mean it is without value. Literary criticism does not detract from the value of Amos whose healthy protestantism promises a more universal religion and individual spiritual experience.

735. Josse, Robert. "Amos: Un bouvier inquiete les satisfaits de toujours." pp. 9-26 in *Prophetes pour un temps d'injustice (VIIIe siecle av.J.C.). Introduction a une lecture d'Amos, Osee, et Michee.* Saint-Brieuc: SOFEC, 1977. 91 pp. The introduction reviews astrology, the origin of biblical oracles, the people of God, the land, the prophets' passion for justice. Discusses trade, economic development, false religion, politics. A closing chapter discusses the elements for a prophetic church today.

736. Jouon, Paul. "Notes de critique textuelle (Ancien Testament)." *Melanges de l'universite Saint Joseph* (Beirut) 4 (1910), 19-32. Amos 5:16-17 is on p. 30. Exegesis.

737. Jouon, P. "Notes de lexiographie hebraique." *Melanges de L'Universite Saint Joseph* = MUSJ (Beirut) 10, No. 1 (1925), 1-46. Amos 3:9, pp. 16-17. Comparative exegesis.

738. Jozaki, Susamu. "The Secondary Passages of the Book of Amos." *Kwansei Gakuin University Annual Studies* (Nishinomiya) 4 (1956), 25-100.

739. Julian of Eclanum (c 380-455 CE). "Commentarius in Amos Prophetam." PL 21 (1867), cols 1057-1104. Translation, critical notes, exegesis, commentary. A general introduction (cols 959-962) gives background. The section title is, "Pseudo-Rufini d'Aquilee Commentarius in Oseam, in Joel, in Amos." This work is sometimes attributed to Rufinus of Aquileia (c 345-410 CE). Julian was born in Apulia in southern Italy and became bishop of Eclanum in Apulia in 416. He defended Pelagianism and was exiled in 418, finally settling in Sicily in 431. An accomplished exegete, he also wrote on Hosea and Joel. PL 21 (1849), cols 1167-1172 are on Julianus Eclanensis.

740. Junker, Hubert. "Amos, der Mann, den Gott mit unwiderstehlicher Gewalt zum Propheten machte." *Trierer Theologische Z* 65, No. 6 (1956), 321-328.

741. Junker, Hubert. "Amos und di 'opferlos Mosezeit': Ein Beitrag zur Erklarung von Amos 5:25-26." *Theologie und Glaube* 27 (1935), 686-695. Textual analysis, noting earlier studies.

742. Junker, Hubert. "'Leo rugiet, quis non timebit? Deus locutus est, quis non prophetabit?' Eine textkritische und exegetische Untersuchung uber Amos 3:3-8." *Trierer Theologische Z* 59 (1950), 4-13.

743. Junker, Hubert. "Text und Bedeutung der Vision Amos 7:7-9." Bib 17, No. 3 (1936), 359-364. Discusses various scholarly interpretations, compares other prophets, exegesis and commentary.

744. Justi, Karl Wilhelm. *Amos. Neu ubersetzt und erlautert.* Leipzig: Barth, 1820. xvi + 256 pp. Bound with Joel, Micah, Nahum with separate pagination. A commentary with detailed exegesis.

745. Juynboll, T.G.J. *Disputation de Amoso.* Leiden: Brill, 1828.

K.

746. Kafang, Zamani B. A Study of the Theological Nature of the Hymnic Elements of the Book of Amos 4:13; 5:8, 9; and 9:5, 6. MA Thesis. Trinity Evangelical Divinity School, 1987. viii + 140 pp. Available on microfiche. Literature review, notes limits of hymnic elements, concludes they are descriptive and creation categories, notes the life setting, theological concepts. The hymnic elements extol Yahweh as the Creator and Sustainer of the universe.

747. Kahlert, H. "Zur Frage Nach der Geistigen Heimat des Amos. Eine Pruefung der These von Hans Walter Wolff." *Dielheimer Blatter zum AT* (Dielheim) 4 (1973), 1-12.

748. Kaimakis, Dimitris. "The Lord's Day for the Prophets of the OT" (Greek). *Epistemonike Epeteris Thessalonikis* 29 (1988), 207-289. Amos 5:18

749. Kaiser, Otto. "Amos." pp. 215-218 *Introduction to the Old Testament* by Kaiser. Minneapolis: Augsburg, 1975. xvii + 420 pp. original, 1969. (rev, by author, to 1973). A general introduction to prophecy is followed by literary types, and a discussion of spoken to written form. Gives a bibliography. Discusses the prophet (home, date, whether he considered himself a prophet, his message), the book (collected over time).

750. Kaiser, Otto. "Das Buch Amos." pp. 118-126 in *Grundriss der Einleitung in die kanonischen und deutero-kanonischen Schriften des Alten Testament. Band. 2. Die Prophetischen Werke.* Gutersloh: Gutersloh Verlagshaus Gerd Mohn, 1994. 198 pp. Kaiser reviews the collection of the Twelve (pp. 103-107), comparing MT, LXX, Vulgate, chronology, unity, editorial history, theology. For Amos, he discusses the unity, message, the place of the book among the

160   The Book of Amos

Twelve, historical background, structure, unity, origin of the book,
literary problems, earlier studies, the man.

751. Kaiser, Walter C. "The Davidic Promise and the Inclusion of the
     Gentiles (Amos 9:9-15 and Acts 15:13-18): A Test Passage for
     Theological Systems." JETS 20, No. 2 (June 77), 97-111. Who are
     the people of God and what is the kingdom of God? The latter
     includes Jews and Gentiles. Kaiser describes "evangelicalism," or
     "promise theology," the total plan of God. James quoted Amos on
     this and settled the debate. It's a charter for all humanity, which
     includes Jews and Gentiles, covenant theologians and
     dispensationalists.

752. Kallikuzhuppil, John. "Liberation in Amos and Micah." Bible
     Bhashyam (Kerala) 11 (1985), 215-223. These prophets criticized
     the social crimes of their day on the basis of their religion. They did
     not advocate reform or political liberation. Rev, OTA 10 (1987),
     176.

753. Kapelrud, Arvid Schou. "Amos." Vol. 1:col 85 in Biblisch-
     historisches Handworterbuch, 3 vols, ed Bo Reicke and Leonhard
     Rost. Gottingen: Vandenhoeck & Ruprecht, 1962. 1:xvi pp. + 616
     cols. Amos' name, home, historical context, message, encounter
     with Amaziah. Amos' destiny is unknown.

754. Kapelrud, Arvid Schou. "Amosbuch." Vol. 1:cols 85-87 in
     Biblisch-historisches Handworterbuch, 3 vols, ed Bo Reicke and
     Leonhard Rost. Gottingen: Vandenhoeck & Ruprecht, 1962. 1:xvi
     pp. + 616 cols. Amos' place among the prophets, the unity of the
     book, oracles against the nations, relationship to other prophets.

755. Kapelrud, Arvid Schou. "Amos og hans omgivelser." Norsk
     Teologisk Tidsskrift 84, No. 3 (1983), 157-166. The Day of the
     Lord is based on the New Year festival. A review essay of Hans M.
     Barstad, Studies in the Religious Polemics in the Book of Amos.
     Oslo, 1981.

756. Kapelrud, Arvid Schou. Central Ideas in Amos. Oslo: Oslo
     University Press, 1961. 86 pp. Reprint, 1956 original. Amos was
     not just a simple shepherd but a high official in charge of the

temple herds. He was well educated and knew the religious traditions and the temple cult. His idea of a universal God goes back to El in the Ras Shamra texts. God as righteous was not new either but the idea that the relationship of God and people depended on morality was new. Amos' expectation that other nations should follow these standards was also new. He transformed the cultic concept of the Day of Yahweh into a day of judgment.

757. Kapelrud, Arvid Schou. "God as Destroyer in the Preaching of Amos." JBL 71, No. 1 (Mar 52), 33-38. This is not a new idea. The ANE gods did not hesitate to destroy their own people but the moral element is new. The prophets reacted to the luxury and extravagance of their day. They foretold the disaster for this immorality, while ANE records refer to the destruction as caused by the gods, after the fact.

758. Kapelrud, Arvid Schou. "New Ideas in Amos." pp. 193-206 in *Volume du Congres Geneve 1965*. VTS 15 ed G.W. Anderson, et al. Leiden: Brill, 1966. vii + 326 pp. His words were retained in poetic form so we really have here ideas from 760 BCE, which we can consider without the usual disagreements of the scholars. His new ideas are the oracle of doom based on concern for a just society. Amos and the great prophets turned Yahweh's judgment on his own people based on morality and the covenant or their immoral breaking of the covenant. Neither morality nor covenant were new but the close connection was. The covenant did not have a dominant role in his day. Amos' proclamation that the Day of the LORD would be dark and not light, his concern for the poor, etc. took old ideas and gave them new meaning. Amos was an intelligent man devoted to the service of Yahweh.

759. Kapelrud, Arvid Schou. "Profeten Amos og hans yrke." *Norsk Teologisk Tidsskrift* 59 (1958), 76-79. A comparative study.

760. Karlsbad, I.Z. *Die Propheten Amos und Hosea*. Frankfurt am Main: Kaufmann, 1913.

761. Katzoff, Louis. "Noblesse Oblige." *Dor le Dor* (Jerusalem) 16, No. 4 (Sum 88), 213-216. Amos' refrain caught attention and led to his message of social justice, Amos 3:2 is the most famous "therefore"

in history. God demands higher rather than lower standards of goodness. The higher the privilege, the greater the responsibility, and the more inexcusable the failures. Chosenness is not superiority but double responsibility for service.

762. Kearley, F. Furman. "Difficult Texts From Amos, Obadiah and Jonah." pp. 404-414 in *Difficult Texts of the Old Testament* ed Wendel Winkler. Hurst, TX: Winkler Publications, 1982. 446 pp. Discusses (pp. 405-409) Amos 9:11-15. Is the tabernacle of David yet to be established? It is a future idyllic age. Reviews the various theories - critical, figurative, premillennial. Kearley's view is conditional-multiple meaning of future blessings, e.g., people must repent. The lack of the latter left many prophecies unfilled. The message was literal to people in Amos' time. It has its ultimate fulfillment in Christ.

763. Keddie, Gordon J. *The Lord is his Name*. Welwyn Commentary Series. Welwyn, Hertfordshire, England: Evangelical Press, 1986. 137 pp. The cover has a subtitle, "Studies in Amos." A statue of the Scottish preacher Thomas Guthrie has the words of Amos 5:8. Amos has a message of new life though it comes in the context of a nation under judgment. Israel was prosperous like the Christian "neo-pagan" West today. He offers no comfort to those doing their own thing but great encouragement for true followers of the Lord Jesus. The introduction reviews the man and his time, provides a map, an outline of his prophecy, a time chart giving his context between 1200-600 BCE. Each chapter of the commentary has study questions for discussion.

764. Kee, A. Alistair. "Amos and Affluence." *The Furrow* (Maynooth, Ireland) 38, No. 3 (Mar 87), 151-161. We find Amos appealing through a careful selection of verses for our private religion. His denunciation of public sin is disturbing. The rich are condemned for oppressing the poor. Religion was doing very well. The cult is a barrier to seeking God. Sections of Amos are morally objectionable. Amos announced judgment, not only on Amaziah the priest but on Amaziah's wife and children. This is not the God of Jesus Christ. We do not hear the word of God in such verses because we have heard later words.

765. Keel, Othmar. "Rechttun oder Annahme des Drohenden Gerichts? (Erwagungen zu Amos, dem Fruhen Jesaja und Micha)." BZ ns 21 (1977), 200-218. Notes earlier studies and compares Isaiah and Micah.

766. Kegler, Jurgen. "Prophetischer widerstand." pp. 90-141 in *Prophetie und Widerstand* ed Volker Eid. Theologie zur Zeit 5 ed Peter Eicher, et al. Dusseldorf: Patmos, 1989. 294 pp. Amos (pp. 102-107) is an example along with Elijah, Elisha, Micah, Isaiah, Jeremiah, Ezekiel and Jonah, of prophetic resistance. JHWH called him to preach against the leadership which opposed Him. Kegler discusses historical background (dynasty of Jehu; Amaziah the priest, the accumulation of wealth and social sins) and the theology of prophetic resistance.

767. Keil, Carl Friedrich. "Amos." pp. 233-336 in *The Twelve Minor Prophets*, Vol. I. Biblical Commentary on the Old Testament by Keil and Franz Delitzsch. Grand Rapids: Eerdmans, 1949 (6th printing, 1967). A general introduction gives an overview of the Twelve and the historical background. Amos is dated between 810-783, the fourth prophet after Obadiah, Joel and Jonah. The introduction to Amos discusses the man, his vocation, historical background, his book (structure, composition). The commentary reprints the text with exegesis and exposition.

768. Keil, Carl Friedrich. *Biblischer Commentar uber die Zwolf Kleinen Propheten*, 3rd ed. BC 3/4. Leipzig: Dorffling und Franke, 1888. (original, 1866) Reprint, *Die zwolf kleinen Propheten*, 3rd ed, 1888. Giessen, Brunnen, 1985. viii + 718 pp.

769. Keimer, Ludwig. "Eine Bemerkung zu Amos 7:14." Bib 8, No. 4 (1927), 441-444. Discusses MT, LXX and Vulgate, on the interpretation of sycamore and Amos' work as a dresser of its fruit. Notes earlier studies and gives a drawing of the fruit before and after.

770. Keller, Carl A. "Notes bibliques de predication sur les textes du prophete Amos." *Verbum Caro* 15 [Issue No. 60], No. 4 (1961), 390-398. Gives notes on selected texts, homiletic considerations,

plans for sermons on the God of faith, the significance of worship, etc.

771. Kellermann, Ulrich. "Der Amosschluss als Stimme deuteronomistischer Heilshoffnung." EvT 29 (1969), 169-183. Surveys earlier opinions, translates Amos 9:8-15 with commentary.

772. Kelley, Page Hutto. *The Book of Amos. A Study Manual.* Shield Bible Study Series. Grand Rapids: Baker, 1966. 98 pp. Reprinted, *Amos: Prophet of Social Justice.* Contemporary Discussion Series. Grand Rapids: Baker, 1972. 134 pp. The introduction gives historical and personal background, the theme, an outline. The commentary is divided into crime and punishment, God's controversy with his people, privilege and responsibility, the fallen mighty, visions of the end. The reprint has discussion questions after each chapter.

773. Kelley, Page Hutto. "Contemporary Study of Amos and Prophetism." R&E 63, No. 4 (Fall 66), 375-385. Reviews the literature on the prophets and biblical criticism, the cult, ecstasy, origin and function of the office as background for the study of Amos.

774. Kelly, Joseph G. "The Interpretation of Amos 4:13 in the Early Christian Community." pp. 60-77 in *Essays in Honor of Joseph P. Brennan* ed Robert F. McNamara. Rochester, NY: Saint Barnard's Seminary, 1976. 158 pp. The Greek Fathers cite Amos 204 times. Amos 4:13 is the most cited (26 times) as well as being the most cited in Jewish rabbinic literature. The former cited the LXX version which they used to teach the orthodox doctrine of creation and guide believers away from gnosticism and Manicheism. The wind is created, not the Holy Spirit. There are different interpretations of "his anointed." Three Fathers anticipate the historical-critical method.

775. Kelly, William. "Amos." pp. 116-166 in *Lectures Introductory to the Study of the Minor Prophets.* London: Broom, 1874. xxxvi + 540 pp. The preface condemns Christianity for failing to search the Scriptures. The general introduction discusses the Twelve as a

group. The study includes commentary with exegesis, comparative textual studies, history, relevance to Christianity and for today.

776. Kelso, James L. "Amos. A Critical Study." BS (St Louis, MO) 85, No. 337 (Jan '28), 53-63. Reviews Amos' personality, his message, the lifestyle of his audience. Gives a detailed outline of the text. The doxologies speak of God's work as Creator. Repentance must be shown in good works. The prophet is God's human agent for reconciliation.

777. Kessler, Rainer. "Die angeblichen Kornhandler von Amos 8:4-7" (The Supposed grain dealers of Amos 8:4-7). VT 39, No. 1 (Jan 89), 13-22. They were dishonest dealers getting people into debt.

778. Kida, Kenichi. "The Sovereignty of God and the Destiny of the Nations in the Prophecies of Amos, Isaiah and Jeremiah." pp. 169-181 in *Konsequente Traditionsgeschichte: Festschrift fur Klaus Baltzer zum 65. Geburtstag* ed Rudiger Bartelmus, et al. Orbis Biblicus et Orientalis 126 ed Othmar Keel, et al. Freiburg, Switzerland/Gottingen: Universitatsverlag/Vandenhoeck & Ruprecht, 1993. v + 401 pp. Gives the historical background, the world of nations in this period, discusses prophecy and the divine council. The pre-exilic prophets kept basic principles of social ethics as the common ground, and refused the optimistic nationalism of their day. They tried to save their people from simply following the traditional and disappearing as empires come and go. Today, we should take history more seriously.

779. Kim Young Il. "Language of Jewish Worship in the Book of Amos" (Korean). *Sinhak Sasang* (Seoul) 65 (1989), 259-290.

780. Kinet, Dirk, ed. *Der aufhaltbare Untergang: Hosea - Joel - Amos - Micha*. Bibelauslegung fur die Praxis 14. Stuttgart: Katholisches Bibelwerk, 1981. 157 pp.

781. King, David M. "The Use of Amos 9:11-12 in Acts 15:16-18." *Ashland Theological J* 21 (1989), 8-13. In Acts 15, James quoted Amos in the LXX. It was a faulty translation but he did not violate the author's intent. The LXX is not inspired as Augustine claimed. After judgment has fallen on Israel, Yahweh will raise the fallen

house of David and enlarge the kingdom to include the nations
(*goyim*). The LXX misreads vs 12 but the Gentiles are still
included.

782. King, Frederick LaRue. "A Destructive Critic's Perverse
Interpretation of the Scriptures." *The Bible Student and Teacher*,
3rd series, 5, No 1 (July '06), 17-23. A critic said Jer 7:22, Amos
5:25 and Ps 40:6 agree in denying the Mosaic institution of
sacrifices. Amos does not deny sacrifices. The issue is true and
acceptable sacrifices.

783. King, George Brockwell. "The Changing World of Amos' Day -
and of Ours." *The Canadian J of Religious Thought* (Toronto) 8,
No. 4 (Sep-Oct '31), 397-406. Describes Amos and Bethel and how
things might have appeared in those days, the popular religion,
historical background. The world was changing - politically,
religiously, etc. So is ours. In the midst of change, we can respond
with force and perish by the sword, or withdraw, or grow from
within in justice and love.

784. King, Philip J. "Amos." pp. 245-252 in *The Jerome Biblical
Commentary* ed Raymond E. Brown, et al. Englewood Cliffs, NJ:
Prentice-Hall, 1968. xxxviii + 637 OT, 889 NT. The book has been
edited but Amos is the author. He preached against social evil.
Worship without morality has no value. See Barre, for The New
Jerome.

785. King, Philip J. *Amos, Hosea, Micah - An Archaeological
Commentary*. Philadelphia: Westminster, 1988. 176 pp. King
illustrates these prophets with archaeological data from the Iron II
Age (1000-586 B.C.), including history, geography, architecture,
fortifications, war, religion, agriculture, flora and fauna, etc.

786. King, Philip J. "The *Marzeah* Amos Denounces - Using
Archaeology to Interpret a Biblical Text." *Biblical Archaeology
Review* 15, No. 4 (July/Aug 88), 34-44. Translates revelry or
banquet, a pagan ritual in the form of a social and religious
association. The term may be the group or the building. The
feasting might last for days and included excessive drinking. It was
a funerary cult at Palmyra. Jer 16:5 refers to the house of mourning

(*beth merzeah*). Amos refers to ivory beds, reclining, eating, drinking, singing and music, and anointing with oil. King illustrates and discusses ivory, music, eating and drinking bowls, olive oil presses.

787. King, Philip J. "The *Marzeah*: Textual and Archaeological Evidence." EI 20 (1989), 98*-106*. The Yigael Yadin Memorial Volume. Discusses various definitions for the word, e.g., banquet, perhaps an annual feast. A *byt mrzh* is a house of mourning. The term appears in Amos 6:7 and Jer 16:5. Gives a commentary on each and discusses Num 25:3-9 (Pope describes the festivities as a *marzeah*), the Madeba map with Betomarsea (*byt mrzh*), Kuntillet 'Arjud (described by Pope as a *byt mrzh*).

788. Kitto, John. *Daily Bible Illustrations being Original Readings for a Year, on Subjects from Sacred History, Biography, Geography, Antiquities, and Theology. Vol VI. The Prophets*. NY: Carter, 1855. 418 pp. Discusses (pp. 376-380) Amos as a peasant prophet.

789. Klausner, Joseph (1874-1958). *The Book of Amos* (Heb). Tel Aviv: Jizreel, 1943.

790. Kloppers, M.H.O. "Amos 5:1-17" (Afrikaans). *Acta Theologica* (Bloemfontein) 12, No. 2 (1992), 85-94. Looks at whole book, this pericope, chiastic structure, tradition history, literary form (lament), detailed exegesis, theme. Rev, OTA 16, # 2 (June 93).

791. Knabenbauer, Iosepho. "Amos." Vol. 1:249-338 in *Commentarius in Prophetas Minores*, 2 vols. Cursus Sacrae Scripturae: Commentariorum in V.T. Pars III in Libros Propheticos ed R. Cornely, et al. Paris: Lethielleux, 1886. viii + 486 pp. 2nd ed, with M. Hagen, 1924. A general introduction gives an overview of the prophets and a review of earlier studies. The introduction to Amos gives the historical background, relationship with other biblical texts, earlier studies. The commentary is in three parts with sub-divisions of small units, exegesis, comparative studies. Notes the oracles against the nations, the visions, divine judgment, the persecution of the prophet.

792. Knapp, Charles. *Amos and his Age Together with Some Suggestions on the Teaching of the Old Testament*. London: Murby [sic], 1923. ix + 38 pp. The introduction notes this volume was prepared for teaching the OT in schools, and discusses the moral and historical importance of Amos plus assignments. The study is in eight units: Israel among the nations, social and religious conditions, the man Amos, his place among the prophets, God's judgment on the nations, the sins of Israel and their punishment (2 weeks), five visions of judgment. An appendix gives direction for an examination paper, plus bibliography.

793. Knierim, Rolf P. "'I will not cause it to return' in Amos 1 and 2." pp. 163-175 in *Canon and Authority: Essays in Old Testament Religion and Theology* ed George W. Coats and Burke O. Long. Philadelphia: Fortress, 1977. xvii + 190 pp. A review of the interpretations of the suffixed object pronoun -*nu* in Amos' prophetic poem against the nations. The "it" is God's anger. Harper said this in 1905, following a hypothesis of Vater in 1810.

794. Knudson, Albert C. "Amos the Prophet of Moral Law." pp. 56-88 in *The Beacon Lights of Prophecy: An Interpretation of Amos, Hosea, Isaiah, Jeremiah, Ezekiel, and Deutero-Isaiah*. NY: Methodist Book Concern, 1914. xii + 281 pp. For the general reader. Assumes the results of modern biblical scholarship except that eschatology preceded literary prophecy, i.e., there are Messianic passages in pre-exilic prophets. The latter preached repentance and the coming kingdom of God. A general introduction studies the history and nature of prophecy. The unit on Amos considers the influence of his home area on his mental development, his occupation and its influence on his intellectual development, his call, moral evil, trust in ceremonialism, message of doom and hope. The latter is authentic Amos. It may seem inconsistent for us but was not so for the prophet.

795. Koch, Hermann. *Wenn der Lowe brullt: Die Geschichte von Amos, dem Mann, der kein Prophet sein wollte: eine dramatische Erzahlung*. Stuttgart: Junge Gemeinde, 1978. 342 pp.

796. Koch, Klaus, et al. *Amos. Untersuch mit den Methoden einer strukturalen Formgeschichte*, 3 vols. Alter Orient und Altes

Testament 30, ed Kurt Bergerhof, et al. Kevelaer/ Neukirchen-Bluyn: Butzon & Bercker/Neukirchener, 1976. Teil 1. Programm und Analyze (Prospectus and Analysis) xiii + 292 pp. The introduction reviews the status of exegesis in the prophets, the language problems, primary and secondary literature, parallelism and syntax, manuscripts and lower criticism, typology, etc. The text is presented and thoroughly analyzed. Teil 2. Synthese. vii + 159 pp. Commentary with studies of the hymnic elements, the Yahweh names, the Day of the Lord, prophetic speech, predictions, etc. Teil 3. Schlussel (key). 32 pp. Teil 2 and 3 are bound together.

797. Koch, Klaus. "Amos." pp. 36-76 in *The Prophets. Volume One: The Assyrian Age*. Philadelphia: Fortress, 1982. 224 pp. Discusses Amos and his offensive speeches, oppressive visions of downfall, the exploitation of the poor, criticism of the cult, prediction of the fall of Israel and neighboring countries, and the restoration of the Davidic kingdom. Amos speaks in the historical moment out of his experience with God. He is not speaking about salvation history or metaphysics. Koch is concerned with the prophets as thinkers.

798. Koch, Klaus. "Die Rolle der hymnischen Abschnitte in der Komposition des Amos-Buches." ZAW 86, No. 3 (1974), 504-537. The hymn segments in Amos 4:13, 5:8, 9:5-6 were borrowed from a psalm tradition. The first marks the fall of the high places. The second upholds *mishpat*. The third is a theophany leading to destruction.

799. Kockert, Matthias. "Das Gesetz und die Propheten in Amos 1-2." pp. 145-154 in *Alttestamentliche Glaube und Biblische Theologie: Festschrift fur Horst Dietrich Preuss zum 65. Geburtstag* ed Jutta Hausmann and Hans-Jurgen Zobel. Stuttgart/Berlin/Cologne: Kohlhammer, 1992. 376 pp. Surveys various interpretations, comparisons (e.g., Dt 18:16-20), the authoritative word of God. This section was collected by a deuteronomic editor.

800. Kockert, Matthias. "Jahwe, Israel und das Land bei den Propheten Amos und Hosea." pp. 43-74 in *Gottesvolk: Beitrage zu einem Thema biblischer Theologie*. Festschrift "Siegfried Wagner zur Vollendung des 60. Lebensjahres gewidment," ed Arndt Meinhold and Rudiger Lux. Berlin: Evangelische Verlagsanstalt, 1991. 246

pp. There were four views of the land. It was: promised by God, a gift from God, liberated in war by God, Yahweh's possession. Amos has the third view. Cites many scholarly opinions.

801. Koehler, August. "Amos." Vol. 1:157-158 in *The New Schaff-Herzog Encyclopedia of Religious Knowledge* ed Samuel Macauley Jackson et al. Grand Rapids: Baker, 1977, reprint. (original 1909). Outlines the book, reviews the history of Amos and his times. The prophet was especially concerned with the reprehensible behavior of the high and mighty, and the idolatrous, perverted religion.

802. Koehn, Horst. "Die Glaubensaussagen Israels im Spiegel der vorexilischen Schriftprophetie." pp. 171-186 in *Das Alte Testament und seine Botschaft: Geschichte - Literatur - Theologie*, 2nd ed, by Hans-Jurgen Zobel, et al. Berlin: Evangelische Verlagsanstalt, 1984. 372 pp. (original, 1981) Koehn's study is Sec 3 of Ch 2. It is on the divided kingdom with a section on the pre-exilic prophets. The introduction discusses prophecy, its origins (including outside of Israel) and development, e.g., groups (bands) of prophets, the classical prophets. The general discussion includes the prophetic call, self-understanding, message, social criticism, false prophets, the cult, the message of salvation, the covenant and their use of the early traditions. A later section discusses the role of the deuteronomic editors. Koehn discusses the basic faith and the interpretations of the individual prophets, Amos (pp. 176-177), Hosea, Isaiah, Micah and Jeremiah. The message is discussed by Scholl, pp. 146-154. The redaction history is discussed (by Eggebrecht) on pp. 202-205.

803. Kohata, F. "A Stylistic Study on the Metaphors of Amos" (Japanese) pp. 147-161 in *The Bible, Its Thoughts, History and Language: Essays in Honor of Masao Sekine* ed S. Arai et al. Tokyo: Yamamoto Shoten, 1972.

804. Kohler, A. "Amos." vol 1 (1896), 460-463 in *Realencyklopadie fur protestantische Theologie und Kirche*, 3rd ed, 24 vols, ed Albert Hauck. Leipzig: Hinrichs, 1896-1913. 1:iv + 801 pp. Gives a literature review. Discusses the name, the oracles against the

nations, origin, visions, integration of the text, the theological implications of Yahweh's rule of the world.

805. Kohler, Kaufmann and Louis Ginzberg. "Amos - In Rabbinical Literature." Vol. 1:533 in *The Jewish Encyclopedia* ed Cyrus Adler, et al. NY: KTAV, reprint, n.d. (original, 1901). Amos was a stutterer. Moses had 613 commandments. Amos reduced these to one: Seek Me and live. He was killed by King Uzziah. According to pseudo-Epiphanius, he was killed by Amaziah the priest at Bethel.

806. Kohler, Ludwig. *Amos*. Zurich, 1917. Reprinted from "Amos." *Schweizerische Theologische Z* (Zurich) 34 (1917), No. 1:10-21; No. 2:68-79; No. 3:145-157; No. 4:190-208. = *Amos*. Zurich, 1917. Reviews earlier studies, literary analysis, German translation and commentary by small units. The fourth article is on Amos' proclamation.

807. Kohler, L. "Amos-Forsuchungen von 1917 bis 1932." *Theologische Rundschau* 4, No. 4 (1932), 195-213. Literature review.

808. Kolbusz, Stanislaus F. "Amos 1983." BT 21, No. 6 (Nov 83), 406-408. A modern oracle in the style of Amos, against the United States in the days of Ronald Reagan. God will judge for polluting the environment, for prostitution, greed, war.

809. Komlos, Y. "On the Exegesis of Targum Jonathan to Amos" (Heb). pp. 7-9 in *Aramaeans, Aramaic, and the Aramaic Literary Tradition* ed Michael Sokoloff. Bar-Ilan Studies in Near Eastern Languages and Cultures. Ramat Gan: Bar-Ilan University, 1983. 143 (Eng) + 41 (Heb) pp.

810. Konig, A. *Die Profeet Amos*. Koort Verklarings oor die Ou Testament. Kaapstad/Pretoria: Kerk Uitgewers, 1974. 136 pp.

811. Kooij, A. van der. "De tent van David, Amos 9:11-12 in de Griekse bijbel." pp. 49-56 in *Door het oog van de profeten. Exegetische studies aangeboden aan prof. dr. C. van Leeuwen* ed Bob (Bernard Engelbert Jan Hendrik) Becking, et al. Utrechtse Theologische Reeks 8. Utrecht: Faculteit der Godgeleerdheid, Rijksuniversiteit te

Utrecht, 1989. 171 pp. Notes earlier opinions, compares MT and LXX, translation and exegesis.

812. Koonthanam, George. "An Indian Understanding of Prophet Amos Today." *Jeevadhara* (Kerala) 68 (Mar-Ap 82), 111-128. Amaziah was right when he said the land could not bear all Amos' words. India today is like Israel in Amos' time. The church in India is a sick sect out for money and cheap popularity, perverting justice. Church and state are separate but cooperate in a multiplicity of crimes. Amos' judgment on pride and greed applies to India today.

813. Kopp, Johanna. "Soziale Probleme vor 3000 Jahren - Der Prophet Amos." pp. 47-57 in *Israels Propheten - Gottes Zeugen heute: Zugange zu den Prophetenbuchern des Alten Testaments*. Paderborn: Bonifatius, 1991. 247 pp. + maps. Discusses the historical background, the message of doom, God's rejection of the cult.

814. Kraeling, Emil G. "The Book of Amos." pp 143-181 in *Commentary on The Prophets. Vol II. Daniel to Malachi*. Based on the Revised Standard Version by Kraeling. Camden, NJ: Nelson, 1966. 335 pp. A verse by verse commentary. Amos was probably neither unique and original as an older scholarship claimed nor merely repeating tradition as newer scholarship suggests but both. His material was written down by others and later edited with oracles first instead of the visions of chs 7-9.

815. Kraeling, Emil G. "Amos, Harbinger of Judgment." pp. 25-47 in *The Prophets*. NY: Rand McNally, 1969. 304 pp. Hebrew historians do not mention Amos. We only know of him through his book. The LXX calls him a goatherd and a scraper of sycamore trees, i.e., as in Egypt, he nipped the fig with a knife to hasten ripening. Sycamores do not grow in Tekoa. Jewish tradition says he owned property on the coast. He was well educated, which we do not usually associate with shepherds. The point, however, is that he was not a professional prophet.

816. Kraft, C.E. "Strophic Structure in the Book of Amos." JAOS 59, No. 3 (1939), 421. A paper read at the Dec 38 meeting of the Middle West Branch of the AOS in Chicago. Strophic analysis is

useful as a textual criterion and in discovering the artistry and logical thought of the poet. Notes the couplet-triad and two-triad stanzas and use of quatrains (two couplets) in Amos.

817. Kraft, Charles F. "The Book of Amos." pp. 465-476 in *The Interpreter's One-Volume Commentary on the Bible* ed Charles M. Laymon. Nashville: Abingdon, 1971. xv + 1386 pp. Reviews the man, his time and his message. His purpose was to penetrate the veneer of self-satisfied complacency to the rotten core of society. A deadly Day of Yahweh would shake them up. Destruction was inevitable but perhaps if they sought the Lord and let justice roll down like waters, a remnant could be saved. Amos was no country bumpkin started into prophecy when he discovered urban wickedness. He had a remarkable grasp of the history of his world. He was the pioneer of a long succession of prophets.

818. Kraft, Robert A. "P.Oxy. VI 846 (Amos 2, Old Greek) Reconsidered." *Bulletin of the American Society of Papyrologists* (NY) 16, No. 3 (1979), 201-204. Amos 2:6-12 in the LXX. The ms is No. 906 in the Gottingen/ Rahlfs system, University Museum (Philadelphia, PA) No. E 3074, perhaps sixth century. It's from the upper part of a leaf from a papyrus codex, uncial script. Gives a transcription, with critical readings. No translation or critical apparatus.

819. Krause, Gerhard. *Studien zu Luthers Auslegung der kleinen Propheten.* Beitrage zur Historischen Theologie 33, ed Gerhard Ebeling. Tubingen: Mohr, 1962. ix + 417 pp. The general introduction discusses the sources of our information and Luther's general approach to the prophets. The scripture index shows Amos cited frequently by Krause. Shows the importance of this and all the minor prophets in Luther's thought. Compares Luther's early and later translations, and other translations of the time. Luther was heavily influenced by the translation of Hans Denck and Ludwig Hatzer.

820. Krause, Hans Helmut. "Die Gerichtsprophet Amos, ein Vorlaufer des Deuteronomisten." ZAW 50, ns 9, No. 4 (1932), 221-239. Compares earlier studies, the relationship of Amos and the

Deuteronomist, comparisons within Amos and with other texts. Discusses Amos' claim he is not a prophet.

821. Krause, Martin. Das Verhaltnis von Sozialer Kritik und Kommender Katastrophe in den Unheilsprophezeiungen des Amos. Diss. University of Hamburg, 1972. iv + 168 + xiv (bibliography). DAI (1978-79) C 39, No. 590. Focuses on Amos 8:4-8, 2:6b-16, with further examples from 3:9-11, 5:11ff, 4:1-3.

822. Krech, Volkhard. "Prophetische Kritik am Beispiel von Amos 5:21-27." *Deilheimar Blatter zum Alten Testament und seiner Rezeption in der Alten Kirche* = DBAT 23 (1986), 121-155.

823. Kroeker, Jakob. "Amos, der Kunder gottlicher Gerchtigkeit." pp. 67-126 in *Die Propheten oder das Reden Gottes (vorexilisch): Amos und Hosea. Kunder der Gerechtigkeit und Liebe*, 2nd ed, ed Hans Brandenburg. Das lebendige Wort 4. Giessen & Basel: Brunnen, 1960. (original 1932). The general introduction to the volume reviews the prophets and their times, the inner spiritual impulse, difficulties and conflicts. The Amos study notes the relationship of North Israel and world history, Amos' personal background, his main ideas, e.g., the Day of the Lord, relationship to the cult, etc., and his visions.

824. Kuhl, Curt. *The Prophets of Israel*. Richmond, VA: Knox, 1960. iv + 199 pp. Tr *Israels Propheten*, 1956. Introductory chapters describe prophecy in the ANE, the prophet and his ministry, words and works of the prophets, the early prophets. Amos (pp. 59-65) is in a section (pp. 58-92) on eighth century prophets. An introduction gives the historical background. We have only a small portion of Amos' sayings which include condemnation for social sin, replacing rituals with true faith, forgetting what Yahweh has done. The note of hope at the end is a later addition.

825. Kuntz, Manfes. Ein Element der Alten Theophanieuberlieferung und seine Rolle in der Prophetie des Amos. Diss. University of Tubingen, 1968. 265 pp. TLZ 94 (1969), 387-389. Kuntz discusses the problem of cult and prophet, the relationship of theophany and vision, tradition and situation. Comparative textual studies, e.g., Amos and Isaiah.

826. Kunz, Marilyn and Catherine Schell. *Amos: Prophet of Life-Style.*
Neighborhood Bible Studies. Wheaton, IL: Tyndale House, 1978.
55 pp. The work opens with directions on how to use the study
guide, sketches the historical background for Amos, provides a
chart showing the divisions of the book. Each of the nine units asks
a series of discussion questions with suggestions for related study
and prayer. Many of the questions raise or show the relevance of
Amos for today.

827. Kutal, Bartholomaeus. *Libri Prophetarum Amos et Abdiae.*
Commentarii in Prophetas Minores 3. Olmutz: Lidove, Zavody
Tiskarske e Nakladatelske, 1933.

L.

828. Labuschagne, C.J. "Amos' Conception of God and the Popular Theology of His Time." pp. 122-133 in *Studies on the Book of Amos: Papers Read at 8th Meeting of Die Ou Testamentiese Werkgemeenskap in Suid-Afrika Held at Pretoria University 1965* ed A.H. van Zyl. OTWSA 7-8 (1964-1965). Potchefstroom: Pro Rege - Pers Beperk, 1965. pp. 113-169 pp. Bound with *Studies on the Book of Hosea*, the 7th Congress of the OTWSA, 111 pp., with continuous pagination for a total of 169 pp. The prophets were not systematic theologians so we rely on interpretations of their message. Amos' idea of God was Mosaic. The popular idea had become official and is defended by Amaziah. It was a Baalized form of Yahwism. Yahwism emphasizes morality while Baalism emphasizes privilege.

829. Lach, Stanislaw. "Amos." Vol 1 (1985), col 465-466 in *Encykolopedia Katolicka* ed Feliksa Gryglewicza, et al. Lublin: Catholic University, 1985. 1:xvii + 44* + 1312 cols (original 1973) Notes the name, historical background. Bibliography.

830. Lach, Stanislaw. "Amosa Ksiega." Vol 1 (1985), col 466-467 in *Encykolopedia Katolicka* ed Feliksa Gryglewicza, et al. Lublin: Catholic University, 1985. 1:xvii + 44* + 1312 cols (original 1973) Discusses the parts of the book, Amos' conflict with Amaziah the priest and other content. Bibliography.

831. Laetsch, Theodore Ferdinand K. "Amos." pp. 136-192 in *The Minor Prophets*. Bible Commentary. St. Louis, MO: Concordia, 1956. xv + 566 pp. Part 2 of a new commentary of the Bible by The Lutheran Church - Missouri Synod. The earliest reference to the Book of the 12 Prophets is Ecclesiasticus 49:10 (LXX and Vulgate, 49:12). The Latin writers call them *Prophetae Minores*, minor prophets. They are inspired by God. Paul quoted Hab 2:4. Peter

quoted Amos 9:11. The wise men were directed to Bethlehem by Micah 5:1. The general introduction (pp. 1-8) gives the historical background to the prophets by tracing the history of Israel, Egypt, Assyria, Babylonia and Syria from Genesis to the NT. The text is given in small units for each biblical book, with grammatical and textual notes, plus commentary.

832. Lamsa, George Mamishisho. "Amos." pp. 885-897 in *The Old Testament Light: The Indispensable Guide to the Customs, Manners, & Idioms of Biblical Times* (subtitle varies with publisher) by Lamsa. St. Petersburg Beach, FL/Philadelphia/Englewood Cliffs: Aramaic Bible Society/ Holman/Prentice-Hall, 1964. xv + 976 pp. Reprinted, San Francisco: Harper & Row, 1985. A selective commentary (Aramaic *nohara*, "to enlighten") based on the Aramaic or Peshitta (= "clear, true, original") Text. The Bible contains spiritual truths which cannot be seen with the eye but are understood through the mind. A spiritual truth can be imparted through a parable, an allegory, in figurative speech, e.g., Jacob wrestled in his mind - he had a guilty conscience. Biblical idioms are not to be taken literally any more than English idioms. Amos began prophesying c 783 BCE. He was an uneducated herdsman and gatherer of wild figs. Amos 9:3 recognizes God as universal. A universal kingdom ruled by Messiah Christ will embrace all people and Israel will be restored.

833. Landsberger, Benno. "Tin and Lead: The Adventures of Two Vocables." JNES 24, No. 3 (July '65), 285-296. Reviews the history of interpretation.

834. Landy, Francis. "Vision and Poetic Speech in Amos." *Hebrew Annual Review* 11 (1987), 223-246. A study of the anti-poetic in poetry, the stylistic openness, the artlessness, e.g., Amos 7:7-9. Biblical characters are constantly misquoting each other. It is no surprise that Amaziah tells the king of the threat to the crown but not to the sanctuaries. In contrast to Amaziah's aggrandizement, Amos denigrates himself and undercuts Amaziah's claims. In the sequence of the visions, the voice of the prophet is silenced foreshadowing Yahweh's ultimate silence.

835. Lang, Bernhard. "Prophetie und Okonomie im alten Israel." see Lang, "The Social. . ."

836. Lang, Bernhard. "Sklaven und Unfreie im Buch Amos (2:6, 8:6)." VT 31, No. 4 (1981), 482-488. Reviews the interpretations of the texts. Compares Ruth 4:7f, Ps 60:10 and ANE materials.

837. Lang, Bernhard. "The Social Organisation of Peasant Poverty in Biblical Israel." JSOT 24 (1982), 47-63. Expanded as "Prophetie und Okonomie im alten Israel." pp. 53-73 in *Vor Gott sind alle gleich"* Soziale Gleichheit, soziale Ungleichheit und die Religionen ed Gunter Kehrer. Dusseldorf: Patmos, 1983. 248 pp. A longer version of JSOT 24. Reprinted, revised, pp. 114-127 in *Monotheism and the Prophetic Minority: An Essay in Biblical History and Sociology* by Lang. The Social World of Biblical Antiquity Series 1, ed James W. Flanagan. Sheffield, England: Almond Press, 1983. 191 pp, and, pp. 83-99 in *Anthropological Approaches to the Old Testament* ed Bernhard Lang. Issues in Religion and Theology 8 ed Douglas Knight, et al. Philadelphia: Fortress, 1985. xi + 175 pp. Amos may have tried a coup d'etat against King Jeroboam. Notes Amos' concern with equality and discusses rent capitalism and Amos. A general survey of social economic conditions of the poor at the mercy of the rich, is reflected in Amos. The rich are often townspeople living in shameless luxury, exploiting the peasants.

838. Lardet, Pierre. "Culte astral et culture profane chez S Jerome: A propos d'Une tournure suspecte [errore combibimus] et d'allusions non Elucidees du *Commentaire sur Amos.*" *Vigiliae Christianae* (Amsterdam) 35, No. 4 (1981), 321-345. A discussion of Jerome's Commentary on Amos. The initial study is pp. 321-328 plus notes, plus three appendices, e.g., "Le salaire de la corruption."

839. Lattes, Dante. "Amos, prophete de la justice." *Madregoth* 1 (1940), 23-31.

840. Laurie, A.G. "Some Misconstrued Texts." *Universalist Quarterly and General Review* (Boston, 1844-1891), ns 11 (1874), 424-438. Amos 4:12, pp. 424-425.

841. Leahy, Michael. "Amos." pp. 658-665 in *A Catholic Commentary on Holy Scripture* ed Bernard Orchard, et al. London/NY: Nelson, 1953. xvi + 1312 pp. The introduction provides bibliography, historical background, discussion of Amos (date, private and public life), social and religious conditions (the very rich and the very poor; the entire cult at Bethel will be destroyed), doctrine (Yahweh is the Creator of the universe, God of all nations, in a special way the God of Israel, who seeks justice and mercy). The commentary gives notes on the text in sections. Hope for the future is accepted as genuine.

842. Leahy, Michael. "The Popular Idea of God in Amos." *Irish Theological Quarterly* 22, No. 1 (1955), 68-73. The people had different ideas from Amos. For them, God's favor was assured through zealous ritual rather than moral conduct. They were free to oppress the poor. The belief in ritual was shared by their heathen neighbors. They thought God was their patron deity concerned with others only when they attacked Israel. Amos shattered these popular misconceptions.

843. Lehming, Sigo. "Erwagungen zu Amos. I nb' bei Amos." *Z fur Theologie und Kirche* 55, No. 2 (1958), 145-169. Exegetical studies of selected portions with a review of the literature.

844. Lehrman, Simon Maurice. "Amos." pp. 80-124 in *The Twelve Prophets: Hebrew Text, English Translation and Commentary* ed A. Cohen. The Soncino Books of the Bible ed A. Cohen. Bournemouth, Hants., England: Soncino, 1948. ix + 368 pp. 2nd ed, 1952. Tekoa is 12 miles from Jerusalem, near caravan routes. Amos (perhaps a short form of Amaziah) was a herdsman, a peasant, whose work sharpened his powers of observation. He prophesied 765-750. The eclipse of the sun in 8:9 took place in 763. His book shows the lazy selfish parasitic rich and the grinding poverty of the masses. The universal God will punish Israel more severely than other nations because Israel violated the covenant. Ritual will not save them. Society needs justice. The book is in three parts: a preamble (chs 1-2), the charge against Israel (3-6), his visions (7-9). An epilogue, 9:11-15, pictures a Golden Age in the future. Amos may have retired to Tekoa to write his memoirs. One tradition says he was killed by Amaziah the priest of Bethel with a

blow on the temple, while another says Uzziah hit him in the forehead with a red hot iron.

845. Leimbach, K.A. *Die Weissagungen des Osee, Amos und Michaas ubersetzt und kurz erklart*, 2nd ed. Biblische Volksbucher 3. Fulda: Aktiendrukkerei, 1922. 169 pp.

846. Lempp, Walther. "The Nations in Amos." *South East Asia J of Theology* (Singapore) 1, No. 3 (Jan 60), 20-33. Analyzes the word nation(s), and the nations and places in Amos. The nations are in rebellion against God and stand under his judgment. They are a temptation for Israel but they are not inferior.

847. Leslie, Elmer Archibald. "Amos of Tekoa." pp. 13-39 in *The Prophets Tell Their Own Story*. NY: Abingdon, 1939. 307 pp. Each chapter has a prophet speaking in the first person. Amos describes his home, visions, call, preaching, return home to write his book.

848. Levey, Samson H. "Amos in the Rabbinic Tradition." pp. 55-69 in *Tradition as Openness to the Future: Essays in Honor of Willis W. Fisher* ed Fred O. Francis and Raymond Paul Wallace. Lanham, MD: University Press of America, 1984. x + 225 pp. Cites a number of the many references to Amos. Some interpretations are "novel, some rather naive, some interesting." One of these is that King Jeroboam honored Amos as a prophet.

849. Levi, Gerson B. "Amos, Book of." Vol. 1:533 in *The Jewish Encyclopedia*, 12 vols, ed Isadore Singer, Cyrus Adler, et al. NY: KTAV, n.d. (original, 1901). The nations are called to witness the sins of Israel. The women have been cruel to the poor and needy. For injustice and riotous living, the nation will be destroyed. Amos is told to go back home to Judah. The book ends with words of comfort - a remnant will be saved.

850. Levin, C. "Amos und Jerobeam I." VT 45, No. 3 (July 95), 307-317. A comparative study including the confrontation with Amaziah.

851. Levin, S. "The Idea of Social Justice in the Prophecies of Amos and First Isaiah" (Heb). pp. 120-133 in *Sefer Neiger* ed Arthur Biran, et al. Jerusalem: Kiryat Sepher, 1959. 387 pp.

852. Lewis, Jack Pearl. "Archaeology and the Book of Amos." Evangelical Theological Society Papers, micropublished by the Theological Research Exchange Network. Portland, Oregon, 1988. 34 pp. Archaeology does not prove the Bible but illustrates it. Studies the artifacts and history, peoples, warfare, daily life, Amos' indictment of Israel, threats, ANE treaties, literary devices and the vocabulary.

853. Lewis, Jack Pearl. "The Prophet Amos." pp. 16-23 *The Minor Prophets*. Grand Rapids: Baker, 1966. 103 pp. Discusses the man, structure of the book, Israel's neighbors, the sins of Israel, the Day of the Lord, the NT connection. Discussion questions at the end include the relationship of privilege and responsibility, comparison of Israel and the Church today, sin in Amos' time and ours, whether God is a God of judgment or mercy. Bibliography.

854. Lewis, Ralph Loren. "Amos." pp. 14-75 in The Persuasive Style and Appeals of the Minor Prophets Amos, Hosea, and Micah. Diss. Ann Arbor: University of Michigan, 1958. v + 222 pp. DAI 20, No. 4 (Oct 66), 1483. The general introduction gives an overview of the study and discusses style as a way of getting a response. This includes logic, authority, ethos, emotion (fear, guilt, security, sympathy), etc. For each prophet, Lewis discusses personality, setting (political, social, religious), the speeches. The personal includes training, characteristics, contributions. Amos shared ideas of justice, judgment, suffering and redemption. The study of the speeches reviews moral principles, content, style, vocabulary, sentence structure, metaphors, rhetoric. The speeches we have are probably abstracts or summaries rather than complete speeches. The final conclusion compares the three prophets in their style and usage.

855. Lewis, Ralph Loren. "Four Preaching Aims of Amos." *Asbury Seminarian* (Wilmore, KY) 21, No. 2 (Ap 67), 14-18.

856. Limburg, James. "Amos." pp. 79 in *Hosea - Micah* by Limburg.
Interpretation: A Bible Commentary for Teaching and Preaching ed
James Luther Mays, et al. Atlanta: Knox, 1988. xi + 201 pp.
Limburg outlines the text with snappy titles like "A Roaring,
Rolling Stream," "The Customer is Always Wronged," "Who Do
You Think You Are?" But the message of doom is the same to
Israel and the surrounding nations, with just a touch of hope at the
end. The new element in the message to Israel is the retelling of the
past - the Exodus, guidance through the wilderness, the conquest,
the sending of the prophets. The prophetic task is to predict
(foretelling), address the present (forthtelling) and recall the past.
A new element is predicting God's punishment of his own people.
Because they are chosen, they have a higher standard but they have
iniquity and they will be punished. The busyness of religion will
not save them. They must do justice. They haven't so they will be
conquered and deported. Some day, however, God will rebuild the
kingdom of David.

857. Limburg, James. "Amos 7:4: A Judgment with Fire?" CBQ 35, No.
3 (July 73), 346-349. There is no need to emend the MT. Tr:
"Yahweh was calling for the making of a complaint, to be followed
by the sending of fire." It could be "judgment with fire" but not
"judgment by fire."

858. Limburg, James. "Sevenfold Structures in the Book of Amos." JBL
106, No. 2 (June 87), 217-222. The use of seven (symbolizing
completeness) is deliberate, e.g., 2:6-8 (accusations), and may
indicate authentic Amos sayings. He was using a stylistic device to
build up a climactic declaration. There are 49 divine speech
formulas in Amos, seven in each major section (one has 14). The
"three and for four" means totality.

859. Lindblom, Johannes. "Buch der Revelationen des Propheten
Amos." pp. 66-97 in *Die literarische Gattung der prophetischen
Literatur. Eine literargeschichtliche Untersuchung zum Alten
Testament*. Uppsala Universitets Arsskrift. Teologi 1. Uppsala:
Lundequist, 1924. iii + 122 pp. Discusses the general problem of
revelation and the prophetic literature as literature of revelation.
Amos is an example. Gives exegesis, literary criticism,

commentary, scholarly interpretations. The closing discussion is on the form of the prophetic oracle.

860. Lindhagen, Stig. *Profeten Amos.* Stockholm: Verbum, 1971. 91 pp. The introduction discusses the background, Amos' identity, the composition of the book. The commentary gives a translation and brief observations.

861. Loader, James A. "The Prophets and Sodom: The Prophetic Use of the Sodom and Gomorrah Theme." *Hervormde Teologiese Studies* 47 (Mar 91), 5-25.

862. Lods, Adolphe. "Amos." pp. 79-87 in *The Prophets and the Rise of Judaism.* London: Kegan Paul, Trench, Trubner, 1937. xxiv + 378 pp. Tr *Les prophetes d'Israel et les debuts du Judaisme.* Paris, 1935. The prophets and the concept of prophecy are considered in the context of history. Lods discusses the prophet's life and mission. His experience included earthquake and storm, shepherding that does not exclude culture, a Judean was not a prophet. His mission was embodied in the visions. Yahweh reproaches his people for ingratitude. The unforgivable sin is exploitation of the small by the great. The comfort passage contradicts everything else Amos has said.

863. Loewenstamm, Samuel Ephraim (1907-1987). "*klub qyts.* A Remark on the Typology of the Prophetic Vision (Amos 8:1-3)" (Heb). *Tarbiz* 34 (July 65), 319-322, ii (Eng summary). Reprinted, pp. "Kelub Qayis (Am 8:1-3)." pp. 22-27 in *From Babylon to Canaan: Studies in the Bible and its Oriental Background,* ed [Preface by] Yitzhak Avishur and Joshua Blau. Publication of the Perry Foundation for Biblical Research. Jerusalem: Magnes Press, Hebrew University, 1992. xvii + 495 pp. Review of earlier studies and exegesis. The basket of fruit is not a symbol of the end though much strained exegesis has tried to make it this. One seeks the underlying idea. Amos worried about the end, *qts.* His vision was *klub qyts,* summer fruit. The divine interpretation is "The end is come upon my people." Compares Alexander's dream of a satyr. He was told it meant *se Turos,* "thine is Tyre," his underlying desire. Compares several dreams reported by Freud.

864. Loewenstamm, Samuel Ephraim. "Ostracon 7 from Arad, Attesting the Observance of the New-Moon Day?" (Heb). BM 21 [Issue No. 66], No. 3 (Ap-June 76), 330-332, 494 (Eng summary). Reprinted, pp. 131-135 in *From Babylon to Canaan: Studies in the Bible and its Oriental Background* ed [Preface by] Yitzhak Avishur and Joshua Blau. Publication of the Perry Foundation for Biblical Research. Jerusalem: Magnes Press, Hebrew University, 1992. xvii + 495 pp. Transcription and translation of Nos. 7 and 4. Notes earlier studies and difficulties. The reference is to a rest day on the New Moon as in Amos 8:5. The order of the ostracon is necessary because the government storerooms would have been closed and only opened for an emergency. Even then, the recording of the provision of supplies had to be postponed until the next day.

865. Lofthouse, W.F. "The Call of Amos." Exp 8th ser, 24, No. 2 (1922), 45-51. The minor prophets do not record a "call." The story of Amaziah (told in the third person) in Amos is in between visions (first person), probably inserted by an editor. The visions (discusses each) may have been part of the call but they seem to imply the call has already come.

866. Lohmann, Paul. "Einige Textkonjekturen zu Amos." ZAW 32, No. 2 (1912), 274-277. Notes earlier studies and suggests emending Amos 8:5, 6:5, 9-10. For 6:5, cf. Elhorst, ZAW 35 (1915), 62-63.

867. Lohr, Max. *Untersuchungen zum Buche Amos*. BZAW 4. Giessen: Ricker (Topelmann), 1901. vi + 67 pp. The material is in three parts: the text of Amos (and related problems), the theological significance of the book, and a study of Yahweh Sabaoth.

868. Longacre, Lindsay B. *Amos: Prophet of a New Order*. Life and Service Series ed Henry H. Meyer. NY: Methodist Book Concern, 1921. 105 pp. The book opens with suggestions for using the lessons and the place of the prophets in human life. The lessons include the man and his time, the God of nations and men, the chosen people, the deceitfulness of riches, true worship, prophet visions, the blessed future, the prophets and the church. The last unit is on notes that interpret Amos, e.g., reality, progress, Christ. Each unit closes with study questions.

869. Loretz, Oswald. "Amos 6:12." VT 39, No. 2 (Ap 89), 240-242. The question in the first part of vs 12 is an example of *parallelismus membrorum* and is to be answered positively.

870. Loretz, Oswald, "Die babylonischen Gottesnamen *Sukkut* und *Kajjamanu* in Amos 5:26. Ein Beitrag zur judischen Astrologie" (The Babylonian divine names Sukkut and Kajjamanu in Amos 5:26. A contribution to Jewish astrology). ZAW 101, No. 2 (1989), 286-289. Discusses the context of vss 21-27, and the history of interpretation.

871. Loretz, Oswald. "Die Berufung des Propheten Amos (7:14-15)." UF 6 (1974), 487-488. Discusses the work of Hermann Schult on Amos 7:15, gives a transliteration of vss 14-15 with commentary, comparative textual analysis, study of literary motifs.

872. Loretz, Oswald. "Die Entstehung des Amos-Buches im Licht der Prophetien aus Mari, Assur, Ishchali und der Ugarit-Texte. Paradigmenwechsel in der Prophetenbuchforschung." UF 24 (1992), 179-215. Discusses the ur-text, structure, historical background, the visions, the author of the book, Amaziah, pre-exilic and later prophecy, whether there is hope for the future. An extensive bibliography.

873. Loretz, Oswald. "Exodus, Dekalog und Ausschliesslichkeit Jahwes im Amos- und Hosea-Buch in der Perspektive ugaritischer Poesie." UF 24 (1992), 217-248. Extensive literature review, background and analysis of the poetry. Amos is pp. 221-232, 242-244.

874. Loretz, Oswald. "Ugaritische und Hebraische Lexikographie." UF 13 (1981), 127-135. Unit 7.1 is a study of "*slm* in Am. 5:22 und das *shlmjm* Opfer" with transliteration, translation, exegesis, comparison of other text, numerous notes on earlier studies.

875. Loretz, Oswald. "Ugaritisch-biblisch *mrzh* 'Kultmahl, Kultverein' in Jer 16:5 und Am 6:7." pp. 87-93 in *Kunder des Wortes: Beitrage zur Theologie der Propheten. Josef Schreiner zum 60. Geburtstag* ed Lothar Ruppert, et al. Wurzberg: Echter, 1982. 333 pp. Notes the scholarly interpretation of these verses. The concept is in the Canaanite tradition.

876. Loretz, Oswald. "Vergleich und Kommentar in Amos 3:12." BZ ns 20, No. 1 (1976), 122-125. Discusses the meter in relation to earlier views.

877. Loscalzo, Craig. "Preaching Themes From Amos." R&E 92, No. 2 (Spr 95), 195-206. Notes several cautions such as distinguishing between the prophet and ourselves. Homiletic commentary on summer fruit, communism, Day of the Lord, etc.

878. Loss, Nicolo Maria. *Amos e introduzione al profetismo biblico; versione, introduzione, note.* Nuovissima Versione 29. Rome: Paoline, 1979. 270 pp.

879. Loss, Nicolo Maria. "Uso e Valore Dei Nomi di Dio e Dei Nomi del Populo nel Libro di Amos." *Salesianum* 41, No. 3 (July-Sep 79), 425-440. 2568: "The Use and Significance of the Names of God and the Names of the People in the Book of Amos." Discusses earlier views, the terms for God (generic [Elohim], personal [Yahweh], honorary [Lord], titular [Lord of Hosts]) and the people. These names have theological significance and show Amos' theology.

880. Luneberger, L.O. "Amos: The Preacher of the Gospel of Law." BS (St Louis, MO) 84, No. 336 (Oct '27), 402-410. God is both love and law, love and justice. Reviews the life of Amos and the religious conditions of the day.

881. Luria, Ben Zion. "Amos - Prophet and Worldly Man." *Dor le Dor* 10, No. 3 (Spr 82), 183-186. Amos never mentioned Assyria but he knew his world. Word studies show names of places, identity of objects, and Assyria as the enemy.

882. Luria, Ben Zion. Amos 4:2b (Heb). BM 12 [Issue No. 30], No. 2 (Mar 67), 6-11.

883. Luria, Ben Zion. "The Prophecies unto the Nations in the Book of Amos from the Point of View of History" (Heb) BM 18 [Issue No. 54], No. 3 (Ap-June 73), 287-301, 421-422. Eng summary. Reprinted, pp. 199-219 in Studies in the Minor Prophets ed B.Z. Luria. Jerusalem: Kiryat Sepher, 1981. In Amos' time,

Aram/Damascus had already surrendered to the Assyrians so the references to them, Ammon and Moab are unlikely. The names Beth Eden and Bik'at Aven are designations for Damascus. The reference to Moab is from the time of Jehoshaphat. Those to the Philistines, Tyre and Edom are from the time of the destruction of the temple.

884. Luria, B.Z. "Teqoa - The City of Amos" (Heb). pp. 104-115 in *Sepher E. Auerbach* ed Arthur Biram. Jerusalem: Kiryat Sepher, 1956.

885. Luria, Ben Zion. "Who Calls the Waters of the Sea and Spills Them on the Face of the Earth (Amos 5:8, 9:6)" (Heb). BM 30 [Issue No. 101], No. 2 (Jan-Mar 85), 259-262. There are several references to earthquakes in Amos. There may also be a tidal wave (tsunami) in 5:8 and 9:6. Rev, OTA 9 (1986), 77.

886. Lust, Johan "Remarks on the Redaction of Amos 5:4-6, 14-15." OTS 21 (1981), 129-154. This volume of OTS is titled: *Remembering All the Way* by B. Albrektson, et al. Vss 4-5 refer to the cultic reform by Josiah while vss 14-15 were added by a Deuteronomic redactor, no longer interested in the cult but in offering people a moral choice.

887. Luther, Martin. "Lectures on Amos." pp. 125-190 in *Lectures on the Minor Prophets. I. Hosea, Joel, Amos, Obadiah, Micah, Nahum, Zephaniah, Haggai, Malachi* ed Hilton C. Oswald. Luther's Works 19 ed Jaroslav Pelikan, et al. St. Louis: Concordia, 1975. xii + 436 pp. Translates the Latin Altenburg Text, with preface. The detailed commentary is exposition and homilies, with exegesis and comparative references.

888. Luther, Martin. "Preface to the Prophet Amos. 1532." Vol. VI:426-427 in *Works of Martin Luther With Introductions and Notes* The Philadelphia Edition, 6 vols. Grand Rapids: Baker, 1982. VI:521 pp. (original, ed C.M. Jacobs, et al. Philadelphia: Muhlenburg Press, 1930-43) Amos denounces the people of Israel throughout the book until the end when he predicts Christ. No prophet does so little promising and so much threatening. It is said the priest Amaziah had him beaten to death with a rod. The three and four

sins are one sin, repeated seven times, and then starting over. The NT quotes Amos (Acts 7 and 15) on Israel's sin and failure to keep the law.

889. Luthi, Walter. *Dies ist's, was der Prophet Amos gesehen hat*, 10th ed. Basel: Reinhardt, 1946. 131 pp. (original, 1938) Eng tr, *In the Time of Earthquake. An Exposition of the Book of the Prophet Amos in Relation to our own Times.* London: Hodder and Stoughton, 1940. 143 pp. "It is a time of earthquake. Events are pressing and moving quickly." "Amos utters God's word to men threatened with earthquake - to all men threatened with earthquake in all places and at all times." The Church is threatened. It is being shaken with a sieve. "There is but one consolation here: He who shakes the sieve is also the One who called poor sinners to His table." A chapter by chapter commentary.

890. Lyndon, E.I. "The Gospel for the Restless Heart." pp. 21-29 in *Prophetic Spokesmen: Studies in the Twelve Minor Prophets.* London: Epworth, 1930. 95 pp. A sermon on Amos 5:8.

891. Lyngdoh, Bosetin Cross. The Demand of Social Justice in the Prophecy of Amos and its Meaning for Socio-Political Structure of India. Diss. Calvin Theological Seminary (Grand Rapids, MI), 1985. vii + 103 pp. Rev, *Calvin Theological J* 20 (Nov 85), 361. Amos' message is justice. God champions the cause of the poor, the humble, the oppressed. He gives His justice and righteousness to man. Only the righteous man can do justice.

M.

892. Maag, Victor. "Amos." RGG 1 (1957), cols. 328-330. 3rd ed. A review of his life, office and message. RGG, 1st ed (1909), cf Baentsch; 2nd ed (1927), cf Balla.

893. Maag, Victor. "Amosbuch." RGG 1 (1957), cols. 330-331. 3rd ed. The book is in the third place among the 12 prophets.

894. Maag, Victor. *Text, Wortschatz und Begriffswelt des Buches Amos.* Leiden: Brill, 1951. xv + 254 pp. Detailed study of the text and interpretation, grammatical elements (prepositions, conjunctions, particles), single words, concepts (e.g., beginning and end, heaven, people, war).

895. Maag, Victor. "Zur Ubersetzung von Maskil in Amos 5:13, Ps 47:8 und in den Uberschriften Einiger Psalmen." *Schweizerische Theologische Umschau* 13, No. 5 (Dec '43), 108-115. A comparative study, with exegesis, noting earlier studies.

896. McCaughey, J. Davis. "Imagination in the Understanding of the Prophets." pp. 161-174 in *Religious Imagination* ed James P. Mackey. Edinburgh: Edinburgh University Press, 1986. iv + 217 pp. The prophet does not eliminate the vision (Amos 7-9) but shapes it by word and deed. Prophets know a word that creates reality. The book of Amos is the product of many hands over centuries. The later text is not corrupt. Life gets more complicated. We do not just write the truth. We write it for and to someone. Historical and literary analysis helps us see the subtle development, inter-relation and gathering rhetorical force of the five visions. We need to re-write Amos in order to hear him.

897. McComiskey, Thomas E. "Amos." Vol 7 (1985), 267-331 in *Expositor's Bible. Vol. 7. Daniel, Minor Prophets*, 12 vols, ed

Frank E. Gaebelein, et al. Grand Rapids, MI: Regency (Zondervan), 1985. xvi + 725. The introduction reviews the historical background, unity (it is), authorship, date, theological values (God is sovereign, the election of Israel, the Day of the Lord), and gives a bibliography and outline. The commentary follows the grammatico-historical approach, attention to grammar in historical context to determine meaning at the time of writing, with an evangelical approach (divine inspiration, complete trustworthiness and full authority of the Bible) but not an inflexible literalism. The text of the NIV is given with exegetical notes and commentary.

898. McComiskey, Thomas Edward. "The Hymnic Elements of the Prophecy of Amos: A Study of Form-critical Methodology." pp. 105-128 in *A Tribute to Gleason Archer* ed Walter C. Kaiser, Jr. and Ronald F. Youngblood. Chicago: Moody, 1986. 324 pp. Reprinted, JETS 30, No. 2 (June 87), 139-158. Calls for objective use of form criticism, notes earlier studies of hymnic elements, the problem of their intrusive nature (they are not), their sophisticated theology (YHWH as Creator), their use of divine titles, their setting, undisputed Amos material (repetition of similar clauses). The hymnic elements are authentic.

899. MacCormack, J. "Amos 7:14." ET 67, No. 10 (July 56), 318. Amos said, "I *was* [am] no prophet, neither was [am] I a prophet's son." I was not a prophet but am now after the Lord called me.

900. McCullough, W.S. "Some Suggestions About Amos." JBL 72, No. 4 (Dec 53), 247-254. A paper given at the Society's 86th meeting, Union Theological Seminary, 28 Dec 50. Cf JBL 70 (1951), xii. Notes earlier studies, claims the text of Amos is authentic, discusses the order and context of the oracles, the audience (both Judah and Israel), current Yahwism (a universal God who had a special purpose for Israel), the Day of the Lord, a remnant. The later addition of Amos 9:8d-15 is congruent with his hope.

901. McCurdy, J.F. "Light on Scriptural Texts from Recent Discoveries." HR 32, No. 1 (July 1896), 24-27. Amos 3:3. Discusses the historical background of the area, the rising dominance of the Aramaeans and their destruction by the Assyrians. This saved both Israel and Judah.

902. Macdonald, D.B. "Old Testament Notes. 2. Amos 5:25." JBL 18, Nos. 1&2 (1899), 214-215. Detailed exegesis, concerned with worship with the heart.

903. McFadyen, John Edgar. *A Cry for Justice: A Study in Amos.* The Short Course Series ed John Adams. Edinburgh: Clark, 1912. viii + 151. (reprinted, 1927). The book is divided into nine sections for preachers and congregations to study, e.g., the lion's roar, the divine demand, unslaked thirst, dark and dawn.

904. McFadyen, John Edgar. "An Old Testament Message." Exp, 8th Ser, 21, No. 1 (Jan '21), 1-18. The OT message is Amos. McFadyen discusses the character of the nation and of God, and preparation to meet God.

905. McKeating, Henry. "The Book of Amos." pp. 12-70 in *The Books of Amos, Hosea and Micah.* Cambridge Bible Commentary on the New English Bible ed Peter R. Ackroyd, et al. Cambridge: Cambridge University Press, 1971. x + 198 pp. For teachers and students as well as the general reader. There is a general introduction to these 8th century prophets. Each book has an introduction which is followed by short sections of the text and explanatory notes. The content of the book is from Amos, including the order, but it was written down later, the bulk of it in a single operation shortly after 722 BCE. The hopeful passages were added later.

906. Mackenzie, H.S. "The Plumb-Line (Amos 7:8)." ET 60, No. 6 (Mar 49), 159. It's an object lesson. Small mistakes in the beginning of the wall, and of life, become greater in time.

907. McKenzie, John L. "Amos." pp. 27-28 in *Dictionary of the Bible.* Milwaukee: Bruce, 1965. xix + 954 pp + 17 maps. Gives historical and personal background, an outline of the text. Discusses the visions, the doxologies (not by Amos), the future, God's demand for morality.

908. McKim, Randolph H. "The Radical Criticism Tested by Amos, Hosea and Ezekiel." *The Bible Student and Teacher* 5, No. 4 (Oct '06), 267-272. These prophets hold the same scheme of history as

earlier works. They do not support the Graf-Wellhausen hypothesis. One writer counted 45 references to Moses in Amos. Amos knew elements usually assigned to the Priestly Code, which dates c 550 BCE.

909. Maclagan, P.J. "Amos 9:3." ET 26, No. 5 (Feb '15), 237. Refers to the abundance of harvest rather than rapid growth a la Driver #399.

910. Maclaren, Alexander. "Amos." pp. 143-176 in *Ezekiel, Daniel, and the Minor Prophets*. Expositions of Holy Scripture 9 by Maclaren. NY: Hodder & Stoughton/Doran, n.d. (received in library, 1952) viii + 370 pp. Volume title and number varies. Eerdmans, 1959, vol 4; Baker's 1974 reprint, vol 6. Original, 17 vol. Useful sermonic comment on selected portions of the book, e.g., 3:3.

911. Maclean, Hector. "Amos and Israel." *Reformed Theological Review* (Hawthorn, Victoria, Australia) 18, No. 1 (Feb 59), 1-6. Amos differed from other prophets in his delivering a message to a foreign nation, unless Jonah is considered history. This helps explain references to Judah. He says Israel is doomed. There will be nothing left. He has limited hope and only a limited call to repentance.

912. Macpherson, Ann. "Amos and Hosea." Vol. I (1971), 1-54 in *Prophets*, 2 vols. Scripture Discussion Commentary 2 and 4, ed Laurence Bright. Chicago/St. Louis: ACTA Foundation/Sheed & Ward, 1971-2. ACTA = Adult Catechetical Teaching Aids. Commentary, pp. 5-28, on four sections of Amos: oracles against Israel and the nations, injustice and hypocrisy, woe to injustice, the visions. It is possible that the visions were originally Amos' call to prophecy.

913. MacRae, Allan A. "Scientific Approach to the Old Testament - a Study of Amos 9 in Relation to Acts 15." BS 110, No. 440 (Oct 53), 309-320, last in a series of four, starting vol 110, No. 437 (Jan-Mar 53), 18-24. Amos is not prominent in the other three. Reprinted, pp. 111-122 in *Truth for Today* ed J.F. Walvoord. 1963.

914. Maggioni, B. "Il profeta Amos." *Rivista del Clero Italiano* (Milan) 73 (1992), 590-599.

915. Maier, Walter A. "Eighteenth Sunday After Pentecost. Amos 8:4-7. Sep 25, 1983." CTQ 47, No. 2 (Ap 83), 164-165. Amos rebuked his contemporaries for wicked business practices, strange in a nation supposed to be a people of God. As the people of God today, we need to guard against "The Fearful Sin of Covetousness" (sermon outline).

916. Maier, Walter A. "Nineteenth Sunday After Pentecost. Amos 6:1-7. Oct 2, 1983." CTQ 47, No. 2 (Ap 83), 165-166. Each of us has been born into the world as the crown of God's creation, to become His child. Sermon outline on "God is Serious About Our Living in Love." The affluent leaders lived in luxury without love of neighbor.

917. Maigret, Jacques. "Amos et le sanctuaire de Bethel." *Bible et Terre Sainte* 47 (May 62), 5-6. Describes the historical background, the royal sanctuary at Bethel, Amos the Judahite burgher, the festival, a God who values justice.

918. Malamat, Abraham. "Amos 1:5 in the Light of the Til Barsip Inscriptions." BASOR 129 (Feb 53), 25-26. Translated from "'The Sceptre-Holder from Beth Eden' and the Inscriptions from Til-Barsib." BIES 16, Nos. 1/2 (1951), 42-45, with Eng summary, p. III. Bet-Eden is Bit-Adini, the Aramaean state on the Middle Euphrates near the great bend. Til Barsip (Tell Ahmar) was the capital. In Amos' time, it was governed by an Assyrian noble named Shamshi-ilu. The center of his province was Harran which the LXX names instead of Beth-Eden. The rise to power of Tiglath-pileser III in 746 eliminated the power of such nobles as he rearranged provinces to reduce their power.

919. Mallau, Hans Harald. "Las reacciones frente a los mensajes profeticos y el problema de la distincion entre profetas verdaderos y falsos. A Proposito de Amos 7:10-17." *Rivista Biblica* (Buenos Aires) 1 (1972), 33-39.

920. Mamie, Pierre. "Le livre d'Amos. Les chatiments et le 'reste d'Israel'." *Nova et Vera* 37, No. 3 (1962), 217-223.

921. Manakkatt, Matthew. "The Intercessary Prayer of Amos in Amos 7:1-6." *The Living Word* (Kerala, India) 100 (1994), 182-191.

922. March, Wallace Eugene. "Amos 1:3-2:16. The Exegesis of a Tradition." *Austin Seminary Bulletin* 90, No. 6 (Mar 75), 7-34. Offers a translation, analyzes the structure, the background and the theological importance of the tradition.

923. Margolis, Max L. "Another Haggadic Element in the Septuagint." AJSL 12, No. 2 (Ap-July 1896), 267. Amos 1:11 LXX. Exegesis.

924. Margolis, Max L. "Notes on Semitic Grammar. III. An Abnormal Hebrew Form in Amos 9:1" AJSL 19, No. 1 (Oct '02), 45-48. Exegesis.

925. Margolis, Max L. "Notes on Some Passages in Amos." AJSL 17, No. 3 (Ap '01), 170-171. Exegesis on 3:12, 4:3, 5, 5:6.

926. Markert, Ludwig. "Amos/Amosbuch." Vol. 2 (1978), 471-487 in *Theologische Realenzyklopadie*, 24+ vols. Berlin: de Gruyter, 1977ff. Reviews the person, the office, the book and its continuing influence.

927. Markert, Ludwig. *Struktur und Bezeichnung des Scheltworts. Eine gattungskritische Studie anhand des Amosbuches.* BZAW 140 ed Georg Fohrer. Berlin: de Gruyter, 1977. xii + 330 pp. Diss. Friedrich-Alexander-Universitat (Erlangen-Nurnberg), 1974. The introduction discusses the typology approach and invective as a type, its characteristics, various interpretations. Ch 2 is a structural analysis of Amos. Ch 3 enlarges the discussion of invective in German and Hebrew, form criticism, ANE parallels.

928. Marsh, John. "The Book of Amos." pp. 25-75 in *Amos and Micah: Thus Saith the Lord.* Torch Bible Commentaries ed Marsh and Alan Richardson. London: SCM, 1959. (reprint, 1967). 128 pp. The general introduction reviews prophecy and the making of a prophetic book. Amos and Micah were lone wolves rather than part

of the sons of the prophets tradition. The books began with an oral tradition expanded in time. The task of exegesis is not distinguishing between genuine and what is not. The whole book is the authenticity of a long lived tradition. This is neither the old conservatism nor the more recent historicism. The introduction to Amos reviews the historical background and outlines the book. The comments are by section and small units. Amos is dated 760 B.C. Ch 9:11-15 was added later, not just as a happy ending but to refer back to the lesson - obey God.

929. Marti, Karl. "Amos." pp. 144-227 in *Das Dodekapropheton erklart*. Kurzer Hand-Commentar zum Alten Testament 13 ed Marti et al. Tubingen: Mohr, 1904 xvi + 492 pp. A general introduction reviews the place of the minor prophets in the canon, the history of their collection and their significance in the history of the religion of Israel. The introduction to Amos reviews the man, his time, his significance, the original book, secondary elements.

930. Marti, Karl. "Zur Komposition von Amos 1:3-2:3." pp. 323-330 in *Abhandlungen zur semitischen Religionskunde und Sprachwissenschaft. Wolf Wilhelm Grafen von Baudissin zum 26. September 1917* ed Wilhelm Frankenberg and Friedrich Kuchler. BZAW 33. Giessen: Topelmann, 1918. xi + 436 pp. Notes the exegetical problems, history of interpretation, the historical situation, problems of originality, comparison with other texts.

931. Martin, George. "Streams of Justice and Mercy." *New Covenant* 23 (Sep 1993), 34.

932. Martin-Achard, Robert. *Amos: l'homme, le message, l'influence*. Publications de la Faculte de Theologie de l'Universite de Geneve 7. Geneva: Labor et Fides, 1984. 320 pp. The introduction discusses the man (name, Tekoa, work, episode at Bethel, etc), his message (language, inauthentic texts, the cult, the visions, the nations) and the continuing influence of Amos (Qumran, NT, early church and Reformation, modern times). The commentary follows the outline of the book with exegesis on individual verses.

933. Martin-Achard, Robert. "The End of the People of God." pp. 1-71 in *God's People in Crisis: A Commentary on the Book of Amos*

and a Commentary on the Book of Lamentation by Robert Martin-
Achard and S. Paul Re'emi. International Theological Commentary
ed George A.F. Knight and Fredrick Carlson Holmgren. Grand
Rapids/Edinburgh: Eerdmans/Handsel, 1984. viii + 134 pp.
Reviews the historical situation of the book and Amos' origins. The
Church saw in Amos a witness to Christ and the Church. The
Jewish, Marxist philosopher Ernst Bloch saw Amos as witness to
an oppressive society supported by the Church. Savonarola
preached from Amos and was executed. The commentary reviews
the oracles against the nations and against Israel and its elite. But
the epilogue predicts salvation. The latter was added by a distant
disciple under the inspiration of the Spirit in the post-exilic age. It
is a "nevertheless" to Amos' pronouncement of doom. The
profound reality of God's grace is demonstrated for Christians by
the Cross and the Resurrection. One commentator thought Amos
and Lamentations were bound together as an accident of
publication schedules while another thought it was because the
human situation of these 2 books is similar. The latter view is not
clear.

934.   Martin-Achard, Robert. *L'homme de Teqoa: Message et
       Commentaire du Livre d'Amos.* Aubonne: Moulin, 1990. 105 pp. A
       condensation of Amos, 1984.

935.   Martin-Achard, Robert. "La Predication d'Amos. Remarques
       Exegetiques et Homiletiques." ETR 41, No. 1 (1966), 13-19.
       Discusses numerous earlier studies, Amos' relationship with the
       wisdom tradition, application for today.

936.   Masterman, J.H.B. and G.H. Box, eds. "Amos." pp. 39-47, 123-127
       in *The Minor Prophets: A Little Library of Exposition with New
       Studies.* London: Cassell, 1929. xii + 144 pp. The volume has three
       parts. Masterman provides an overview of the Twelve. The second
       part is a series of statements from many sources, arranged by
       section of the text of each prophet. Box provides a critical study,
       pp. 115-144, which includes a review of content.

937.   Matheson, George. "Studies in the Minor Prophets. III. Amos." Exp
       2nd ser, vol 3 (May, 1882), 338-352. There are three phases of
       reaction in the life of every developed nation: physical, intellectual,

moral. They came together in the age of the Jewish Reformation: the rise of the prophets of Israel. The three reflect the importance of the individual, truth, conscience. Viewed from the human side, the prophets were poets expressing their faith. Amos is foremost in this movement. He is not an innovator but speaks in the true spirit of early Judaism true to the Mosaic spirit. Amos and other prophets knew the Garden of Eden story, with its double message of glory and sin, so Amos told of the destruction of the old ideal, called people to give up selfish joy. Then they would see the day of the Lord in glory.

938. Mauchline, John. "The Book of Amos." pp. 26-32 in *Prophets of Israel (3): The Twelve*. Bible Guides 9, ed William Barclay and F.F.Bruce. London/Nashville: Lutterworth/Abingdon, 1964. 94 pp. Reviews the purpose (Yahweh's real demands), plan and historical setting of the book. Gives an exposition and discusses the power of the book (the demand for justice).

939. Mauchline, J. "Implicit Signs of a Persistent Belief in the Davidic Empire." VT 20, No. 3 (July 70), 287-303. The oracles against the nations reflect an earlier day when the neighboring people had a covenant relationship with Israel/Judah, perhaps under David, or even earlier in the patriarchal period. Amos could announce punishment in the name of Yahweh because of this. The punishment is for violation of brotherly obligation, as in covenant relationships. Other references reflect the Davidic tradition also, e.g., God hides his people in his pavilion, i.e., royal pavilion. Jerusalem will be like Sinai, drawing people together in relation to God. Compares Amos with Isaiah, and others.

940. Maurer, Franz Joseph Valentin Dominik. (1795-1874). "Amos." Vol 2:331-383 in *Commentarius Grammaticus Criticus in Vetus Testament in Usum Maxime Gymnasiorum et Academiarum adornatus*, 5 vols. Leipzig: Volckmar, 1838. Vol 2:745 Latin study on grammar, exegesis, comparative textual analysis - MT, Greek, Latin - and notes on earlier studies. Gives historical background, parallels in other texts.

941. Mays, James Luther. *Amos. A Commentary*. OT Library ed Peter Ackroyd, et al. Philadelphia: Westminster, 1969. viii + 168 pp. 4th

ed, 1978. Reviews the prophet and his time, his words and message (next time the fire!), and the book. Amos is known only through his book and we know little about him. He was a sheepherder which probably means he was an owner in charge of other shepherds and significant person in the community. He was well informed in history and religious tradition. His message was the end of Israel. The leaders lived in pride and luxury in shocking contrast to the plight of the poor. The larger part of the book is Amos' but the book was edited later.

942. Mays, James Luther. "Words about the Words of Amos." INT 13, No. 3 (July 59), 259-272. There are far more words about Amos than by Amos - a review of the literature about Amos.

943. Mazar, E. "Archaeological Evidence for the 'Cows of Bashan Who Are in the Mountain of Samaria.'" pp. 151-157 in *Festschrift Reuben R. Hecht: Studies in Honor of His 70th Birthday* ed B. Azkin, et al. Jerusalem: Koren, 1979.

944. Meek, Theophile J. "The Accusative of Time in Amos 1:1" JAOS 61, No. 1 (1941), 63-64. It represents duration of time, e.g., Amos prophesied for two years.

945. Meek, Theophile J. "Again the Accusative of Time in Amos 1:1." JAOS 61, No. 3 (1941), 190-191. It represents a point of time, not duration as stated earlier.

946. Mehlman, Bernard. "Amos 9:6." *J of Reform Judaism* (NY) 25 (Sum 78), 47-50. The term *va-agudato* is variously translated as His vault or His congregation. It is used in midrashim and aggadot about Sukkot and means the community of the people. The term *agudah* is one of the 70 names of God.

947. Meinhold, Johannes. *Studien zur Israelitischen Religionsgeschichte. Band 1. Der Heilige Rest, Teil 1: Elias, Hosea, Amos, Jesaja.* Bonn: Weber, 1903. viii + 160 pp. Diss. Marburg, 1903. Amos, pp. 33-63. Discusses the remnant in Amos including Judah as the remnant.

948. Meinhold, Johannes and Hans Lietzmann. *Der Prophet Amos.*
      Hebraisch und Griechisch. Kleine Texte fur theologische und
      philologische Vorlesungen und Ubungen 15/16. Bonn: Marcus and
      Weber, 1905.

949. Melugin, Roy F. "Amos." pp. 735-749 in *Asbury Bible*
      Commentary ed Eugene E. Carpenter and Wayne McCown. Grand
      Rapids, MI: Zondervan, 1992. 1246 pp. Based (for the most part)
      on the New International Version. The introduction notes the man,
      time, message (judgment on Israel for its injustice with a note of
      hope at the end), structure (part A uses "people of Israel" while part
      B uses "house of Israel"). Each part has a doxology praising God
      as the creator. The beginning and end of the book focus on Judah.
      The postscript moves from judgment to salvation. The commentary
      is by sections with details on the verses.

950. Melugin, Roy F. "Amos." pp. 720-725 in *Harper's Bible*
      Commentary ed James L. Mays, et al. San Francisco: Harper &
      Row, 1988. xviii + 1326 pp. In the introduction, Melugin discusses
      the proclamation of judgment, written down later by others. The
      opening and closing reflect Jerusalem but the main part of the book
      is Israelite in focus. The commentary is in small units with subject
      or theme headings.

951. Melugin, Roy F. "The Formation of Amos: An Analysis of
      Exegetical Method." Vol I (1978), 369-391 in *SBL 1978 Seminar*
      Papers ed Paul J. Achtemeier. SBL Seminar Papers Series 13 ed
      Achtemeier. Missoula, MT: Scholars Press, 1978. vii + 415 pp.
      There were two volumes in 1978 (II:vii + 346) from the 114th
      Annual Meeting, held in New Orleans. Reviews the history of
      scholarship, especially Wolff and Koch. A fresh analysis includes
      structural analysis, analysis of genre (oracles, proclamations,
      instruction), layers of redaction with new material added.

952. Melugin, Roy F. "The Vision Reports in Amos." p. 205 in
      Abstracts: American Academy of Religion/Society of Biblical
      Literature 1986 ed Kent Harold Richards and James B. Wiggins.
      Atlanta, GA: Scholars Press, 1986. i + 269 pp. The SBL section is
      pp. 169-262 from the 122nd Annual Meeting. Four vision reports
      are arranged in pairs, with a fifth vision, and expansions in the third

and fourth. The latter insertions relate to the theology of Amos as a whole. The pairing reflects a theological understanding of Yahweh's historical activity.

953. Merwe, B.J. van der. "A Few Remarks on the Religious Terminology in Amos and Hosea." pp. 143-152 in *Studies on the Book of Amos: Papers Read at 8th Meeting of Die Ou Testamentiese Werkgemeenskap in Suid-Afrika Held at Pretoria University 1965* ed A.H. van Zyl. OTWSA 7-8 (1964-5). Potchefstroom: Pro Rege - Pers Beperk, 1965. pp. 113-169. Bound with *Studies on the Book of Hosea*, the 7th Congress of the OTWSA, 111 pp., with continuous pagination for a total of 169 pp. Reviews the interpretations of "transgress," "sin," "law," "covenant." Amos saw the cult as evil. Hosea thought it had sinned, i.e., it was once legitimate. The relationship of Yahweh and Israel was formal for Amos but personal for Hosea.

954. Michalski, Wilhelm. *Amos. Introduction, new version, commentary* (Pol). Lvov: Bibljoteka religijna, 1922. x + 96 pp.

955. Michel, Diethelm. "Amos." pp. 179-209 in *Israels Glaube im Wandel: Einfuhrungen in die Forschung am Alten Testament* by Michel. Berlin: Verlag "Die Spur" Dorbandt, 1968. 302 pp. Reviews the general characteristics of "prophet" from a variety of texts as a context for the discussion of Amos. In 7:10-17, Amos is an outsider. Michel translates with commentary, with additional pericope, noting God's "no" to the people's social injustice, their cult, their holy history, their faith, their existence. In the end, there is a promise of restoration.

956. Milik, J.T. "Amos." pp. 173-174 in *Les "Petits Grottes" de Qumran* by M. Baillet, et al. Discoveries in the Judean Desert of Jordan 3. Oxford: Clarendon Press, 1962. xiii + 317 pp. Transcription of the text (from Cave 5) and critical apparatus.

957. Millard, Alan R. and John H. Stek. "Amos." pp. 1345-1359 in *The NIV Study Bible: New International Version* ed Kenneth L. Barker, et al. Grand Rapids, MI: Zondervan, 1985. xxiii + 1950 + 157 (appendices) The introduction discusses the author, date,

background, theme and message. Gives an outline. Annotated NIV text.

958. Miller, Charles H. "Amos and Faith Structures: A New Approach." BT 19, No. 5 (Sep 81), 314-319. Discusses edited strata, identifying the values of the writers, the "School" of Amos, his faith, faith development. Draws on Hans W. Wolff, Jean Piaget, Lawrence Kohlberg and James W. Fowler for group study of Amos.

959. Miller, John W. "Amos of Tekoa." pp. 39-64 in *Meet the Prophets: A beginner's guide to the books of the biblical prophets - their meaning then and now.* NY: Paulist, 1987. ix + 250 pp. A general introduction reviews the nature of prophecy, its historical setting, and how to study a prophetic book. Each unit closes with questions for review. For Amos, Miller looks at the book as a whole, the man (name, job, home, life style, theology, his call, historical setting), his message and its relevance.

960. Miller, Patrick D., Jr. "Amos." pp. 21-25 in *Sin and Judgment in the Prophets: A Stylistic and Theological Analysis.* SBL Monograph 27, ed James L. Crenshaw. Chico, CA: Scholars, 1982. x + 143 pp. The general introduction reviews the lawsuit of God against his people, the *talion*, the correspondence of sin and judgment and scholarly interpretations. The closing sections of the text discusses the source, setting, classification of the patterns of correspondence. God's retribution is poetic justice but its purpose is purifying, reclaiming, renewing. He considers this common imagery in Amos 5:7, 10-11, etc, including literary problems. Amaziah will be punished for specific sin, not just be caught up in the larger catastrophe.

961. Miller, P.W. "Amos." *The Evangelical Quarterly* (London) 12, No. 1 (15 Jan 40), 48-59. Discusses Amos' judgment on the sins of the day which are like those of our time, including totalitarianism. But there is hope. Jehovah will raise up his broken people.

962. Mishael, Yosef. "Behold the Days are Coming Upon You" (Heb). BM 36 [Issue No. 125], No. 2 (Jan-Mar 91), 160-165. Amos 4:1-3. Mishael notes earlier studies, the structure ABCDE F E'D'C'B'A'.

963. Mitchell, H.G. *Amos: An Essay in Exegesis*. Boston: Bartlett, 1893. 2nd ed, 1900. In addition to translation and commentary, introductory studies review the man, his time, the book, while supplementary studies consider his relationship to the Hexateuch and to the prophets, and his theology. Even if he owned his flocks, he was probably poor, living on a bit of bread and a few figs. His simplicity is striking in the text. He was fearless and discerning. The book has been called the most orderly of the prophets. There are numerous references to the history and events and laws of the Hexateuch, J, E, D and probably P. His theology was complete. He refers to Yahweh 52 times. God is the Creator with power over nature and all humanity. Later prophets were influenced by Amos.

964. Mitchell, H.G. "The Idea of God in Amos." JBL 7 (Dec 1887), 33-42. YHWH is the God of all men and things. Jehovah is omnipotent, omniscient, omnipresent. He is good and merciful.

965. Mittmann, Siegfried. "Amos 3:12-15 und das Bett der Samarier." *Z des Deutschen Palastina-Vereins* 92, No. 2 (1976), 149-167. Gives transliteration, German translation, notes earlier studies, seven illustrations of beds and decoration.

966. Mittmann, Siegfried. "Gestalt und Gehalt einer prophetischen Selbstfertigung (Am 3:3-8)." *Theologische Quartalschrift* 151, No. 2 (1971), 134-145. Gives a German translation, discussion of earlier views, style and structural analysis, form criticism, comparison to other texts.

967. Moeller, Henry R. "Ambiguity at Amos 3:12." BTr 15, No. 1 (Jan 64), 31-34. Discusses the problems and various translations. Suggests the scribes fused two words, so follows Isaac Rabinowitz and translates "a piece of couch and a part from a bed's leg." This fits the context.

968. Moffatt, James. "Literary Illustrations of Amos." Exp 8th series, 9 (Mar '15), 272-288. Draws on quotations across the ages as parallels, explanation and exposition of Amos' illustrations.

969. Moller, W. "Amos ein Volksprophet u. unsere Zeit." *Vortrag: Nach dem Gesetz u. Zeugnis* 29 (1929-1930), 359-365, 425-435.

970. Monloubou, J. *Amos et Osee, Saintete de Justice, Saintete d'Amour*. Sous la Main de Dieu 8. Paris: Cerf, 1964. viii + 256 pp.

971. Monloubou, L. "Prophetes d'Israel: Amos." Vol 8 (1972), cols 706-724 in *Dictionnaire de la Bible, Supplement*, 12 + vols, ed Louis Pirot, et al. Paris; Letouzey et Ane, 1928-1993 + 8:vi pp. + 1475 cols. Reviews earlier studies, discusses Amos and his book, Tekoa, the prophet, his message. This includes the oracles against the nations, the visions, authenticity, doxologies, the epilogue, professional prophets. Extensive bibliography.

972. Montgomery, James A. "Notes from the Samaritan (2) the Root *prt*, Amos 6:5." JBL 25, No. 1 (1906), 51-52. It means "sing."

973. Montgomery, James A. "Notes on Amos." JBL 23, Part 1 (1904), 94-96. Word studies including *noqed*, shepherd or prince.

974. Montgomery, James A. "Notes on the Old Testament. 6. *mblyg*, Amos 5:9." JBL 31, No. 3 (1912), 143. Exegesis. The word is related to come in, live.

975. Moon, Cyris Hee Suk. *A Korean Minjung Theology: An Old Testament Perspective*. Maryknoll, NY: Orbis, 1985. x + 83 pp. Discusses Amos (pp. 41-45) in a chapter on "Prophets and the Helpless, Poor, and Oppressed." These three groups are the *minjung* or common people. Amos' message was to the elite, the oppressing ruling classes on behalf of the oppressed in the name of God. The oppression was economic, political, legal, religious. All persons and institutions are accountable to Yahweh.

976. Moon, Cyris Hee Suk. "An Old Testament Understanding of Minjung." pp. 119-135 in *Minjung Theology: People as the Subjects of History* ed Kim Yong Bock. Singapore: The Commission on Theological Concerns, The Christian Conference of Asia, 1981. iv + 196 pp. According to Amos, the upper class took from the middle which took from the poor. God will judge the unpardonable sins of political, social and economic oppression by the rulers against the minjung. Amos and Micah stood on the side of the oppressed. They were commoners, not professional prophets,

who lived and identified with people. People today must follow in the footsteps of the true prophet.

977. Moore, Michael S. "Yahweh's Day." *Restoration Quarterly* 29 (Abilene 1987), 193-208.

978. Moore, R. Kelvin. "Amos: An Introduction." *TE* 52 (Fall 95), 27-36. Amos judged the entire society and surrounding nations as well. The book reads like a morning newspaper. Moore discusses the name, date, the man, historical background, theology. God is sovereign, a Judge, One who elects. He is the God of hope. Gives an outline of Amos and bibliography.

979. Morag, Shelomo. "'Latent Masorah' in oral language traditions." *Sefarad* (Madrid) 46 (1986), 333-344. This volume is a festschrift for Federico Perez Castro.

980. Moreau, Madeleine. "Sur un commentaire d'Amos: De Doctrina christiana IV, VII, 15-21, sur Amos 6:1-6." pp. 313-322 in *Saint Augustine et la Bible* ed Anne-Marie la Bonnardiere. Bible de Tous les Temps. Paris: Beauchesne, 1986. 462 pp. Includes translation of passages from *Da Doctrina christiana* with commentary.

981. Moreno, C.A. "Amos." *Theologia y Vida* 4 (1963), 23-35.

982. Morgan, G. Campbell. "Amos - National Accountability." pp. 41-57 in *The Minor Prophets: The Men and Their Messages*. Old Tappan, NJ: Revell, 1960. 157 pp. New in book form, these are lectures delivered at the Northfield Conference and published in the *Northfield Echoes* in 1902-1903. The biblical text is printed followed by commentary on the prophet and his times, oracles against the nations (Amos 1-2), Israel's sin (3-4), laments (5-6), visions (7-9), restoration (9:11-15), the message (Judah and Israel will be more severely judged than other nations) and the permanent message. The latter is that God still governs the nations. Those with the clearest light have the greatest responsibility. God despises sins like cruelty, hatred, slavery, violence, corruption.

983. Morgenstern, Julian. "The Address of Amos - Text and Commentary." HUCA 32 (1961), 295-350. [= Amos IV] Amos

delivered only one address. The book reflects this. It is not a miscellaneous collection. Gives the text in Hebrew, translation in English, commentary (exegesis, word studies), Amos' lifestyle and message, secondary passages (e.g., the denunciation of Judah).

984. Morgenstern, Julian. "Amos Studies I." HUCA 11 (1936), 19-140. Notes the problems of oral tradition with poets forgetting their own words and preservation by others in different verse order, etc. Applies this for portions of Amos, gives the text in Hebrew metrics. Discusses the visions, the editing of 1:1-2, problems of chronology.

985. Morgenstern, Julian. *Amos Studies. Parts I, II, and III*, Vol. 1. The Sigmund Rheinstrom Memorial Publications II. Cincinnati: Hebrew Union College, 1941. xi + 428 pp. Reprinted from HUCA 11 (1936), 19-140; 12/13 (1937-1938), 1-53; 15 (1940), 59-305. The three parts are the biographical sections of the book, the date of Amos' prophecy and the historical antecedents to it. Amos delivered a single address, on New Year's Day, in 751 BCE, at the Northern sanctuary of Bethel. The stranger's words may have taken 30 minutes. Amos preached a new universalism. Yahweh is more than a national deity. He is concerned with all the nations. Part IV = HUCA 32 (1961), 295-350.

986. Morgenstern, Julian. "The Historical Antecedents of Amos' Prophecy." HUCA 15 (1940), 59-305. [= Amos III] Surveys Hebrew history from David and Solomon to Jeroboam and Uzziah, and the social and religious context of Amos.

987. Morgenstern, Julian. "The Loss of Words at the Ends of Lines in Manuscripts of Biblical Poetry." HUCA 25 (1954), 41-83. The loss is because metrical units were written on a single line, with the left hand margin occasionally lost. The missing thought or word may be recovered through the study of meter, parallelism or chiasm. The hypothesis is tested on Amos 8:13, 2:13 and Isaiah. Careful analysis of the first suggests: "On that day the beautiful maidens shall faint, And the vigorous youths grow weary; The young people shall become exhausted and stumble, And shall fall, to rise no more." The second becomes: "Behold, I will cause you to topple over, Just as the full cart topples over To which a sheaf is added."

988. Morgenstern, Julian. "The Sin of Uzziah, the Festival of Jeroboam, and the date of Amos." HUCA (Cincinnati) 12-13 (1937-1938), 1-53. [= Amos II] Uzziah's sin (leaving the high places intact) was punished by leprosy, even though other kings were not punished. The real sin, presumably was offering incense in the temple. This brought on the earthquake in 749 BCE. Amos' prophecy was on New Year's Day in 751, two years to the day before this earthquake. Jeroboam I burned incense on the 15th of the eighth month. He dedicated his new, royal sanctuary at Bethel in the same way, same occasion, as Solomon dedicated the temple 30 years earlier. The deuteronomic editors condemned him for changing the date of the festival. Jeroboam, Uzziah and Amos' last vision are all at the same time in the festival.

989. Morgenstern, Julian. "The Universalism of Amos." pp. 106-126 in *Essays Presented to Leo Baeck on the Occasion of His Eightieth Birthday*. London: East & West Library, 1954. xiii + 211 pp. Reviews scholarly opinions on this and the monotheism of Amos. Amos 9:7 says God controlled the movement of other nations. This verse belongs between 3:1a and 3:2. Amos thought only the land of Israel was clean [he himself was from Judah according to most commentators]. Later Jeremiah said people in a foreign land could pray to Yahweh. Thorough universalism came with Deutero-Isaiah. But Amos took the first step.

990. Mosley, Harold R. "The Oracles Against the Nations." TE 52 (Fall 95), 37-45. Discusses the function (got Israel's attention), structure, the formula (for three... for four...), the crimes of the nations (violated human decency), the crimes of Israel and Judah (violated the covenant: injustice, oppression, rebellion against God).

991. Moss, Howard. "Amos." pp. 210-221 in *Congregation: Contemporary Writers Read the Jewish Bible* ed David Rosenberg. NY: Harcourt Brace Jovanovich, 1987. xiv + 526 pp. Israel thought that as the Chosen People, they were immune from God's wrath but Amos damned Israel with the news it was not special. It would be judged by the same standards as its neighbors. Amos is that odd combination of Oriental poetry and democratic agitprop that characterizes Whitman - a blend of image, catalogue, message, parallel constructions and contrast. If history begins with the story

of others, Amos was the first historian, seeing Israel as a nation among nations, helping enlarge a tribal consciousness into a broader sense of a world dominated by God's will and a moral view. Reading Amos, one feels little has changed.

992. Motyer, Alec. *Amos. Le rugissement de Dieu.* Lausanne: Presses Biblique Universitaires, 1982. 176 pp.

993. Motyer, J.A. "Amos." pp. 726-741 in *The New Bible Commentary Revised,* ed Donald Guthrie, et al. Grand Rapids, MI: Eerdmans, 1970. xv + 1310. (original, by Bussey, 1953) Reviews Amos' times, teaching, book. He never uses the word covenant though he clearly understood Israel to be the covenant people. His monotheism is based on God as Creator who is the Judge of the world. Doom does not mean there is no hope but the basic problem was a people who were outwardly very religious. The book is a very carefully edited piece of literature - all by Amos.

994. Motyer, J.A. *The Day of the Lion: The Message of Amos.* The Bible Speaks Today, ed Motyer and John R.W. Stott. Downers Grove, IL: InterVarsity, 1974. 208 pp. Amos put in hours of study and learned all about world affairs before preaching his sermons. The mind of the nation was coming under his spell. What a pity we have only the distilled essence of what he said. Our first task is exegesis. The second is exposition. The latter comes out of pulpit work. May God graciously stoop to use this book for the benefit of his church. There is a full commentary on the book of Amos, divided into three parts.

995. Moulton, Richard G. "Amos." pp. 91-113, notes pp. 249-256, in *Daniel and the Minor Prophets.* The Modern Reader's Bible 16. NY: Macmillan, 1898. A literary approach using the Revised Version. The general introduction describes the prophets' personal lives, history, ideas, literary forms. The text is divided into sections with thematic headings. The notes look at the work as a whole. Moulton says Amos is a single prophetic sentence which he calls "rhapsody." In this case, its a rhapsody of judgment but it moves beyond to a vision of restoration.

996. Mousset, Pacifique. "La pedagogie d'un prophete: Amos." *Catechistes* 27 (1956), 267-277.

997. Mowinckel, Sigmund. "Amos-Boken." Oversaettelse med Tekstritiek Kommentar." *Norsk Teologisk Tidsskrift* 28 (1927), 1-31. Translation with annotation, exegesis and commentary.

998. Mowinckel, Sigmund Olaf Plytt (1884-1965). A review article of Seierstad, *Die Berufungserlebnisse...* in *Norsk Teologisk Tidsskrift* 49 (1948), 120-128. The book's title is *Die Offenbarungserlebnisse*. Mowinckel reviews the book, includes his own opinion, notes earlier ones.

999. Mowinckel, Sigmund Olaf Plytt. "Amos." pp. 618-652 in *De Senere Profeter* by Mowinckel and N. Messel. Det Gamle Testamente 3 by S. Michelet, et al. Oslo: Aschehoug (Nygaard), 1944. 834 pp. A major introduction (pp. 9-62) discusses prophecy in Israel and the ANE, its origins and characteristics, the rise of apocalyptic, the books of the prophets. The section on the minor prophets has a brief introduction on the collection plus a bibliography. The introduction to Amos notes the man, his call, the historical background, content, bibliography. The annotated translation with critical notes, has marginal sigla to indicate sources, e.g., Amos, redactors, a gloss, etc.

1000. Mowvley, Harry. "Amos." pp. 3-91 in *The Books of Amos & Hosea*. Epworth Commentaries ed Harold F. Guite and Ivor H. Jones. London: Epworth, 1991. xix + 168 pp. The general introduction notes prophecy as prediction, the gift of the Holy Spirit (I Co 12), and prophetic preaching. These ideas distort the function of the Hebrew prophets, messengers of God. While Amos and Hosea are called writing prophets, they probably wrote very little or nothing. Their words were collected by others. The introduction to Amos continues the review of prophecy in Israel, and neighboring areas, and gives the historical background for Amos, the man and his time. The comments are in sections and small units. The hope added at the end is an important part of the message of doom. Both have their place in the Christian gospel.

1001. Mowvley, Harry. "Which is the Best Commentary? XVI, Amos and Hosea." ET 103, No. 12 (Sep 92), 364-368. Discusses commentaries in general, larger vs smaller types, specifically those related to Amos and Hosea, e.g., Harper, Wolff, Anderson & Freedman, Hayes, Polly, his own, et al.

1002. Mulder, Martin Jan. "Ein Vorschlag zur Ubersetzung von Amos iii 6b." VT 34, No. 1 (Jan 84), 106-108. Exegesis with a review of interpretations.

1003. Muller, David Heinrich (1846-1912). *Die Propheten in ihrer ursprunglichen Form. Die Grundgesetze der ursemitischen Poesie erschlossen und nachgewiesen in Bibel, Keilinschriften und Koran und in ihren wirkungen erkannt in den Choren der Griechischen Tragodie,* 2 vols. Vienna: Holder, 1896. Vol 1 is the prolegomena and epilegomena and 2 (bound together) gives selections from the Hebrew and Arabic (Syriac) texts. Vol 1 reviews the structure of Babylonian, Assyrian, Neo-Babylonian, Quranic and Hebrew prophetic poetry. The last includes Amos (pp. 62-73) with translation and comparative textual study. Another unit considers origin and historical development (Amos, pp. 193-195, 209). Portions of the NT and the Greek classics are also analyzed.

1004. Muller, Hans Peter. "Ein Paradigma zur Theorie der alttestamentlichen Wissenschaft: Amos, seine epigonen und Interpreten" (A Paradigm for the Theory of OT Studies: Amos, His Followers and Interpreters). *Neue Z fur Systematische Theologie und Religionsphilosophie* 33, No. 2 (1991), 112-138. English summary, p. 138. Amos did not proclaim a utopia. This idea comes later from deuteronomic imitators.

1005. Muller, Hans Peter. "Phonizien und Juda in exilisch-nachexilischer Zeit." *Die Welt des Orients* 6, No. 2 (1971), 189-204. Amos 1:9-10. Begins his survey with Amos' oracles against the nations as reflecting the latter's situation.

1006. Muntag, Andor. *Amosz konyve, forditas es magyarazat.* Budapest: Lutheran Church, 1979.

1007. Muntag, Andor. Amosz konyve es mi (The Book of Amos and Us). *Liber Pontificalis* 49, No. 1 (1974), 641-652.

1008. Muntag, Andor. "Amosz Tortenelmi Szerepe" (The Historical Role of Amos). *Liber Pontificalis* 49 (1974), 584-591.

1009. Muntingh, L.M. "Political and International Relations of Israel's Neighboring Peoples according to the Oracles of Amos." pp. 134-142 in *Studies on the Book of Amos: Papers Read at 8th Meeting of Die Ou Testamentiese Werkgemeenskap in Suid-Afrika Held at Pretoria University 1965* ed A.H. van Zyl. OTWSA 7-8 (1964-5). Potchefstroom: Pro Rege - Pers Beperk, 1965. pp. 113-169 pp. Bound with *Studies on the Book of Hosea*, the 7th Congress of the OTWSA, 111 pp., with continuous pagination for a total of 169 pp. Reviews the history of interpretations of Damascus, Philistines, etc. in government, slavery, exile, migration.

1010. Muraoka, Takamitsu. "Is the Septuagint Amos 8:12-9:10 a Separate Unit?" VT 20, No. 4 (Oct 70), 496-500. Refutes G. Howard's view (VT 20 [1970], 108-112) that this is a separate unit (see #681).

1011. Murray, William D. *The Message of the Twelve Prophets*. NY: YMCA, 1904. ix + 197 pp. + chart. The chart has fill in blanks for each of the Twelve for key thought, word, text, outline. Studies originally prepared for a business men's Bible class. There is a one page lesson for each day. Each lesson has the verses for the day, commentary, study questions, relevant scripture from other books, sometimes a prayer, sometimes the message for today, definitions, NT quotations of or related to the prophet. Amos (pp. 1-35) is covered in 5 weeks. The book uses the American Standard Edition of the Revised Version.

1012. Murtonen, Andre E. "The Prophet Amos - A Hepatoscoper?" VT 2, No. 2 (1952), 170-171. Detailed denial of Bic in VT 1 (1951), 293.

1013. Muss-Arnolt, W. "Amos 5:26 (21-27)." Exp 6th ser 2, No. 6 (Dec 1900), 414-428. Commentary and exegesis with rearrangement of the text. Vs 26 is an editorial addition. The editor was sarcastic and educated.

1014. Myers, Jacob Martin. "The Book of Amos." pp. 97-149 in *Hosea, Joel, Amos, Obadiah, Jonah.* Layman's Bible Commentary 14. London/Richmond: SCM/Knox, 1960. 176 pp. For the general reader with the RSV, using modern scholarship. The authorship of the book has never been questioned but some content may have been added later. It is doubtful he *wrote* any part of the book but he delivered the oracles and shared the visions and may have included the hymnal fragments. The liturgical materials, e.g., 1:3-2:16 may have been his poetry. There are editorial elements, e.g., 1:1-2a. The purpose of the book was to preserve the words of Amos. His purpose was to deliver the judgments of God. Outlines the book in four sections: call, oracles against the nations, sermons (Israel's sin/God's judgment) and Amos' visions. He preached c 750, 10-20 years before Hosea in a time of stability which he knew could not last.

1015. Myers, Jacob M. "A Niagara of Righteousness (Amos)." pp. 97-102 in *Invitation to the Old Testament.* Garden City, NY: Doubleday, 1966. xi + 252 pp. Discusses the historical background, the man, the message, judgment of bankrupt deceptive religion.

N.

1016. Naastepad, Th.J.M. *Amos*. Verklaring van een Bibjbelgedeelte. Kampen: Kok, 1977. 103 pp. Translation and commentary, divided into 13 units.

1017. Nagele, Sabine. *Laubhutte Davids und Wolkensohn: Eine auslegungsgeschichte Studie zu Amos 9:11 in der judischen und christlichen Exegese*. Arbeiten zur Geschichte des Antiken Judentums und des Urchristentums 24 ed Martin Hengel, et al. Leiden: Brill, 1995. Diss. Eberhard Karls University (Tubingen), 1993. Eng summary, pp. 223-238, "The Booth of David and The Son of the Clouds." Reviews the history of interpretation, including Qumran, rabbinic literature, the NT, early Church, Middle Ages and Reformation period and up to modern times. Compares the translations of the versions - LXX, Vulgate, Targum, Syriac, MT - and interpretive methods - literary criticism, redaction history, the deuteronomic redaction, tradition history the question of unity.

1018. Namiki, K. "The Images of Amos" (Japanese). *Sources and Development of Western Spirit. Festschrift for T. Kanda*. Tokyo: Pediraviumu-kai, 1976. iv + 212 pp.

1019. Nagah/Nageh, Rivka. "Are You Not Like the Ethiopians to Me (Amos 9:7)" (Heb). BM 27 [Issues 89-90], Nos. 2/3 (1981/1982), 174-182. Discusses many interpretations including the idea that the verse praises Israel. Nagah rejects the last and does not think universalism started with Amos. She thinks the verse is an expression of shock and despair. Rev, OTA 6 (1983), 75.

1020. Nash, Kathleen. "Let Justice Surge." BT 31, No. 5 (Sep 93), 265-271. Amos refers to the Exodus three times. The Exodus (and the gratitude expected) and the Sinai covenant are two poles of his thought. Liberation and responsibility go together. The Israelites have rejected the covenant. They are moral failures. God is a liberator concerned with the weak and oppressed. Seek good and not evil is a morality for today.

1021. Navarro Peiro, Angeles and Federico Perez Castro. "Amos." pp. 19-31 in *Biblia Babilonica: Profetas Menores. Edicion critica segun Manuscritos Hebreos de Puntuacion Babilonica.* Textos y Estudios "Cardenal Cisneros" de la Biblia Poliglota Matritense 16 ed Federico Perez Castro. Madrid: Instituto "Arias Montano" C.S.I.C., 1977. xvii + 106 pp. CSIC = Consejo Superior de Investigaciones Cientificas. The introduction reviews the manuscripts used for this critical edition, describes their fragmentary condition, notes earlier studies, gives a summary of the Babylonian punctuation, a list of variants. Hebrew text of several manuscripts of Amos with critical apparatus.

1022. Neal, Marshall. "The Folly of Failing to Respond to God's Judgment." BV 27, No. 2 (Nov 93), 9-16. Discusses the judgment, the emptiness of external religion, God's displeasure. Samaria had every chance to repent but refused. This is our situation today.

1023. Neher, Andre. *Amos: Contribution a l'etude du prophetisme.* Paris: Vrin, 1950. xv + 299 pp. 2nd ed., 1951. A study of the man, his life and message, his visions, historic antecedents (e.g., the Rechabites), and a general study of prophecy (social function, ethics, metaphysics).

1024. Neil, William. "Amos." pp. 289-292 in *Harper's Bible Commentary* by Neil. NY: Harper & Row, 1962. 544 pp. Gives the historical background and the religious situation, Amos' call, denunciation of evil, intuitive insights, focus on justice.

1025. Neiman, David. "Sefarad: The Name of Spain." JNES 22, No. 2 (1963), 128-132.

1026. Nel, W.A.G. "Amos 9:11-15: An Unconditional Prophecy of Salvation during the Period of the Exile." OTE 2 (1984), 81-97. Not from Amos. The Exilic or post-exilic writer is consoling his people of the southern kingdom. The unconditional salvation is based on their political view of God.

1027. Neteler, B. (1821-1912). "Amos." pp. 30-41 in *Die Gliederung des Buches der zwolf Propheten als Grundlage ihrer Erklarung*. Munster: Niemann, 1871. 118 pp. A general introduction gives historical background to the prophetic movement, compares LXX, MT, and other versions. Treatment of individual prophets includes exegesis, commentary, more detail on history and interpretation.

1028. Neubauer, Karl Wilhelm. "Erwagungen zu Amos 5:4-15." ZAW 78, No. 3 (1966), 292-316. (Eng summary) Vss 4-7, 10-12, 14-15, are a unit created by Amos. These combine Amos and a sharp attitude toward cultic salvation. The promise of life is in seeking God.

1029. Neuberg, Frank J. "An Unrecognized Meaning of Hebrew *dor*." JNES 9, No. 4 (Oct 50), 215-217. The word means generation and dor wa-dor means eternity. It also means assembly, council, in Ugaritic and Phoenician. The latter applies in Amos 8:14, Ps 84:11, etc.

1030. Neufeld, D.F. [Close of probation] [Amos 3:7] [Question and Answer] *Advent Review and Sabbath Herald* 154 (4 Aug 77), 9.

1031. Neumann, Frederick. *Where Do We Stand? A Selective Homiletical Commentary on the Old Testament. Vol. II. Faith and Reality in History. The Historical Books and the Prophets*. Brooklyn, NY: Gaus, 1978. xi + 282 pp. Includes two sermons on Amos, one for Memorial Day and one for daily life.

1032. Newcome, William. "Amos." pp. 14-58 in *An Attempt towards an Improved Version, Metrical Arrangement, and an Explanation, of the Twelve Minor Prophets*. London: Tegg, 1836. xlv + 408 pp. The preface discusses prophecy in general, earlier studies, rules for translation. The text is translation with critical notes and exegesis.

1033. Newman, Louis Israel. "Parallelism in Amos." Part I:1-209 in *Studies in Biblical Parallelism*. Semicentennial Publications of the University of California. Berkeley: University of California, 1917. x + 388. Also published as *University of California Publications in Semitic Philology* 1, Nos. 2 and 3:57-444. Reviews poetic parallelism in Finnish and Chinese as well as Near Eastern traditions. Amos has numerous examples - complete and incomplete, four term variation, alternate, synonymous, synthetic, triplets and monostichs, strophic formations. Amos 1:3-2:8 is analyzed in detail. Sheer prose is rare. If the original text were known, we might find even more parallelism but then the Prophet may also have followed other rhetorical laws, or inner impulses.

1034. Newton, J.C. Calhoun. "Studies in Amos and Hosea." *Southern Methodist Review* 22 (1897), 75-92.

1035. Nichol, Francis D. "Amos." pp. 21-22, 951-984 in *The Seventh-day Adventist Bible Commentary*, vol 4, ed Nichol et al. Washington, DC: Review and Herald, 1955. 1184 pp. Vol. 4 (of seven vols; four on the OT) is on the prophets. General articles are on the role of Israel in OT prophecy (spiritual Israel replaced physical Israel), Daniel (in addition to the commentary on Daniel) and the chronology of the prophets. A convenient chart is on p. 18. The 17 maps are helpful. There is a short introduction to each prophet. Neither the general articles nor the commentaries are signed. Each biblical book has a commentary which includes an introduction (title, authorship, historical setting and outline) and by chapters a translation, comments and references to the writings of Ellen G. White. Amos (767-753 BCE) was a herdsman. Though poor, he was independent. The theme of the book is the call to repentance. Corruption will bring divine judgment but he closes the book with a glorious picture of the ultimate triumph of righteousness.

1036. Niditch, Susan. *The Symbolic Vision in Biblical Tradition.* Harvard Semitic Monographs 30. Chico, CA: Scholars Press, 1980. xii + 258 pp. Diss. Harvard, 1978. Stage I is the symbolic vision form illustrated by Amos (pp. 21-41) and Jeremiah. Stage II is literary-narrative (Zechariah). The baroque stage is illustrated by Dan 7-8, 2 Baruch and 4 Ezra. While the basic form continues, over time it varies and develops, e.g., in Stage II, the seer asks for an explanation while in Stage I, he is the passive instrument of the message. The symbols become more mythologized. Stage III adds more detail, e.g., the emotional state of the seer. Amos 7:7-9 and 8:1-3 are translated, critically annotated and analyzed. God sends the vision and interprets it himself.

1037. Niehaus, Jeff. "Amos." pp. 315-509 in *The Minor Prophets: An Exegetical and Expository Commentary. Vol 1. Hosea, Joel, and Amos* ed Thomas Edward McComiskey. Grand Rapids, MI: Baker, 1992. x + 509 pp. Amos is largely faceless. He did not seek to be a prophet. His ministry was in the early 760s BCE in the midst of prosperity from successful conquest, a quiescent Assyria. The style and structure is appropriate. A covenant-lawsuit messenger uses this form of address, common in the ANE. Niehaus lists phrases common to the Pentateuch as covenant background. Amos used poetry skillfully. In theology, God is sovereign over the world. The loving God desires life, not death for sinful people. Amos' anthropology emphasizes sin, especially idolatry and social injustice. Detailed outline plus a select bibliography. The commentary has Niehaus' translation (a literal rendition of the section that follows) in one column with the New RSV in the other. The exegesis is a study of the words and phrases giving the Hebrew or Greek with English translation. The exposition amplifies the exegesis, discussing related theological and hermeneutical issues, with homiletics.

1038. Nielsen, Eduard. "Om formkritik som hjaelpemiddel i historisk-genetisk forskning, belyst ved eksempler fra Amos 1-2 og Mika 1." *Dansk Teologisk Tidsskrift* 52, No. 4 (1989), 243-250. Translation, exegesis, commentary, review of earlier opinions. English summary: Form Criticism can be done without historical evidence, but the former can corroborate the latter, as is demonstrated in this comparison.

1039. Niemann, Hermann Michael. "Theologie in geographischen Gewand. Zum Wachstumsprozess der Volkerspruchsammlung Amos 1-2." pp. 177-196 in *Nachdenken uber Israel, Bibel und Theologie: Festschrift fur Klaus-Dietrich Schunck zu seinem 65. Geburtstag* ed Hermann Michael Niemann, et al. Beitrage zur Erforschung des Alten Testaments und des Antiken Judentums 37 ed Matthias Augustin and Michael Mach. Bern: Peter Lang, 1994. 498 pp. Discusses the oracles against the nations, the themes, the relationships among the oracles and among the nations and Israel. Extensive literature review.

1040. Nishizu, Joseph, and Michael Urano. *Joel, Amos, Obadiah, Jonah, Micah, Nahum, and Habakkuk* (Japanese). Franciscan Biblical Institute. Tokyo: Chuo Shuppansha, 1986. vi + 342 pp. The Franciscan Biblical Institute has translated the Hebrew into Japanese. The oracles can be traced back to Amos himself but editorial additions came later. Rev, OTA 10 (1987), 94.

1041. Nishizu, Teruo J. "Amos 4:4-5, A Post-Exilic Redaction" (Japanese). *Nanzan Theological Journal* 6 (Feb 83), 1-21 (Japanese). Usually considered a Josianic addition, Nishizu sees it as postexilic, reflective of the Jerusalemite priests. Rev, OTA 7 (1984), 73.

1042. Nissinen, Marti. *Prophetie, Redaktion und Fortschreibung im Hoseabuch: Studien zum Wedegang eines Prophetenbuches im Lichte von Hos 4 und 11*. Altes Orient und Altes Testament 121 ed Kurt Bergerhof, et al. Kevelaer/ Neukirchen-Vluyn: Butzon und Bercker/Neukirchener, 1991. xi +406 pp. The introduction reviews methods of research with a focus on the MT. The two chapters are then analyzed with an emphasis on the theological dimension with particular comparisons of the deuteronomic influence, the cult, covenant, cow motif, Baal Peor, Amos, Isaiah, Jeremiah.

1043. Noain, Enrique. "Amos." pp. 498-503 in *Biblia para la iniciacion cristiana: 1. Antiguo Testamento* ed Noain. Madrid: Heroes, 1977. 528 pp. Introduction, unit headings and annotation for Christian initiates - converts, confirmands - with selected portions of the text of *Nueva Biblia Espanola* ed Luis Alonso Schokel and Juan Mateos. The text is illustrated with drawings and poster like sayings. Margins have cross references to other verses of scripture. The introduction notes the justice of God, the judgment on Israel and the nations, the visions of the future, the prediction of restoration.

1044. Noble, Paul R. "'I Will Not Bring "It" Back' (Amos 1:3): A Deliberately Ambiguous Oracle?" ET 106, No. 4 (Jan 95), 105-109. Reviews the debate on the meaning and who or what is "It" with a critique of several scholarly opinions.

1045. Noble, Paul R. "Israel among the Nations." *Horizons in Biblical Theology* 15, No. 1 (June 93), 56-82. Amos 1:3-3:2. Contre Barre, the theology is not covenant or treaty terminology. The nations are condemned for inhuman cruelty rather than Israelite law. To be the people of God, means following common moral standards but also more than this. In rejecting God's law, Judah and Israel have rejected that which makes them unique among the nations. They have rejected God's grace.

1046. Noble, Paul R. "The Literary Structure of Amos: A Thematic Analysis." JBL 114, No. 2 (Sum 95), 209-226. Reviews the literature and notes the book as a whole is united by structural parallelism and themes, not divine speech formulae.

1047. Nogalski, James. "Amos." pp. 74-122 in *Literary Precursors to the Book of the Twelve*. BZAW 217 ed Otto Kaiser. Berlin: de Gruyter, 1993. ix + 301 pp. Diss (part of), University of Zurich, 1991. The Twelve are related via catchwords at the end which lead into the next text. Joel 4:1-21 leads to Amos 1:1-2:16 while Amos 9:1-15 leads to Obad 1-10 (pp. 24-21). Translation, exegetical notes, comparison versions, e.g., LXX and MT, earlier studies. The Amos study reviews macrostructure, literary units, function and growth. The latter includes future restoration, political dominion, eschatological-agricultural abundance.

1048. Nogalski, James D. "A Teaching Outline for Amos." R&E 92, No. 2 (Spr 95), 147-151. Commentary on each of the book's four sections, with notes on earlier opinions and bibliography.

1049. Nogalski, James D. "The problematic suffixes of Amos 9:11." VT 43, No. 3 (July 93), 411-418. A feminine plural, masculine singular and feminine singular all seem to refer to the booth of David. LXX reads all three as feminine singular. Scholars have followed the LXX or tried to avoid the problems. Nogalski notes the use of feminine singular nouns with plural adjectives and delineates the structure to show the reference is to the cities destroyed in the Babylonian destruction. The material is a later addition to the text.

1050. Nola, Alfonso M. di. "Amos, Libro di." Vol. 1 (1970), cols 306-309 in *Enciclopedia delle Religioni* ed Mario Gozzini, et al. Firenze:

Vallecchi, 1970-1976. Discusses the title, Amos' status as a prophet, historical context (Jeroboam II, the shrines, Hosea), his message, bibliography.

1051. Notscher, Friedrich. "Amos." Vol 3:714-741 in "Zwolfprophetenbuch oder Kleine Propheten." Vol 3:665-851 in *Die Heilige Schrift in Deutscher Ubersetzung* [Echter-Bibel] ed Friedrich Notscher, et al. Wurzburg: Echter, 1958. (original, *Zwolfprophetenbuch oder Kleine Propheten.* Echter Bibel. Wurzburg, 1948. 187 pp.) Translation and commentary.

1052. Nowack, Wilhelm. "Amos." pp. 118-175 in *Die kleinen Propheten ubersetzt und erklart*, 2nd ed. Handkommentar zum Alten Testament In Verbindung mit anderen Fachgelehrten, Part 3. Die prophetischen Bucher, Vol. 4, ed Nowack. Gottingen: Vandenhoeck und Ruprecht, 1903. vi + 446 pp. (original, 1897; 3rd ed, 1922) The introduction reviews the man, his time, the book, his significance in the history of religious development.

O.

1053. O'Brien, J. Randall. "Amos." pp. 24-26 in *Mercer Dictionary of the Bible* ed Watson E. Mills, et al. Macon, GA: Mercer University Press, 1990. xxx + 987 + 64 [maps, photographs] pp. Amos was not a venal "prophet for profit" hired by the king. The false prophets and kept priests were immoral. Amos was stunned by the social ills. Those in true covenant with Yahweh show it by ethical living. Perhaps because his message was rejected, he put it in writing to seek vindication in time. He is not mentioned elsewhere in the Bible. Amos was a highly literate person with analogy, metaphor, vivid imagery, with gifts as an orator and thinker of the highest order. His book is a typical sermon and his ministry may have been no longer than 30 minutes. He wailed his woe-cry over Israel, a lament for the dead. Israel's hour of grace was past. The Day of the Lord is darkness but he left the door open for repentance.

1054. O'Brien, J. Randall. "Amos, Book of." pp. 26-27 in *Mercer Dictionary of the Bible* ed Watson E. Mills, et al. Macon, GA: Mercer University Press, 1990. xxx + 987 + 64 [maps, photographs] pp. The earliest surviving collection in book form. Gives an outline of the book. Ch 1-6 are the words of Amos while 7-9 are his visions. He prophesies the doom of Israel. There is a note of hope but scholars debate its authenticity.

1055. O'Connell, Robert H. "Telescoping N + 1 Patterns in the Book of Amos." VT 46, No. 1 (Jan 96), 56-73. Outlines the book as a series of these, e.g., "for three transgressions and for four" - judgment, woe, vision, eschatological promises.

1056. Odelain, O. and R. Sequineau. "Amos." p. 26 in *Dictionary of Proper Names and Places in the Bible*. Garden City, NY: Doubleday, 1981. xli + 481 pp. A native of Tekoa whom God called to go to Bethel to preach even though he was not a professional prophet. He attacked the luxury of the rich, oppression of the poor, formalistic worship. Quoted twice in the NT Book of Acts.

1057. Oesterley, W.O.E. "Amos 2:8. 'Pledged Clothes'." ET 13, No. 1 (Oct '01), 40-41. Exegesis with transcription of the Hebrew, comparison with LXX and other OT sources for clothes or cloth beside the altar, and ANE practices. In Amos' verse, the clothing spread out by corrupt priests is an offering to Asherah.

1058. Oesterley, W.O.E. *Studies in the Greek and Latin Versions of the Book of Amos*. Cambridge: University Press, 1902. viii + 112 pp. Thesis, B.D., Jesus College, Cambridge. Reviews the text of uncial Q (Hesychian) and cursive 22 (Lucianic) with critical apparatus in parallel columns (pp. 25-61), the Greek versions of Aquila, Theodotion and Symmachus, other manuscripts, as well as the Old Latin and Vulgate. The study shows the Greek text was fluid with enormous variety.

1059. Oesterley, W.O.E. "The Symbolism of the 'Pair of Shoes' in Amos 2:6." *Society of Biblical Archaeology, Proceedings* (London) 23, No. 172 (Jan 1901), 36-38. The shoe is a conventional symbol in legal transactions. "To cast over" is to take possession. "To take off" or "give up" is renunciation. The rich took the shoe or forced the peasant to give it up, i.e., give up his land. George Adam Smith said Amos' era was very "modern."

1060. Oesterley, W.O.E. and Theodore H. Robinson. "The Book of Amos." pp. 363-368 in *An Introduction to the Books of the Old Testament*. Living Age Books. NY: Meridian, 1958. xvi + 454 pp. (original 1934) Reviews the historical background, structure and contents, date and authorship, man and message. Outwardly people were rich but the society was rotten. Discusses the oracles against the nations, the law of causation, the visions. Most of the book is from Amos. Amos may have witnessed an eclipse, which would be June 763 BCE. He came from rugged country and work, and could see the spiritual dangers in Israel. He had a remedy in justice. Religiosity is no substitute for God's moral demands. MT is well preserved but LXX is helpful at points.

1061. Oettli, Samuel. *Amos und Hosea: Zwei Zeugen gegen die Anwendung der Evolutionstheorie auf die Religion Israels. Drei theologische Ferienkursvortrage mit einem textkritischen Anhang.* Beitrage zur Forderung Christlichen Theologie 5, No. 4 ed U. Schlatter and H. Cremer. Gutersloh: Bertelsmann, 1901. iii + 107. Exegesis and commentary, Amos (pp. 64-77). The introduction discusses the evolutionary theory of the development of Israelite religion, the main ideas of the two prophets and the relationship of the nation's history and the religious significance of the prophets.

1062. Oettli, Samuel. "Der Kultus bei Amos und Hosea." pp. 1-34 in *Griefswalder Studien. Theologische Abhandlungen Hermann Cremer.* Gutersloh: Bertelsmann, 1895. iv + 356 pp. Discusses the historical background, various interpretations, animal sacrifices, cult personnel. The prophetic polemic against the cult is not yet an absolute ban but an attempt to relate it to the heart of God.

1063. Ogden, Daniel Kelly. "The Earthquake Motif in the Book of Amos." pp. 69-80 in *Goldene Apfel in silbernen Schalen: Collected Communications to the XIIIth Congress of the International Organization for the Study of the Old Testament, Leuven 1989* ed Klaus-Dietrich Schunck and Matthias Augustin. Beitrag zur Erforschung des Alten Testaments und des antiken Judentums 20, ed Matthias Augustin and Michael Mach. Frankfurt am Main: Lang, 1992. 179 pp. [Pr 25:12 golden apples in a silver setting]. Ogden cites archaeological evidence for earthquakes, which may be the one in the reign of King Uzziah. Describes, discusses seismic language and imagery and other natural phenomena in the Book of Amos.

1064. Ogilvie, Lloyd J. "Amos." pp. 261-364 in *Hosea, Joel, Amos, Obadiah, Jonah.* The Communicator's Commentary 20 ed Ogilvie. Dallas, TX: Word, 1990. xiv + 436 pp. The introduction reviews the political, social and religious background, the man, his book, his teaching. Amos was a sheep breeder, cattle man and fig grower with big flocks/herds. His business took him to the northern kingdom of Israel. He preached two years before the earthquake, which dates him to 762 BCE. Amos brings us to Calvary with humility and repentance.

1065. Ohlsen, Woodrow, ed. "Amos." pp. 182-206 in *Perspectives on Old Testament Literature*, ed Ohlsen. NY: Harcourt Brace Jovanovich, 1978. xiii + 450 pp. Gives an introduction to Amos, followed by three reprints (Harper, Anderson, Smith), concluded with suggested readings and discussion questions.

1066. Old, Hughes Oliphant. "Calvin's Theology of Worship: The Prophetic Criticism of Worship." pp. 73-87 in *Calvin Studies III: Papers Presented at a Colloquium on Calvin Studies at Davidson College and Davidson College Presbyterian Church, 1986* ed John H. Leith. Davidson, NC: Davidson College, 1986. 99 pp. The title in the text is "John Calvin and the Prophetic Criticism of Worship." Amos 5:21-24 is a major example. Calvin did not despise solemn assemblies, songs, organ music. He knew many OT passages say God is pleased with sacrifice, the smell of incense. The difference is the inner attitude with which one worships. God wants a sincere heart.

1067. Olmo Lete, Gregorio del. "La Vocacion de Amos (Amos 7:10-17; 9:1-4)." pp. 179-207 in *La Vocacion del Lider en el Antiguo Israel. Morfologia de las Relatos Biblicos de Vocacion*. Bibliotheca Salmanticensis III, Studia 2. Salamanca: Universidad Pontificia Salamanca, 1973. 467 pp. Diss. Universidad Pontificia Salamanca, 1973. The author discusses the concept of election and calling, gives a general overview of scholarly interpretations, analyzes the calling of Abraham, Amos, et al. The focus of the essay on Amos is Amos the *nabi*, with an introduction to the texts, Spanish translation, critical apparatus, a study of the structure of the text, the visions, the relationship of visions and call, the form and theological significance of the visions. The entire study refers to scholarly perspectives specifically related to the passage.

1068. Olyan, Saul M. "The Oaths of Amos 8:14." pp. 121-149 in *Priesthood and Cult in Ancient Israel* ed Gary A. Anderson and Olyan. JSOT Supplement 125 ed David J.A. Clines and Philip R. Davies. Sheffield: JSOT, 1991. 217 pp. This is ch 1 of his Problems in the History of the Cult and Priesthood in Ancient Israel. Diss. Harvard University, 1985. 232 pp. DAI 47, No. 1 (July 86), 211. Gives a transcription and translation, review of the literature and debates, exegesis, textual comparison, MT and LXX, the identification of the gods, the sanctuary of Beersheba, the bull icons at Dan and Bethel, pilgrimage. The oaths in Amos are critical of the pilgrimage, lacking covenant, and covenant behavior. "Pilgrims may seek Yahweh from Dan to Beersheba but they will not find him."

1069. O'Neill, Dennis Michael. The Attitudes of Amos, Hosea, Jeremiah, and Deutero-Isaiah concerning the Man/God relationship: A Study in Hebraic Monotheism. Ann Arbor, MI: University Microfilms, 1979. viii + 137 pp. Diss. Michigan State University, 1979. Available in microfilm, 1 reel, 35 mm. DAI 40,No. 4 (Oct 79), 2126. Monotheism as currently used is inadequate (scholars debate when "it" began with no consensus of what "it" is). O'Neill expands it via Ludwig Feuerbach to the essential nature of God as isomorphically related to that of man. To know God is to become one with him. The proper function of the Hebrew discloses the nature of God. The essential nature of both is the same. The text reviews the types of monotheism promulgated by scholars. A review of Aristotle's theology shows that his system of thought fulfills the criteria for an expanded concept of monotheism - there is one God whose nature is simple and a unity. An analysis of 31 relevant passages in the four prophets shows only Jeremiah is monotheistic.

1070. Ongaro, Giovanni. "Amos." vol 1 (1948), cols 1110-1112 in *Enciclopedia Cattolica*. Vatican City: Vatican, 1948. Discusses the name, the prophet's personal background ("I am not a prophet"), the book (content, structure, epilogue of hope).

1071. Oort, Henricus. "Amos." Vol 2 (1901), 865-881 in *Het Oude Testament opnieuw uit den Grondtekst Overgezet en van Inleidingen en Aanteekeningen Voorzien. Tweede Deel. Job - Maleachi* by Abraham Kuenen, et al. Leiden: Brill, 1899-1901. xii + 1105 pp. The introduction gives historical background, comparative textual study. The translation is annotated. Short introductions to sections of the text highlight history, main features and related matters.

1072. Oort, Henricus. "Amos and the Prophets by Profession (Amos 7; Num 11)." pp. 209-220 in *The Bible for Learners. Vol. II. From*

228   The Book of Amos

David to Josiah; From Josiah to the Supremacy of Mosaic Law by Oort, et al. Boston: Roberts, 1888. 1:vii + 546; 2:vii + 616 pp. Vol. II is by Oort. The English copyright is 1878. Tr from Dutch (n.d.). Amos was very poor but also very learned - he could speak and write very well. He knew history and theology. Oort discusses the content, the meeting with Amaziah, Amos' response, the nature of prophecy and prophets, Moses' hope that all people could be Yahweh's prophets. Oort calls the latter tradition a legend.

1073. Oort, Henricus. "De Echtheid van Amos 4:13, 5:8,9; 9:5,6." *Theologisch Tijdschrift* 25 (1891), 125-126.

1074. Oort, Henricus. "Het Vaderland van Amos." *Theologisch Tijdschrift* 25 (1891), 121-125. Discusses the homeland and work of Amos, notes earlier studies, and exegesis.

1075. Oort, Henricus. "De profeet Amos." *Theologisch Tijdschrift* 14 (1880), 114-158. Selected studies in Amos. An index gives the verses cited.

1076. Oosterhoff, Berend J. "Amos." pp. 252-253 in *The World of the Old Testament*. Bible Handbook 2 ed A.S. van der Woude, et al. Grand Rapids, MI: Eerdmans, 1989. xi + 300 pp. tr from the Dutch, *Bijbels Handboek, Deel IIa: Het Oude Testament*. Kampen: Kok, 1982. A general introduction notes the prophets did more than predict the future. They proclaimed the word of God, a call to love and justice. The discussion of Amos includes the man, his time, book, preaching. The latter included judgment for sin - injustice, oppression. There will be a remnant but only to show the effectiveness of judgment, not as a blessing.

1077. Orchard, W.E. "Amos." pp. 11-52 in *Oracles of God: Studies in the Minor Prophets*. London: Clarke, 1922. 244 pp. Reviews the historical and personal background, the danger of chosenness (some think it gives license to be immoral), the problems of ritual, Amaziah the priest, the harshness of the message but Amos broke the false connection of worship and injustice.

1078. Orelli, Conrad von (1846-1912). "Amos." pp. 103-155 in *The Twelve Minor Prophets*. Minneapolis: Klock & Klock, 1977. vii +

405 pp. Reprint, Edinburgh: Clark, 1897. 3rd ed, 1908. Tr (1893) of *Die zwolf kleinen Propheten.* Kurzgefasster Kommentar zu den heiligen Schriften Alten und Neuen Testamentes, Series A, 5:2, ed Hermann Strack und Otto Zockler. Munich: Beck, 1888. 2nd ed, 1896. vi + 224 pp. The general introduction notes the Twelve have been together as one book, at least since Eccles 49:10. Orelli suggests they were collected soon after Malachi and it is probable that the majority were found together before the Exile. Translation plus notes (exegesis), followed by exposition at appropriate intervals. The introduction to the book of Amos reviews the man and his time, the well arranged book (by Amos himself).

1079. Orienti, Sandra. "Amos: Iconografia." vol 1 (1961), cols 1027-1028 in *Bibliotheca Sanctorum,* 12 volumes. Rome: Istituto Giovanni XXIII of the Pontificia Universita Lateranense, 1961-1970 (including Index). Discusses the representation of Amos in church art.

1080. Orlinsky, Harry M. and Milton Weinberg. "The Masora on *'anawim* in Amos 2:1." pp. 25-36 in *Estudios Masoreticos (V Congreso de la IOMS) Dedicados a Harry M. Orlinsky* ed Emilia Fernandez Tejero. Textos y Estudios "Cardenal Cisneros" de la Biblia Poliglota Matritense 33, ed Federico Perez Castro, et al. Madrid: Instituto "Arias Montano" C.S.I.C., 1987. 250 pp. CSIC = Consejo Superior de Investigaciones Cientificas. Amos 2:7. Examines the variation between *'nwim* and *'nwiim* and the Massora concern with what is written as compared with what is read, with a note that this is a mistake. The authors conclude that the warning of a mistake is itself a mistake.

1081. Orlinsky, Harry M. and Milton Weinberg. "Notes on some *Masora Parva* of Amos." *Sefarad* (Madrid) 46, Nos. 1-2 (1986), 381-390. This volume is a festschrift for Federico Perez Castro. The *masora parva* are not what they appear to be. They draw on the Cairo, Aleppo, Petrograd, Leningrad codices, the 2nd edition of the *Biblia Rabbinica,* the 3rd edition of the *Biblia Hebraica* (BHK) and *Biblia Hebraica Stuttgartensia* (BHS), the *masora magna* (MM), the *masora finalis* (MF), the *masora parva* (MP), plus scholars such as Frensdorff and C.D.Ginsburg.

1082. Orton, Job (1717-1783). "The Book of the Prophet Amos." Vol 6:336-366 in *A Short and Plain Exposition of the Old Testament with Devotional and Practical Reflections for the Use of Families,* 6 vols. Shrewsbury: Eddowes, et al., 1741. Vol 6:xxxii + 519. Published from manuscripts by Robert Gentleman. 2nd ed, 1791; 3rd ed, 1822. A short introduction gives historical background with a summary of Amos. Prints the text chapter by chapter with annotations to the text and reflections, including application, e.g., to families, in Orton's day.

1083. Osborn, Andrew R. "The Responsibility of Privilege." Amos 1-3:2." *Biblical Review* 16, No. 4 (Oct '31), 574-578. Notes ancient and more recent atrocities, and our responsibility for them. We cannot plead noblesse oblige, or our chosen place in the universe. Our responsibility is the exact opposite. Notes Amos' background and character.

1084. Osswald, Eva. Urform und Auslegung im Masoretischen Amostext. Ein Beitrag zur Kritik an der Neueren Traditionsgeschichtlichen Methode. Diss. Jena, 1951. Reviewed in TLZ 80, No. 3 (Mar 55), 179. Reviews the history of interpretation of Amos.

1085. Osswald, Eva. "Die Botschaft der Propheten des 8. Jahrhunderts V. Chr. - Amos - Hosea - Jesaja - Micha." pp. 84-112 in *Von Bileam bis Jesaja. Studien zum Alttestamentlichen Prophetie von ihren Anfangen bis zur 8. Jahrhundert V. Chr. Im Auftrag der Alttestamentlichen Arbeitsgemeinschaft in der DDR* ed Gerhard Wallis. Berlin: Evangelische Verlagsanstalt, 1984. 128 pp. A general discussion including the broken relationship with God, the paradox of Israel, the intervention of Yahweh, the problem of the repudiation of Israel, the remnant. Her discussion draws on all four prophets.

1086. Osten-Sacken, Peter von der. "Die Bucher der Tora als Hutte der Gemeinde. Amos 5:26f. in der Damaskusschrift." ZAW 91, No. 3 (1979), 423-435. On CD VII:13-19.

1087. Osty, Emile. "Amos." pp. 1343-1353 in *La Bible de Jerusalem: La Sainte Bible traduite en francais sous la direction de l'Ecole Biblique de Jerusalem, Nouvelle edition revue et augmentee.* Paris:

Cerf, 1977. 1844 pp. The revision has moved the introductory material to a general introduction (pp. 1069-1091) to the prophets edited and revised by Roland de Vaux. Amos is pp. 1085-1086. The text of Amos is divided into four sections: oracles against the nations, judgment on Israel, Amos' visions, the future hope. The text is extensively annotated.

1088. Osty, Emile. "Amos." pp. 7-60 in *Amos. Osee*, 2nd ed. La Sainte Bible traduite en francais sous la direction de l'Ecole Biblique de Jerusalem (this fascicle was under the direction of J. Trinquet and Michel Carrouges). Paris: Cerf, 1960. 123 pp. (original, 1952) The introduction notes the book's place in the canon, the prophet himself, his message, the book with analytical outline, its influence, the problems of text and translation. The commentary provides a French translation with annotation. It is in four sections: judgment on the nations, threats to Israel, the visions, the restoration.

1089. Osty, E. and J. Trinquet. *La Bible. Les Petits Prophetes: Osee, Joel, Amos, Abdias, Jonas, Michee, Nahum, Habacuc, Sophonie, Aggee, Zacharie, Malachie*. Lausanne: Rencontre, 1972. 434 pp.

1090. Osty, Emile and Joseph Trinquet. *La Bible: Traduction francaise sur les textes originaux introductions et notes*. np: Seuil, 1973. They give a short introduction to the minor prophets, p. 1939. Amos is pp. 1972-1990. An introduction gives an outline and discusses authorship, sources. The text is French translation with annotation.

1091. Otzen, Benediki. "Amos og afguderne." *Norsk Teologisk Tidsskrift* 84, No. 3 (1983), 167-185. Amos was a reformer. A review essay on Hans M. Barstad, *Studies in the Religious Polemics in the Book of Amos*. Oslo, 1981. Rev, OTA 7 (1984), 72.

1092. Ouellette, Jean. "Le mur d'etain dans Amos 7:7-9." RB 80, No. 3 (July 73), 321-331. It's a wall of tin.

1093. Ouellette, Jean. "The Shaking of the Threshholds in Amos 9:1." HUCA 43 (1972), 23-27. There is no need to postulate the threat of an earthquake. More likely it is a threat of someone, Yahweh in this case, who will force their way into the temple at Bethel to lay hands on those who have taken sanctuary there. Discusses the Akkadian cognates, the pivot stones of the door posts, altars of refuge, the certainty of divine judgment.

1094. Overholt, Thomas W. "Commanding the Prophets: Amos and the Problem of Prophetic Authority." CBQ 41, No. 4 (Oct 79), 517-532. Part of the prophet's authority is divine (7:15, etc.) but part is social - the response of the people. Comparative study includes a prophet Wodziwob among the Paiute Indians of Nevada (founder of the Ghost Dance of 1870), Handsome Lake (founder of the Long House religion of the Iroquois), and the Cargo cults of New Guinea.

1095. Owens, John Joseph. "Exegetical Studies in the Book of Amos." R&E 63, No. 4 (Fall 66), 429-440. Study of selected passages.

P.

1096. Paas, Stefan. "De HERR als Schepper en koning: de hymnen in Amos." *Nederlands Theologisch Tijdschrift* 49, No. 2 (Ap 95), 124-139. A discussion of the hymns of Amos, their style, content, background, comparison with Jeremiah and others.

1097. Paas, Stefan. "'He Who Builds His Stairs into Heaven...' (Amos 9:6a)." UF 25 (1993), 319-325. Kings often sat on a throne situated on a platform, with stairs leading to the throne. In Egyptian symbolism, both represent the Primeval Mound. The god ascended the stairs and then turned the chaos into cosmos. Amos' imagery reflects this tradition, applied to Yahweh.

1098. Padilla, Washington. "Amos." pp. 9-201 in *Amos-Abdias*. Comentario Biblico Hispanoamericano ed Justo L. Gonzalez, et al. Miami, FL: Editorial Caribe, 1989. 244 pp. Rev, pp. 15-226. 1993. 271 pp. The introduction reviews the man, his time, the book, his message. A detailed outline divides the book into three parts. In addition to the translation and commentary, excursi give in depth studies of injustice, society, visions, etc.

1099. Pannier, E. "Amos." Vol 1 (1903), cols 1117-1120 in *Dictionnaire de Theologie Catholique* (DTC), 15 vols, ed A. Vacant, et al. Paris: Letouzey and Ane, 1903-1950. 1:xii pp. + 2664 cols. Discusses the name, the man, the historical background, geography, divisions of the book, messianic prophecies, texts, versions and commentaries.

1100. Park, Yune Sun. "Amos." pp. 171-226 in *A Commentary on the Minor Prophets*. Seoul, Korea: Yung Eum Sa, 1969. 514 pp.

1101. Parker, Bernice. "From Sound to Sense (1992)." pp. 9-10 in *Many Voices: Multicultural Responses to the Minor Prophets* ed Alice Ogden Bellis. Lanham, MD: University Press of America, 1995.

xiv + 101 pp. The writers in this book try to apply the minor prophets today. An Amos type oracle of judgment against talk and worship that does not translate into living - rap with no map.

1102. Parker, Simon B. "Amos." pp. 367-374 in *The Books of the Bible.* Vol. 1. *The Old Testament/Hebrew Bible* ed Bernhard W. Anderson. NY: Scribner's, 1989. xix + 435 pp. The first prophet whose words were collected as an independent literary work. Reviews the background in northern Israel and the response to his message. Amos responded to their indifference, complacency and hostility. He begins with something they can agree with and then exposes their guilt and the coming punishment. Gives an outline of the content and reviews the major issues in interpretation and various views on these. The message is presented as coming from God. Interpreters give historical and psychological descriptions of it. It is not clear if he was merely announcing bad news or if he was hoping to change people. There is disagreement on how much of the book is from Amos and how much is by others.

1103. Parmentier, R. "Amos reecrit pour 1978." *Dialogue* 79-80 (Paris) (1978) = pp. 49-70 in *Actualisation de la Bible.* Paris, 1982.

1104. Paterson, John. "Amos: Prophet of Righteousness." pp. 11-37 in *The Goodly Fellowship of the Prophets: Studies, Historical, Religious, and Expository in the Hebrew Prophets.* NY: Scribner's, 1948. xiii + 313 pp. A general introduction on prophecy is followed by individual treatment of each. Discusses the man, his prophet status as a new thing, his personal history, his thought (steeped in nature, insight), historical background, his ministry (pleas for mercy, call for justice), teaching (Yahweh vs Canaanite culture; justice not sacrifice). Whether Amos was a monotheist is less important than God as a world God. Israel as elected has greater responsibility but has sinned in exploiting the poor, lacking justice, flaunting wealth, mechanical religion, pride. Judgment is coming.

1105. Paton, Lewis Bayles. "Amos 5:14." BW 13, No. 3 (Mar 1899), 196-197. Amos and people agreed God was with them, but they thought this meant regardless of morality. Amos said God's continuing presence depended on righteousness.

1106. Paton, Lewis Bayles. "Amos at Bethel." pp. 207-220 in *The Bible as Literature* ed Richard G. Moulton, et al. NY: Crowell, 1896. xviii + 375 pp. Gives background of history and of Amos as a sheep-master, who through his call was led to a higher idea of God as the first cause. Describes the wealth and the sins of Israel, and God's judgement. The book is not a single sermon but the substance of his preaching which was offensive to all classes of society. He went back to Tekoa and wrote the book.

1107. Paton, Lewis Bayles. "Did Amos Approve the Calf-Worship at Bethel?" JBL 13, No. 1 (1894), 80-90. The author of Kings condemns calf worship but recognizes that King Jeroboam was using the bull as a symbol of Yahweh and not idolatry. Amos does not mention the calves. The worship of Yahweh at Bethel, Dan, Gilgal, Beersheba was legitimate. Bethel and its people will be destroyed. But it is not some detail that is erroneous. The entire popular idea of Yahweh is wrong. Hosea is the first to mention the calves but he too saw the whole system as corrupt.

1108. Paul, Shalom M. *Amos: A Commentary on the Book of Amos*, ed Frank Moore Cross. Hermeneia, ed Cross, et al. Minneapolis: Fortress, 1991. xxvii + 408 pp. The introductory material gives a general overview, discusses literary origins, authenticity. The commentary gives translation, commentary and notes, exegetical and reference. There are three sectional introductions, two excursi (the doxologies and the visions), 69 pp. general bibliography. The closing oracles are often ascribed to a late editor but Paul shows how they are in Amos' language and represent his concerns.

1109. Paul, Shalom. "Amos: A Commentary on the Book of Amos." *Shofar* 12, No. 4 (Sum 91), 145-147.

1110. Paul, Shalom M. *Amos: Introduction and Commentary* (Heb). Mikra LeYisrae'el: A Bible Commentary for Israel ed Moshe Greenberg and Shmuel Ahituv. Tel Aviv/Jerusalem: Am Oved/Magnes (Hebrew University), 1994. vi + 162 pp. Bound with Mordechai Cogan's *Joel*.

1111. Paul, Shalom M. "Amos 1:3-2:3: A Concatenous Literary Pattern." JBL 90, No. 4 (Dec 71), 397-403. Reviews the history of interpretation. Notes a pattern in which catch words and ideas are common only to contiguous units. The oracles are welded together by this pattern, whether by Amos or a later editor.

1112. Paul, Shalom M. "Amos 3:3-8: The Irresistible Sequence of Cause and Effect." *Hebrew Annual Review* 7 (1983), 203-220. Amos draws his audience into the flow of the relationship of all events and happenings. The prophet is compelled by God to speak. Prophecy is also cause and effect. It is useless for people to threaten him to keep quiet. Once commanded, he must speak. Amos adapted the style of the wisdom teacher to this pericope but it remains unique. Paul shows a literary pattern characterized by symmetry and concatenation. Gives a transcription of the Hebrew with exegesis and commentary.

1113. Paul, Shalom M. "Amos 3:15 - Winter and Summer Mansions." VT 28, No. 3 (July 78), 358-359. The wealthy followed the example of royalty and built separate homes for summer and winter.

1114. Paul, Shalom M. "Fishing Imagery in Amos 4:2." JBL 97, No. 2 (June 78), 183-190. Reviews the varied attempts to understand this verse. Paul translates "And you will be transported in baskets and the very last one of you in fisherman's pots."

1115. Paul, Shalom M. "A Literary Reinvestigation of the Authenticity of the Oracles Against the Nations in Amos." pp. 187-205 in *De la Torah au Messie. Etudes d'exegese et d'hermeneutique bibliques offertes a Henri Cazelles pour ses 25 annees d'enseignement a l'Institut Catholique de Paris (Octobre 1979)* ed Maurice Carrez, et al. Paris: Desclee, 1981. 648 pp. The oracles are related in literary fashion with catch words, phrases and ideas. This shows unity and authenticity. Amos's "poetic devices and rhetorical skill are ever a source of admiration."

1116. Payne, J. Barton. "Amos." pp. 412-418 in *Encyclopedia of Biblical Prophecy. The Complete Guide to Scriptural Predictions and Their Fulfillment*. NY: Harper & Row, 1973. In 144 pages, Payne reviews nature and identification of prediction and of fulfillment. Gives the historical background of Amos. The book is in two parts: messages of judgment in chs 1-6, and, the rest of the book with visions of wrath, grace, visions. The doom of Samaria appears in 47 of the 85 vss of prediction (58% of the book's 146 vss), with 25 other topics. Verse-by-verse analysis of predictions in pp. 413-418.

1117. Peckham, Brian. "Amos." pp. 158-183 in *History and Prophecy: The Development of Late Judean Literary Traditions*. The Anchor Bible Reference Library. NY: Doubleday, 1993. xiv + 880 pp. Amos is presented as one of the prophetic paradigms. Isaiah challenged beliefs while Amos challenged practice. A revisor brought it up to date to include the fall of Judah, restrict punishment for the guilty and pardon for the innocent. Peckham reviews the structure and organization, language and style, compositional process, sources and interpretation. Amos wanted justice. He called on his hearers to seek Yahweh and live. The editor had different ideas. People had sinned by worshipping other gods. Amos' Israel came to an end but the editor's did not. Amos is discussed on p. 706.

1118. Peifer, Claude J. "Amos the Prophet: The Man and His Book." BT 19, No. 5 (Sep 81), 295-300. God will destroy Israel for their crimes against their own brothers and sisters. Describes the structure, the man, the making of the book. The latter was edited by Judahites after the fall of Samaria. In the exile, two salvation oracles were added. So were oracles against Tyre, Judah and Israel. The book gives us Amos' message and also tells us what it meant for succeeding generations. Amos condemned sin and prophesied destruction.

1119. Pelser, H.S. "Amos 3:11 - A Communication." pp. 153-156 in *Studies on the Book of Amos: Papers Read at 8th Meeting of Die Ou Testamentiese Werkgemeenskap in Suid-Afrika Held at Pretoria University 1965* ed A.H. van Zyl. OTWSA 7-8 (1964-1965). Potchefstroom: Pro Rege - Pers Beperk, 1965. pp. 113-169 pp. Bound with *Studies on the Book of Hosea*, the 7th Congress of the OTWSA, 111 pp., with continuous pagination for a total of 169 pp. An exegetical study of *usebib*, "round about"in 3:11, "An adversary (there shall be) even round about the land." This is the only instance of *sabib* used as a preposition or adverb in the singular construct state with the copula *u*. Notes various translations, MT,

LXX, etc., the history of interpretation, arguments pro and con, comparisons with other texts.

1120. Perez Castro, Federico, et al., eds. "Amos." pp. 49-71 in *El Codice de Profetas de el Cairo. Tome VII. Profetas Menores. Edicion de su Texto y Masoras*. Textos y Estudios "Cardenal Cisneros" de la Biblia Poliglota Matritense 20, ed Federico Perez Castro, et al. Madrid: Instituto "Arias Montano" C.S.I.C., 1979. 186 pp. CSIC = Consejo Superior de Investigaciones Cientificas. Hebrew text with critical apparatus. Part of the Cairo codex, the oldest (895 CE) of the Ben Asher codices. The Cairo codex is owned by the Karaite community in Cairo.

1121. Perez, Q. "El profeta Amos." *Sal Terrae* 9 (1920), 686-693, 804-811.

1122. Perlitt, Lothar. "Amos, Micha, Jesaja." pp. 135-139 in *Bundestheologie im Alten Testament*. Wissenschaftliche Monographien zum Alten und Neuen Testament 36, ed Gunther Bornkamm and Gerhard von Rad. Neukirchen-Vluyn: Neukirchener, 1969. viii + 300 pp. Discusses Deuteronomy (with exegesis of 2 Kgs 22f, 2 Kgs 17, Jer 11, Josh 23, Dt 29, the themes of the land, idols, the law, the promise to David, etc), the 8th century prophets (Amos, Micah, Isaiah, Hosea, etc), Sinai, Josh 24. Notes the history of interpretation for Amos, the lack of the terminology and the problem of the prophets and the covenant, the interpretation of Amos 3:2 as "You only have I recognized by covenant."

1123. Peters, John P. "Amos 5:6, 6:2." *Hebraica* 2, No. 3 (Ap 1886), 175. Amos 6:2 indicates a date of 711. Amos was still alive, or his disciples prepared his book to be included in Hezekiah's library.

1124. Peters, John P. "Miscellaneous Notes." *Hebraica* 1, No. 4 (Ap 1885), 242-243. Exegetical studies. Amos 1:6. Gaza is to be punished because they took Hebrews as captives and sold them as slaves in a time of peace. Amos 5:25-27. A pairing of opposites, e.g., the worship of the true God in the past, and, idolatry in the future.

1125. Pfeifer, Gerhard. "Amos und Deuterojesaja denkformenanalytisch verglichen." ZAW 93, No. 3 (1981), 439-443. A comparison of Amos 3:1-2 and Isaiah 45:18-19 in their understanding of Yahweh's word, the world and history, their thought pattern.

1126. Pfeifer, Gerhard. "Die Ausweisung eines lastigen Auslanders Amos 7:10-17" (The banishment of a troublesome foreigner, Amos 7:10-17). ZAW 96, No. 1 (1984), 112-118.

1127. Pfeifer, Gerhard. "Die Denkform des Propheten Amos (3:9-11)." VT 34, No. 4 (Oct 84), 476-481. An example of analysis using the patterns of thought.

1128. Pfeifer, Gerhard. "Denkformenanalyse als exegetische Methode, erlautert an Amos 1:2-2:16." ZAW 88, No. 1 (1976), 56-71. (Eng summary) Discusses this method and gives an example in Amos, with a review of earlier studies. The "movement of thought" aids exegesis, following the thought through literary units, noting development and connections. In Amos, we find repetition, concreteness, consistency interspersed among other "movements."

1129. Pfeifer, Gerhard. "Die Fremdvolkerspruche des Amos - spater *vaticinia ex eventu*?" VT 38, No. 2 (Ap 88), 230-233. A response to Volkmar Fritz. The oracles against the nations date before their destruction.

1130. Pfeifer, Gerhard. "Die Gottesnamen im Amosbuch." pp. 64-70 in *Haim M.I. Gevaryahu Memorial Volume*. Jerusalem: World Jewish Bible Center, 1990. The English-French-German section (iv + 145 pp.) is ed Joshua J. Adler. The Hebrew section (iii + 154 pp.) is ed Ben Zion Luria. Cites all the references and compares them with the LXX and earlier studies.

1131. Pfeifer, Gerhard. "'Ich bin in tiefe Wasser geraten, und die Flut will mich ersaufen' (Ps 69:3): Anregungen und Vorschlage zur Aufarbeitung wissenschaftlicher Sekundarliteratur." VT 37, No. 3 (July 87), 327-339. Proposes a bibliography of secondary literature for Amos. Gives (pp. 332-339) categories for Amos 2:4-5.

1132. Pfeifer, Gerhard. "Das Ja des Amos." VT 39, No. 4 (Oct 89), 497-503. A response to Smend's "No of Amos," EvT (Munich) 23 (1963), 404-423 (see #1373). Amos says yes to God's lawsuit against him, against his people and against the people of the world.

1133. Pfeifer, Gerhard. "Jahwe als Schopfer der Welt und Herr ihrer Machte in der Verkundigung de Propheten Amos." VT 41, No. 4 (Oct 91), 475-481. A study of the doxologies in Amos 4:13, 5:8-9, 9:5-6. Could be authentic.

1134. Pfeifer, Gerhard. "Das nachgestellte erlauternde Partizip - eine Stileigentumlichkeit des Amosbuches." Z fur Althebraistik (Stuttgart) 6 (1993), 235-238. Amos strives for preciseness in his statements by using the postpositive illustrative participle.

1135. Pfeifer, Gerhard. "'Rettung' als Beweis der Vernichtung (Amos 3:12)." ZAW 100, No. 2 (1988), 269-277. Denkformen analysis of Amos 3:12, an independent unit, with German translation and exegesis, review of earlier scholarly opinions, and related to Pfeifer's other essays on Amos. Only fragments will be left in Samaria as an example of its destruction.

1136. Pfeifer, Gerhard. Die Theologie des Propheten Amos. Frankfurt am Main: Peter Lang, 1995. 147 pp. A commentary on Amos, followed by analysis of the names used for God, the transactions of God with Amos (call, visions, etc.), Israel (the land, the end), the people (God as Lord), the world (doxologies, destruction).

1137. Pfeifer, Gerhard. "Uber den Unterschied Zwischen Schriftstellern des Zwanzigsten Jahrhunderts nach und des ersten Jahrtausends vor Christus. Zur entstehung des Amosbuches." VT 41, No. 1 (Jan 91), 123-127.

1138. Pfeifer, Gerhard. "Unausweichliche Konsequenzen: Denkformenanalyse von Amos 3:3-8." VT 33, No. 3 (July 83), 341-347. German translation with exegesis. Understanding of the patterns of thought help us identify the words of God, and of Amos.

1139. Pfeifer, Robert H. "The Book of the Twelve. 3. Amos." pp. 577-584 in Introduction to the Old Testament. NY: Harper & Brothers,

1941. xii + 909 pp. Gives the historical background, notes the brief character of Amos' ministry, his use of imagery, the message of destruction, his tears for the doom of Virgin Israel, editorial additions by Jews of Jerusalem between 500-250 BCE.

1140. Philippe, Elie. "Amos." Vol 1, Part 1 cols 512-518 in *Dictionnaire de la Bible*, 5 vols, ed Fulcran Vigouroux, et al. Paris: Letouzey et Ane, 1895-1912. Part 1:lxiv + 832 cols; Part 2:cols 833-1984. Each volume has two parts for a total of 10. Discusses the life of Amos, date and character of the prophecy, authenticity, outline, style, history of the text, messianism. Bibliography.

1141. Phillips, John. "Amos: The Cowboy Prophet." *Moody Monthly* (Chicago) 77, No. 7 (Mar 77), 35-37. Describes the fierce Assyrians, peaceful Egyptians, urbanized soft Israelites. Amos saw that their prosperity was superficial hiding injustice, idolatry. People were glad to hear him condemn their neighbors but objected when he condemned them. Within 50 years the predicted disaster fell.

1142. Phillips, J.B. "The Book of Amos." pp. 1-24 in *Four Prophets: Amos, Hosea, First Isaiah, Micah. A Modern Translation from the Hebrew*. London/NY: Bles/Macmillan, 1963. xxvii + 161 pp. + 2 maps. E.H. Robertson provides an essay on historical background. The general introduction discusses some problems, e.g., the LXX, the difficulty of the Hebrew, questions of style, the importance of the prophets. The introduction to Amos tells about him (a shepherd in the howling wilderness, a hard Calvinist), the theme of doom and denunciation, the only hope in the far future. The readable translation has no notes.

1143. Pigott, Susan M. "Amos: An Annotated Bibliography." SWJT 38, No. 1 (Fall 95), 29-35. Reviews general introductions, books, commentaries.

1144. Pilcher, Charles Venn. "Amos." pp. 135-206 in *Hosea, Joel, Amos: A Devotional Commentary*. London: Religious Tract Society, 1929. 207 pp. The study is divided into 17 units, with text and commentary, noting the various ways of interpreting the prophet.

1145. Pleins, J. David. Biblical Ethics and the Poor: The Language and
Structures of Poverty in the Writings of the Hebrew Prophets
(Oppression, Exploitation, Justice, Injustice). Diss. University of
Michigan, 1986. x + 336 pp. DAI 47, No. 6 (Dec 86), 2201.
Available in microfiche. Studies words for poor. Poverty is an
unjust structure of society. For Amos (pp. 163-181), Pleins
discusses creditors and debts, market practices, legal practices, the
judgment of God. Economic interests have replaced Yahwistic
ethics. There is irony in the situation. So many rich people will die,
their funerals will need poor people to mourn.

1146. Pollard, Edward Bagby (1864-1927). "Other Traditional
Misinterpretations." *Crozer Quarterly* (Chester, PA, 1924-52) 4,
No. 2 (Ap '27), 204-206. Amos 3:3. In a sparsely settled area,
people do not often travel the same way by chance. There was
agreement to meet, not agreement in doctrine.

1147. Polley, Max E. "Amos and the Davidic Empire." pp. 204-205 in
*Abstracts: American Academy of Religion/Society of Biblical
Literature 1986* ed Kent Harold Richards and James B. Wiggins.
Atlanta, GA: Scholars Press, 1986. i + 269 pp. The SBL section is
pp. 169-262 from the 122nd Annual Meeting. See his book same
title, NY: Oxford University, 1989. xii + 243 pp. (annotated in
entry #1148). The oracles against the nations are based on violation
of their covenant with David, the basis of his empire. Amos
supported a reunited empire. The oracle against Judah is a
Deuteronomic addition but the others are all by Amos. The north
will be exiled but will return to reunite with the south, accepting
rule over the whole area by David's descendants.

1148. Polley, Max E. *Amos and the Davidic Empire: A Socio-Historical
Approach.* NY: Oxford University, 1989. xii + 243 pp. Recent
scholarship has focused on the book as a literary work. Polley notes
recent research shows Amos' oracles fit in 8th century Canaan. He
reviews the historical background of kingship and state religion in
Egypt, Mesopotamia, Canaan, Judah and Israel. It is only then that
he looks at Amos' oracles against the nations and northern shrines.
Amos' concern is social justice and the just king. On this basis he
calls for repentance. The idea of a just king is also found in Ps 72,
Prov 16 and 29 and Isaiah 9 and 11. Amos castigated the state and

the wealthy for failing to live by this standard established presumably in the Davidic line of kings. He called the north to repent, and to reunite with the south. In the reborn nation, true religion centered in Jerusalem would be honored and the ideal Davidic king would establish justice.

1149. Pomykala, Kenneth E. *The Davidic Dynasty Tradition in Early Judaism: Its History and Significance for Messianism*. SBL Early Judaism and Its Literature 7 ed William Adler. Atlanta, GA: Scholars Press, 1995. Diss. Claremont Graduate School, 1992. Notes many earlier scholarly views. Reviews the biblical background (pre-exilic, exilic, post-exilic), Qumran and other sources. Amos 9:11-15 (pp. 61-63) is post-exilic. This is not an oracle about the Davidic dynasty but about Jerusalem. This is the only appearance of "booth of David" in the Hebrew Bible. There are two oracles, vss 11-12 on the booth of David, and 13-15 on future prosperity. Isaiah calls Jerusalem a booth.

1150. Poole, Matthew. "Amos." 2:898-921 in *A Commentary on the Holy Bible. Vol. II. Psalms-Malachi*. McLean, VA: MacDonald, n.d. Reprint. 2:ii + 1030 pp. A general introduction is followed by short notes and outline at the head of each chapter, and verse by verse commentary. Amos pronounced judgment on Israel and all the nations but closed with the promise of a spiritual state under the Messiah, full of grace and peace.

1151. Pope, M.A. "Le MRZH a l'Ugarit et ailleurs." *Annales Archeologiques Arabes Syriennes* 28/30 (1978-1980), 141-143.

1152. Porter, J.R. "*Bene-hannebi'im*." JTS 32, No. 2 (Oct 81), 423-429. This expression appears 10 times in the OT, nine of the examples with Elisha. The tenth is 1 Kgs 20:35. In Amos 7:14 there is a unique *ben-naby'* which most scholars relate to the longer form. If there is a connection, it may be that the sons of the prophets were opposed to the monarchy and so was Amos.

1153. Potter, Roland. "Spirituality of the Judean Desert III: Amos of Tekoa." *Life of the Spirit* (London) 14 (1959-1960), 349-358.

1154. Power, E. "Note to Amos 7:1." Bib 8, No. 1 (1927), 87-92. The word *lqs* means late grain from the Jan-Feb planting. The locusts are coming to destroy this crop.

1155. Prado, Juan. "Amos." Vol. 1 (1963), cols. 435-436 in *Enciclopedia de la Bible*, 6 vols, ed Juan Antonio Gutierrez- Larraya. Barcelona: Ediciones Garriga, 1963-1965. Reviews the life of Amos, including the accusation that he was an agitator and a seditionist.

1156. Prado, Juan. "Amos, Libro de." Vol. 1 (1963), cols. 436-440 in *Enciclopedia de la Bible*, 6 vols, ed Juan Antonio Gutierrez-Larraya. Barcelona: Ediciones Garriga, 1963-1965. Discusses the history of exegesis and the authenticity of the book, its literary and theological value.

1157. Prado, Juan. *Amos, el Profeta Pastor: Introduccion, version y commentario teologico popular*. Madrid: El Perpetuo Socorro, 1950. Cf. "'Emissiones Biblicas' de Radio Madrid." *Biblia y Predicacion* 2 (May-June 44).

1158. Praeger, Mirjam. "Amos, der Hirte aus Tekoa." *Bibel und Liturgie* 36 (1962-1963), 84-96, 164-172, 243-255, 295-308.

1159. Praetorius, Franz. "Bemerkungen zu Amos." ZAW 35, No. 1 (1915), 12-25. Exegesis of selected verses.

1160. Praetorius, Franz. *Die Gedichte des Amos: Metrische und Textkritische Bemerkungen*. Halle: Niemeyer, 1924. iii+ 46 pp. A study of poetic structure.

1161. Praetorius, Franz. "Zum Texte des Amos." ZAW 34, No. 1 (1914), 42-44. Exegesis of selected verses.

1162. Preminger, Alex and Edward L. Greenstein, eds. "Amos." pp. 270-275 in *The Hebrew Bible in Literary Criticism*. NY: Ungar, 1986. xvi + 619 pp. This is not literary criticism in the biblical studies sense of the term but a listing of writers who refer to Jonah - literary references in novels, biblical scholars, etc., e.g., St. Augustine, William R. Harper, Samuel Sandmel.

1163. Priero, G. "Super tribus sceleribus Damasci et super quattuor non convertam (Am 1:3)." *Palestra del Clero* (Roviga, Italy, 1921) 13, No. 1 (1934), 449-452.

1164. Priest, John. "The Covenant of Brothers." JBL 84, No. 4 (Dec 65), 400-406. The phrase appears in Amos 1:9. Brotherhood played a prominent role in ANE covenants as well as in Israel, e.g., with David and Jonathan. Tyre and Israel had such a treaty and the oracles against Tyre and Edom are both authentic to Amos.

1165. Prignaud, J. "Caftorim et Keretim." RB 71, No. 2 (1964), 215-229. Discusses the context for these peoples and various proposals for their identity.

1166. Procksch, Otto Caesar (1874-). *Die Geschichtsbetrachtung bei Amos, Hosea und Jeremia*. Konigsberg i. Pr.: Hartung, 1901. 44 pp. Available on microfilm. Amos is discussed on pp. 2-12, analyzing earlier studies, history, geography, relationship to other biblical materials.

1167. Procksch, Otto. *Geschichtsbetrachtung und Geschichtliche Uberlieferung bei den Vorexilischen Propheten*. Leipzig: Hinrichs, 1902. viii + 176 pp. Amos is considered as part of the decline of Ephraim (pp. 7-13) and under historical tradition (pp. 109-118) of this type of story, e.g., Sodom and Gomorrah. Notes numerous earlier studies, the role of the Patriarchs and Amos' use of the tradition.

1168. Procksch, Otto. "Amos." pp. 62-98 in *Die Kleinen Prophetischen Schriften vor dem Exil*. Erlauterungen zum Alten Testament 3 ed for Calwer Verlagsverein. Calwer/Stuttgart: Verlag der Vereinsbuchhandlung, 1910. 175 pp. 2nd ed. Stuttgart: Deichert [Scholl], 1929. A general introduction reviews the nature of prophecy, the historical background and the prophetic movement as a whole for this period. The introduction for Amos gives the immediate historic context, his background in Tekoa, his preaching at Bethel. The commentary is in sections with smaller sub-units with German translation, exegesis, comparison of relevant texts.

1169. Puech, Emile. "Milkom, le dieu ammonite, en Amos 1:15." *VT* 27, No. 1 (Jan 77), 117-125. Compares MT and LXX with that of Jer 49:3 (LXX 30:3) and other uses of the terms.

1170. Pusey, E.B. "Amos." 1:223-341 in *The Minor Prophets. A Commentary Explanatory and Practical. Vol. 1. Hosea, Joel, Amos, Obadiah and Jonah. Vol. 2. Micah, Nahum, Habakkuk, Zephaniah, Haggai, Zechariah and Malachi.* Grand Rapids, MI: Baker, 1950. 1:427 2:504. 1:10th printing, 1972. 2:11th printing 1971. (original 1860) The commentary is for the general reader. Technical matters are in the footnotes. The introduction reviews Amos' life, birthplace of Tekoa, prophecies at Samaria, God's power of nature, Amos' simple eloquence. Amos predicted the conversion of all the heathen after the fall of the Davidic dynasty. People did not believe it then and did not when He came.

1171. Putnam, Frederic. "Historical Amos." *Eternity* 33, No. 11 (Nov 82), 37-38. Gives the historical background, outline of the text, the history of redemption focusing on the covenant, archaeology (Beersheba, Ugarit, Samaria, Beth Eden, Kerioth), restoration and study tips.

R.

1172. Rabin, C. "The Language of Amos and Hosea" (Heb). pp. 115-136 in *Studies in the Minor Prophets* ed Ben Zion Luria. Jerusalem: Kiryat Sepher, 1981.

1173. Rabinowitz, Isaac. "The Crux at Amos 3:12." VT 11, No. 2 (Ap 61), 228-231. Emends to read "As the shepherd 'rescues' out of the lion's mouth two legs, or a piece of ear, So shall the Israelites who dwell in Samaria be 'rescued' - in the form of a corner of a couch, and of a piece out of the leg of a bed!"

1174. Radanovsky, Eva. "Time: The Priceless Gift of God as Seen in Amos." *The Hartford Quarterly* (Hartford, CT) 4, No. 4 (Sum 64), 65-68. Sermon on Amos 7:7-9. A nation that has lost its history has forfeited its divine election. God gave them more time to repent. They refused.

1175. Rahmer, Moritz. "III. Amos." pp. 1-27 in *Die hebraischen Traditionen in den Werken des Hieronymus. Zweiter Theil: Die Commentarii zu den XII kleinen Propehten. Heft I. Hosea, Joel, Amos.* Berlin: Poppelauer, 1902. vi + 48 pp. Separate pagination for each prophet. Hosea to Micah bound together in book form. Available on ATLA microfiche 1987-3049. Reprinted from *Monatschrift fur Geschichte und Wissenschaft des Judentums* 42 (1898), 1-16, 97-107, 200 (corrections). MGWJ is available on microfilm [#393-414 at PTS]. The foreword gives an overview of the concern with Jerome. An overview of the series is given on p. 2 of the Hosea study. Exegesis of selected terms and phrases, with commentary, notes on earlier studies and Jerome's usage. An appendix (pp. 28-39) adds additional study. A second appendix (pp. 42-48) discusses biblical place names in the Onomasticon of Jerome. MGWJ 42:197-199 is a essay, "Welcher biblische

Ortsname ist 'Cedson' im Onomastikon des Hieronymus?" attached, p. 200, are corrections for the Amos essay, pp. 97-107.

1176. Rahtjen, Bruce D. "A Critical Note on Amos 8:1-2." JBL 83, No. 4 (Dec 64), 416-417. Amos' play on words, summer fruit//the end, is similar to the last line in the Gezer calendar where the unpointed text can be read as the month of summer fruit but it is also the last word in the poem.

1177. Ramsay, William M. "Amos." pp. 234-240 in The Westminster Guide to the Books of the Bible. Louisville, KY: Westminster/John Knox, 1994. xi + 564 pp. The introduction gives background. A chart shows the relationship between the parts, notes date, purpose, significance. The main text reviews the content - oracles against the nations, against Israel, five visions of judgment to come, the added promise - perhaps by Amos, perhaps another inspired prophet.

1178. Ramsey, George W. "Amos 4:12 - A New Perspective." JBL 89, No. 2 (June 76), 187-191. Discusses the rib, the situation in Amos, and translates, "Prepare to call your 'gods,' O Israel."

1179. Randellini, Lino. "Il profeta Amos, defensore del poveri." Bollettino del l'Amicizia Ebraico-Cristiana di Firenze 6 (1971), 35-43.

1180. Randellini, Lino. "Ricchi e Poveri nel libro del Profeta Amos." Studium Biblicum Franciscanum Liber Annuus 2 (1951-1952), 5-86. Describes Amos' time, social conditions, Amos' style, prophecies against Israel, oppression and punishment, fraudulent merchants, Amos' religious doctrines, future salvation. Notes various scholarly interpretations.

1181. Rashi. "Amos." Miqra'oth Gedoloth [The Rabbinic Bible]. NY: Pardes, 1961.

1182. Ratcliff, Edward Craddock. "Amos." pp. 569-579 in A New Commentary on Holy Scripture Including the Apocrypha ed by Charles Gore, et al. NY: Macmillan, 1928. xv + 697 (OT), iii + 158 (Apocrypha), iii + 743 (NT) pp. The introduction summarizes what little we know about Amos himself, the historical background, his message and main ideas. He does not actually say he is a monotheist but it is clear there is only one God, who is in covenant with Israel. He boldly declares the Day of Jehovah will be one of humilation rather than the glory of Israel. The authenticity of the book cannot be seriously disputed. However, scholars are agreed on a number of verses that come later and the material has been rearranged. The commentary is on small units of text.

1183. Ravasi, Gianfranco. "Amos, il profeta della giustizia." pp. 45-62 in *I Profeti*. Milan: Editrice Ancora Milano, 1975. 287 pp. Discusses the background of Amos, his personal life, visions, universal morality, problems of luxury, rituals, the prayers (entreaties) of Amos. Numerous quotations from Jeremiah; no notes on earlier studies.

1184. Rector, Larry J. "Israel's Rejected Worship: An Exegesis of Amos 5." *Restoration Quarterly* 21, No. 3 (1978), 161-175. Detailed exegesis of the text with reviews of earlier studies. One oracle was given in Samaria and another in Bethel. People had separated liturgy from morality. Amos objected. Immoral actions negate the liturgy.

1185. Reed, Oscar F. "The Book of Amos." vol 5 (1966), 105-145 in *Beacon Bible Commentary*, 10 vols. Kansas City: Beacon Hill Press, 1966. 5:453 The introduction reviews earlier studies, the author and historical background, Amos and his message, and gives an outline. The commentary is by small units with brief explanations.

1186. Reeves, Talata. "A Prophetic Reconception of God for our Time." pp. 153-159 in *One Faith, Many Cultures: Inculturation, Indigenization, and Contextualization* ed Ruy O. Costa. Boston Theological Institute Annual 2. Maryknoll, NY/Cambridge, MA: Orbis/BTI, 1988. xvii + 162 pp. Discusses contextualization, the need for a prophet like Amos, et al. Postulates a prophetic reconception of God through the message of the prophets, e.g., Amos 5:18-20. God is a God of justice and not external ritual. The church's mission is making disciples for Christ. The major obstacle has been the culture of the disciple, the failure to recognize the cultural limits.

1187. Refer, K. *Amos. Die Worte des Propheten Ubersetz und Gedeutet.* Munich: Kaiser, 1927. 56 pp.

1188. Reider, Joseph. "Contributions to the Scriptural Text.'" HUCA 24 (1952-1953), 85-106. His studies include Amos (pp. 94-96). Translates Amos 2:7 as "who grind (or crush) to the dust of the earth the needy and the poor." Amos 5:6 is "lest a fire lick the house of Joseph and consume it, and there be none to quench it in the house of Israel." Amos 9:9 is "like as corn is sifted in a sieve."

1189. Reider, Joseph. "*dmsq* in Amos 3:12." JBL 67, No. 3 (Sep 48), 245-248. A paper given at the Society's 83rd meeting, 30 Dec 47, at Union Theological Seminary, NYC. Cf JBL 67, No. 1 (Jan 48), vi. Two words, both meaning leg or support, have coalesced to look like Damascus. The original may have been *d'm*, a rare word. A scribe explained it with a marginal *sq* which was later incorporated into the text.

1190. Reider, Joseph. "Etymological Studies in Biblical Hebrew." VT 4, No. 3 (1954), 276-295. Amos 1:13, p. 279. Exegesis. Notes scholarly opinions. It refers to stony tract, e.g., northern Arabia.

1191. Reimer, Haroldo. "Agentes y Mecanismos de Opresion y Explotacion en Amos." *Revista de Interpretacion Biblica Latin-Americana* = RIBLA (San Jose, Costa Rica) 12 (1992), 69-81. Discusses the identity of the oppressors - the agents of exploitation - the state (soldiers, priests, king) oppresses people with forced labor, taxes. Israelites also oppress each other.

1192. Reimer, Haroldo. *Richtet auf das Recht! Studien zur Botschaft des Amos.* Stuttgarter Bibel-Studien 149 ed Helmut Merklein and Erich Zenger. Stuttgart: Katholisches Bibelwerk Gmbh, 1992. 256 pp. The introduction studies the interpretation of prophecy from a Latin American perspective. The following chapters consider the composition and social history analysis of selected portions of Amos, e.g., the anti-Samaria complex, the visions, etc. The closing section discusses the message and theology of Amos.

1193. Reinke, Laurenz (1797-1879). "Die messianischen Ausspruche des Propheten Amos." Vol. 3 (1861), 184-208 in *Die messianischen*

Weissagungen bei den grossen und kleinen Propheten des A.T.
Vorbemerkungen, Grundtext und Eubersetzung nebst einem
philologisch-kritischen und historischen Commentar, 4 vols.
Giessen: Ferber, 1859-1862. 3:vii + 604. The introduction gives
historical background, discusses the imagery of Amos's writing,
notes earlier studies, extensive bibliography. The commentary is on
selected passages with exposition, exegesis, comparative textual
studies, comparison of MT, LXX, Syriac, Arabic, Ethiopic, etc.

1194. Renaud, Bernard. "Genese et Theologie d'Amos 3:3-8." pp.
353-372 in *Melanges bibliques et orientaux en l'honneur de M.*
Henri Cazelles ed Andre Caquot and Matthias Delcor. Altes Orient
und Altes Testament 212 ed Kurt Bergerhof, et al. Neukirchen-
Vluyn/Kevelaer: Neukirchener/Butzon & Bercker, 1981. xii + 543
pp. Analyzes the literary structure and theology in the several
stages of development.

1195. Renaud, Bernard. "Prophetic Criticism of Israel's Attitude to the
Nations: A Few Landmarks." pp. 35-43 in *Truth and Its Victims* ed
William Beuken, et al. Concilium: Religion in the Eighties 200.
Edinburgh: Clark, 1988. xiv + 160 pp.

1196. Rendtorff, Rolf. "Zu Amos 2:14-16." ZAW 85, No. 2 (1973),
226-227. Eng summary. There were three normal verses of two
stichs, but the arrangement has been disturbed. Put 15a after 14a
and the verses have a clear parallelism in material and form.

1197. Rendtorff, Rolf. "Amos." pp. 71-76 in *Men of the Old Testament.*
Philadelphia: Fortress, 1968. 156 pp. (Ger original, 1967) We have
stories about earlier prophets and a minimum of their words. The
opposite tradition begins with Amos. We do not know how long he
prophesied or what happened to him. His words from the Lord
were offensive to the powers that be, especially the royal court.
Like all the prophets, Amos was not an innovator but upheld
ancient Israelite traditions. But while people understood traditions
like the Day of the Lord as favorable to Israel, Amos had the
opposite interpretation.

1198. Reuss, Eduard (1804-1891). "Amos." Vol 2 (1892), 64-84 in *Die*
Propheten. Die Alte Testament ubersetzt, eingeleitet und erlautert,

7 vols by Reuss. Braunschweig: Schwetschke, 1892-1894. 2:576 pp. Tr from *Les Prophetes*, 1:ii + 574; 2:ii + 403, 1876. La Bible: Traduction Nouvelle avec Introductions et Commentaires. Paris: Sandoz and Fischbacher, 1874-1881. A general introduction to Hebrew prophecy reviews its origins, character, preaching, predicting, role in the OT in relation to people, state (theocracy, etc.), religion, with examples drawn from many of the prophets. The introduction to Amos reviews the content, historical background, oracles against the nations, confrontation with Amaziah, visions, judgment, future hope. The commentary has a translation with critical notes.

1199. Reventlow, Henning Graf. *Das Amt des Propheten bei Amos.* Forschungen zur Religion und Literatur des Alten und Neuen Testaments 80 ed Ernst Kasemann and Ernst Wurthwein. Gottingen: Vandenhoeck & Ruprecht, 1962. 120 pp. The question about Amos' prophet office turns on his encounter with Amaziah, his visions and rituals, e.g., curse ritual (4:6-11), blessing (9:13-15).

1200. Reynolds, H.R. and P. Whitehouse. "Amos." Vol 5 (1905), 447-467 in *A Bible Commentary for Bible Students*, 8 vols ed Charles John Ellicott. London: Marshall, 1905. 5:viii + 609 pp. original, Cassell, 1884. Reprinted (various titles) several times, including pp. 636-641 in Ellicott's Bible Commentary in One Volume, ed and condensed by Donald N. Bowdle. Grand Rapids, MI: Zondervan, 1971. vi + 1242 pp. with condensed commentary notes, no introduction, biblical texts or reference to Reynolds and Whitehouse. The introduction reviews the life and work of Amos, historical background, idolatry and corruption. Gives an outline. The biblical text is followed with phrase by phrase commentary explaining, offering alternate translation, comparing with other texts. Amos was not a prophet, i.e., not a professional member of the guild. Several excursi give an expanded study of selected problems.

1201. Riach, John L. "The Story of Amos in Dialogue." ET 55, No. 7 (Ap 44), 191-194. Amos is written in an imaginary dialogue, which is paraphrased in a village in Germany, 1938, when the Nazis said no to the OT.

1202. Rice, Gene. "Was Amos a Racist?" *J of Religious Thought* 35, No. 1 (Spr-Sum 78), 35-44. No. Rice analyzes the arguments pro and con. The Ethiopians were never Israel's enemies. The archaeological data from Amos' day shows the Ethiopians had an advanced culture. Amos was showing the love of God for all known peoples, including those near and far.

1203. Richard, Earl. "The Creative Use of Amos by the Author of Acts." *Novum Testament* (Leiden) 24, No. 1 (1982), 37-53. Acts 7 and 15 make extensive use of Amos 5:25-27 and 9:11-12 from the LXX. It is not clear if Luke read Amos to support his own ideas or if diligent study of the Scriptures profoundly influenced his writing.

1204. Richardson, H. Neil. "Amos's Four Visions - Of Judgment and Hope." *Bible Review* 5, No. 2 (Ap 89), 16-21. In the first two, Amos intercedes (successfully), but not the latter two. Translates in the third, "someone stood beside the heat holding tin in his hand." Richardson finds hope in the visions of locusts and fire as well as the conclusion of Amos.

1205. Richardson, H. Neil. "Amos 2:13-16: Its Structure and Function." Vol I (1978), 361-368 in *SBL 1978 Seminar Papers* ed Paul J. Achtemeier. SBL Seminar Papers Series 13 ed Achtemeier. Missoula, MT: Scholars Press, 1978. vii + 415 pp. There were two volumes in 1978 (II:vii + 346) from the 114th Annual Meeting, held in New Orleans. Gives the Hebrew, discusses the form, textual criticism, length of stichs, parallelism, repetition, function. The function of the unit is to conclude the war oracles and to separate these from the rest of the book which lacks war language.

1206. Richardson, H. Neil. "Apart from Justice and Righteousness There Is No Life: An Exegetical Study of Amos 5." *Wesleyan Studies in Religion* (Buckhannon, WV) 62 (1969-70), 5-11. He notes Amos' knowledge of history, geography, Hebrew literature, wisdom language and thought, e.g., cause and effect. Amos was an original poet. His message is clear: unjust and unrighteous deeds lead to destruction and death.

1207. Richardson, H. Neil. "A Critical Note on Amos 7:14." JBL 85, No. 1 (Mar 66), 89. The *lamedh* is an emphatic particle rather than the negative *lo'* so Amos said, "I am a prophet but not a seer."

1208. Richardson, H. Neil. "SKT (Amos 9:11): 'Booth' or 'Succoth' ?" JBL 92, No. 3 (Sep 73), 375-381. Surveys uses of the term and concludes it is the town of Succoth as a symbol of David's success and the restoration of the two kingdoms.

1209. Richardson, Paul A. "Worship Resources for Amos." R&E 92, No. 2 (Spr 95), 207-217. Discusses passages for reading, relevant hymns and other musical elements, prayers.

1210. Richter, Georg. "Amos." pp. 66-96 in *Erlauterungen zu dunkeln Stellen in den Kleinen Propheten*. Beitrage zur Forderung christlicher Theologie = BFCT 18, Nos. 3-4, ed D.A. Schlatter and D.W. Lutgert. Gutersloh: Bertelsmann, 1914. 199 pp. = BFCT 18:275-473. Transcriptions, translations, exegesis and commentary, comparing earlier opinions, MT, LXX.

1211. Richter, Wolfgang. "Amos." pp. 86-133 in *Biblia Hebraica transcripta (BH^t) das ist das ganze Alte Testament transkribiert, mit Satzeinteilungen versehen und durch die Version tiberisch-masoretischer Autoritaten bereichert, auf der sie grundet 10. Kleine Propheten*. Munchener Universitatsschriften. Arbeiten zu Text und Sprache im Alten Testament 33.10 ed Richter. St. Ottilien: EOS, 1993. v + 357 pp. The Hebrew and transliteration are on facing pages. The text is given for each, line by line, e.g., 1:5 is divided into 5 units, a-e, and there are five lines. The text as a whole has a few critical notes.

1212. Ridderbos, Jan. "Amos." Vol 1 (1952), 169-257 in *De Kleine Profeten Opnieuw Uit den Grondtekst Vertaald en Verklaard. Eerste Deel: Hosea, Joel, Amos*, 3 vols, 2nd ed. Korte Verklaring der Heilige Schrift met Nieuwe Vertaling, ed Gerhard Charles Aalders, et al. Kampen: Kok, 1949-1952. 1:260. (original, 1932-35) The introduction considers the man, the background, the content and outline of the book. The commentary has a Dutch translation with comparison of other biblical texts.

1213. Ridderbos, Nic.H. Beschouwingen naar Aanleiding van Wolffs "Die Stunde des Amos." *Gereformeerd Theologisch Tijdschrift* 72, No. 1 (1972), 1-18. A review essay discussing Amos, his background, his message, exegesis of Amos 3 and 4, preaching, the significance of the Book of Amos.

1214. Riedel, Wilhelm. "Bemerkungen zum Buche Amos." Vol 1:19-36 in *Alttestamentliche Untersuchungen*. Leipzig: Deichert, 1902. v + 103 pp. Discusses the literary problems and specific verses. Exegesis and commentary, compares MT and LXX, structural analysis.

1215. Riedel, Wilhelm. "Miscellen 7. Amos 9:10." ZAW 20, No. 3 (1900), 332. Exegesis, comparative textual study.

1216. Rieger, Julius. *Die Bedeutung der Geschichte für die Verkundigung des Amos und Hosea*. Giessen: Topelmann, 1929. viii + 116 pp. Amos is discussed in ch 1 while Hosea is studied in ch 2. The history of the people is reviewed in and for each, and together.

1217. Ries, Claude A. "The Book of Amos." pp. 609-635 in *The Wesleyan Bible Commentary*. Vol. 3. [The Latter Prophets]. Peabody, MA: Hendrickson, 1986. Reprint, original 1979. ix + 806 pp. The commentary is nonsectarian and non-polemical, produced by nine denominations including the Church of God, Free Methodists, Wesleyan Methodists, etc., in the spirit of John Wesley and Adam Clark, with the best tools of present-day Bible scholarship, sound but practical rather than technical. Ries provides a complete outline of Amos and reviews the man, his world, the integrity of the book, its message. He was a poor farmer who was a master of the purest and most classical Hebrew, rhetorical, oratorical, epigrammatical, metaphorical with imagination glowing with eloquence of heaven-born convictions. He preached in a time of military and economic prosperity. The nation became more and more corrupt. Amos' message is judgment. God hates sin. God is loving, patient, ready to forgive, and seeks the fellowship of men of all races. Samaria must be destroyed.

1218. Riessler, Paul. "Der Prophet Amos." pp. 63-100 in *Die kleinen Propheten oder das Zwolfprophetenbuch nach dem Urtext ubersetzt und erklart.* Rottenburg a.N.: Bader, 1911. vi + 294 pp. The introduction notes the historical background, the prophet's home in the southern kingdom of Judah, Amos' personal background as told to Amaziah, comparison with Hosea. The commentary gives the German translation by chapters, with extended notes.

1219. Rinaldi, Giovanni (1906-1994). "Due note ad Amos." *Rivista degli Studi Orientali* (Rome) 28 (1953), 149-152. Exegesis for Amos 3:11b (Vulgate) and 7:4 (Heb), noting earlier studies, comparing TM, LXX, Vulgate.

1220. Rinaldi, Giovanni. "De III et IV Visione Libri Amos (Amos 7:7-9; 8:1-3)." VD 17 (1937), No. 3 (Mar 37), 82-87; No. 4 (Ap 37), 114-116. Text of the Vulgate and Latin translation of MT, with exegesis and commentary, discussion of earlier studies.

1221. Rinaldi, Giovanni. "Amos." Vol I (1953), 121-218 in *I Profeti minori.* La Sacra Bibbia, ed Salvatore Garofalo. Turin: Marietti, 1953. xvi + 218 + 12 pls. The first of three volumes on the minor prophets, vol 2 (1960); vol 3 (1968). The three vols are reviewed in JBL 89, No. 3 (Sep 70), 355-356. This volume includes a general introduction on the prophetic movement, inspiration, religion, prophetic literature. There is an extensive general bibliography as well as a separate one for Amos. The introduction to Amos discusses the man, his time, his book (composition, etc.), his revelation. The commentary gives the translation in Italian with exegesis and exposition.

1222. Rinaldi, Giovanni. "Note ebraiche." *Aegyptus* (Milan) 34, No. 1 (Jan-June 54), 35-62. Amos 8:5, 9:1 on pp. 39-42. Exegesis.

1223. Rinaldi, G. "La parola 'anak." *Bibbia e Oriente* (Milan) 4 (1962), 83-84. Amos 7:7-9, exegesis, discussion of other views on tin or lead.

1224. Rinaldi, G. "Saggio storico religioso sul profeta Amos." *Aevum* 26 (1949), 316-356.

1225. Roberts, J.J.M. "Amos 6:1-7." pp. 155-66 in *Understanding the Word: Essays in Honor of Bernhard W. Anderson* ed James T.

Butler, et al. JSOT Supplement 37. Sheffield, England: JSOT, 1985. 391 pp. A correct analysis of the structure is the key to solving the textual and other problems of the *hoy* oracle ("hey") Cf 5:18-20 for the other *hoy* oracle. Kullane, Hamath and Gath were destroyed or diminished in 738 BCE when Azariah expanded his power but failed to halt the Assyrians. Israel's luxury loving nobility will also be destroyed for ignoring the suffering of the poor.

1226. Roberts, Jimmy J.M. "A Note on Amos 7:14 and Its Context." *Restoration Quarterly* 8, No. 3 (1965), 175-178. Review of the literature, exegesis, commentary. Amos said, "I was not a prophet."

1227. Roberts, J.J.M. "Recent Trends in the Study of Amos." *Restoration Quarterly* 13, No. 1 (1970), 1-16. Discusses earlier views, focusing on Amos the cultic prophet and Amos' attitude toward the cult. Amos was too complex a character to be encompassed in one view such as cult prophet. This insight should be preserved but not be allowed to hinder other insights.

1228. Robertson, Edwin Hanton. *Amos, Hosea, Micah, Isaiah 1-39*. Mowbray's Mini-commentary 8. London: Mowbray, 1968. 70 pp.

1229. Robertson, James. "Amos." Vol 1 (1976), 120-125 in *The International Standard Bible Encyclopedia*, 5 vols, ed James Orr, et al. Grand Rapids: Eerdmans, 1939. 1:xx + 508. (original, 1915), reprint 1955, 1976; rev, 1979 (see #1230) Reviews the man, his mission, date (c 760) and book. He knows God and the history of his people but there is no indication as to how he knows. The book tells about social and religious conditions of the time including rituals, ethics, the prophetic order, i.e., the book shows what prophecy was in ancient Israel. Prophetic religion did not begin with Amos. There is no crudeness of expression, no struggling up from naturalism or a tribal god. God rules nature and the nations, examines human hearts, treats people with equal justice and is most severe on the privileged.

1230. Robertson, James and Carl Edwin Armerding. "Amos." Vol. 1 (1979), 114-117 in *The International Standard Bible Encyclopedia*, 3rd ed, 4 vols, ed Geoffrey W. Bromiley et al. Grand Rapids, MI:

Eerdmans, 1979-1988. Vol. 1:xxv + 1006. Reviews the prophet (name, home, personal history, preparation, date [760-750 BCE]) and the book (divisions, theology, historical and critical value). The book reflects contemporary religion and society. There is no ethics apart from the Pentateuch and no false assurance of God's choice apart from covenant responsibility.

1231. Robertson, O. Palmer. "Hermeneutics of Continuity." pp. 89-108 in *Continuity and Discontinuity: Perspectives on the Relationship Between the Old and New Testaments: Essays in Honor of S. Lewis Johnson, Jr.* ed John S. Feinberg. Westchester, IL: Crossway Books, 1988. 410 pp. Amos 9:11-15 is useful for interaction between dispensational and nondispensational interpretation of prophecy. Discusses the original meaning. There is continuity with Abraham and salvation by grace, but discontinuity with the past for Esau is now among the elect. The NT (Acts 15) continues this teaching. A dispensational view sees fulfillment in the future. This view is based on the "great parenthesis" idea that the prophetic clock stopped and now it's starting again. One alternative is to see the fulfillment of Amos' prophecy occurring in the present. Believers in Christ ultimately shall participate in the restoration of all things.

1232. Robinson, George L. "Amos the Prophet of Justice." pp. 47-60, 177-178 in *The Twelve Minor Prophets*. NY: Smith, 1930. 203 pp. (original, Doran, 1926). Reprinted, Grand Rapids: Baker, 1974. Tr, *Los Doce Profetas Menores*. El Paso, 1982. Discusses the man, early occupation, call, period, literary style, message (destruction of Samaria for injustice), analysis and content (judgments; visions), permanent value of his message (morality of God; insincere worship an insult to God; social justice; privilege involves responsibility), special verses. The appendix cites earlier studies on the later additions to Amos, especially the elements of hope. Robinson sees the latter as intrinsic to Amos.

1233. Robinson, Henry Wheeler. "Amos." pp. 775-783 in *The Abingdon Bible Commentary* ed Frederick Carl Eiselen, et al. NY: Abingdon, 1929. xvi + 1452. He was not a cleric but a true prophet. He resented social injustice and had an abnormal psychical experience. Robinson outlines the moral and religious corruption. People lived luxuriously instead of in simple Rechabite nomadic style. Society was cruel and unjust to the helpless. There was religious ritual without moral living. Prosperity brought evil. But justice is a divine foundation for society. Privilege implies responsibility. Elaborate worship without moral standards of living, is an insult to God.

1234. Robinson, Theodore H. "Amos." pp. 60-71 in *Prophecy and the Prophets in Ancient Israel*, 3rd ed with a new bibliography by G.W. Anderson. London: Duckworth, 1979. viii + 231 pp. (original 1923) Amos saw the luxury of the rich and the oppression of the poor. It seemed as if nothing could touch the conscience of Israel. No honest critic could secure a hearing. Amos did not denounce the system as system. Judah learned to plow and Samaria to trade but both had forgotten Yahweh. Amos spoke of the universality of Yahweh. This is not yet monotheism but it grew into that. God would punish neighboring countries, not for crimes against Israel but for crimes against humanity.

1235. Robinson, Theodore Henry. "The Book of Amos." pp. 106-121 in *Old Testament. Vol. III. The Decline and Fall of the Hebrew Kingdoms: Israel in the Eighth and Seventh Centuries B.C.* The Clarendon Bible. Oxford: Clarendon, 1926. xx + 263 pp. Robinson provides a commentary on Amos 3-7. The introduction notes three kinds of materials: oracles and narrative by the prophet and materials about him. The visions, Amos 7ff, are an example of the second. Men thought ritual was more important than justice but Amos reversed the order.

1236. Robinson, Theodore H. *The Book of Amos. Hebrew Text Edited with Critical and Grammatical Notes.* Texts for Students 30. London: SPCK, 1923, 1951. 61 pp. There is a useful vocabulary. The text is that of the Massorah, freely emended where necessary. About half of the corrections come from the LXX with some reference to the Peshitta and Vulgate. The introduction reviews the nature of Hebrew poetry, sounds, rhythms. Each beat is a stichos. Two beats per line is a Distich; three a Tristich. A Stichos with two beats is a Dimeter and with three, a Trimeter, etc. A longer unit is a strophe or stanza.

1237. Robinson, Theodore H. "Amos." pp. 71-108 in *Die Zwolf Kleinen Propheten, Hosea bis Micha* by Robinson, and, *Nahum bis Maleachi* by Friedrich Horst. Handbuch zum Alten Testament, Erste Reihe, 14, ed Otto Eissfeldt. Tubingen: Mohr, 1938. vi + 267 pp. 2nd ed, 1954; 3rd ed 1964. A general introduction gives an overview of the minor prophets, the name, the literature. The introduction to Amos reviews the book, the prophet (style, time, message), the text, the literature. The commentary gives a German translation, exegetical notes, detailed discussion.

1238. Robscheit, Hellmuth. "Die thora bei Amos und Hosea." EvT 10, No. 1 (1950), 26-38. Draws on history, politics and the cult.

1239. Roesler, A. "Prophetenbilder. 1. Amos." *Theologisch Praktische Quartalschrift* (Linz, Austria) 69, No. 1 (1916), 1-13. A comparative study with homiletic.

1240. Rohkramer, Martin. "Gottesdienst in der Welt: Eine Predigt uber Amos 5." pp. 43-50 in *Wort und Gemeinde. Probleme und Aufgaben der Praktischen Theologie: Eduard Thurneysen zum 80. Geburtstag* ed Rudolf Bohren and Max Geiger. Zurich: EVZ, 1968. Compares the historical context of Amos with recent European history and thought.

1241. Romer, Thomas. "Amos: Les fondements de sa Prophetie, ou: Le Probleme de son 'enracinement spirituel'." *Foi et Vie* [Cahier Biblique 23] 83, No. 5 (Sep 84), 26-34. Reviews several scholarly opinions, the oracles against the nations and against Israel, prophecy as social criticism, prophecy and theology.

1242. Rosel, Hartmut Nahum. *The Book of Amos* (Heb). Haifa, Israel: Ach, 1990. 316 pp. A full commentary on the text in Hebrew.

1243. Rosel, Hartmut Nahum. "Kleine Studien zur Entwicklung des Amosbuche." VT 43 (Jan 93), 88-101. Exegetical analysis with reviews of earlier studies.

1244. Rosenbaum, Stanley N. *Amos of Israel. A New Interpretation.* Macon, GA: Mercer University Press, 1990. xii + 129 pp. Reviews Amos' time, origin, occupation, and the sociology of Samaria, the unity and authenticity of the book, its languages and dialect. Amos was a citizen of Israel, a middle level employee (a district inspector of government herds and sycamores) with sufficient social standing to command an audience and wrote in a northern dialect. The entire book is by Amos. Suggestions for redaction are superfluous. After he spoke (20 minutes), he left for exile in Tekoa in Judah. Later he was joined there by members of his "guild" who formed a colony of exiles. Rosenbaum says "Biblical scholarship is a form of worship undertaken by those who cannot sing."

1245. Rosenbaum, Stanley N. "Northern Amos Revisited: Two Philological Suggestions." *Hebrew Studies* 18 (1977), 132-148. Amos was a native of Israel, not Judah, as shown by the priest's order to flee *from* his native land, and the accusation of treason, i.e., against Israel. If he were a Judahite, his prophecy of Jeroboam's death would not be treason. Detailed exegesis and bibliography.

1246. Rosenmuller, Ernst Friedrich Karl (1768-1835). "In Amosum Prooemium." pp. 1-271 in *Prophetae minores: Annotatione Perpetua. Volumen Secundum. Amos, Obadias et Jonas.* Scholia in Vetus Testamentum 7. Leipzig: Barth, 1812. Vol 7/2:ii + 420. The introduction to Amos gives the historical background, the history of interpretation (Jewish and Christian) and bibliography. The commentary has exegesis, word study, comparative textual study including versions such as MT, LXX, Syriac, Vulgate, and discussion of earlier scholarly analysis such as Jerome, Theodoret, et al.

1247. Rosler, Aug. "Prophetenbilder. 1. Amos." *Theologisch Praktische Quartalschrift* 69, No. 1 (1916), 1-13. Compares OT, NT, the present, earlier studies, the Amaziah incident, Yahweh's control of nations.

1248. Rost, Leonhard. "Zu Amos 7:10-17." pp. 229-236 in *Festgabe fur Theodor Zahn.* Leipzig: Deichert, 1928. v + 238 pp. Commentary with discussion of various scholarly interpretations, comparison with LXX, etc.

1249. Rothstein, Gustav. "Amos und seine Stellung innerhalb des israelitischen Prophetismus (Mit einem Exkurs uber: Ort und Dauer der Wirksamkeit des Amos)." TSK (Gotha) 78, No. 3 (1905), 323-358. Notes earlier studies, the Moabite King Mesha as a shepherd, various versions.

1250. Rottzoll, Dirk U. "II Sam 14:5 - eine Parallele zu Am 7:14f." ZAW 100, No. 3 (1988), 413-415. "I am" is found in both verses. In each, a statement is made and answered.

1251. Routtenberg, Hyman J. *Amos of Tekoa: A Study in Interpretation.* NY: Vantage Press, 1971. 194 pp. Diss. Rabbinic Interpretation of Amos. Boston University, 1943. A commentary on Amos based on rabbinic sources followed by a critique of these interpretations. Describes the Jewish tradition of oral law and notes the references to Amos in the Haggadah (why he was called Amos, how God tested him, his death, who wrote the book). The name is from *amas*, "to press." He was so named because he stammered. Both he and his father were prophets, *contra* his own statement. He was a wealthy man (and so were all the prophets) who *owned* the flocks and sycamore trees. He was killed by King Uzziah (Louis Ginsberg says this is a Christian source). His book was written by the Men of the Great Assembly [Synagogue].

1252. Routtenberg, Hyman J. Rabbinic Interpretation of Amos. Diss. Boston University, 1943. Not available from UMI.

1253. Rowley, Harold Henry. "Was Amos a Nabi?" pp. 191-198 in *Festschrift fur Otto Eissfeldt zum 60. Geburtstag 1. September 1947* ed Johann Feuck. Halle an der Saale: Niemeyer, 1947. v + 233 pp. Discusses Amos 7:14-15 with many scholarly opinions, LXX and Peshitta Syriac (both past tense), Rowley's own preference for past tense. The latter is possible but cannot be demanded. In 3:7, Amos implicitly claims to be a nabi. So he is saying to Amaziah that he *was* not a prophet, that he is not now prophesying for money, but speaks for God.

1254. Rudolph, Wilhelm. "Amos." pp. 93-292 in *Joel - Amos - Obadja - Jona.* Kommentar zum Alten Testament 13.2 ed Rudolph, et al. Gutersloh: Mohn, 1971. 400 pp. A chronological chart is by Alfred Jepsen. The introduction discusses the historical background, the person, the book. There is an extensive bibliography.

1255. Rudolph, Wilhelm. "Amos 4:6-13." pp. 27-38 in *Wort - Gebot - Glaube. Beitrage zur Theologie des Alten Testaments. Walther Eichrodt zum 80.* Geburtstag ed Hans Joachim Stoebe, et al. Abhandlungen zur Theologie des Alten und Neuen Testaments 59 ed Oscar Cullmann and Stoebe. Zurich: Zwingli, 1970. 331 pp. Reviews the history of interpretation, analyzes the structure of the text, notes the deuteronomic and chronicler traditions.

1256. Rudolph, Wilhelm. "Die angefochtenen Volkerspruche in Amos 1 und 2." pp. 45-49 in *Schalom. Studien zu Glaube und Geschichte Israels. Alfred Jepsen zum 70.* Geburtstag ed Karl-Heinz Bernhardt. Arbeiten zur Theologie 1st series, vol 46, ed Theodor Schlatter, et al. Stuttgart: Calwer, 1971. Discusses the oracles against the nations with a review of several interpretations.

1257. Rudolph, Wilhelm. "Gott und Mensch bei Amos." pp. 19-31 in *Imago Dei: Beitrage zur theologischen Anthropologie. Gustav Kruger zum siebzigsten Geburtstage am 29. Juni 1932* ed Heinrich Bornkamm. Giessen: Topelmann, 1932. v + 232 pp. Discusses earlier studies and notes God is the Lord and Israel the servant; see Romans 9:16.

1258. Rudolph, Wilhelm. "Schwierige Amosstellen: Dem Bearbeiter des Zwolfprophetenbuchs in der neuen Biblia Hebraica." pp. 157-162 in *Wort und Geschichte: Festschrift fur Karl Elliger zum 70. Geburtstag* ed Hartmut Gese and Hans Peter Ruger. Alter Orient und Altes Testament 18 ed Kurt Bergerhof, et al. Kevaelaer/ Neukirchen-Vluyn: Butzon & Bercker/Neukirchener, 1973. x + 215 pp. Exegesis of selected passages with a review of interpretations.

1259. Ruiz Gonzales, Gregorio (d. 1984). "Amos 5:13: Prudencia en la Denuncia Profetica?" *Cultura Biblica* 25, No. 253 (Nov-Dec 73), 347-352. Discusses the authenticity of the verse, and its interpretation, with an extensive review of earlier opinions.

1260. Ruiz Gonzalez, Gregorio. *Comentarios Hebreos Medievales al Libro de Amos (Traduccion y notas a los Comentarios de Rasi, E. de Beaugency, A. 'ibn 'Ezra', D. Qimhi, J. 'ibn Caspi).* Publicaciones de la Universidad Pontificia Comillas Madrid. Series I: Estudios, 31. Teologia I,20. Madrid: UPCM, 1987. liii + 300 pp.

Quotes the text of Amos verse by verse with the exegesis (if known) of each of these medieval rabbis for that verse. Dr. Maria Teresa Ortega Monasterio completed the manuscript after Ruiz' death, and wrote the introduction with a biography of each scholar.

1261. Ruiz Gonzales, Gregorio, ed/tr. *Don Isaac Abrabanel y su Comentario al Libro de Amos. Texto hebreo del manuscrito de El Escorial, traduccion y notas.* Publicaciones de la Universidad Pontificia Comillas Madrid Series I. Estudios, 30, Teologia I, 16 ed A. Vargas-Machuca. Madrid: Universidad Pontificia Comillas, 1984. clx + 271 pp. Based on the Escorial (Spain) ms G-I-11. Ruiz reproduces the Hebrew and gives a translation into Spanish with annotation of Abrabanel's (1437-1508) commentary on Amos. The introduction includes a biography of Abrabanel, a leader of Spanish Judaism at the time of expulsion in 1492, as well as the manuscript itself. The commentary is in four parts.

1262. Rupprecht, Eberhard. "Das Zepter Jahwes in den Berufungsvision von Jeremia und Amos." ZAW 108, No. 1 (1996), 55-69. Jer 1:11-14 was originally behind 4:21. The scepter represents authority and power. Compares 1:13 to Gen 22. Amos' visions of natural disasters reflect images of military destruction, the warrior and the scepter.

1263. Rusche, Helga. *Der Prophet Amos*, 2nd ed. Geistliche Schriftlesung 4, ed Hermann Eising and Hans Lubsczyk. Dusseldorf: Patmos, 1986. 148 pp. (original, 1963) The introduction discusses the prophet and his book with an outline overview. The commentary has introductory remarks, translation, discussion, exegesis, review of earlier studies, extensive notes.

1264. Rusche, Helga. "Wenn Got sein Wort entzieht. Meditation zu Amos 8:11-12." *Bibel und Leben* (Dusseldorf) 10 (1969), 219-221. Devotional.

1265. Ryan, D. "Amos." pp. 693-701 (Sec 555-560) in *A New Catholic Commentary on Holy Scripture*, rev, ed Reginald C. Fuller, et al. London: Nelson, 1969. xix + 1377 pp. (original, ed Bernard Orchard, et al. London/NY: Nelson, 1953. xvi + 1312 pp.) The introduction provides bibliography, discussion of the date (between 780-740), Amos' life, social and religious conditions, doctrine

(Yahweh is Creator and Controller of the Universe, God of all Nations), composition (oracles, biography, doxologies). The commentary is by small units.

1266. Ryken, Leland. "Amos." pp. 337-347 in *A Complete Literary Guide to the Bible* ed Ryken and Tremper Longman III. Grand Rapids: Zondervan, 1993. 528 pp. Discusses Amos as satire, satiric strategies (fat cows of Bashan), satiric structure (oracles against the nations), satiric imagination (a lion roars, come to Bethel and transgress), satire in every part of the Bible, e.g., Proverbs, the NT gospels.

S.

1267. Sacon, K.K. "Amos 5:21-27. An Exegetical Study" (Japanese) pp. 278-299 in *The Bible, Its Thoughts, History and Language. Essays in Honor of Masao Sekine* ed S. Arai. Tokyo: Yamamoto Shoten, 1972.

1268. Sampey, John R. "Notes on Amos." R&E 30, No. 3 (July 33), 284-295. Exposition, homiletic. Discusses the man, historical background, Amos as orator.

1269. Sanders, Frank Knight and Charles Foster Kent. "The Message of Amos." pp. 21-44 in *The Messages of the Earlier Prophets Arranged in the Order of Time, Analyzed, and Freely Rendered in Paraphrase.* The Messages of the Bible 1, ed Sanders and Kent. Philadelphia: Wattles, 1898. xv + 304 pp. A general introduction to the volume discusses the beginnings of Hebrew prophecy, characteristics of prophetic writings, and how to use a paraphrase. Samuel linked the old order and the new, followed by Nathan, Elijah and others. We know only a few of the considerable number. In the prophets, the supremacy of the moral element revolutionized religious thinking. Reviews the man and his people, the sins of Israel, no excuse, ritual as useless, visions, the immediate and distant future. He was a rude shepherd from the south facing sophisticated, luxury loving greed. His mere presence would be resented. Because his charges were true, he surely aroused great resentment. They silenced his lips but not his pen "and thus rendered his words immortal."

1270. Sanders, Henry A. "Amos." pp. 52-67 and 153-165 in *The Minor Prophets in the Freer Collection and The Berlin Fragment of Genesis* by Sanders and Carl Schmidt. University of Michigan Studies, Humanistic Series 21. NY: Macmillan, 1927. xv + 436 pp.

Part 1 is on the minor prophets; part 2 on Genesis. Part 1 gives a history of the Washington Manuscript (Greek ms V.1, in the Freer Collection of the Smithsonian), reviews palaeography, the subscription, the character of the text, marginal glosses. The text itself is then reprinted, pp. 49-151, with notes (critical apparatus), pp. 152-229. The reprint is based on Sanders' collation and consists of the original text with corrections, glosses etc in footnotes. Five plates show the first appearance of the papyrus (28 leaves), fragments, Micah 5:8-6:10, Zech 3:4-4:7. The ms was bought in Cairo in 1916 but kept in a bank vault until 1920.

1271. Sanders, Joseph P. "Amos Speaks at Communion Service." *Wesleyan Studies in Religion* 62 (1969-1970), 13-17. Communion represents unity, among all people. The wheat is united into flour for bread and the grapes are united into juice for wine. The minister's prophetic role is to speak out for God. Amos is a good source for sermons for the communion service, e.g., on grain in 5:11, poverty in 4:1, etc. Here are studies in overconfidence in riches, worship without justice is sacrilege, etc. Holy communion is not just a time of personal piety but of unity against hatred and injustice.

1272. Sanderson, Judith E. "Amos." pp. 205-209 in *The Women's Bible Commentary* ed Carol A. Newsom and Sharon H. Ringe. London/Louisville, KY: SPCK/ Westminster/John Knox, 1992. xix + 396 pp. The introduction reviews author, outline, and problems for women. Amos condemned rich women for oppressing the poor but failed to champion poor women. The commentary discusses women and children suffering regardless of innocence. He does note God's judgment on those that rip open pregnant women. He objects to father and son having intercourse with the same "girl" but the fate of the girl is not considered. His reference to "fat cows of Bashan" suggests he held women accountable for their sin, though Amaziah's wife will suffer for her husband's sin.

1273. Sandmel, Samuel. "Amos." pp. 55-69 in *The Hebrew Scriptures. An Introduction to their Literature and Religious Ideas*. NY: Knopf, 1963. xviii + 552 + xviii [index] pp. Reviews editorial additions (including Amos 7:10-17), the visions, content (excerpts of 34 addresses), denunciations (of greed, injustice, cruelty, oppression of the poor), the day of Yahve, call to repentance, universalism, special position means special punishment, the development of the book.

1274. Sandrock, Charles W. "The Prophet Amos Speaks to 1942." *J of Theology of the American Lutheran Conference* (Minneapolis) 7, Nos. 9-10 (Sep-Oct 42), 684-694. Notes that a stranger has come to town in 1942. Writes the Book of Amos, his message, its application, as if he were in town for 1942.

1275. Sansoni, Carlo. "Amos, uomo del suo Tempo." *Bibbia e Oriente* (Genoa) 10, No. 6 (1968), 253-265. Discusses doctrinal presuppositions, Amos and the Rechabites, contemporary study with an extensive review of earlier works.

1276. Sant, C. "Religious Worship in the Book of Amos." *Melita Theologica* 3, No. 2 (1950), 75-93; 4, No. 1 (1951), 34-48.

1277. Saregianne, Chr. "Den eimai Nabi (Amos 7:14)" (Greek). pp. 632-646 in *Ponema Eugnomon, Fs B.M. Bella* [Vellas]. Athens: Apostolica Diakonia, 1969.

1278. Sargent, James E. *Hosea, Joel, Amos, Obadiah and Jonah.* Nashville, TN: Graded Press (Cokesbury), 1988. 157 pp. Each book has an introduction with the commentary in several sections, each of which has an introduction. Provides an outline, word studies, theological interpretation and a summary of the message. For Amos, he discusses the man and his audience.

1279. Sasowski, Reinhard. "Dann wende ich das Schicksal meines Volkes." *Bibel und Kirche* 22, No.4 (1967), 116-119. Amos 9:11-15.

1280. Sauer, Georg. "Amos 7:10-17 und Mesopotamischer Briefstil." pp. 119-128 in *Haim M.I. Gevaryahu Memorial Volume.* Jerusalem: World Jewish Bible Center, 1990. The English-French-German section (iv + 145 pp.) is ed Joshua J. Adler. The Hebrew section (iii + 154 pp.) is ed Ben Zion Luria. Utilizes third, second and especially first millennium BCE materials for data, notes earlier studies, other biblical examples, makes comparisons of parallels in

Amos. Gives transliterations, some translation, transcription of the Hebrew.

1281. Sauermann, O. "Der Prophet der sozialen Gerechtigkeit." Der Seelsorger 24 (1954), 229-235, 273-278.

1282. Sawyer, John F.A. "'Those Priests in Damascus': A Possible Example of Anti-Sectarian Polemic in the Septuagint Version of Amos 3:12." pp. 123-130 in *Annual of the Swedish Theological Institute* 8 (1970-1971) ed Hans Kosmala. Leiden: Brill, 1972. v + 183 pp. The end of Israel will be tatters of a sheep or goat after wild animals have killed it. The reference to Samaritans, and the priests of Damascus (cf Qumranites), reflect the time of John Hyrcanus. The verse makes good sense at an early stage in the history of the LXX.

1283. Sawyer, John F.A. "The Prophets (III): Daniel to Malachi." pp. 102-125 in *Prophecy and the Prophets of the Old Testament*. Oxford Bible Series ed Peter R. Ackroyd and Graham N. Stanton. Oxford: Oxford University Press, 1987. xii + 163 pp. Rev, 1993. pp. 113-138 in *Prophecy and the Biblical Prophets*. xii + 180 pp. Amos, pp. 111-113/123-125, was not a country bumpkin. He has a fresh literary expertise blending legal idiom, the messenger speech form, creation hymns, a lament, fine poetic expressions. His message is one of judgment. The last few verses of hope were added later.

1284. Scharbert, Josef. "Amos." pp. 91-133 in *Die Propheten Israels bis 700 v. Chr.* Cologne: Bachem, 1965. 359 pp. This is ch 8. Ch 10 (pp. 185-193) compares Hosea and Amos. Discusses the sources of the book, Amos's biography, his relationship to the people, "that Day," oracles of woe, key words such as "Hear!" German translations with commentary.

1285. Schaumberger, J.B. "Grundgedanken und Charakterbild des Propheten Amos." *Kirche und Kanzel* 14 (1931), 1-16.

1286. Schedl, Claus. "The Prophet Amos, Champion of Right and Justice." Vol. 4:151-168 in *History of the Old Testament*, 5 vols. Staten Island, NY: Alba House, 1972. 4: xxi + 473 pp. Section 1 reviews the historical background and prophecy from 931-814 BCE while Section 2 carries this to 648. Section 3 is "Under the Hammer of Babylon." Amos (Sec 2) preached justice. He could not keep silent in the face of Israel's sin. The book is composed of sections from his preaching, perhaps preserved by his disciples. His powerful oratory heralds the destruction of Israel but he also has a word for the remnant.

1287. Schegg, Peter (Petrus Johannes, 1815-1885). "Amos." pp. 213-362 in *Die kleinen Propheten Uebersetzt und erklart. Erster Theil. Osee - Michaas.* Regensburg: Manz, 1854. viii + 583 pp. The introduction reviews Amos' work and call, the content, relationship with other texts, historical background, earlier studies. The commentary provides German translation with the text divided into three sections, with exegesis and analysis.

1288. Schenker, Adrian. "Steht der Prophet unter dem Zwang zu weissagen, oder steht Israel vor der Evidenz der Weisung Gottes in der Weissagung des Propheten? Zur Interpretation von Amos 3:3-8." BZ 30, No. 2 (1986), 250-256. Amos does not have to prophesy but people should listen.

1289. Schlesinger, S. "Zu Am 3:15." *Monatsschrift fur Geschichte und Wissenschaft des Judentums* 67, Nos. 1/3 (Jan/Mar 1923), 137. Exegesis. The journal is available in both reprint and microfilm.

1290. Schmid, Hans Heinrich. "Amos. Zur Frage Nach der 'Geistigen Heimat' des Propheten." *Wort und Dienst* ns 10 (1969), 85-103. Reprinted, pp. 121-144 in Altorientalische Welt in der alttest. Theologie. Zurich: TVZ, 1974. Reviews the history of interpretation, notes the relationship with the covenant, old Israelite tradition, other biblical texts, the wisdom tradition.

1291. Schmid, Herbert. "Nicht Prophet bin ich, noch Prophetensohn. Zur Erklarung von Amos 7:14a." *Judaica* 23, No. 2 (1967), 68-74. Exegesis and review of earlier studies.

1292. Schmid, Rudolf. "Amos 6:1a, 4-7 (26. Sonntag des Jahres)." Vol. 3 (1971), 75-82 in *Die alttestamentlichen Lesungen der Sonn- und Festtage Auslegung und Verkundigung* ed Josef Schreiner.

Schriftleitung Erich Zenger. 20. Sonntag des Jahres bis Christkonig Lesejahr C. Vol. 3. in den Verlagen Echter Katholisches Bibelwerk. Wurzberg: Echter, 1971. 169 pp. Discusses the text and the situation, theological implications (the prophet as social critic) and suggested outlines for preaching.

1293. Schmidt, Daniel. "Critical Note: Another Word-Play in Amos?" *Grace Theological J* (Winona Lake, IN) 8, No. 1 (Spr 87), 141-142. Discusses the destruction of Israel and a word play that runs through the book. The root is *'mts* which appears in 2:14, 16, where the prophet speaks of human power which is futile before God. It is part of Amaziah's name and he will be destroyed.

1294. Schmidt, Hans. "Die Herkunft des Propheten Amos." pp. 158-171 in *Karl Budde zum siebzigsten Geburtstag am 13. April 1920* ed Karl Marti. BZAW 34. Giessen: Topelmann, 1920. vii + 194 pp. Compares various interpretations, MT and LXX, other prophets, details on Amos' description of himself.

1295. Schmidt, Hans. *Der Prophet Amos*. Sechs Vorlesungen an Einem Kriegschochschulkurs. Tubingen: Mohr, 1917.

1296. Schmidt, Nathaniel. "On the Text and Interpretation of Amos 5:25-27." JBL 13, Nos. 1&2 (1894), 1-15. Exegesis with comparison of MT, LXX, Vulgate, the history of interpretation, comparison with other texts. Amos thought the earlier period of the Wilderness Wandering did not have a sacrificial cult. It probably did but it was not the center of the faith.

1297. Schmidt, Werner H. "Die deuteronomistische Redaktion des Amosbuches. Zu den theologischen Unterschieden zwischen dem Prophetenwort und seinem Sammler." ZAW 77, No. 2 (1965), 168-193. Surveys previous opinions, studies the theological significance of the deuteronomic passages of the book. Uses content, language and history to identify deuteronomic editorial verses. These give the time and place of the prophetic activity, note the message as from God, refer to the divine history of Israel, acknowledge the wrong done to the prophets of God, repeat the charges against the nations and the tribes of Israel. Vs 3:7 has a different understanding of God.

1298. Schmidt, Werner H. "'Suchet den Herrn, so werdet ihr leben': Exegetische Notizen zum Thema 'Gott suchen' in der Prophetie." pp. 127-140 in *Ex orbe religionum: Studia Geo Widengren*, vol 1, ed C.J. Bleeker, et al. Studies in the History of Religion 21. Leiden: Brill, 1972. vii + 479 pp. Notes the history of interpretation. Compares Amos 5:4 with the OT concern to seek God and live.

1299. Schmitt, Armin. *Ein offenes Wort: Das Prophetenbuch Amos fur unsere Zeit ershclossen.* Regensburg: Pustet, 1985. 87 pp.

1300. Schmitt, John J. "Samaria in the Books of Prophets of the Eighth Century BCE." pp. 115-121 in *Proceedings of the Eleventh World Congress of Jewish Studies. Jerusalem, June 22-29, 1993. Division A. The Bible and Its World* ed David Assaf. Jerusalem: The World Union of Jewish Studies, 1994. vi + 246 (Eng), iv + 158 (Heb) Both Jerusalem and Samaria were thought to be inviolate and both are called whores by the prophets. Amos announces the destruction of Samaria. His sharpest words are for the elite.

1301. Schmitt, John J. "The Virgin of Israel: Meaning and Use of the Phrase in Amos and Jeremiah." p. 122 in *Program and Abstracts of the XII Congress of the International Organization for the Study of the OT*. Jerusalem: IOSOT, 1986.

1302. Schmitt, John J. "The Virgin of Israel: Referent and Use of the Phrase in Amos and Jeremiah." CBQ 53, No. 3 (July 91), 365-387. The phrase first occurs in Amos 5:2 (though he did not invent it) and is generally seen as a metaphor for Israel. In Jer 31:4, etc., it might be Jerusalem. Schmitt says it refers to capital cities, alternately Samaria and Jerusalem. It does not really mean "virgin" but simply refers to a city as a woman.

1303. Schmoller, Otto. "The Book of Amos." 62 pp. tr and enlarged, Talbot W. Chambers, from Schmoller's *Die Propheten Hosea, Joel und Amos.* Theologisch- homiletisches Bibelwerk. Bielefeld, 1872. The English edition is vol 14 of the OT, containing the minor prophets, edited by Philip Schaff. NY: Scribner's, 1902. Reprinted as vol 7, with Ezekiel, Daniel and the Twelve, of John Peter Lange, *Commentary on the Holy Scriptures: Critical, Doctrinal and Homiletical*, tr, ed, with additions, by Philip Schaff. Grand Rapids,

MI: Zondervan, 1960. Separate pagination of each book. Schmoller's introduction reviews the personal relations of Amos (name, occupation), historical background, the book (contents, style). Both introduction and commentary review the history of interpretation. The commentary has a translation, critical notes on text and grammar, exegesis, a section on doctrine and ethics, one on homiletics and the practical. Each section of the commentary opens with a summary heading.

1304. Schneider, A. "Amos und Luther. Eine Gegenuberstellung." *Pastoralblatter* 106 (1966), 418-434.

1305. Scholl, Karl. "Der Prophetismus der vorexilischen Zeit." pp. 138-170 in *Das Alte Testament und seine Botschaft: Geschichte - Literatur - Theologie*, 2nd ed, by Hans-Jurgen Zobel, et al. Berlin: Evangelische Verlagsanstalt, 1984. 372 pp. (original, 1981) The introduction discusses prophecy, its origins (including outside of Israel) and development, e.g., groups (bands) of prophets, the classical prophets. The general discussion includes the prophetic call, self-understanding, message, social criticism, false prophets, the cult, the message of salvation, the covenant and their use of the early traditions. A later section discusses the role of the deuteronomic editors. Scholl discusses the prophet message in Amos and Hosea (pp. 146-149), etc. Amos and Hosea both worked in the northern kingdom, both were concerned with social injustice. Gives an outline of Amos noting the five visions, the word of salvation, etc. Amos' message includes both God's universal concern for others and Israel's special place. The latter brings God's special wrath. The basic faith is discussed by Koehn (pp. 176-177P); redaction history discussed by Eggebrecht (pp. 202-205).

1306. Schottroff, Willy. "Amos - Das Portrat. . ." see his "The Prophet. . ." (#1308).

1307. Schottroff, Willy. "'Auferstanden aus Ruinen...' Bibelarbeit uber Amos 6:1-14." pp. 107-124 in *Die kostbare Liebe zum Leben* ed Luise Schottroff, et al. Biblische Inspirationen. Munich: Kaiser, 1991.

1308. Schottroff, Willy. "The Prophet Amos: A Socio-Historical Assessment of His Ministry." pp. 27-46 in *God of the Lowly: Socio-Historical Interpretations of the Bible* ed Schottroff and Wolfgang Stegemann. Maryknoll, NY: Orbis, 1984. iv + 172 pp. Tr "Der Prophet Amos: Versuch der Wurdigung seines Auftretens unter sozialgeschichtlichem Aspekt." pp. 39-66 in *Der Gott der kleinen Leute: Sozialgeschichtliche Bibelauslegungen* vol 1. Altes Testament, and vol. 2. Neues Testament ed W. Schottroff and W. Stegemann. Munich: Kaiser, 1979. This essay expands and develops "Amos - Das Portrat eines Propheten (I-V)." *Stimme der Gemeinde* 24 (1972), 113-115, 145-146, 193-196, 225-227, 289-292. Discusses Amos' identity, his book, his historical context, the social background of his message. His ability to express himself and his knowledge of tradition suggest that he was not too lowly. He may have owned or merely herded livestock, etc. The rich of society were exploiting the poor and Amos said God objects to that. He wants justice and righteousness. He seeks a just society. Amos was the first to enunciate a basic theme of the history of Western society.

1309. Schottroff, Willy. "Warum Amos kein Gehor fand." *Stimme der Gemeinde* (Frankfurt) 24 (1972), 113-115, 145-146, 193-196, 225-227, 289-292.

1310. Schoville, Keith N. "A Note on the Oracles of Amos against Gaza, Tyre and Edom." pp. 55-63 in *Studies in Prophecy* ed D. Lys, et al. VTS 26. Leiden: Brill, 1974. vii + 169 pp. The crime of the three was in 841 BCE in retaliation when Jehu submitted to Assyria and broke the alliance against Assyria.

1311. Schoville, Keith N. "The Sins of Aram in Amos 1." Vol 1:363-375 in Division A, *The Proceedings of the Sixth World Jewish Congress of Jewish Studies held at The Hebrew University of Jerusalem 13-19 August 1973 under the auspices of The Israel Academy of Sciences and Humanities* ed Avigdor Shinan. Jerusalem: World Union of Jewish Studies, 1977. vii + 427 (Eng) + vii + 221 (Heb) Reviews the opinions that the oracles against the nations are not a unit while others think this is a unit. The oracles follow a traditional pattern (cf Egyptian sources) with Aram first reflecting an historical event. The countries were in alliance - covenant - but these parity treaties were broken when Jehu submitted to Assyria. The nations had broken their oath.

1312. Schrade, Hubert. "Der Hammer schwingende Gott des Amos." pp. 157-163 in *Der verborgen Gott. Gottesbild und Gottesvorstellung in Israel und im alten Orient.* Stuttgart: Kohlhammer, 1949. 316 pp. + 43 pls. Amos' relationship to the northern kingdom, his vision of God, his relationship to the Canaanite cult, the Day of Yahweh, ancient Egypt.

1313. Schult, Hermann. "Amos 7:15a und die Legitimation des Aussenseiters." pp. 462-478 in *Probleme biblischer Theologie. Gerhard von Rad zum 70. Geburtstag* ed Hans Walter Wolff. Munich: Kaiser, 1971. 690 pp. Survey of interpretations and comparative data. The verse is not history but the legitimation of an outsider.

1314. Schulte, A. "Die koptische Übersetzung der kleinen Propheten." *Theologische Quartalschrift* 76, No. 4 (1894), 605-642, and, vol 77, No. 2 (1895), 209-229. Amos, pp. 628-632. An exegetical study. A general introduction gives background on the Coptic tradition, manuscripts, earlier studies, comparative examples with the corpus of the minor prophets, other versions (MT, LXX, etc.).

1315. Schultes, J.L. "Gott redet auch durch sein Schweigen. Bibel Meditation zu Amos 8:4-7, 11-12." *Bibel und Liturgie* 48 (1975), 256-259.

1316. Schultes, Josef L. *Herr ist sein Name. Eine Arbeitsheft zum Buch Amos.* Gesprache zur Bibel 9. Klosterneuburg: Osterreichisches Katholisches Bibelwerk, 1979. 40 pp. The book is in 10 sections for study, song, prayer, focus on living today. Rev, OTA 3 (1980), 251.

1317. Schultz, Arnold C. "Amos." Vol 2:301-309 in *The Biblical Expositor: The Living Theme of The Great Book*, 3 vols, ed Carl F.H. Henry. Philadelphia: Holman, 1960. 2:vii + 402 pp. Reprinted, pp. 683-691, in one volume, 1973. xxvii + 1282 pp. A section by section commentary. God punishes but there is the hope of restoration (9:11-15). There is no prediction of a personal Messiah.

1318. Schultz, Arnold C. "Amos." pp. 829-837 in *The Wycliffe Bible Commentary* ed Pfeiffer and Everett F. Harrison. Chicago: Moody, 1962. xvii + 1525 pp. Uzziah reigned successfully "and for a time the influence of Amos was spiritually constructive." "It is generally believed that Amos prophesied" c 760 BCE. It "was a time of political security for Israel, which was reflected in the pride and carelessness of the ruling classes." Amos' writing is in the finest literary style and shows he was not an untutored rustic. His message is a cry for justice. People must repent and seek the Lord. Because people will not repent, there is nothing left but destruction. The Day of the Lord asserts the claims of God's moral character. When this is recognized, the glory of the promised Davidic kingdom will come. That day is inevitable. [The contradiction of will be destroyed and will be restored, is not discussed.]

1319. Schuman, N.A. "Amos on de Traditie." pp. 17-29 in *Amos. Een Aanklacht de profeet en Zijn betekenius nu*. Amsterdam: Vrije Universiteit, 1979.

1320. Schuman, N.A. *Getuigen van tegenspraak; profetie uit de mond van Ams en Jesaja*. Baarn: Ten Have, 1981. 157 pp.

1321. Schumpp, Meinrad. "Der Prophet Amos." pp. 95-145 in *Das buch der zwolf Propheten*. Herders Bibelkommentar. Die Heilige Schrift fur das Leben Erklart, 10/2, ed Edmund Kalt and Willibald Lauck. Freiburg im Breisgau: Herder, 1950. xi + 408 pp. The introduction reviews the man, his time, his book, his religion. The text gives a German translation and verse by verse commentary.

1322. Schungel-Straumann, Helen. *Gottesbild und Kultkritik vorexilischer Propheten*. Stuttgarter Bibelstudien 60, ed Herbert Haag, et al. Stuttgart: KBW [Katholisches Bibelwerk], 1972. 144 pp. Reviews the lordship of Yahweh in Israel and cultic institutions, the imageless God, the covenant God, the pre-state period, the Canaanite cult, divine images, stones and asherah, alters and sacrifices. Discusses Amos' critique of the cult (pp. 30-34) and of the priests, prophets and participants in the cult (pp. 52-53), and, the religious basis for the criticism (pp. 71-87) in his concept of God and "seek the good" as the real service of God.

1323. Schutte, J. "Bible Study on Amos." *Church and Liberation* ed David Jacobus Bosch. Missionalia 5. Pretoria: South Africa Missiological Society, 1977. 126 pp. Rev, *Calvin Theological J* 14 (1979), 87-88.

1324. Schuurmans Stekhoven, J.Z. *De Alexandrijnsche Vertaling van het Dodekapropheton*. Leiden: Brill, 1887. viii + 137 pp. Diss. State University of Gronigen, 1887. An exegetical study. Gives a general discussion of the LXX, earlier studies especially Lagarde, different Greek versions compared to MT citing numerous references from the minor prophets, the work of Jerome and other early scholars, the general character of the LXX version of the minor prophets with many citations from the Twelve. Ch 5 offers variations from Vollers and a more extended treatment of individual prophets, e.g., Amos, pp. 59-60. The Scripture index lists specific citations in the text.

1325. Schuurmans Stekhoven, J.Z. "Het Vaderland van Amos." *Theologische Studien* 7, No. 3 (1889), 222-228. Discussion of Tekoa and the area, earlier writers, description, later tradition, OT references.

1326. Schwantes, Milton. *Amos: Meditacoes e Estudos*. Sao Leopoldo/ Petropolis: Sinodal/Vozes, 1987. 124 pp. *Das Land kann seine Worte nicht ertragen: Meditationen zu Amos*. Tb 105. Munich: Kaiser, 1991. 186 pp. Discusses the historical background of the time of Jeroboam, Amos' experience of God, the message of Amos, its doom, God as Creator.

1327. Schwantes, Milton. "Jacob el Pequeno Visiones en Amos 7-9: En Homenje al Pastor Werner Fuchs." *RIBLA: Revista de Interpretacion Biblica Latinoamericana* (San Jose, Costa Rica) 1 (1988), 87-99. Discusses the context of the visions, and adds commentary on each, noting the dialogue between Amos and Yahweh, compassionate concern, his pastoral background.

1328. Schwantes, Milton. "Profecia e Organizacao: Anotacoes a luz de um texto (Am 2,6-16)." *Estudos Biblicos* 5 (1985), 26-39, at the end of *Revista Eclesiastica Brasileira* (Petropolis, Brazil) 45, Issue No. 177 (Mar 85), 1-224. EB 5 (69 pp.) is subtitled "Biblia E

Organizachao Popular." It is attached to REB after p. 224. Translation and commentary, noting earlier studies, comparisons with other texts. Amos knew people who suffered the crimes listed. The peasant movement is the interpretive medium for Amos' threats against the army and the generals, against the state which impoverishes the peasants. Rev, OTA 10 (1987), 177.

1329. Schwantes, Siegfried J. "Note on Amos 4:2b." ZAW 79, No. 1 (1967), 82-83. The Heb *tsnnoth* is translated by *hopla* in the LXX. The Hebrew is translated "hooks" but *hopla* means ropes which makes more sense in context. The Hebrew also relates to the Assyrian for rope.

1330. Sebok (Schonberger), Mark. "Amos." pp. 32-41 in *Die syrische Uebersetzung der zwolf kleinen Propheten und ihr Verhaltniss zu dem Massoretischen Text und zu den Alteren Uebersetzungen Namentlich den LXX und dem Targum*. Breslau: Preuss und Junger, 1887. iii + 75 pp. Diss. Leipzig: Leipzig University, 1887. A general introduction gives background for the study in MT, LXX, the Peshitta and Targums. An exegetical study with notes on relevant chapters and verses.

1331. Sedding, E.D. *The Eyes of the Lord. The Message of Amos*. London: SPCK, 1946.

1332. Seesemann, Otto. "Amos." pp. 1-17 in *Israel und Juda bei Amos und Hosea nebst einem Exkurs uber Hos 1-3*. Theologische Habilitationsschrift. Leipzig: Dieterich, 1898. iv + 44 pp. Analysis and review of scholarship.

1333. Segert, Stanislav. "Zur Bedeutung des Wortes *noqed*." pp. 279-283 in *Hebraische Wortforschung: Festschrift zum 80. Geburtstag von Walter Baumgartner* ed Benedikt Hartmann, et al. SVT 16 ed G.W. Anderson, et al. Leiden: Brill, 1967. x + 429 pp. Reviews the history of interpretation, compares ANE languages, discusses King Mesha of Moab as a *noqed*, perhaps with a cultic function, and the implications for Amos.

1334. Segert, Stanislav. "A Controlling Device for Copying Stereotype Passages? (Amos 1:3-2:8, 6:1-6)." VT 34, No. 4 (Oct 84), 481-482.

D.N. Freedman noted two passages with seven similar sections. In both series, the fifth member is different. This is not a mistake. It's a check on the copyist to get it right.

1335. Seidel, M. "Four Prophets Who Prophesied at the Same Time" (Heb). pp. 195-238 in *Hiqre Mikra*. Jerusalem: Mosad HaRav Kook, 1978.

1336. Seidl, Theodor. "Heuschreckenschwarm und Prophetenintervention: Textkritische und syntaktische Erwagungen zu Am 7:2." BN 37 (1987), 129-138. Discusses the context in vss 1-3, various interpretations.

1337. Seierstad, Ivar P. "Amosprophetien i ljoset av nyare gransking" (The Prophecy of Amos in the Light of New Discoveries). *Tidsskrift for teologi og kirke* (Oslo) 2, no. 1 (1931), 111-127. Discusses Weiser (1929) and Cramer (1930) and a variety of other sources.

1338. Seierstad, Ivar P. "Erlebnis und Gehorsam beim Propheten Amos." ZAW 52, ns 11, No. 1 (1934), 22-41. Cites earlier studies, the question of ecstasy, Amos' description of his call in 7:10-17.

1339. Seierstad, Ivar P. *Die Offenbarungserlebnisse der Propheten Amos, Jesaja und Jeremia. Eine Untersuchung der Erlebnisvorgange unter besonderer Berucksichtigung ihrer religios-sittlichen Art und Auswirkung.* Skrifter utgitt av det Norske Videnskaps-Akademi i Oslo II. Hist.-Filos. Kl. 1946. No. 2. Oslo: Dybwad, 1946. 2nd ed, Oslo: Universitetsforlaget [Scandinavian University Books], 1965. 271 pp. A general review of the topic is followed by an overview of each prophet, the psychological form of their witness, details of their proclamation, personal dimensions, the criterion of the Word of God and the question of ecstatic prophecy.

1340. Seierstad, Ivar P. "Oplenelse oglydighet hosprofeten Amos." pp. 77-97 in *Budskapet: Et utvalg au gammeltesttamentlige artikler.* Oslo: Universitets forlaget, 1971.

1341. Seilhamer, Frank H. "Amos: Judgment, Justice, and Renewal." pp. 41-49 in *Prophets and Prophecy: Seven Key Messengers* by

Seilhamer. Philadelphia: Fortress, 1977. x + 85 pp. Reprinted from *The Lutheran* (1976). The story is retold for lay persons. He notes that Amos pronounced doom but pled with God to forgive rather than destroy the people. However, God would shake Israel like grain in a sieve. Yet his unsinkable love would keep him from obliterating his creation. The land was to be covered with corpses but one day it will be a garden spot.

1342. Seilhamer, Frank H. "The Role of Covenant in the Mission and Message of Amos." pp. 435-451 in *A Light Unto My Path: Old Testament Studies in Honor of Jacob M. Myers* ed Howard N. Bream, et al. Gettysburg Theological Studies 4. Philadelphia: Temple University Press, 1974. xxv + 529 pp. Compares scholarly views that the prophets were innovators. Ideas like the covenant are too sophisticated for desert dwellers. Others note such ideas were ancient when Abraham left Ur. Amos' words reflect violations of the covenant, for both Judah and Israel. The covenant is seen in both the terminology used by Amos and in the sins for which people are guilty. The covenant curses are about to happen.

1343. Sell, Canon [Edward]. "Amos." pp. 10-16 in *The Minor Prophets*. Madras: Diocesan Press, 1922. xiii + 77 pp. Describes Amos' concern for justice, his call, his call to the people to repent, God's rejection of ritual, the doom to come, the hope in the future for the repentant nation.

1344. Sellin, Ernst. "Antisamaritanische Auslegungen im Texte des Amosbuches." *Orientalistische Literaturzeitung* = OLZ 17, No. 4 (Ap '14), cols 155-156. Exegesis of 5:26 and related OT verses.

1345. Sellin, Ernst. "Drei Umstrittene Stellen des Amosbuches." *Z des Deutschen Palastina-Vereins* 52 (1929), 141-148. Amos 5:13, 6:2, 9:1. Exegesis.

1346. Sellin, Ernst. "Der Prophet Amos. pp. 144-225 in *Die Zwolfprophetenbuch ubersetzt und erklart*. Kommentar zum Alten Testament 12 ed Sellin, et al. Leipzig: Deichert, 1922. ix + 568 pp. Later editions are in multiple volumes, e.g., *Erste Halfte: Hosea - Micha*, 2 vols, 3rd ed. Leipzig: Quelle und Meyer, 1930. A general introduction discusses the Book of the Twelve, the significance of the Twelve in the history of religion, rhythm (poetry) in the Twelve. The introduction to Amos reviews the man, his time, his book, the rhythm of the language. The commentary gives a German translation, critical notes, exegesis.

1347. Selms, A. van. "Amos' Geographic Horizon." pp. 166-169 in *Studies on the Book of Amos: Papers Read at 8th Meeting of Die Ou Testamentiese Werkgemeenskap in Suid-Afrika Held at Pretoria University 1965* ed A.H. van Zyl. OTWSA 7-8 (1964-1965). Potchefstroom: Pro Rege - Pers Beperk, 1965. pp. 113-169 pp. Bound with *Studies on the Book of Hosea*, the 7th Congress of the OTWSA, 111 pp., with continuous pagination for a total of 169 pp. Geographic poetry centers on a place, e.g., Jerusalem, Samaria, or, a whole series of places. Amos has 73 names of which 29 are Judah or Israel; 23 transjordanian; 21 cisjordanian (9 Judah; 12 Israel). Israel had recently captured or recaptured transjordanian territory from Damascus. Amos knew of places within a 500 mile radius.

1348. Selms, A. van. "Isaac in Amos." pp. 157-165 in *Studies on the Book of Amos: Papers Read at 8th Meeting of Die Ou Testamentiese Werkgemeenskap in Suid-Afrika Held at Pretoria University 1965* ed A.H. van Zyl. OTWSA 7-8 (1964-1965). Potchefstroom: Pro Rege - Pers Beperk, 1965. pp. 113-169 pp. Bound with *Studies on the Book of Hosea*, the 7th Congress of the OTWSA, 111 pp., with continuous pagination for a total of 169 pp. There are two references: Amos 7:9, 16. Here are two of the four times the name is spelled with a *sin* compared with 107 spellings with a *tsade*. The latter is a literary tradition and the former an oral tradition. In Amos, the usage is related to the Jacob cycle including Bethel and the transjordan holy places like Penuel.

1349. Servert, Maria Josefa de Azcarraga. *Minhat Say de Y.S. de Norzi: Profetas Menores: (traduccion y anotacion critica).* Textos y Estudios "Cardinal Cisneros" 40. Madrid: Instituto de Filologia, C.S.I.C., Departamento de Filologia Biblica y de Oriente Antigua, 987. lxix + 259 pp. Reviews Norzi's life and the origin of his work known as the *Minhat Say*, "Offering of Shelomo Yedidiah (Norzi)." The original title *Goder Peres*, "Repairer of the Breach" (Isaiah 58:12) indicates its purpose - to establish the correct text. Servert's critical commentary discusses Norzi's sources and how he used them.

1350. Shapiro, David S. "The Seven Questions of Amos." *Tradition* (NY) 20, No. 4 (Wint 82), 327-331. The seven are in Amos 3:3-8. They all relate to the prior statement that God has known Israel alone, so Israel will be destroyed. The examples relate to harmony, and cause and effect. People should live in harmony with God but instead they go in the opposite direction. God warns them of the result in hopes they will repent.

1351. Shaskolsky, Rinah Lipis. "The Prophets as Dissenters." *Judaism* 19, No. 1 (Wint 70), 15-29. Gives several examples from Amos, Hosea, Micah and Jeremiah.

1352. Shelley, John C. "Amos." pp. 743-755 in *Mercer Commentary on the Bible* ed Watson E. Mills, et al. Macon, GA: Mercer University Press, 1995. xxii + 1347 pp. The introduction reviews the author (a cattle rancher, not a poor shepherd), setting, problems of interpretation. Amos was a poet rather than a systematic theologian. Gives an outline of the content. The commentary is in small units, based on the New Revised Standard Version of the Bible.

1353. Shy, Hadassa. "Amos" (Heb). pp. 70-99 in *Tanhum Ha-Yerushalmi's Commentary on the Minor Prophets: A Critical Edition with an Introduction translated into Hebrew and Annotated* (Heb). Publication of the Perry Foundation for Biblical Research. Jerusalem: Magnes Press, The Hebrew University, 1991. lxii + 376 pp. Tanhum ben Joseph died in 1291.

1354. Sicre, Jose L. "Amos." pp. 87-168 in *"Con Los Pobres de la Tierra": La justicia social en los profetas de Israel.* Madrid: Ediciones Cristiandad, 1984. 506 pp. Gives an overview of justice concerns in the ANE, then in individual prophets and then in a synthesis on a vision of society, victims, concrete problems, who is responsible, solutions. For Amos, Sicre analyzes Amos' personality, his time, oracles against the nations, the encounter with God, the grand alternative ("Seek me and live"), the "woe" section, the denunciation of the merchants. He discusses a vision of society, with Amos' condemnations, the victims of injustice, responsibility for oppression, was Amos a social critic. Sicre gives a thorough review of earlier theories and a special discussion of Robert Coote's theory.

1355. Sicre, Jose L. "Los dioses olvidados. Poder y riqueza en los profetas preexilicos." pp. 109-115 in *Estudios de Antiguo Testamento* 1. Madrid: Cristiandad, 1979.

1356. Sicre, J. "Weissage uber mein Volk Israel. Der Prophet Amos - Zeit, Persohnlichkeit, Botschaft." pp. 110-123 in *Gericht und Umkehr. Die Botschaft des Propheten Amos.* Neukirchen-Vluyn: Neukirchener, 1967.

1357. Sievers, Eduard and Hermann Guthe. *Amos, metrisch bearbeitet.* Der Abhandlungen der Philologisch-Historischen Klasse der Konigl. Sachsischen Gesellschaft der Wissenschaften 23, No. 3. Leipzig: Teubner, 1907. ii + 92 pp. The text in Hebrew and transliteration, both with critical notes, a study of the poetry and style and a general introduction to the text.

1358. Sievi, Josef. "Weissage uber mein volk Israel. Der Prophet Amos - Zeit, Personlichkeit, Botschaft." *Bibel und Kirche* 22, No. 4 (1967), 110-116.

1359. Sigg, Ferdinand. "Amos: Herr, dir ist niemand zu vergleichen." pp. 18-20 in *Zwolf Heilege Menschen Gottes: Zum Studium der Zwolf Kleinen Propheten.* Zurich: Christliche Vereinsbuchhandlung, n.d. 48 pp. Opening units give a general introduction to the prophets, discuss God's word, historical background, and who were the prophets. Includes a chronological table and map for the period of the Twelve, and discussion questions on each. The discussion gives a general overview of Amos, with opposition to the Canaanite tradition and the future restoration.

1360. Simeon, Charles. "Amos." pp. 189-245 in *Expository Outlines on the Whole Bible. Vol 10. Hosea through Malachi.* Grand Rapids, MI: Zondervan, 1956. viii + 631 pp. Reprint, from 8th ed, London: Bolm, 1847. Original title, *Horae Homileticae.* Sermons on selected texts, listed in the Table of Contents with sermon titles. The Expository Outlines are numbered. Amos has Nos. 1186-1196.

Each "Outline" reprints a text, e.g. Amos 2:13, with a sermon outline, containing illustrations, discussion of concepts, application.

1361. Simmons, J. Sam. "Spiritual Leadership and the Integrity Factor: How Amos Challenges Contemporary Spiritual Leaders." *Mid-America Theological J* 19 (1995), 99-113. Develop personal discipline (do not be at ease in Zion), confidence in God (not Samaria), value for things in perspective (beds of ivory), an awareness of the danger of slavery to pleasure (those who drink wine from sacrificial bowls), a renewal of God's vision (do not grieve over the ruin of Joseph). Integrity and effective spiritual leadership are inseparable.

1362. Simon, Uriel. "Amos." pp. 177-265, 299-313 in *Abraham Ibn Ezra's Two Commentaries on the Minor Prophets. An Annotated Critical Edition. 1. Hosea, Joel, Amos* (Heb). The Institute for the History of Jewish Bible Research, Sources and Studies 4. Ramat-Gan, Israel: Bar-Ilan University Press, 1989. 332 pp. Abraham Ibn Izra (1089-1164). A general introduction reviews the commentary tradition and the work as a whole. S.C. Reif (VT 42, No. 2 (Ap 92), 278) notes the text of the standard commentary written in France in 1156, based on MS Montefiore at Jews' College, London. It is a newly published "alternative version" composed 12 years earlier in Italy and transcribed in simple terms by a pupil; follows MS Heb 217 at Bibliothéque Nationale, Paris. Other manuscripts, later commentators and printed editions are used and evaluated. A detailed introduction will be provided in a future volume.

1363. Sinclair, L.A. "The Courtroom Motif in the Book of Amos." JBL 85, No. 3 (S 66), 351-353. The heavenly council, the *rib* pattern and the covenant are background for Amos' oracles.

1364. Sinker, R., ed. "Amos." pp. xix-xxi + 82-99 in *The Book of Daniel & the Minor Prophets*. Philadelphia/ London: Lippincott/ Dent, 1901. xxxiv + 242 pp. The kingdom was strong but Amos predicted its doom. The reference to the earthquake suggests the book was published at once as complete. Amos' God was not just Israel's but the God of all the earth. His message endures because the evils he preached against have endured through the ages.

1365. Sklba, Richard J. *Pre-Exilic Prophecy: Words of Warning, Dreams of Hopes, Spirituality of Pre-Exilic Prophets.* Message of Biblical Spirituality 3, ed Carolyn Osiek. Collegeville, MN: Liturgical Press [A Michael Glazier Book], 1990. vii + 183 pp. Sklba reviews prophecy in terms of "mysterious beginnings" (visions; call), zealous for the Lord, voices for the poor, liturgy, judgment, salvation, images of God, the community. He discusses Amos' call, his message of justice and righteousness vs social evil, judgment on the nation and the later editorial addition of Judah to Amos' message.

1366. Smalley, William A. "Discourse Analysis and Bible Translation." BTr 31, No. 1 (Jan 80), 119-125. Discourse analysis is a term for efforts to study larger organizations of texts. The theory of dynamic equivalence translation (meaning in context) is not very helpful in this. Vague generalities apply rather than precise understanding. Smalley compares translations of Amos to show how modern translations may destroy the Hebrew structure, patterning, repetition. Suggests an English rhetorical style. This type of analysis shows that not all examples will be the same in all languages and on all levels of language.

1367. Smalley, William A. "Recursion Patterns and the Sectioning of Amos." BTr 30, No. 1 (Jan 79), 118-127. Shows how patterns, e.g., chiasm, relate smaller sections, and larger groups. It's a common device for giving form to otherwise loosely connected sayings or stories. This provided unity, cohesion, aesthetic form. Translators should show these relationships. Uses many examples from Amos.

1368. Smalley, William A. "Translating the Poetry of the OT." BTr 26, No. 2 (Ap 75), 201-211. From the introduction of Jan de Waard and Smalley, *A Translator's Handbook on Amos.* Uses Amos as examples of parallelism, picture language, meter, emotion, making the reader think without saying something directly, subject matter. Gives suggestions on translating poetry as poetry.

1369. Smalley, William A. "Translating 'Thus saith the Lord'." BTr 29, No. 1 (Jan 78), 222-224. Uses Amos for examples to show different ways of translating to give the words more authority. The prophets spoke so the modern translator should listen to the words read or spoken out loud to catch the oratorical style. Sometimes "thus saith the Lord" should be left out and at times changed in position to give the intended effect.

1370. Smart, James D. "Amos." Vol 1:116-121 in *The Interpreter's Dictionary of the Bible* ed George A. Buttrick, et al. Nashville: Abingdon, 1962. xxxi + 876 pp. Discusses a new epoch in prophecy (first separate book), the man and his background, date (between 760-745 BCE), the book, style, theology (covenant, remnant, universalism, Day of Yahweh).

1371. Smart, James D. *Servants of the Word: The Prophets of Israel.* Westminster Guides to the Bible ed Edwin M. Good. Philadelphia: Westminster Press, 1960. 95 pp. Gives a general introduction to Amos, historical background, structure of the book, attack on false religion. We hear nothing more of him but his words were edited in Judah.

1372. Smelik, K.A.D. "The Meaning of Amos 5:18-20." VT 36, No. 2 (Ap 86), 246-248. The Day of the Lord is a future event in which God will crush his enemies who include the false prophets. People think it will be Israel's victory but instead God will use the enemy armies to punish his people.

1373. Smend, Rudolf. "Das Nein des Amos." pp. 85-103 in *Die Mitte des Alten Testaments: Gesammelte Studien Band 1.* Beitrage zur Evangelischen Theologie 99 ed Eberhard Jungel and Smend. Munich: Kaiser, 1986. 246 pp. Reprinted from EvT 23, No. 8 (1963), 404-423. Compares Amos' no, or Yahweh's no through Amos, with Micah, other prophets, and today. The parallel is with the social situation. Discusses the covenant and Israel as the people of Yahweh, Amos and the cult as per the modern discussion of cult prophets.

1374. Smend, Rudolf. "'Das Ende is gekommen': Ein Amoswort in der Priesterschrift" pp. 67-72 in *Die Botschaft und die Boten. Festschrift fur Hans Walter Wolff zum 70. Geburtstag* ed Jorg Jeremias and Lothar Perlitt. Neukirchen: Neukirchener, 1981. ix + 426 pp. Reprinted pp. 154-159 in *Die Mitte des Alten Testaments: Gesammelte Studien Band 1.* Beitrage zur evangelischen Theologie

99 ed Eberhard Jungel and Smend. Munich: Kaiser, 1986. 246 pp. Compares Amos 8:2 with Gen 6:13 and other texts with a review of scholarly interpretations.

1375. Smith, Billy K. "Amos." pp. 89-129 in *Hosea, Joel, Amos, Obadiah, Jonah*. Layman's Bible Book Commentary 13. Nashville, TN: Broadman, 1982. 153 pp. The publisher notes the series is primarily concerned with the meaning of the Bible for today. The Table of Contents gives a detailed outline of each book. The author's introduction describes the prophet (his name, not a professional prophet), the times, the prophecies (words, visions). The commentary is in many small units, which include exegesis, description and explanation of the content of Amos, and very little reference to the present, no footnotes, no bibliography.

1376. Smith, Billy K. "Amos." pp. 22-170 in *Amos, Obadiah, Jonah* by Smith and Frank S. Page. The New American Commentary 19B ed E. Ray Clendenen, et al. Nashville, TN: Broadman & Holman, 1995. 304 pp. The introduction reviews the historical background, the man himself (discusses *noqed*), the book, language, message (God's sovereignty, the end of Israel, judgment, Day of the Lord, restoration). The commentary is divided into title and theme, Amos' words, his visions.

1377. Smith, Gary V. *Amos: A Commentary*. Library of Biblical Interpretation. Grand Rapids, MI: Regency Reference Library (Zondervan), 1989. xv + 307 pp. The introduction surveys the historical context, the man and the book (text, style, structure, theological themes). The theology centers on the acts of God whose concern is moral righteousness. The commentary is divided into three parts, reflecting the text, chs 1-2, 3-6, 7-9. Each is introduced and discussed in terms of unity, structure, interpretation and theological developments. The translation is in a column paralleled by a verse by verse analytical outline. Each unit within the parts provides introduction, background, structure, interpretation, theological development. The hopeful epilogue at the end is part of the message. It is hope for the righteous remnant, consistent with other prophets. Extensive notes and bibliography provide both confirmatory and alternate points of view.

1378. Smith, Gary V. "Amos 5:13. The Deadly Silence of the Prosperous." JBL 107, No. 2 (July 88), 289-291. No emendation is necessary. Just translate, "Therefore, at that time the prosperous person will be silent, for it will be an evil time."

1379. Smith, Gary V. "Continuity and Discontinuity in Amos' Use of Tradition." JETS 34, No. 2 (Mar 91), 33-42. Recent scholarship has emphasized continuity, e.g., covenant treaties, but they also had new words for a new day. Amos is an example of both in literary forms of speech, theology and application. Amos used the Exodus story but in his time, God killed the young men of Israel rather than Egypt. Sin is more important than the exodus in determining the future.

1380. Smith, Gary V. "The Vision Report in Amos 9." p. 205 in *Abstracts: American Academy of Religion/Society of Biblical Literature 1986* ed Kent Harold Richards Melugin and James B. Wiggins. Atlanta, GA: Scholars Press, 1986. i + 269 pp. The SBL section is pp. 169-262 from the 122nd Annual Meeting. The vision reports end with 9:10.

1381. Smith, George Adam. "Amos." 1:55-216 in *The Book of the Twelve Prophets, Commonly Called the Minor. Vol. 1. Amos, Hosea, and Micah. With an Introduction and a Sketch of Prophecy in Early Israel*, 2 vols, rev. The Expositor's Bible 4. NY: Harper & Brothers, 1928. 1:xx + 478 + foldout chronology; 2:xx + 529 + 2 foldout chronologies (original 1896-98) Smith provides a new translation and reviews the book, the man, atrocities, civilization and judgment, the false peace of ritual, doom or discipline, common sense and law. The bulk of the book is genuine but over 50 vss have been questioned. The atrocities are those of the nations with Judah and Israel condemned last. The latters' doom is the heavier because they have been the more privileged.

1382. Smith, George Adam. "Common Sense and the Reign of Law." pp. 202-205 in *Perspectives on Old Testament Literature* ed Woodrow Ohlsen. NY: Harcourt Brace Jovanovich, 1978. xiii + 450 pp. Reprinted from Smith, *The Book of the Twelve Prophets*. Amos sees cause and effect in God's actions against Israel. He has a sense of law, of moral necessity.

1383. Smith, John. "The Burden of Amos." ET 11, No. 2 (Nov 1899), 83-88. The prophets drew on Abraham and Moses. God worked through Amos, a peasant. Anyone can see external events. The new element was the light God gave on the events, and the discovery of God himself in this new time. There is judgment on nations as well as individuals, on the moral decay of civilization, e.g., people dedicated to nothing more than making money.

1384. Smith, John Merlin Powis (1866-1932). "Amos and Hosea." pp. 55-84 in *The Prophets and Their Times*, 2nd ed, by Smith (1st ed) and William A. Irwin (2nd ed). Chicago: University of Chicago Press, 1941. xvii + 342 pp. (original, 1925) The 2nd preface is dated Thanksgiving Day, 1940. Amos is discussed on pp. 57-69. Reviews the history of the times and Amos' denunciation of corruption, conspicuous consumption and external ritual. The Day of the Lord will be one of disaster rather than triumph. The only hope is right conduct and genuine religious attitude. He probably would not have done away with sacrifice but his religion was ethical or theological. He objected to the magical ideas.

1385. Smith, John Merlin Powis (1866-1932). "A Commentary on the Book of Amos." pp. 1-68 in *A Commentary on the Books of Amos, Hosea, and Micah* by Smith. The Bible for Home and School ed Shailer Mathews. NY: Macmillan, 1914. ix + 216 pp. The introduction gives an outline, discusses the unity of the text (Amos has suffered little at the hands of the editors), literary style (vigorous, effective), date, historical background, the man and his message. The latter was counter to all the beliefs of his day. He opposed corruption, injustice, oppression. He pronounced judgment but the very fact that he preached shows that he hoped, he cared. He failed to save Israel but his ability to diagnose the problem was established. The commentary is based on the Revised Version of 1881 with exegetical footnotes and critical notes on the text. Amos 7:14 is translated, "I was no prophet," i.e., he was not a professional prophet seeking personal gain.

1386. Smith, Ralph L. "Amos." pp. 81-141 in *The Broadman Bible Commentary*. Vol. 7. *Hosea-Malachi* ed Clifton J. Allen, et al. Nashville, TN: Broadman, 1972. xiv + 394 pp. The introduction reviews the man, times, book, theology. Amos was a shepherd, a *noqed*, a word used elsewhere in the OT only for King Mesha (2 Kgs 3:4). There was political stability in his time with the rich getting richer. People were religious but in an external way. The book is in two parts. There are sermonettes, a dirge, doxologies, prayer, rhetorical questions (which show influence from the wisdom movement). Amos 7-9 has five visions - more than any other book of OT prophecy. His theology is judgment. The end of Israel is near. The other nations are also judged. There is a ray of hope in 9:11-15, which many scholars see as a later addition but it is difficult to believe Amos was only a messenger of doom. The commentary is on units rather than verse by verse.

1387. Smith, Ralph L. "The Theological Implications of the Prophecy of Amos." SWJT 9, No. 1 (Fall 66), 49-56. The Book of Amos is not a systematic theology on the nature of God, man, sin and salvation. Instead he proclaims what God is going to do - destroy Israel. He also reminds people of what God has done (covenant) and what the nations and Israel have done (sin). His Messianic oracle is hope for the future when Israel and Judah will be re-united.

1388. Smith, Roy L. *The Bible and the First World State: Amos, Hosea, Isaiah, Micah*. Know Your Bible Series 2 ed Elmer A. Leslie, et al. NY: Abingdon, 1943. 64 pp. A general introduction claims the prophets spoke for their own time rather than some mystical future, but the time to which they spoke was very similar to our own [NB: Smith spoke to 1943; over 50 years later, his statement is more, not less true]. Smith uses a question/answer or catechetical format and fits in scripture at appropriate places. Historically he describes the change from an agricultural to commercial economy, the rising tide of immorality, the corruption of the worship of Yahweh. For Amos (pp. 21-34), Smith discusses the man, his private life, book, preaching, era, visions, Bethel, the Day of Jehovah, politics, morality, condemnation and hope. Instead of sacrifice of rams and bulls, Amos demanded just and fair treatment of others. He condemned graft, corruption, cruelty, prostitution, drunkenness. He called for righteous living. Priests and those in high places rejected him.

1389. Smith, W. Robertson. "Amos and the House of Jehu." pp. 90-143 in *The Prophets of Israel and Their Place in History to the Close of the Eighth Century B.C.* NY: Appleton, 1882. xvi + 444 pp. Detailed discussion of the historical background and the religious situation as Amos came on the scene. Reviews our knowledge of Amos' person and message, lack of knowledge of God, God's universalism, the judgment, hope for the future.

1390. Smythe, H.R. "The Interpretation of Amos 4:13 in St. Athanasius and Didymus." JTS ns 1, No. 2 (Oct 50), 158-168. These two were orthodox. Their opponents denied the divinity of the Holy Spirit and appealed to this verse. Athanasius decides that *pneuma* without the article or additional words, does not indicate the Holy Spirit. He noted context, different usages for a word, different ways to interpret. Didymus follows Athanasius, that this verse does not refer to the Holy Spirit. While they did not know Hebrew, their interpretation is pre-eminently sane, not forcing interpretation of single words. The doctrinal issue does not depend on mere literalness.

1391. Snaith, Norman H. "Amos." pp. 11-51 in *Amos, Hosea and Micah.* Epworth Preachers' Commentaries, ed Greville P. Lewis, et al. London: Epworth, 1956. 112 pp. The commentary series attempts to explain the original meaning of the text and indicate its relevance. Part of the latter is that the prophets knew sin when they saw it. The commentary is divided into small units which Snaith sees as independent, i.e., context is not helpful in understanding. He notes a number of later additions to the text including the hope for restoration in ch 9. The editor thought faithful Israelites would be saved but did not think sinners would be. There is debate over the origin of the phrase, "the Day of the Lord." The best explanation is that originally it referred to New Year's Day and the Harvest Feast.

1392. Snaith, Norman H. *The Book of Amos.* Part I. *Introduction.* Part 2. *Translation and Notes,* 2 vols. Study Notes on Bible Books. London: Epworth, 1945-1946. 1:48; 2:147 pp. Reprinted, 1957-1958. Vol 1 discusses the historical background, the economic conditions in Israel, the canon, the construction of the book, Amos the man and prophet, the message. The latter includes the rejection of Israel, charges against the rich, worship and wickedness, the God of righteousness, Jehovah the Savior. Amos clearly had a bias for the poor and needy. The translation in vol 2 is presented in small units of 1-3 verses with exegesis and commentary. In the confrontation with Amaziah, Amos says he is not a professional prophet. The hopeful verses at the end are understood as later additions to the text.

1393. Snyder, George. "The Law and Covenant in Amos." *Restoration Quarterly* 25, No. 3 (1982), 158-166. Compares the ANE treaty pattern with the Sinai covenant and the prominence of the covenant in Amos.

1394. Snyman, S.D. "Amos 6:1-7 as an intensification of Amos 3:9-11." *In Die Skriflig* (Potchefstrom, S Africa) 28, No. 2 (June 94), 213-222. Reviews earlier opinions including Jeremias (Amos 3-6) who separated chs 3-4 from chs 5-6. Snyman's structural analysis confirms this.

1395. Snyman, S.D. "A Note on Ashdod and Egypt in Amos 3:9." VT 44, No. 4 (Oct 94), 559-562. Reviews the history of interpretation. Suggests (traditio-historical) that Ashdod represents the Conquest and Egypt the Exodus.

1396. Snyman, S.D. "Politiek in die preek? 'n Illustrasie uit Amos 3:9-15." *Ned Geref Teologiese Tydskrif* 33, No. 2 (June 92), 150-156. Discusses political preaching with Amos as an example, including NT perspectives. Amos 3:9-15 illustrates how this can be done.

1397. Snyman, S.D. "'Violence' in Amos 3:10 and 6:3." ETL 71, No. 2 (Ap 95), 30-47. Exegesis comparing other passages in Amos and the Bible in the context of violence in the Bible as whole. The second pericope here intensifies he first.

1398. Soares, T.G. "Social Sins and National Doom. An Exposition of Amos 5:18-6:14." BW 31, No. 1 (Jan '08), 62-67. The study includes false thinking, selfish indifference, inevitable consequences.

1399. Soden, Wolfram von. "Zu einigen Ortsbenennungen bei Amos und Micha." *Z fur Althebraistik* 3, No. 2 (1990), 214-220. Suggests emendations in Amos 6:2 (*sijjon* to *'ijjon* as in Ps 133:3) and in Micah 1:10ff.

1400. Soggin, J. Alberto. "Amos 6:13-14 und 1:3 auf dem Hintergrund der Beziehungen zwischen Israel und Damascus im 9. und 8. Jahrhundert." pp. 433-441 in *Near Eastern Studies in Honor of William Foxwell Albright* ed Hans Goedicke. Baltimore: Johns Hopkins, 1971. xxvii + 474 pp. Discusses the historical background.

1401. Soggin, J. Alberto. "Das Erdbeben von Amos 1:1 und die Chronologie der Konige Ussia und Jotham von Juda." ZAW 82, No. 1 (1970), 117-121. (Eng summary) Traces of an earthquake were found in Hazor in 1956, identified with Amos 1:1, dated 760 BCE. Zech 14:4-5 refers to it years later. Josephus IX, x, 14 connects it on a cultic transgression by Uzziah, for which he was smitten with leprosy, which required the co-regency with Jotham. Begrich and Jepsen figured out a date of 759 for this, almost identical with the excavations at Hazor. A chronological chart shows the sequence for the different sources.

1402. Soggin, J. Alberto. *The Prophet Amos: A Translation and Commentary*. London: SCM, 1987. xix + 150 pp. Tr of *Il profeta Amos*. Brescia: Paideia, 1982, revised and updated to constitute a second edition. The introduction considers the man and his time, literary genres, style, composition, origins of the book, Amos' thought, the LXX and ancient versions. A new translation is followed by a philological-critical commentary for the translation which is followed by an historical and exegetical commentary. The note of hope at the end is post-exilic, popular eschatology. General bibliography and also for each unit.

1403. Solari, J.K. "Amos, Book of." Vol 1:453-454 in *New Catholic Encyclopedia*, 16 vols, ed William J. McDonald, et al. NY: McGraw-Hill, 1967 (Vol 16, Supplement, 1974). Reviews the historical background, divisions of the book, its composition, content and doctrine. Most of the book is by Amos. References to Judah and other fragments were added later. The messianic promise of restoration, 9:8c-15, was probably added in the exile after the destruction of both kingdoms. With rustic candor, he exposes the greed of the wealthy. Sincere repentance and a return to Yahweh might save them. His theme is righteousness in contrast to Hosea's emphasis on love, *chesed*, a term which is not found in Amos.

1404. Soper, B. Kingston. "For Three Transgressions and for Four: A New Interpretation of Amos 1:3, etc." ET 71, No. 3 (Dec 59), 86-87. Discusses numerical sayings and parallels in Homer and Ugaritic and various interpretations of Amos. Amos is not a numerical saying. Follows the Talmudic interpretation which emphasizes four. One gets away with it three times but not the fourth.

1405. Sowada, John. "Let Justice Surge Like Water..." BT 19, No. 5 (Sep 81), 301-305. Israel kept the outward forms but abandoned the essence of her faith. Amos condemned the indulgent spirit of the powerful used to exploit the powerless. Cultic observance was a cultic charade. Election entails responsibility.

1406. Speidel, Kurt. "Hunger nach Gottes Wort. Meditation zu Amos 8:11-12." Bibel und Kirche 22, No. 4 (1967), 120-122.

1407. Speier, Salomon. "Bemerkungen zu Amos." VT 3, No. 3 (July 53), 305-310. Exegetical notes on Amos, e.g., Tekoa. This is unit I. See Homenaje for unit II.

1408. Speier, Salomon. "Bemerkungen zu Amos, II." 2:365-372 in Homenaje a Millas-Vallicrosa, 2 vols ed R. Almagia and M. Almagro. Barcelona: Consejo Superior de Investigaciones Cientificas, 1956. 582 pp. Discusses Jewish interpretations of Amos - Hebrew commentaries (Qimhi, Rashi, Malbim), the Mishna (Ta'anit Pereq III), the work of Azarja dei Rossi.

1409. Speier, Salomon. "Did Rashi have Another Vorlage on Amos 4:10 than is found in the Usual Editions?" (Heb). Leshonenu 33, No. 1 (Oct 68), 15-17, 111 (Eng summary). Rashi read kederek and not bederek, with the meaning "as on the way." This is found in seven manuscripts.

1410. Speiser, Ephraim Avigdor. "Note on Amos 5:26." BASOR 108 (1947), 5-6. Notes some of the problems interpreters have found but suggests the verse clearly refers to astral idolatry.

1411. Sperber, Alexander. The Bible in Aramaic Based on Old Manuscripts and Printed Texts. IVB. The Targum and the Hebrew

Bible. Leiden: Brill, 1973. xv + 417 pp. The introduction discusses the orgin of the Targum, followed by problems of editing, the Targumic interpretation of the Bible, critical apparatus, variants and sources of confusion, related translations, e.g., Peshitta. "The Hebrew 'Vorlage' of the Targum" presents textual variants for the Pentateuch and the Prophets (pp. 294-351). Amos is pp. 344-345.

1412. Sperber, Alexander. "Amos" (Aramaic). pp. 417-432 in *The Bible in Aramaic Based on Old Manuscripts and Printed Texts. III. The Latter Prophets According to Targum Jonathan*. Leiden: Brill, 1962. xii + 505 pp. The introduction discusses the basic text, Ms. Or. 2211 with additions from Ms. Or. 1474, both in the British Museum, and other sources. The text is transcribed with critical apparatus: Upper (phonetic variants), Lower (consonantal variants) and Testamonia.

1413. Sperber, D. "Varia Midrashica IV. 1. Esau and His Mother's Womb - A Note on Amos 1:11." *Revue des etudes juives* 137, Nos. 1&2 (Jan-June 78), 149-153. Esau cut his mother's *metra* so she could not conceive again. Discusses defective and plene readings. The *kethib* is largely forgotten, replaced by the *qere*.

1414. Spiegel, Shalom. "Amos vs. Amaziah." pp. 38-65 in *The Jewish Expression* ed Judah Goldin. New Haven: Yale University, 1976. (original, 1970) Reprinted from *Essays in Judaism* 3. NY: Jewish Theological Seminary, 1957. Translates the text and compares it with Marbury vs Madison in American history, the semantics of justice, rite and rights, the legacy of justice and peace.

1415. Spradlin, Michael R. "Righteousness and Justice in The Book of Amos." *Mid-America Theological J* 19 (1995), 51-55. Discusses the various meanings of the terms, contrasts the injustice and unrighteousness of unregenerate humanity rebelling against God, God's call to spiritual life.

1416. Spreafico, Ambrogio. "Amos: Struttura Formale e Spuntii per una Interpretazione." *Rivista Biblica* (Brescia, Italy) 29, No. 2 (Ap-June 81), 147-176. Notes earlier studies. Gives detailed analysis of the structure.

1417. Spreafico, Ambrogio. *I Profeti. Introduzione e Saggi di Lettura.* Lettura pastorale della Bibbia 27. Bologne: Dehoniane, 1993. 144 pp. An introduction with a summary of the prophet's life and time, with a pericope in translation and discussed in more detail. Rev, OTA 17, No. 2 (June 94), # 1581.

1418. Sprenger, Hans Norbert. "Commentarius in Amosum." Part 2:105-156 in *Theodori Mopsuesteni Commentarius in XII Prophetas. Einleitung und Ausgabe. Teil I. Einleitung; Teil II. Textausgabe* by Sprenger. Gottinger Orientforschung veroffentlichungen des sonderforschungsbereiches orientalistik and der Georg-August-Universitat Gottingen: Series 5, Biblica et Patristica; Vol 1. Wiesbaden: Harrassowitz, 1977. The parts have separate pagination. 1. vii + 174 pp; 2. ii + 475 pp. Part 1 reviews the Greek and Syriac manuscripts of Theodore including the Nestorian literature in the 8/9th centuries, the biblical text he was using and his exegesis. The latter includes historical-grammatical, typological and theological. The biblical text, his commentary and critical apparatus are presented in Greek. His bibliography includes the versions of the commentary on the 12 prophets published in the 19th century, e.g., PG 66 (1864), 1-662. Cf Theodore.

1419. Staerk, Willy (1866-1946). *Amos-Nahum-Habakuk herausgegeben.* Ausgewahlte poetische Texte des Alten Testaments 2. Leipzig: Hinrichs, 1908.

1420. Stamm, Johann Jakob (1910-1993). "Der Name des Propheten Amos und sein Sprachlicher Hintergrund." pp. 137-142 in *Prophecy: Essays Presented to Georg Fohrer on His Sixty-fifth Birthday 6 September 1980* ed John Adne Emerton. BZAW 150 ed Georg Fohrer. Berlin/NY: de Gruyter, 1980. vii + 202 pp. Analyzes the name, compares Ugaritic, Akkadian and many earlier opinions.

1421. Staples, W.E. "Epic Motifs in Amos." JNES 25, No. 2 (Ap 66), 106-112. General discussion of motifs notes a logical reason for destruction (overpopulation, etc), an intercessor. Suggests the motifs are from literature and prophetic writings are too.

1422. Steinle, W. *Amos, Prophet in der Stude der Krise.* Stuttgart: Steinkopf, 1979. 125 pp.

1423. Steinmann, Andrew. "The Order of Amos's Oracles Against the
      Nations 1:3-2:16." JBL 111, No. 4 (Wint 92), 683-689.
      Reviews earlier studies, geographical order, concatenous (catch words)
      patterns, characteristics of the nations. The oracles were all by one
      person.

1424. Steinmann, Jean. *Le Prophetisme Biblique des Origines a Osee.*
      Lectio Divina 23. Paris: Cerf, 1959. 260 pp. Reviews the historical
      background of the Conquest, the contact between the Israelites and
      the Canaanites, and prophecy from the Judges to Hosea. Amos (pp.
      139-186) is discussed in terms of his historical background and
      ministry, the main oracles on injustice and the cult, God's judgment
      on Israel, and Amos himself - his character, culture, opposition to
      ritual, monotheism and poetry.

1425. Steinmueller, John E. and Kathryn Sullivan. "Amos." p. 62 in
      Catholic Biblical Encyclopedia, Old Testament. NY: Wagner,
      1956. xviii + 1166 + xiii [appendix] Discusses Amos, his life and
      historical background.

1426. Steinmueller, John E. and Kathryn Sullivan. "Amos, Book of." pp.
      62-64 in *Catholic Biblical Encyclopedia, Old Testament.* NY:
      Wagner, 1956. xviii + 1166 + xiii [appendix] Discusses the theme
      (God's sovereignty over all creation), contents, date, authenticity,
      divine authority (it's quoted in the NT).

1427. Stenzel, Meinrad. "Das Dodekapropheton in Ubersetzungswerken
      lateinsicher Schriftsteller des Altertums." TZ 9, No. 2 (Mar/Ap 53),
      81-92. Part 5 of his Dissertation. Notes earlier studies. A
      comparative study of Rufinus of Aquila and Irenaeus, citing
      relevant verses from the Twelve.

1428. Stevenson, Dwight E. "Justice or Death: The Book of Amos." pp.
      187-193 in *Preaching on the Books of the Old Testament.* NY:
      Harper & Brothers, 1961. xiii + 267 pp. The introduction discusses
      the OT as the Word of God. The basic concern in the text is
      preaching on whole books of the Bible rather than fragmented
      texts, even when one preaches many sermons on the same biblical
      book. The text should be within the larger context. For Amos,
      Stevenson describes the historical setting, the man, outline of the

books, suggestions for reading (begin with the visions), the main themes (social wrong, call to repent), key verse (5:24), cardinal idea (if prosperity cloaks injustice, disaster may follow), a preaching outline, a modern title.

1429. Stevenson, Herbert F. "Amos: The Peasant Prophet." pp. 49-93 in *Three Prophetic Voices: Studies in Joel, Amos and Hosea.* London: Marshall, Morgan & Scott, 1971. 158 pp. A general review of the content of the book of Amos. The hope at the end is not a sentimental happy ending but a preview of the millennial kingdom. "What a prospect for the redeemed!"

1430. Steveson, Pete. "Visions of Judgment (Amos 7)." BV 27, No. 2 (Nov 93), 29-34. Discusses the vision of the locust plague, the fire, the plumbline, the accusation by Amaziah. God's messengers will often face rejection.

1431. Stibitz, George. "The Message of the Book of Amos." BS 68, No. 260 (Ap '11), 308-342. Surveys the man, historical background, the book, the visions, hope. God is an ethical being who upholds impartial justice on the nations and on Israel.

1432. Stoebe, Hans-Joachim. "Noch einmal zu Amos 7:10-17" (Once again on Amos 7:10-17). VT 39, No. 3 (July 89), 341-354. Discusses Amaziah and Amos' response. He was not a seer or cult prophet.

1433. Stoebe, Hans-Joachim. "Der Prophet Amos und sein burgerlicher Beruf." *Wort und Dienst* ns 5 (1957), 160-181. Reprinted, pp. 145-166 in Stoebe's *Geschichte, Schicksal, Schuld und Glaube* ed Heinz-Dieter Neef. Athenaum Monografien Theologie Bonner Biblische Beitrage 72, ed Frank-Lothar Hossfeld and Helmut Merklein. Frankfurt am Main: Athenaum, 1989. 339 pp. Studies the text in relation to other OT texts, Ugaritic and the ANE context, the history of interpretation.

1434. Stoebe, Hans Joachim. "Uberlegungen zu den geistlichen Voraussetzungen der Prophetie Amos." pp. 209-225 in *Wort - Gebot - Glaube. Beitrage zur Theologie des Alten Testaments. Walther Eichrodt zum 80. Geburtstag* ed Stoebe et al.

Abhandlungen zur Theologie des Alten und Neuen Testaments 59 ed Oscar Cullmann and Stoebe. Zurich: Zwingli, 1970. 331 pp. Reprinted, pp. 167-183 in Stoebe's *Geschichte, Schicksal, Schuld und Glaube* ed Heinz-Dieter Neef. Athenaum Monografien Theologie Bonner Biblische Beitrage 72, ed Frank-Lothar Hossfeld and Helmut Merklein. Frankfurt am Main: Athenaum, 1989. 339 pp. Reviews the history of interpretation, analyzes the text, compares the LXX, exegesis and commentary.

1435. Story, Cullen I.K. "Amos - Prophet of Praise." VT 30, No. 1 (1980), 67-80. Detailed exegesis and review of earlier studies. These brief but buoyant hymns affirm Yahweh as creator and judge with a covenant renewal theme. The context is crucial to understanding the material.

1436. Strange, John O. "Preaching from Amos." SWJT 9, No. 1 (Fall 66), 69-79. Discusses the plan of the book, preaching values - many ideas for sermons.

1437. Strange, M. *The Books of Amos, Osee and Michea, with a Commentary.* Pamphlet Bible Series 26. NY: Paulist, 1961.

1438. Struik, Felix. "Justicia integral: El mensaje social de los profetas pre-exiloicos." *Biblia y fe* 17, No. 50 (May-Aug 91), 171-193. Discusses the mosaic ideal, adaption to Canaan, the monarchy, eighth century prophets. Amos is discussed on pp. 180-182.

1439. Stuart, Douglas. "Amos." pp. 273-400 in *Hosea-Jonah.* Word Biblical Commentary 31 ed David A. Hubbard, et al. Waco, TX: Word Books, 1987. xlv + 537 pp. One of the best commentaries available. Thorough bibliography with both general and specific (at sections). A general introduction notes the prophetic dependency on the Pentateuch. The text is divided into sections and subdivided into small units with bibliography, translation, notes, form/structures/setting, comment, explanation. The purpose of all this is the theological meaning of the text with directly relevant data for this. Notes scholarly views but the primary concern is the text. The introduction to the book of Amos reviews the historical background, the man, his style, the structure of the book, his message (covenant, history, Yahweh's sovereignty, foreign nations, geography (he knew it; presumably so did his audience), economics (concern for the poor; decadence of the rich), corrupt judges, idolatry, immorality, unity of north and south, exile (he never mentions Assyria), previous research on Amos. Amos was a cattle and sheep breeder and not just a peasant shepherd watching the sheep. The oracles of hope are genuine Amos.

1440. Stuart, Douglas. "Amos." pp. 63-87 in *Hosea-Jona*. Word Biblical Themes ed David A. Hubbard, et al. Dallas: Word, 1989. x + 121 pp. A general introduction summarizes each of the five. Themes discussed include God's sovereignty, social justice, exploitation of the poor, corporate sin, God's prosecution of those who violate the covenant, exile, the prophet as messenger and intercessor.

1441. Stuart, Douglas K. "The Poetry of Amos." pp. 197-213 in *Studies in Early Hebrew Meter* by Stuart. Harvard Semitic Monographs 13, ed Frank Moore Cross, Jr. Missoula, MT: Scholars Press, 1976. viii + 245 pp. Less than a fourth of Amos is clearly metrical poetry. Most of it is prose oracles with neither meter nor consistent parallelism. There are remnants of the latter but only a minute percentage compared to early poetry. Presents a number of examples with discussion, Hebrew in one column, transliteration in a parallel column, followed by translation.

1442. Stuhlmueller, Carroll (1923-1994). "Amos, Desert-Trained Prophet." BT No. 4 (Feb 63), 224-230. Life in the desert made him a tough, out-spoken, gruff, biting character. Today, we need to be shaken up by this plainspoken man of God.

1443. Stuhlmueller, Carroll. "The Book of Amos." pp. 7-30 in *Collegeville Bible Commentary*. Vol 15. *Amos, Hosea, Micah, Nahum, Zephaniah, Habakkuk*. Collegeville, MN: Liturgical Press, 1986. 120 pp. The Commentary is available as a single volume, ed Dianne Bergant and Robert J. Karris. Liturgical Press, 1989. ix + 1301. The text is from the *New American Bible*. There are maps of eighth century Palestine, of the Assyrian and Babylonian Empires. A chronological chart gives the kings of Judah, Israel, Assyria and the prophets. The volume closes with a series of review and study questions for each prophet. The introduction to Amos discusses the man (fierce champion of justice), historical background, tradition, literary form. The commentary gives the text and commentary in appropriate units. The promises at the end were added by editors in the post-exilic period.

1444. Stuhlmueller, Carroll. "The Prophetic Price for Peace." pp. 31-44 in *Biblical and Theological Reflections on The Challenge of Peace* ed John T. Pawlikowski and Donald Senior. Theology and Life Series 10. Wilmington, DE: Glazier, 1984. 295 pp. A general review. Amos does not use the word for peace but he is an example because he condemns inhuman warfare and social crimes. His condemnation includes Israel. His view that God is concerned for all people is an extraordinary insight for world peace.

1445. Sunukjian, Donald R. "Amos." pp. 1425-1452 in *The Bible Knowledge Commentary: An Exposition of the Scriptures* by Dallas Seminary Faculty, Old Testament, ed John F. Walvoord and Roy B. Zuck. Wheaton: Victor, 1985. 1589 pp. Tr, *Das Alte Testament erklart und ausgelegt*, 3 vols. Newhausen/ Stuttgart: Hanssler, 1990-1991. Discusses the prophet and his message. Gives an outline, bibliography, detailed commentary.

1446. Super, A.S. "Figures of Comparison in the Book of Amos." *Semitics* 3 (1973), 67-84. Reviews definitions of artists and prophets. Studies Amos' use of metaphors, similes, images. Amos used the known to illustrate the known. Metaphors are more powerful than parallelism.

1447. Sutcliffe, Thomas Henry. *The Book of Amos*. Biblical Handbooks, ed A.W.F. Blunt. London: SPCK, 1939. iv + 88 pp. 2nd ed, 1955. A running commentary on the text with discussions of background, the man himself, what the book means today. The teaching is summarized as belief in one God, and justice including right living.

1448. Sutterlin, W. "Thekoa. Eine geographisch-archaeologisiche Skizze." *Palastinajahrbuch des Deutschen evangelischen Instituts fur Altertumswissenschaft des Heiligen Landes zu Jerusalem* (Berlin) 17 (1921), 31-46. Gives a general description and a review of the history of the site with two pictures of ruins from a later date. The Amos section is p. 44.

1449. Swete, Henry Barclay, ed. "Amos" (Gk). Vol 3 (1894), 16-28 *The OT in Greek according to the Septuagint*, 3 vols. Cambridge University Press, 1887-1894. xx + 879 pp. Reprinted several times. A general introduction gives an overview of manuscripts and sources, the nature of the LXX and its history. Each book has the Greek text, with critical apparatus.

1450. Szabo, Andor. "Nehany uj szemont Amos konyve megertesehez" (A Unified New Perspective for Understanding the Book of Amos). *Theologiai Szemle* (Budapest) 15 (1972), 215-218.

1451. Szabo, Andor. "Textual Problems in Amos and Hosea." VT 25, No. 2a (May 75), 500-524. Makes several suggestions for Amos (pp. 500-508), e.g., Amos' statement he was not a prophet or son of the prophets. The latter means prophecy in Israel had declined. God made a new start in Amos who had not eaten the bread of the prophets.

1452. Szwarc, Urszula. "Hunger for the Word of the Lord. The theological significance of the oracle Am 8:11-12" (Pol). *Ruch Biblijny* (Cracow) 36, No. 2 (1983), 122-131.

1453. Szwarc, Urszula. "The Poor in the Teaching of the Prophet Amos 2:6b-7a; 4:1b; 5:11a-12b; 8:4" (Pol). *Roczniki Teologiczno-Kanoniczne: Annales de Theolgie et du Droit Canon* (Lublin) 35, No. 1 (1988), 5-14. Eng summary. The first part is a detailed analysis concentrating on the terminology. The second part discusses general conclusions. The different terms for the poor are synonymous, e.g., poor, ignored, oppressed, the personal dignity of those held in contempt.

1454. Szwarc, Urszula. "Thirst after God's Word: Exegetical-Theological Analysis of the Text of Am 8:11-12" (Pol). *Roczniki Teologiczno-Kanoniczne: Annales de Theolgie et du Droit Canon* (Lublin) 27, No. 1 (1980), 43-51. Eng summary, p. 51. Notes earlier studies. Amos has prognosticated God's punishment which will be caused by the nation itself because it rejected God's grace allowing them to understand God's instruction. Szwarc sees confirmation of this in Isaiah 6:9-10.

T.

1455. Talmon, Shemaryahu. "The Ugaritic Background of Amos 7:4."
Tarbiz 35, No. 4 (June 65), 301-303. Heb with Eng summary on p.
i. The story of Anat includes her victory over Yam, etc. The
Hebrew writer suppressed the mythical allusions by presenting
natural phenomenon.

1456. Talmon, Shemaryahu and Esti Eshel. "*whmskyl b't hhy'ydos* (Amos
5:13)." *Shnaton* (Jerusalem) 10 (1986-1989), 115-122, xvii-xix
(Eng summary). Usually translated as the wise are silent in an evil
time. But this is the opposite of the prophet's mission. An alternate
is not wise, but singing, so the exhortation is to silence joyful
singing in times of wickedness.

1457. Tangberg, Karl Arvid. *Die prophetische Mahnrede. Form- und
traditionsgeschichtliche Studien zum prophetischen Umkehrruf.*
Forschungen zur Religion und Literatur des Alten und Neuen
Testaments 143 ed Wolfgang Schrag und Rudolf Smend.
Gottingen: Vandenhoeck & Ruprecht, 1987. 215 pp. Reviews the
history of interpretation, clarifies terminology, discusses examples
of the type (gattung) of prophetic warning, compares wisdom,
deuteronomic exhortations.

1458. Tatford, Fredrick A. *Prophet of Social Injustice: An Exposition of
Amos.* Twentieth Century Series. Eastbourne, Sussex: Prophetic
Witness, 1974. 144 pp. Reprinted, *The Minor Prophets*, vol 1.
Minneapolis: Klock & Klock, 1982. The preface surveys the world
in poverty and wealth like Israel in Amos' day. The introduction
discusses the man, date, historical background including external
religiosity, purpose (to prophesy against Israel), style (perfect
symmetry, choice expression, vividness, close acquaintance with
the letter and spirit of the law), the divisions of the book.

1459. Taylor, John. "The Book of Amos." ET 12, No. 7 (Ap '01), 318-319. A review of Max Lohr's strophic translation/restoration, including Lohr's analysis of the 269 OT references to Yahweh Sabaoth, as referring to Yahweh's warlike might and victory.

1460. Taylor, John. "The Book of Amos." ET 15, No. 2 (Nov '04), 64-65. A review of Baumann's *Aufbau der Amosreden*. BZAW 7. cf also BZAW 4 - Lohr.

1461. Taylor, John. "A New Hebrew Lexicon." ET 3, No. 10 (July 1892), 479-480. A review of Siegfried and Stade's Hebraisches Worterbuch, focusing on Amos, comparing their, his own, and others' exegesis.

1462. Taylor, John. "Notes on Siegfried and Stade's New Hebrew Lexicon, II." ET 3, No. 11 (Aug 1892), 520-521. Taylor continues his review.

1463. Taylor, John. "Notes on Siegfried and Stade's New Hebrew Lexicon, III." ET 4, No. 1 (Oct 1892), 48. Amos 3:11. Taylor continues his review.

1464. Taylor, John. "Notes on Siegfried and Stade's New Hebrew Lexicon, IV." ET 4, No. 3 (Dec 1892), 130-132. Amos 3:12, 5:26. Taylor continues his review.

1465. Taylor, John. "A Prophet's View of International Ethics." Exp, 4th Ser, 8, No. 2 (1893), 96-109. A fictional description of Amos' return to Tekoa to write his memoirs. A review of the contents of the Book of Amos. Discussion of crimes against humanity.

1466. Taylor, John B. "Amos." pp. 27-42 in *The Minor Prophets*. Scripture Union Bible Study Books 15. Grand Rapids: Eerdmans, 1970. ii + 94 pp. Each biblical book is divided into daily study units, e.g., Amos 2:6-16 "The Sins of Israel," 4:1-5 "The Cocktail Set." The introduction notes Amos was a shepherd but the Hebrew *noqed* may mean "sheep-breeder" like King Mesha of Moab. Amos was a man of affairs in touch with recent events and sufficient liturgical knowledge to produce the oracles in their present form. He attacked the Israelites for their immoral conduct, their social evils, rather than idolatry (as Hosea did) or ritual problems. Questions for study/discussion appear at the end.

1467. Taylor, Kenneth N. "Amos." pp. 77-94 in *Living Prophecies: The Minor Prophets Paraphrased with Daniel and The Revelation*. Wheaton, IL: Tyndale House, 1965. x + 246 pp. A modern English translation. An appendix to the volume notes prophecies of the Living Christ, fulfilled and yet to be fulfilled. The introduction compares the crime and immorality of today with that of prophetic times.

1468. Taylor, R. Bruce. "Amos." pp. 27-28 in *Dictionary of the Bible* ed James Hastings, et al. NY: Scribner's, 1909. xvi + 992 pp. Reviews the man, his time, contents of the book, his theology. God rules the world, political and natural. He has a special relationship with Israel, which will be destroyed if it does not respond in righteousness. Privilege means responsibility. The Hebrew of the text is pure, written by a keen observer of nature and people. Amos is the first to use the phrase, the day of the Lord. With Amos, prophecy breaks away from tradition to the individual with a direct line to, and responsible to no one except God.

1469. Terrien, Samuel L. "Amos and Wisdom." pp. 108-115 in *Israel's Prophet Heritage: Essays in Honor of James Muilenburg* ed Bernhard W. Anderson and Walter Harrelson. NY: Harper & Brothers, 1962. xiv + 242 pp. Reprinted, pp. 448-455 in Studies in Ancient Israelite Wisdom ed James L. Crenshaw. NY: KTAV, 1976. xvii + 494 pp. Amos uses both language and style from the wisdom movement which was more ancient in Israel than scholars have traditionally assumed. Terrien also notes that prophets, priests and wise lived in the same, interacting environment. They were not isolated from one another.

1470. Terry, Milton S. "The Prophecy of Amos." *Methodist Review* (NY) 72, No. 6 (Nov 1890), 868-885. Discusses the man, historical background, message. Gives an analytical outline, annotated translation.

1471. Tesch, Albert. *Setzt der Prophet Amos Autoritatives Gesetz voraus?* Berlin: np, 1895. Inaugural Diss.

1472. Theiner, J.A. *Die Zwolf Kleineren Propheten. In der Art und Weise des von Brentano-Dereser'schen Bibelwerks Ubersetzt und erklart.* Leipzig: Teubner, 1828. iii + 364 pp. The study of is in two parts, "Einleitung zum Propheten Amos" (pp. 85-89) and the annotated translation (pp. 90-144). The introduction reviews the personal history of Amos, his time, the content of his book, his style, canonical status. The translation has short introductions on the content and background for each chapter and extensive annotation with exegesis, textual comparisons, history, commentary, earlier studies.

1473. Theis, Johannes. "Der Prophet Amos ubersetzt und erklart." 1 (1937), 105-137 in *Die Zwolf Kleinen Propheten, ubersetzt und erklart. I. Halfte: Osee, Joel, Amos, Abdias, Jonas, Michaas,* 2 vols, by Joseph Lippl, et al. Die Heilige Schrift des Alten Testaments VIII. Band, 3. Abteilung, ed Franz Feldmann and Heinrich Herkenne. Bonn: Hanstein, 1937, 1938. 1:xii + 227. A general introduction reviews the Book of the Twelve Prophets as in Sirach 49:10, Josephus, et al., Augustine's use of "Minor" Prophets, their significance, their poetry, and provides bibliography. The introduction to Amos discusses the person (his name, home, his call to be a prophet), his time, content of the book, organization (outline), the significance of Amos in religious history, his language. The commentary has continuous German translation with copious notes, exegesis and discussion.

1474. Theodore of Mopsueste (c 350-428). "In Amosum prophetam commentarius." PG 66 (1864), cols 241-304. The section on the minor prophets opens with a general introduction (cols 105-124), literary, canonical, historical. Each commentary has the Greek and Latin printed in parallel columns with critical notes. Theodore, Bishop of Mopsuestia (392-428), supported the new Nicene orthodoxy (381 CE) and opposed the Arians and Apollinarians. In 553, he was condemned as a Nestorian. Only fragments of his dogmatic writings survived. His commentary on the minor prophets (PG 66:105-632) has been preserved in Greek. He insisted on the autonomy of the OT and interpreted the text at narrative or historical level. Trinitarian interpretations are excluded and predictive prophecy restricted. Only Malachi predicted Christ. However, there is also a spiritual typological meaning which hints at Christ without detracting from the meaning of the text in its own time. Cf Sprenger.

1475. Theodore. "In Amos 2:3-5." *Theodori Mopsuesteni fragmenta syriaca* ed E. Sachau. Leipzig: Englemann, 1869.

1476. Theodoret of Cyr. "Commentarius in Amos prophetam. Opera Omnia 2." PG 81 (1859), cols 1663-1708. Greek and Latin in parallel columns, commentary with notes. Cols 1545-1550 are a general introduction to the minor prophets. Theodoret (393-458 [453? 466?] C.E.), a theologian of the Antiochene school, was bishop of Cyrrus in Osroene Syria (423). He was a friend of Nestorius who thought his friend was misunderstood, and thus opposed St. Cyril. He was deposed in 499 by the Robber Synod of Ephesus but reinstated. He reluctantly voted against Nestorius at Chalcedon (451). Cf. Ashby for a full treatment.

1477. Thiel, Winfried. "Amos." 1 (1986), cols 124-126 in *Evangelisches Kirchenlexikon [EKL]: Internationale Theologische Enzyklopadie*, 3rd ed, 3 vols +, ed Erwin Fahlbusch et al. Gottingen: Vandenhoeck & Ruprecht, 1985 +. 2:xi + 1535. For the 2nd ed., EKL, see Bach. Discusses the man, his book, his message. Amos is a radical from among the people.

1478. Thiel, Winfried. "Verfehlte Geschichte im Alten Testament." *Theologische Beitrage* 17, No. 5 (Oct 86), 248-266. Reviews scholarly opinions. Discusses the Deuteronomic history with the prophets as examples, including Amos, Hosea, Micah and Jeremiah.

1479. Thomas, D.E. "The Experience Underlying the Social Philosophy of Amos." *J of Religion* 7, No. 2 (Mar '27), 136-145. Amos grew up where one had to work hard for a living. The rich oppressed the poor. Justice is in the nature of God. People's sins fell especially hard on the next generation.

1480. Thomas, David Winton. "Note on *no'adu* in Amos 3:3." JTS ns 7, No. 1 (Ap 56), 69-70. Drawing on the Arabic, he translates, "Will two walk together unless they are at peace with one another?"

1481. Thompson, Alden. "A God who Hates Feasts, Sacrifices, and Prayers." *Signs of the Times* 113 (Jan 86), 28. Amos 5.

1482. Thompson, John A. "The 'Response' in Biblical and Non-biblical Literature with Particular Reference to the Hebrew Prophets." pp. 255-268 in *Perspectives on Language and Text: Essays and Poems in Honor of Francis I. Andersen's 60th Birthday* ed Edward W. Conrad and Edward G. Newing. Winona Lake, IN: Eisenbrauns, 1987. xxviii + 443 pp. Discusses the response in non-biblical material, e.g., the Greek chorus, Handel's Messiah, etc., and in the Bible, e.g., Psalms, Job. Amos is a major example. Recognition of this element is a tool for unraveling the mysteries of the MT.

1483. Thompson, Michael E.W. "Amos - A Prophet of Hope?" ET 104, No. 3 (Dec 92) 71-76. Amos preached doom on the rich. But there will be a remnant, e.g., like two legs or a bit of ear rescued from a lion. In his oracles, he is trying to get people to repent. God will destroy but God speaks of "my people" suggesting continuation. The hope in the oracles suggests the note of hope at the end is also from Amos.

1484. Thomson, J.G.S.S. "Amos." pp. 32-33 in *The New Bible Dictionary* ed James D. Douglas, et al. Grand Rapids: Eerdmans, 1962. xvi + 1375 pp. (reprinted, 1974) The Hebrew text has been well preserved. It divides into four parts. His time and history show a prophet's message was bound up with the conditions of the people to whom he preached. Religion was not neglected but perverted. Ritual went hand in hand with immorality. The rich ceremony and sacrifice was at the expense of the poor. Amos has references to tradition - Sodom and Gomorrah, Isaac, Jacob, Joseph, the Exodus, wilderness wandering, the conquest. God is the creator and sustainer of the world who judges the nations. Israel will be judged more severely because God revealed his will to her. The solution is not more ritual but righteousness. Amos failed. No one listened to him.

1485. Thomson, J.G.S.S. and J.A. Motyer, "Amos, Book of." 1:44-45 in *The Illustrated Bible Dictionary*, 3 vols, ed. James D. Douglas, et al. [a revision of *The New Bible Dictionary*. Grand Rapids, MI: Eerdmans, 1962]. Lane Cove, Australia/Leicester/ Wheaton, IL:

Hodder & Stoughton/Inter-Varsity Press/Tyndale House, 1980. 1:xvi + 576. See Thomson, "Amos."

1486. Thorogood, Bernard. *A Guide to the Book of Amos, with Theme Discussions on Judgement, Social Justice, Priest and Prophet.* Theological Educational Fund Study Guide, 4. London: SPCK, 1971. x + 118 pp. The introduction reviews the nations, prophets, suggestions for study, Amos the man and his time, his book. The commentary divides the book in five sections: judgment, preaching, true and false religion, visions, more preaching, followed by an epilogue of hope. Visuals include a map, a time chart for kings and prophets, 24 pictures which relate the prophetic era to today. Study suggestions include word study, contents, application, opinion, research.

1487. Tietsch, A. "Die Botschaft des Amos." *Die Zeichen der Zeit* 26 (1972), 211-217.

1488. Till, Walter, ed. "Amos." pp. 33-40 in *Die Achmimische Version der Zwolf Kleinen Propheten (Codex Rainerianus, Wien) mit Einleitung, Anmerkungen und Worterverzeichnis.* Coptica: Consillio et Impensis Instituti Rask-Oerstediani 4. Hauniae: Gyldendal, 1927. xii + 151 pp. The introduction covers the manuscripts, characteristics of the language, the text, publication. Till gives a transcription of the Akhimimic text with critical notes.

1489. Todd, Vergil H. "The Eschatology of Pre-Exilic Prophets." *The Cumberland Seminarian* 22, No. 3 (Wint 85), 51-69. A general review including Amos, Hosea, Isaiah, Micah, Jeremiah, Zephaniah, Nahum, Habakkuk and Ezekiel. Amos was the first to use the term, "the Day of the Lord," but it would be a day of darkness, not light. His hope (9:9-11) is authentic, a reflection of the eschatological community of which he was a part.

1490. Torczyner, H. "Dunkle Bibelstellen." pp. 274-280 in *Vom Alten Testament, Karl Marti zum Siebzigsten Geburtstage* ed Karl Budde. BZAW 41. Giessen: Topelmann, 1925. viii + 336 pp. Exegesis of Amos 2:7 (pp. 278-279).

1491. Torrey, Charles Cutler. *The Lives of the Prophets: Greek Text and Translation.* JBL Monograph Series 1 ed Robert H. Pfeiffer. Philadelphia: SBL and Exegesis, 1946. iii + 53 pp. Torrey gives the historical background on the manuscripts and what is known of the work including earlier studies of it. It is known in Greek but was originally in Hebrew. It is Palestinian throughout except for Jeremiah which tells of blessings on the Egyptians through Jeremiah. The work is from the first century CE. The items are not biography in the full sense but extended bits of information or folklore, especially miracles, related to the individuals. Torrey gives a collation of the Greek manuscripts plus translation. In the Amos (pp. 26, 40) unit, Amaziah frequently beat Amos. Amos died from a blow from Amaziah's son.

1492. Torrey, Charles Cutler. "Notes on Am 2:7; 6:10; 8:3; 9:8-10." JBL 15, Nos. 1&2 (1896), 151-154. Exegesis, word study with comparison of MT, LXX, Peshitta, the history of interpretations.

1493. Torrey, Charles Cutler. "On the Text of Am 5:25; 6:1, 2; 7:2." JBL 13, No. 1 (1894), 61-63. Exegesis, noting problems with Massoretic pointing, grammar, suggested emendations.

1494. Tos, Aldo J. "Amos: Prophet of the God of Justice." pp. 142-143 in *Approaches to the Bible: The Old Testament.* Englewood Cliffs, NJ: Prentice-Hall, 1963. xxv + 286 pp. Reviews Amos' personal and historical background, judgment, day of the Lord, remnant, a return to monotheism, elements of universalism, his book as an anthology of quotations - oracles he gave at various times.

1495. Tourn, Giorgio and J. Alberto Soggin. *Amos: Profeta della Giustizia.* Turin: Claudiana, 1972. 232 pp. Soggin translated the Hebrew and Tourn wrote the commentary. The introduction surveys the man, his time, his book. The commentary gives the translation, plus related passages, e.g., Amos 1:1 is compared to 7:14-15. The text is followed by commentary on the language, relevant content, and the problems related to the passage. The chapters outline the text in terms of the language of God, the condemnation, the election of Israel, the excuse of religion, false security, the problem of the elite, Yahweh as Creator, the restoration.

1496. Touzard, Jules. *Le Livre d'Amos*. Paris: Bloud, 1909. lxxxv + 119 pp. The introduction gives the historical background, discusses the man, analyzes the book and its authenticity, reviews the doctrines. Vs by vs commentary. Available on microfiche, ATLA 1985-3557.

1497. Towner, W. Sibley. "Amos." p. 45 in *The Dictionary of Bible and Religion* ed William A. Gentz, et al. Nashville: Abingdon, 1986. 1147 pp. Reviews the historical background, Amos' home and occupation.

1498. Towner, W. Sibley. "Amos (Book of)." p. 45 in *The Dictionary of Bible and Religion* ed William A. Gentz, et al. Nashville: Abingdon, 1986. 1147 pp. Discusses the historical background, contents, day of the Lord, judgment, promise. Some say the last is not from Amos but it provides a balance typical of the prophetic canon.

1499. Toy, Crawford Howell. "The Judgment of Foreign Peoples in Amos 1:3-2:3." JBL 25, No. 1 (1906), 25-28. Traditionally, the prophetic attitude towards other people was narrow nationalism, without regard to any morality. At first glance, the atrocities cited by Amos appear to be crimes against humanity but they are actions of war and no worse or better than that of the Israelites.

1500. Trabold, Robert A. "Amos, Micah, and Hosea: Prophets in Crisis." *Focus: A Theological J* (Willowdale, Ontario) 3, No. 2 (1966-1967), 27-37.

1501. Trapiello, Jesus Garcia. "Situacion historica del profeta Amos." *Estudios Biblicos* 26, No. 3 (1967), 249-274. Discusses the geographical problem, the origin of Amos, his prophetic activity, the sociological problem, the chronological problem.

1502. Treu, Ursula. "Amos 7:14, Schenute und der Physiologus." *Novum Testamentum* 10, Nos. 2-3 (1968), 234-240. Compares earlier studies, the Greek text, exegesis and commentary.

1503. Trochon, M. *Les Petites Prophetes*. Paris: Lethielleux, 1883.

1504. Tromp, Nicholas J. "Amos - Profetie als Kritische Funktie." *Ons Geestelijk Leven* 48 (1971), 294-302.

1505. Tromp, Nicholas J. "Amos 5:1-17. Towards a Stylistic and Rhetorical Analysis." *OTS* 23 (1984), 19-38. This volume is titled: *Prophets, Worship and Theodicy, Studies in Prophetism, Biblical Theology and Structural and Rhetorical Analysis and on the Place of Music in Worship* ed Adam Simon van der Woude. Leiden: Brill, 1984. v + 139 pp. The Amos text is chiastic. Rhetorical analysis is what goes on between speaker and hearer. It includes exhortation, an effort to persuade people to act. The idea that total destruction is coming and there is nothing they can do about it, is hyberbole designed to shock. Amos proposes measures to prevent it.

1506. Tromp, N.J. "Vraagtekens bij Amos." pp. 30-40 in *Amos. Een Aanklacht de profeet en Zijn betekenis nu*. Amsterdam: Vrije Universiteit, 1979.

1507. Tromp, N.J. and D. Deden. *De Profeet Amos*. Boxtel: Katholich Bijbelstichting, 1971.

1508. Tsevat, Matitiahu. "Amos 7:14 - Present or Preterit?" pp. 256-258 in *The Tablet and the Scroll: Near Eastern Studies in Honor of William W. Hallo* ed Mark E. Cohen, et al. Bethesda, MD: CDL Press, 1993. xvi + 333 pp. It is present. But the statement does not answer the question of whether Amos is or is not a prophet. Amos is correcting Amaziah's language, repudiating the purpose of Amaziah's statement, that Amos prophesies for personal gain. Amos answers that while some *nbi'im* prophesy for money, Amos is not one of these. He makes his living elsewhere.

1509. Tsumura, David Toshio. "'Inserted Bicolon', The AXYB Pattern, in Amos 1:5 and Psalm 9:7." *VT* 38, No. 2 (Ap 88), 234-236. Amos 1:5 has A and B, the destruction of Damascus and the exile of the people. In between, XY, are two lines about cutting off the king from Beth Eden. Ps 9:7 has the same inserted bicolon pattern.

1510. Tucker, Gene M. "Amos, the Book of." pp. 27-28 in *Harper's Bible Dictionary* ed Paul J. Achtemeier, et al. San Francisco: Harper & Row, 1985. xii + 1178 + 18 (maps) pp. Outlines the book.

Discusses the man and the book. Most of the material is authentic, written down later by those who succeeded the prophet. They added the postexilic verses. Like other prophets, virtually all of Amos' speeches are judgment and punishment. The distinctive elements are that the end is now, his stress on obedience, other nations receive God's care and punishment.

1511. Tucker, Gene M. "The Law in the Eighth-Century Prophets." pp. 201-216 in *Canon, Theology, and Old Testament Interpretation: Essays in Honor of Brevard S. Childs* ed Gene M. Tucker, et al. Philadelphia: Fortress, 1988. xix + 347 pp. A general study. Amos and other prophets claimed their people had violated the laws, especially regarding the covenant.

1512. Tucker, Gene M. "Prophetic Authenticity. A Form-Critical Study of Amos 7:10-17." INT 27, No. 4 (Oct 73), 423-434. Shows the structure in a detailed outline. Discusses genre (prophecy of punishment), setting and intention. "The narrator has Amos confirm his prophetic authority by exercising it." "The authentic prophet is one who has responded to a divine commission."

1513. Tucker, Gene M. "Prophetic Speech." INT 32, No. 1 (Jan 78), 31-45. They announced future events. Amos is a frequent example, and, pp. 40-45, is a test case. He also prayed (intercession) and exhorted people to change.

1514. Turnham, Timothy John. Wealth and Righteousness: Selected OT Teachings on Material Possessions (Ethics, OT), Job, Leviticus, Amos. Diss. Southern Baptist Theological Seminary, 1984. x + 139 pp. DAI 45, No. 12 (June 85), 3664. Available in microfiche. Uses sociology, ethics and comparative texts to study three pericope, e.g., Amos 8:4-8. Gives translation with critical notes and a general introduction to the Book of Amos. The pericope are analyzed through form criticism (structures, genre, setting, intention), tradition criticism, the ethics of the curse and of accusation. Traces the sins of the merchants to the Joseph cycle in Gen 41-47. Joseph practiced the sins Amos condemned. These sins were treason against other Hebrews and rebellion against God. Calls for justice not greed, balance between acquisition and asceticism, labor and leisure, work and worship.

1515. Tweedie, Andrew. *A Sketch of Amos and Hosea: Their Message and Their Times*. Edinburgh and London: Blackwood & Sons, 1916.

1516. Tyciak, Julius. "Amos: Prophet der Gerechtigkeit." pp. 21-33 in *Prophetische Profile: Gestalten und Gedanken des Zwolfpropheten-buches*. Die Welt der Bibel 19 ed Willibrord Hillmann, et al. Dusseldorf: Patmos, 1965. 112 pp. A general discussion, with comparative textual studies, quotations of limited sections.

U.

1517. Uehlinger, Christoph. "Der Herr auf der Zinnmauer zur Dritten Amos-Vision (Am 7:7-8)." *BN* 48 (1989), 89-104. A response to Beyerlin, *Bleilot*... In the third vision, God stands on the wall, not to protect but to defeat the city.

1518. Uffenheimer, Binyamin. "Amos and Hosea: Two Directions in Israel's Prophecy." *Dor le Dor* 5, No. 3 (Spr 77), 101-110. Tr of Hebrew original, pp. 284-320 (Heb) in *Zer Li-Gevurot. The Zalman Shazar Jubilee Volume: A Collection of Studies in Bible, Eretz Yisrael, Hebrew Language, and Talmudic Literature* ed B.Z. Luria. Jerusalem: Kiryat [Kirjath] Sepher, 1973. Amos' condemnations are not based on the international political situation but the sins of society. Hosea's rich imagery is aimed at the sin of idolatry and the fertility cult. He preached the day of repentance and redemption.

1519. Uffenheimer, Benjamin. *Commentary to Amos* (Heb). Biblical Commentaries, Minor Prophets 1 ed S.L. Gordon. Tel Aviv: Gordon, 1968.

1520. Uffenheimer, Benjamin. "Mythological and Rationalistic Thought in Hosea and Amos" (Heb). pp. 155-179 in *Studies in the Minor Prophets* ed B.Z. Luria. Jerusalem: Kiryat Sepher, 1981.

1521. Ulrichsen, Jarl Henning. "Der Einschub Amos 4:7b-8a. Sprachliche Erwagungen zu einem umstrittenen Text." *Orientalia Suecana* (Stockholm) 41-42 (1992-1993), 284-298. Reviews the structure of the text, various hypotheses and earlier studies, the different versions (LXX, Targum, Syriac, Vulgate). Linguistically, the pericope is an intrusion.

1522. Ulrichsen, Jarl Henning. "Oraklene i Amos 1:3ff." *Norsk Teologisk Tidsskrift* 85, No. 1 (1984), 39-54. Detailed study of the oracles against the nations, with a review of earlier opinions and a drawing of their interrelationship as a single unit. Rev, OTA 7 (1984), 277.

1523. Umbreit, Friedrich Wilhelm Carl (1795-1860). "Amos." pp. 131-186 in *Praktischer Commentar uber die Propheten des Alten Bundes. Vierter Band. Die Kleinen Propheten. Erster Theil. Hosea. Joel. Amos. Obadja.* Hamburg: Perthes, 1845. iv + 202 pp. The volume is also titled, *Praktischer Commentar uber die Kleinen Propheten mit exegetischen und kritischen Anmerkungen. Erster Theil. Hosea. Joel. Amos. Obadja.* The introduction discusses Amos' personal background in Tekoa, his use of imagery from nature, the historical background and the northern kingdom, Amos' relationship with other prophets, a summary of his teaching. The commentary gives a translation by sections, with annotation, exegesis, discussion.

1524. Utzschneider, Helmut. "Die Amazjaerzahlung (Am 7,10-17) zwischen Literatur und Historie." BN 41 (1988), 76-101. Notes the history of interpretation of the encounter of Amos and the priest Amaziah, the theme of exile, comparison with 1 Kgs 13. The Amaziah story is on the borderline between fiction and history.

V.

1525. Vaihinger, J.G. "Erklarung schwieriger Stellen des alten Testamentes. V. Amos 5:18-27." *Archiv fur Wissenschaftliche Erforschung des Alten Testaments* 1 (1870), 486-488. A comparative study.

1526. Valeton, J.J.P. "Onderzoek naar den Leeftijd van Joel vooral met het oog op zijne verhouding tot Amos." *Studien* (Gronigen) 1, No. 2 (1875), 122-145. The journal is sub-titled "Theologisch Tijdschrift." A comparative study, e.g., Joel 4:16 and Amos 1:2, and the history of interpretation.

1527. Valeton, J.J.P., Jr. (1814-1906). *Amos und Hosea: Ein Kapitel aus der Geschichte der Israelitischen Religion.* Giessen: Ricker, 1898. Tr, Dutch, *Amos en Hosea een hoofdstuk uit de Gescheidenis.* Nijmegen: Ten Hoet, 1894. Available, ATLA microfiche 1985-3612. Reviews the religious situation in the time of the two and gives an overview of the contents of each prophet. The discussion of Amos includes the origins, the herdsman, not a prophet nor a son of a prophet, his knowledge of God, the service of Yahweh, the judgement, holy preaching. A closing chapter compares the two.

1528. Vanderwaal, Cornelius. "Amos." pp. 31-45 in *Search the Scriptures. Vol. 6: Hosea - Malachi.* St. Catharines, Ontario: Paideia, 1979. 119 pp. Tr from the Dutch, *Sola Scriptura.* Discusses the prophet's life, his appeal to the covenant, oracles against the nations, judgment on the northern kingdom, the apocalypse, messianic promises.

1529. van der Wal, Adri J.O. "Achtergrond en rhetorische functie van Amos 3:1-2" (Background and Rhetorical Function of Amos 3:1-2). *Amsterdamse Cahiers voor exegese en Bijbelse theologie* 6 (1985),

83-90. This is not an independent unit but the conclusion to 2:6 - 3:2.

1530. van der Wal, Adri J.O. "Amos 5:13 - een omstreden tekst." *Nederlands Theologisch Tijdschrift* 41, No. 2 (1987), 89-98. Eng. 156. Vs 13 is authentic Amos. The maskil is a victim of injustice in Amos' time as in Dan 11:33-35 in the time of Antiochus IV Epiphanes.

1531. van der Wal, Adri. *Amos. A Classified Bibliography*, 3rd ed. Applicatio, Computer Application in Theology 3 ed H. Leene and Eep Talstra. Amsterdam: Free University, 1986. xv + 283 pp. (original, 1981) lst ed Dutch; 2nd ed Eng; works published 1800-1983. The 3rd ed has an additional 500 titles. Items are listed with minimal reference, e.g., "Bic, M. Das Buch Amos. Berlin (1969)." The first unit refers to commentaries on the minor prophets. The second is on Amos, and Amos in general. The bulk of the references are sequential, verse by verse.

1532. van der Wal, Adri. "Amos, Een paar Notities." pp. 5-26 in *Amos. Een Aanklacht de profeet en Zijn betekenis nu* by van der Wal, et al. Amsterdam: Vrije Universiteit, 1979. 43 pp.

1533. van der Wal, Adri. "The Structure of Amos." JSOT 26 (June 83), 107-113. Koch determines structure by formulas, doxologies, the one who is addressed. Van der Wal prefers two parts, based on terms, phrases, frequency of perfect consecutive, the use of inclusio. Religious-cultic elements are intertwined with social aspects.

1534. van der Wal, Adri, and Eep Talstra. *Amos. Concordance and Lexical Surveys*. Applicatio, Informatica-toepassingen in de Theologie 2. Amsterdam: Free (Vrije) University, 1984. 136 pp. A computer generated concordance of consonantal text with a separate concordance for prepositions. There are three frequency tables: general, vocabulary of the sections and Amos 5:7-6:12 in context.

1535. Van de Sandt, Huub. "Why is Amos 5:25-27 quoted in Acts 7:42f?" *Z fur die Neutestamentliche Wissenschaft und di Kunde de Alteren*

Kirche 82, Nos. 1/2 (1991), 67-87. Acts, or Luke, quoted the LXX of Amos, not the Hebrew with some variation, e.g., Damascus is replaced by Babylon. The whole is complex but the Amos cite falls into place if the interpretation of the calf narrative is seen in the light of Dt 4. And because the referent there is to the exile, Luke replaces Damascus with Babylon. The meaning of the quote is transformed with the content of the punishment extended to vs 26 and the cause is reduced to vs 25, with the worship of God replaced by the worship of the calf.

1536. van Dyne, J. *Amos - Haggai.* Kansas City: Beacon Hill, 1988.

1537. VanGemeren, Willem A. "Amos." pp. 127-137 in *Interpreting the Prophetic Word.* Grand Rapids, MI: Academic Books [Zondervan], 1990. 545 pp. Discusses Amos and his time, literary form and structure (shown in a structured outline), the message (God's power over creation, judgment, the Day of the Lord, the freedom of the Lord, the remnant, God's kingdom, covenant renewal). VanGemeren closes with a review and study questions and issues.

1538. van Leeuwen, Cornelius. *Amos.* De Prediking van het Oude Testament ed A. van Selms, et al. Nijkerk: Callenbach, 1985. 420 pp. The introduction reviews the man, his time, his book, his style. There are preaching suggestions at the end of each section. In addition to the references inter alia in the detailed discussion, there are 45 pages of notes and 11 pages of bibliography.

1539. van Leeuwen, Cornelius. "Amos." pp. 595-609 in *Tekst Voor Tekst: De Heilige Schrift kort verklaard en toegelicht* ed by B. van Oeveren, et al. 's-Gravenhage: Uitgeverij Boekencentrum B.V., 1987. ix + 1072 pp. The introduction reviews the name and author, historical background, date, themes and outline of content. The commentary studies and develops small units of the text, problems in translation, etc. Headings indicate the substance of the content.

1540. van Leeuwen, Cornelius. "Amos 1:2. Epigraphe du Livre entier ou Introduction aux Oracles des Chapitres 1-2?" pp. 93-101 in *Verkenningen in een Stroomgebied. Proeven van Oudtestamentisch Onderzoek ter gelegenheid van het afscheid van Prof. Dr. M.A. Beek (Explorations in a Stream of Thought: Experiments in Old*

Testament Research on the Occasion of the Departure of Prof. Dr. M.A. Beek) ed M. Boertien, et al. Amsterdam: University of Amsterdam, 1974. ix + 147 pp. An exegetical study. Reviews the history of interpretation and compares the material with its OT context.

1541. van Leeuwen, Cornelius. "De Heilsverwachting bij Amos." pp. 71-87 in *Vruchten van de Uithof. Studies opgedragen aan dr. H.A. Brongers ter gelegenheid van zijn afscheid (16 mei 1974).* Utrecht: Theologisch Institut, 1974. 170 pp. Discusses the various interpretations in the history of exegesis.

1542. van Leeuwen, Cornelius. "Quelques problemes de traduction dans les visions d'Amos Chapitaire 7." pp. 103-112 in *Ubersetzung und Deutung. Studien zu dem Alten Testament und seiner Umwelt Alexander Reinard Hults gewidmet von Freunden und Kollegen with Dominique Barthelemy, et al.* Nijkerk: Callenbach, 1977. 216 pp. Compares translations and the history of interpretation.

1543. van Leeuwen, Raymond C. "De 'Lofprijzingen' in Amos." *Rondom het Woord* 13, No. 3 (1971), 255-267.

1544. van Leeuwen, Raymond C. "The Prophecy of the *Yom YHVH* in Amos 5:18-20." OTS 19 (1974), 113-134. This volume is titled, *Language and Meaning: Studies in Hebrew Language and Biblical Exegesis* ed Adam Simon van der Woude. Leiden: Brill, 1974. v + 150 pp. Reviews the history of interpretation, of scholarly opinions, e.g., a war oracle, an example of covenant with the treaty curses carried out. None of these provide an explanation of the origin of the concept. It's a theophany. Amos reacts to the objections of his audience. They thought God would protect them but they forgot God is the Holy One who would punish them for being unfaithful. The popular view of the Day was blessing, but pre-exilic prophets said judgment. After the exile, the prophets returned to the earlier view with judgment on Israel's enemies. Later it was a day of universal judgment and radical changes in the cosmos. In the broad sense of an end of the present order and the beginning of a new divinely created order, the pre-exilic prophets had an eschatology of doom. In the sense of the end of the world and history, there is no eschatology before the exile.

1545. van Zyl, A.H. "The Consciousness of Sin in Amos" (Afrikaans). *Ned Geref Teologiese Tydskrif* 9, No. 2 (Mar 68), 69-82. The term is "Sondebesef." Notes earlier studies, concept of sin, social injustice, unrighteousness, exploitation of the poor, false worship, misinterpretation of election, wrong ideas about God.

1546. Varadi, M. *Il profeta Amos*. Florence: Casa Editrice Israel, 1947.

1547. Varro, R. "Amos: Les justes, les pauvres et le prophete." *Masses Ouvrieres* 297 (1973), 24-37.

1548. Vasquez, Bernardino. *Dios es Justo y Fiel: Oseas, Amos, Joel, Sofonias, Habacuc* (God is Just and Faithful). Estudio Biblico ELA. Puebla, Mexico: Ediciones Las Americas, 1994. 127 pp. Amos (pp. 40-68) is outlined in three parts: judgment on the people of God and the nations, judgment on Israel, restoration. The latter is all new. Scattered through the texts are boxes with suggestions for further thought and discussion.

1549. Vater, Johann Severin (1771-1826). *Amos ubersetzt und erlautert mit Beifugung des hebraischen Textes und des griechischen der Septuaginta nebst Anmerkungen zu letzterem*. Halle: Hemmerde und Schwetschke, 1810. 75 pp. Hebrew, Greek and German texts with notes on the Greek and German.

1550. Vawter, Bruce. "Amos." pp. 20-22, 29-75 in *Amos, Hosea, Micah, with an Introduction to Classical Prophecy*. OT Message 7, ed Carroll Stuhlmueller and Martin McNamara. Wilmington, DE: Glazier, 1981. 170 pp. The prophetic movement is found throughout the ANE. In Israel, classical prophecy combined experience with the best traditions of the Yahwistic religion and parallels with the surrounding cultures ceased. Vawter discusses Amos (date [c 760-750 BCE], village, message) and text (MT, authenticity, outline). There is only one Amos but the text was edited later. Commentary is by sections with brief overview.

1551. Vawter, Bruce. "Amos of Tekoa." pp. 62-97 in *The Conscience of Israel: Pre-exilic Prophets and Prophecy*. NY: Sheed & Ward, 1961. xii + 306 pp. Discusses the historical background, the prophet from Judah in Israel, oracles against Israel and the nations, varieties of injustice, the nature of religion, election and universalism. Rituals are not condemned as such but must have meaning. Israel was elected to serve the universal God.

1552. Veldkamp, Herman. *The Farmer from Tekoa: On the Book of Amos*. St. Catharines, Ontario, Canada: Paideia, 1977. 239 pp. Tr *De boer uit Tekoa*. Franeker: Wever, n.d. (received in library, 21 Ap 39). 211 pp. A narrative commentary (sermons?) on selected verses in 33 chapters, e.g., "The Calf That Drowned," "God and Culture," "Cut the Knot." Amos was preaching both destruction (for unbelievers; those at ease) and the good news (for believers) of restoration. There is no contradiction. Amos points to Jesus Christ. We ruined His palace but on that day, David's fallen house will be restored.

1553. Veldkamp, Herman. *Paraphrase van het boek van den profeet Amos en van het boek van den profeet Obadjah*. Franeker: Wever, 1940. 72 pp.

1554. Veraszto, Sandor. "Criticism of religion in the Bible." *Theologiai Szemle* (Budapest) 30 (1987), 35-37. Amos 5f.

1555. Verhoeven, P. *Echt rood. Van en vanuit Amos profeet*. Hilversam: Fooi enSticht, 1985. 71 pp.

1556. Vermaak, Petrus S. "The Meaning of *Pesha* in the Book of Amos." pp. 107-114 in *Proceedings of the Eleventh World Congress of Jewish Studies. Jerusalem, June 22-29, 1993. Division A. The Bible and Its World* ed David Assaf. Jerusalem: The World Union of Jewish Studies, 1994. vi + 246 (Eng), iv + 158 (Heb) Discusses "transgression" in Amos and elsewhere. The meaning is not uniform but varies with context, which includes parallels with sin and iniquity.

1557. Vermeylen, Jacques. *Du prophete Isaie a l'apocalyptique: Isaie, I-XXXV, miroir d'un demi-millenaire d'experience religieuse en Israel*, 2 vols. Etudes Bibliques. Paris: Gabalda, 1978. 821 pp. (Vols 1-2, continuous pagination, vol 2:v + 449-821) Amos is discussed, 2:519-569, under "Les relectures deuteronomistes des livres d'Amos et de Michee" (a detailed commentary with an extensive review of earlier opinions as well as comparative study with related texts) and again, 2:632-636, under "Le discours en *hoy* dans la prophetie du viii^e siecle." Notes the authentic Amos compared to the redactors. Amos was the first to use *hoy* at the beginning of his oracles.

1558. Vernes, Maurice. "Amos." pp. 58-61 in *Le peuple d'Israel et ses esperances: Reletives Leur Avenir depuis les origines jusqu'a l'epoque pesane (Le siecle avant J.C.)*. Paris: Sandoz et Fischbacher, 1872. 168 pp. Available in ATLA Microfiche 1985-3633. A general review of prophecies of the future - eschatology, messianism, restoration of the Jews.

1559. Vesco, Jean-Luc. "Amos de Teqoa, Defenseur de l'homme." RB 87, No. 4 (1980), 481-513. Notes numerous earlier studies, translates selected portions, discusses Amos and the covenant and wisdom. Amos condemned social injustice because he knew both the covenant and the wisdom tradition.

1560. Vetter, Paul. "Die Zeugnisse der Vorexilischen Propheten Uber den Pentateuch. I. Amos." *Theologische Quartalschrift* (Ravensburg) 81, No. 4 (1899), 512-552. Discusses the question of the law and how much of the Pentateuch Amos knew, noting scholarly opinions.

1561. Vienney, Amos B. *Amos de Tekoa, son epoque et son livre*. Montauban, 1899.

1562. Viewweger, Dieter. "Zer Herkunft der Volkerworte im Amosbuch unter besonderer Berucksichtigung des Aramaerspruchs (Am 1:3-5)." pp. 103-119 in *Altes Testament Forschung und Wirkung: Festschrift fur Henning Graf Reventlow* ed Peter Mommer and Winfried Thiel. Bern: Peter Lang, 1994. xii + 407 pp. Literature review, historical background, literary context, word studies.

1563. Vischer, Wilhelm. "Amos, citoyen de Teqoa." ETR 50, No. 2 (1975), 133-159. Notes earlier studies, the geography and environment of Tekoa and the way this appears in Amos' language, a comparison of Amos and Hesiod, practical religious in Israel, the evil of the day of the Lord, political poems.

1564. Vischer, Wilhelm. "Perhaps the Lord will be Gracious." INT 13, No. 3 (July 59), 286-295. If we seek the Lord, it may be he will be gracious to us, the remnant of his people.

1565. Vogels, W. "Invitation a revenir a l'alliance et universalisme en Amos 9:7." VT 22, No. 2 (Ap 72), 223-239. Surveys earlier studies and discusses the problems. Compares Isaiah 2:6-16.

1566. Vogt, E. "Waw explicative in Amos 7:14." ET 68, No. 10 (July 57), 301-302. The solution is not in a negative used positively but in the waw explicative, "that is, namely." There were professional and free prophets. Amos said, "I am no nabi, that is, I am no ben-nabi."

1567. Vollborn, Werner. *Innerzeitliche oder Endzeitliche Gerichtserwartung. Ein Beitrag zu Amos und Jesaja.* Kiel: Schmidt & Klaunig, 1938. 55 pp. Diss. Greifswald: Ernst-Moritz-Arndt-Universitat, 1938. Available on microfilm. An overview of the significance of the judgment as the will of God, as fulfillment of the covenant, its eschatological character. The prophets spoke of the nearness of God.

1568. Vollers, K. "Das Dodekapropheton der Alexandriner." ZAW 3, No. 2 (1883), 219-272; ZAW 4, No. 1 (1884), 1-20. A general study comparing LXX and MT with exegesis. Amos is pp. 260-272.

1569. Vollmer, Jochen. "Amos." pp. 8-54 in *Geschichtliche Ruckblicke und Motive in der Prophetie des Amos, Hosea und Jesaja.* BZAW 119, ed Georg Fohrer. Berlin: de Gruyter, 1971. x + 217 pp. Translation, notes, commentary, comparison of different interpretations.

1570. Volz, Paul (1871-1941). "Zu Amos 9:9." ZAW 38, No. 1 (1919), 105-111. An exegetical study.

1571. Volz, Paul. "Amos." pp. 145-161 in *Prophetengestalten des Alten Testaments: Sendung und Botschaft der alttestamentlichen Gotteszeugen.* Stuttgart: Calwer, 1938. 368 pp. Gives a general view of Amos and discusses conflict between prophet and priest, the role of Bethel, the role of the cult, Amos' visions, message for life.

1572. von Rad, Gerhard. "Amos." pp. 102-109 in *The Message of the Prophets*. NY: Harper & Row, 1967. 289 pp. Tr. *Die Botschaft der Propheten*. Siebenstern-Taschen buch 100/101. Munich: Siebenstern Taschenbuch Verlag, 1967. This is a revised version of material from *Theologie des Alten Testament*, tr. *Old Testament Theology*, Vols. I-II. London/Edinburgh: Oliver & Boyd, 1962, 1965. Tekoa was not isolated but a garrison from Rehoboam onward (2 Chr 11:6). [One can note that some do not take Chronicles literally, and a garrison under Rehoboam does not mean forever.] Amos himself was of substance and reputation. The prophetic call is a fact which needs no further discussion. His visions are virtually isolated in prophetic literature. The greater part of his message is based on his own pondering *ad hominem*. All he learned in his visions was that Yahweh would no longer forgive his people. The offences were not named. He says nothing about how Israel knew Yahweh's law. Nothing says people should not recline on ornate beds. The culminating point of his message is that Israel has to deal direct with an unknown Yahweh performing new deeds. The Messianic prophecy of 9:11f is the integration of the old Davidic empire. The foreign nations would suffer for violations of the unwritten law of international relations.

1573. Vonk, C. "Amos." pp. 704-741 in *Hosea - Maleachi*. De Voorzeide Leer. Deel 1Hc. De Heilige Schrift. Uitgave: Liebeek & Hooijmeijer, 1983. iv + 629-976 pp. A selective commentary.

1574. Vriezen, Theodore Christian (1899-1981) with Adam Simon van der Woude. "Amos." pp. 244-246 in *De Literatur van Oud-Israel*. Wassenaar: Servire, 1973. 446 pp. Original, Vriezen, *Oud-Israelitische Geschriften*. The Hague: Servire, 1948, 251 pp. Amos is part of a larger review of the latter prophets (pp. 218-261) and minor prophets (pp. 240-261). Brief introduction reviews the history of the collection of minor prophets, debates on chronological order, MT compared to LXX. Discusses the person of the prophet, his background as a farmer in Tekoa, historical background, brief review of the content (his call, oracles against the nations, visions).

1575. Vriezen, Theodorus C. "Erwagungen zu Amos 3:2." pp. 255-258 in *Archaologie und Altes Testament: Festschrift fur Kurt Galling zum 8. Januar 1970* ed Arnulfe Kuschke and Ernst Kutsch. Tubingen: Mohr, 1970. vi + 363 pp. Exegesis with a review of interpretations and comparison to Amos 9:7.

1576. Vuilleumier-Bessard, Rene. *La tradition cultuelle d'Israel dans la prophetie d'Amos et d'Osee*. Cahiers Theologiques 45. Neuchatel, Switzerland: Delachaux & Niestle, 1960. 95 pp. The two prophets are discussed interchangeably with the culture. Theological concerns include the presence of God and his manifestations, the approval and condemnation of the cult (idolatry, sexual orgies). Discusses the role of the priests, prophets, nazirites, the king, other ministries, the cult in terms of sacrifices, altars, cult objects, festivals. Notes elements of liturgy in the text.

W.

1577. Waard, Jan de. "The Chiastic Structure of Amos 5:1-17." VT 27, No. 2 (Ap 77), 170-177. This is a discourse unit which opens and closes with mourning. Shows how the unit divides into sub-units or paragraphs. The whole discourse is chiastic, with sub-chiasmus in sub-units. Every element falls neatly into place in meaningful relationship.

1578. Waard, Jan de. "A Greek Translation-Technical Treatment of Amos 1:15." pp. 111-118 in *On Language, Culture and Religion: In Honor of Eugene A. Nida* ed Matthew Black and William A. Smalley. Approaches to Semiotics 56. The Hague/Paris: Mouton, 1974. xxvii + 386 pp. Gives a chart of the Greek variants from the MT and discusses the problems. There is no need to presuppose a different Hebrew *Vorlage* or a conflation of Greek texts. All variants can be explained by the translation-technique approach, e.g., the Hebrew *sar* has several meanings, which are included in the Greek text.

1579. Waard, Jan de. "Translation Techniques Used by the Greek Translators of Amos." Bib 59, No. 3 (1979), 339-350. Reflects on the translation of Amos into 100 languages. Techniques include restructuring discourse, objects, components of meaning, style, figures of speech, idioms, dynamic equivalents, etc. Numerous examples in Amos.

1580. Waard de, Jan and Christiane Dieterle. "Le Dieu createur dans l'hymne du livre d'Amos." *Foi et Vie* 83 [Cahier Biblique 23], No. 5 (Sep 84), 35-44. Translation, exegesis, arrangement of the text in chiastic form, extraction of the primitive hymn which was expanded to its present form.

1581. Waard, Jan de and William A. Smalley. *A Translator's Handbook on the Book of Amos.* Helps for Translators. Stuttgart: United Bible Societies, 1979. viii + 274 pp. The introduction reviews the translation of Hebrew poetry as well as the Book of Amos, including paragraphs, headings and cross references and social relationships. The latter is very important in given cultures so the translator needs to understand how superiors speak to inferiors, etc. The RSV and Today's English Version are printed in parallel columns, and are also quoted extensively in the notes, along with other versions. The text is divided according to the structure of the Book of Amos while extensive notes give background for the translation suggestions. A glossary is helpful.

1582. Wagner, Siegfried. "Uberlegungen zur Frage nach Beziehung des Propheten Amos zum Sudreich." TLZ 96, No. 9 (Sep 71), 653-670. A discussion of Amos's origins in the southern kingdom with an extensive review of the literature.

1583. Wainwright, G.A. "The Septuagint's *Kappadokia* for Caphtor." *J of Jewish Studies* (London) 7, Nos. 1-2 (1956), 91-92. Amos 9:7. Caphtor (Keftiu to the Egyptians) was the home of the Philistines. The *'i* is usually interpreted "island" but it also means coastland and sometimes includes the islands off the coast. Thus the identification is not limited to an island, e.g., Crete or Cyprus. At times Cappadocia extended its control to the coast and to islands off the coast.

1584. Waitz, Yosef. "Amos: Sheep Breeder, Cattle Breeder, and Sycamore Fig Slitter" (Heb). BM 13 [Issue No. 33], No. 2 (Jan 68), 141-144. Exegesis with notes on earlier studies. Discusses the terms and their meaning.

1585. Walker, Larry L. "The Language of Amos." SWJT 9, No. 1 (Fall 66), 37-48. Discusses the great variety of rhetorical devices, metaphors, vocabulary, images, used by Amos. He and other prophets did not live in a literary vacuum but were well acquainted with the literature (style and content) of their neighbors.

1586. Walle, R. Vande. "The Minor Prophets as Conscientizers." *Jeevadhara* (Kottayam, Kerala, India) 19, No. 110 (Mar 89), 118-

132. God occupies a central place in the lives and work of Amos, Hosea, Micah. They were men of faith called to a mission, not social workers. God identifies with the poor and conscientizes the oppressors (making them aware of their injustice), censures selfishness, threatens punishment, invites them to change and return to the covenant. A false sense of self-satisfaction induced by empty ritual is unrelated to the most reprehensible behavior in daily life. Amos bluntly indicted those who exploit the powerless. He is not talking about the destitute but those who have meager resources who are being taxed and cheated. The rich are parasites, violating the constitutional order of justice. Their complacency is combined with a sham religiosity of ritualism. God will judge. No guilty person will escape. After weeding out the wild growth, however, God will plant a pure vineyard. The pruning process is medicinal, not vindictive.

1587. Walton, Brian (1600-1661; Bishop of Chester). "Amos." Vol. III:36-55 in *Biblia Sacra Polyglotta, complectentia textus originales, Hebraicum, cum Pentateucho Samaritano, Chaldaicum, Graecum; versionumque antiquarum, Samaritanae, Graece LXXII interp., Chaldaicae, Syriacae, Arabicae, Athiopicae, Perssicae, Vulg. Lat., quicquid comparari poterat,* 6 vols. London: Roycroft, 1656. The third volume contains Job, Psalms, Proverbs, pp. 1-447; Isaiah and Jeremiah, pp. 1-389; Ezekiel and Daniel, pp. 1-227; The 12 minor prophets, pp. 1-149. On two facing pages, the text is given in Hebrew, Latin Vulgate, LXX, Targum Jonathan, Syriac and Arabic. The Heb, Vulgate, LXX, Syriac and Arabic each have a Latin translation. The Targum has a paraphrase in Latin. Koch noted the polyglotta is still used today for Old Translations of the OT.

1588. Walzer, Michael. *An investigation of "yom yhwy" as it relates to the message of Amos.* Cambridge: Harvard, 1987. 96 pp.

1589. Walzer, Michael. "Prophecy and Social Criticism." *Drew Gateway* 55, Nos. 2&3 (Wint 84-Spr 85), 3-27. Amos is a primary source for examples. He was a minimalist monotheist but universalism is not the issue. Israel has failed in its relationships in particular, e.g., oppressing the poor.

1590. Ward, James Merrill. "Amos." pp. 17-140 in *Amos and Isaiah.*
Prophets of the Word of God. Nashville: Abingdon, 1969. 287 pp.
The book focuses on the theological and ethical aspects of these
two contemporaries. Amos' few words have influenced Western
morality out of proportion to their bulk. These are direct utterances
of God. Ward understands Amos to be preaching the authority and
righteousness of God. The text has several liturgical elements
suggesting Amos' role in the cult or at least his use of the liturgy.

1591. Ward, James Merrill. "Amos." pp. 1-49 in *Amos and Hosea.* Knox
Preaching Guides ed John H. Hayes. Atlanta: Knox, 1981. iv + 102
pp. Amos has probably received more attention in classroom and
pulpit than any other book in the OT. The oracles are powerful,
clear, basic ethics. Most commentators now think the traditions of
the Pentateuch were established long before and Amos'
proclamation is rooted in those traditions. Like the modern
preacher, he spoke from within the faith. The priest Amaziah
thought Amos was an outsider. Scholars are still debating whether
Amos was professional or a layman. Either way he serves the truth
of God. The question was not important for Amaziah. He just
wanted Amos out of Bethel. The text is divided into 12 sections,
e.g., many nations, one justice. In a distant hope (9:11-15), Ward
notes not one of them shall escape the judgment. The modern
political state of Israel is seen as fulfillment of the prophecy of
restoration.

1592. Ward, James Merrill. "Amos." pp. 21-23 in *The Interpreter's
Dictionary of the Bible, Supplementary Volume* ed Keith Crim, et
al. Nashville: Abingdon, 1976. xxv + 998 pp. Discusses research on
the cultic dimensions. Disputed passages like the oracles against
Tyre, Edom and Judah, the doxologies and promise of salvation,
hinge on these, e.g., Amos was a cultic prophet and the promises
are part of a liturgy in which the promises balance the judgment.
Sections such as 1:3-2:16 may be a cursing ritual. Rhetorical
questions, formal admonitions, etc. may reflect the wisdom
tradition as well.

1593. Ward, James Merrill. "Amos." pp. 203-214 in *Thus Says the Lord:
The Message of the Prophets.* Nashville: Abingdon, 1991. 282 pp.
Discusses Amos' call and the confrontation with Amaziah, social

justice, the providence of God, worship (repudiated), the Day of YHWH, editorial additions.

1594. Ward, James Merrill. *The Prophets*. Interpreting Biblical Texts ed Lloyd R. Bailey and Victor P. Furnish. Nashville: Abingdon, 1982. 159 pp. Considers several themes such as call and response, worship and idolatry, theodicy and who is like God.

1595. Warmuth, Georg. "Im Buch Amos." pp. 25-36 in *Das Mahnwort. Seine Bedeutung fur die Verkundigung der vorexilischen Propheten Amos, Hosea, Micha, Jesaja und Jeremia*. Beitrage zur biblischen Exegese und Theologie [BET] 1, ed Jurgen Becker and Henning Graf Reventlow. Frankfurt am Main/Bern: Peter Lang/Herbert Lang, 1976. 259 pp. Analyzes the word of warning in several verses in Amos 4 and 5. A general introduction to the text discusses the theme and its form. The function is the focus in the biblical studies.

1596. Warth, Walter. "Bibelarbeit uber Texte aus dem Buch Amos." pp. 332-390 in *Calwer Predigthilfen 5: Ausgewahlte alttestamentliche Texte* ed H. Breit and Claus Westermann. Stuttgart: Calwer, 1966. 392 pp. Selected verses with exegetical notes, commentary.

1597. Waschke, Ernst-Joachim. "Eschatologie als hermeneutischer Schlussel prophetischen Geschichtsverstandnisses." pp. 5-29 in *Hermeneutik eschatologischer biblischer Texte: 21. Konferenz von Hochschultheologen der Ostseelander* ed Dieter Birnbaum. Griefswald: Ernst-Moritz-Arndt-Univsitat, 1982. 162 pp. Notes the history of interpretation, e.g., the OT has been considered law while the NT is the gospel. Obviously the OT is much more than law [in the traditional sense; one could consider both testaments as the word of God]. Uses Amos 5:18 and other passages as examples of the theme, e.g., the Day of the Lord.

1598. Waschke, Ernst-Joachim. "Die funfte Vision des Amosbuches (9:1-4) - Eine Nach-interpretation." ZAW 106, No. 3 (1994), 434-445. Exegesis. Discusses earlier opinions. The unit dates from the Exilic period and confirms the prophet's message for the current generation.

1599. Watts, John Drayton Williams. "Amos: Across Fifty Years of Study." R&E 92, No. 2 (Spr 95), 189-193. A review of the author's study, noting Amos as a standard for how we understand prophecy.

1600. Watts, John Drayton Williams. "Amos, The Man." R&E 63, No. 4 (Fall 66), 387-392. Explores the limited biographical data on Amos and commentators' opinions.

1601. Watts, John D.W. "Amos, The Man and the Message." SWJT 9, No. 1 (Fall 66), 21-26. The two are matched. These include breadth of vision, rooted in the past, God is real, realism in faith including genuine worship, direct obedience, sincere offering.

1602. Watts, John D.W. "Commentaries on Amos: A Review." *Religious Studies Review* 7, No. 2 (Ap 81), 128-132. Discusses Mays (1969), Rudolph (1971), Wolff (1969; 1977), with a general overview of the series and critical comparison of the three volumes. Mays is best for the pastor-expositor, Wolff for the student and professor working with Greek and Hebrew, and Rudolph for balanced criticism.

1603. Watts, John D.W. "A Critical Analysis of Amos 4:1ff." 2:489-500 in *SBL Proceedings: 1972*, 2 vols, ed Lane C. McGaughy. Los Angeles: SBL, 1972. iv + 315-607. A detailed exegesis which sorts out a minimal element for Amos with accretion through various editions to the final form. A Bethel speech is changed into a Samaria speech by adding the mountains of Samaria. Later Judeans objected to the syncretism of the Samaritans. But then the charge of oppressing the needy changed the message from false worship to social injustice.

1604. Watts, John D.W. "Note on the Text of Amos 5:7." VT 4, No. 2 (Ap 54), 215-216. Surveys earlier attempts to translate, relocate, emend, etc. Compares MT and LXX. Translates: It is Yahweh who pours out justice from above and who grants righteousness on earth.

1605. Watts, John D.W. "An Old Hymn Preserved in Amos." JNES 15, No. 1 (Jan 56), 33-39. Gives Hebrew, translation and commentary of hymn fragments 4:13, 5:8, and 9:5-6, and numerous attempts to translate. Shows how the verses are related to their context. The hymn reflects radical Yahwism, rejecting all other powers and religions.

1606. Watts, John D.W. "The Origin of the Book of Amos." ET 66, No. 4 (Jan 55), 109-112. The book includes oracles, autobiographical and biographical materials. Discusses the visions, current scholarship. There are three periods in Amos' ministry. He preached in Judah after he left Bethel. The book is in three parts: a book of messages, a book of visions and the clash with Amaziah. The two books were put together soon, perhaps by the end of the eighth century.

1607. Watts, John D.W. *Studying the Book of Amos.* Nashville: Broadman, 1966. 93 pp. A general reader.

1608. Watts, John D.W. *Vision and Prophecy in Amos.* Leiden/Grand Rapids: Brill/Eerdmans, 1958. viii + 90 pp. Reviews Amos' background, religious experience, relation to the cult, his visions, the two books of Amos, fragments of old hymns (4:13; 5:8; 9:5-6), and his eschatology. Amos became a regular prophet working in the cult, known to the priest. Amos 1-6 was spoken in the north while 6-9 were gathered in the south by disciples. The Day of the Lord and judgement come from the Autumn Festival. The Day means God is creator and judges the nations. Its coming will mean the end of the northern kingdom.

1609. Weathers, Eugene. "An Oracle of God (1990)." pp. 7-8 in *Many Voices: Multicultural Responses to the Minor Prophets* ed Alice Ogden Bellis. Lanham, MD: University Press of America, 1995. xiv + 101 pp. The writers in this book try to apply the minor prophets today. An Amos-type oracle of judgment against irresponsible living - illegitimate children, crack, crime.

1610. Weber, Robert. "Amos Propheta." Vol 2 (1975), 1388-1396 in *Biblia Sacra: Iuxta Vulgatam Versionem. Tomus II. Proverbia - Apocalypsis. Appendix.* 2 vols, ed Bonifatio Fischer, et al. Apparatus by Weber. Stuttgart: Wurttembergische Bibelanstalt, 1975. original, 1969. ii + 1980 pp. Latin text with critical apparatus.

1611. Weigl, Michael. "Eine 'unendliche Geschichte': *'nk* (Amos 7:7-8)."
Bib 76, No. 3 (1995), 343-387. Discusses earlier opinions of this
hapax legomena, oriental background, exegesis.

1612. Weimar, Peter. "Der Schluss des Amos-Buches. Ein Beitrag zur
Redaktions-geschichte des Amos-Buches." BN (Bamberg) 16
(1981), 60-100. A close analysis of Amos 9 with an extensive
review of the history of interpretation. Amos 9:1 and 4b are the
original vision with accretions from the Deuteronomic and early
and late postexilic era.

1613. Weippert, Helga. "Amos/Amosbuch." 1 (1991), cols 92-95 in
Neues Bibel-Lexikon ed Manfred Gorg and Bernhard Lang. Zurich:
Benziger, 1991. 1:xxiii + 965. Originally published in fascicles.
Weippert is Fascicle 1 (1988). Discusses the man (background,
occupations, etc.) and the book (outline, message). Bibliography.

1614. Weippert, Helga. "Amos: His Imagery and Its Background" (Ger).
p. 1-29 in *Beitrage zur Prophetischen Bildsprache in Israel und
Assyrien* with H. Weippert, et al. Orbis Biblicus et Orientalis 64, ed
Othmar Keel, et al.. Freiberg, Switzerland/Gottingen:
Universitatsverlag/ Vandenhoeck & Ruprecht, 1985. ix + 93 pp.
The study extends to the ANE, Egyptian iconography, etc.

1615. Weiser, Artur A. "Amos." pp. 110-180 in *Das Buch der zwolf
kleinen Propheten. I. Die Propheten Hosea, Joel, Amos, Obadja,
Jona, Micha*. Das Alte Testament Deutsch 24, ed Volkmar
Herntrich and Artur Weiser. Gottingen: Vandenhoeck & Ruprecht,
1949. viii + 262 pp. (7th ed, 1979) The introduction gives an
overview of the man and the book. The commentary is a German
translation of small units with extensive notes. Subheadings
indicate content, e.g., the Day of Yahweh.

1616. Weiser, Artur. "Amos." pp. 241-247 *The Old Testament: Its
Formation and Development*; NY: Association, 1961. Tr from the
4th ed of the German edition, 1957 (original, 1948). Published in
England as *Introduction to the Old Testament*. London: Darton,
Longman & Todd, 1961. xv + 492 pp. Discusses the man, the
historical background, the book (visions, oracles). Amos' concept
of God is freedom. In the presence of the transcendent, Israel's

prerogatives collapse. Thus Amos rejects the entire cult system which men think gives them power.

1617. Weiser, Artur A. "Zu Amos 4:6-13." *ZAW* 46, ns 5, No. 1 (1928), 49-59. Reviews earlier studies, problems of translation, the cult, the plague, holy war and other issues.

1618. Weiser, Artur A. "The Background of the Prophecies of Hosea and Amos." *Sinai* 31 (1952), 253-264.

1619. Weiser, Artur A. "Die Berufung des Amos." *Theologische Blatter* 7, No. 7 (July '28), cols 177-182. Analyzes the call and discusses earlier studies.

1620. Weiser, Artur A. *Die Profetie des Amos.* BZAW 53. Giessen: Topelmann, 1929. viii + 332 pp. Discusses the word of Amos in context of visions, language, his understanding of God, the law, the cult, the national religion, the culture.

1621. Weisman, Zeev. "Patterns and Structure in the Visions of Amos" (Heb). BM 14 [Issue No. 39], No. 4 (Sep 69), 40-57. Analysis of Amos 7:1-9:4, noting earlier studies.

1622. Weisman, Zeev. "Stylistic Parallels in Amos and Jeremiah: Their Implications for the Composition of Amos" (Heb). *Shnaton* (Jerusalem) 1 (1975), 129-149, xxiii (Eng summary). Includes epithets, hendiadys, dimeter stichoi, the so-called deuteronomic phraseology. Most of these parallels are unique to Amos and Jeremiah. Part of this is literary influence of Amos on Jeremiah. Part of it suggests the editor of Amos was quite familiar if not actively involved with the composition of Jeremiah's prophecies.

1623. Weiss, Meir. *The Bible from Within: The Method of Total Interpretation.* Publications of the Perry Foundation for Biblical Research in the Hebrew University of Jerusalem. Jerusalem: Magnes, 1984. xiii + 461 pp. cf pp. 102-106, 194-221, 417-421. Tr, updated from original, *HaMiqra Kidemuto* ("The Bible and Modern Literary Theory"). Jerusalem: Bialik, 1962. 3rd ed, 1987. Studies words and phrases ("a prophet's son"), images ("sea to sea"; "LORD roars from Zion"), sentences, units and structure, the literary work in its totality. Among seven appendices, the third reviews the history of interpretation of 7:14. Weiss gives an extensive review of the debates on meaning, interpretation, emendations, etc.

1624. Weiss, Meir. *The Book of Amos* (Heb), 2 vols. Perry Foundation for Biblical Research in the Hebrew University of Jerusalem. Jerusalem: Magnes Press, The Hebrew University, 1992. 1:ix + 301 + ii; 2:iv + 630 + ii. Vol 1 is a commentary. Vol 2 is Notes.

1625. Weiss, Meir. "Concerning Amos' Repudiation of the Cult." pp. 199-214 in *Pomegranates and Golden Bells: Studies in Biblical, Jewish, and Near Eastern Ritual, Law, and Literature in Honor of Jacob Milgrom* ed David P. Wright, et al. Winona Lake, IN: Eisenbrauns, 1995. xxxii + 861 pp. Gives a transcription, literary and structural analysis, and detailed exegesis of Amos 5:21-24. Compares other texts in Amos and elsewhere. Ritual is opposed and righteousness and justice demanded. It does not follow that all ritual everywhere or forever is opposed.

1626. Weiss, Meir. "The Decalogue in Prophetic Literature." pp. 67-81 in *The Ten Commandments in History and Tradition* ed Ben Zion Segal; Eng version ed Gershon Levi. Publications of the Perry Foundation for Biblical Research, The Hebrew University of Jerusalem. Jerusalem: Magnes, 1990. xv + 453 pp. Tr of 1985 Heb ed. Notes the history of interpretation. Compares prophetic concerns, including Amos 3:1-2, with the 10 Commandments and finds traces of the latter.

1627. Weiss, Meir. "In the Footsteps of One Biblical Metaphor (Methodological Remarks and Exegetical, and Historical Notices)." *Tarbiz* 34, No. 2 (Jan 65), 107-128. No. 3 (Ap 65), 211-223. No. 4 (July 65), 303-318. Heb with English summary, pp. I-II of each issue. Part 1 is on Amos; part 2 is on Joel and Jer 35:30; part 3 is on Amos and Joel. "The Lord will roar from on high" and similar words appear in Amos 1:2 (from Zion), etc. For Amos, Weiss reviews a host of opinions and concludes this is an organic unity. In Amos, we have a mind steeped in the pastoral life. The metaphor may be original with him but it's in an independent unit. The reaction is passive/stillness/the end. In Joel, it is active/uproar/dread of the end. In Amos, it is terrifying. In Jeremiah, it is cruelty. In Amos, God shows himself and existence becomes void.

1628. Weiss, Meir. "Methodologisches uber die Behandlung der Metapher dargelegt an Amos 1:2." TZ (Basel) 23, No. 1 (Jan-Feb 67), 1-25. Detailed exegesis, with the history of interpretation, comparison with sources.

1629. Weiss, Meir. "The Pattern of the 'Execration Texts' in the Prophetic Literature." *Israel Exploration J* 19, No. 3 (1969), 150-157. Contra Bentzen and Fohrer, there is no comparison in direction or names or principle between the Texts and Amos' or other prophets' oracles against the nations.

1630. Weiss, Meir. "The Pattern of Numerical Sequence in Amos 1-2: A Re-examination." JBL 86, No. 4 (Dec 67), 416-423. Tr "'Because Three . . . and Because Four' (Amos 1-2)" (Heb). *Tarbiz* 36, No. 4 (July 67), 307-318. Heb with Eng summary, p. i. The pattern is well known in the Bible and the ANE but scholars disagree on Amos' use, e.g., the pattern means four, or, an indefinite number. It is neither but results from *parallelismus memrorum*. The number may be seven, total. There are seven sins, a number which expresses the whole or the largest of all. While following poetic practice, Amos bends the rule to his personal creativity.

1631. Weiss, Meir. "These Days and the Days to Come According to Amos 9:13" (Heb). EI 14 (1978), 69-73. Eng summary, p. 125. When similar concepts are used, their intent may be specific. In Amos, the days will include unceasing labor because of the increased fertility of the land and the blessed state which precedes the curse of the land.

1632. Weitzner, Emil. *The Book of Amos: Prologue, Paraphrase, Epilogue.* NY: n.p., 1963. 45 pp. The preface discusses the ethic of judgement and the message. The prologue is the history and geography of Amos, in verse. The paraphrase modernizes the translation. The epilogue is a drama involving Jeroboam II, Amaziah and Amos, in verse.

1633. Welch, Adam C. "Amos." pp. 107-129 in *Kings and Prophets of Israel*. London: Lutterworth, 1952. 264 pp. Discusses the origins of the book, the historical background, Amos' personal history, his call, the scene at Bethel, God's revelation, the election of Israel, God's concerns with the nations, monotheism (Amos was a monotheist), universal religion.

1634. Wellhausen, Julius (1844-1918). "Amos." pp. 1-10, 67-96 in *Die Kleinen Propheten ubersetz und erklart*, 4th ed. Berlin: de Gruyter, 1963. v + 222 pp. (original, 1892. Skizzen und Vorarbeiten 5. Berlin: Reimer, 1898.) German translation with notes plus detailed commentary.

1635. Wendland, Ernst R. "The 'Word of the Lord' and the Organization of Amos." *Occasional Papers in Translation and Textlinguistics* 2, No 4 (1988), 1-51. Analyzes form and contents together and gives a structural outline of the book. Wendland notes that various interpretations of the structure may distort the Word.

1636. Werner, Herbert. *Amos*. Exempla Biblica 4. Gottingen: Vandenhoeck & Ruprecht, 1969. 203 pp. Commentary on selected passages, e.g., the oracles against the nations, the law of Yahweh, the visions. Detailed notes. The last 35 pages is an essay on Amos in the school curriculum.

1637. Werner, Wolfgang. *Studien zur alttestamentlichen Vorstellung vom Plan Jahwes*. BZAW 173 ed Otto Kaiser. Berlin/NY: de Gruyter, 1988. xi + 334 pp. The review includes Isaiah and the David stories in Samuel and Kings. The 4th chapter discusses other prophetic texts, e.g., Amos 3:3-8 (pp. 167-181), with translations, analysis, comparison of scholarly opinions, vs 7 as a gloss, and its theological background.

1638. Westermann, Claus. "Amos." pp. 185-190 in *Handbook to the Old Testament*. Minneapolis: Augsburg, 1976. xvi + 285 pp. (original Ger, 1962) The structure of Amos is simple: judgment on Israel and the nations; discourses on judgment against Israel; reports on visions, Amos and Amaziah; promise of welfare. The judgments against the nations are for infractions of international law. The doxologies put together form a psalm of creation.

1639. Westermann, Claus. "Amos 5:4-6, 14, 15: Ihr Werdet Leben!" pp. 107-118 in *Ertraege der Forschung am Alten Testament. Gesammelte Studien III* by Westermann, ed Rainer Albertz. Theologische Bucherei 73 ed Gerhard Sauter. Munich: Kaiser, 1984. 228 pp. Discusses various interpretations, comparisons with other texts, exposition, structure. The text of ch 5 moves from dirge to search to woe to doxology to wisdom. The text of the book moves from Judah to the nations and Israel to the prophet to judgment on Israel to a focus on God, and back in reverse order.

1640. Westermann, Claus. "Amos: Prophet to Society." pp. 200-212 in *A Thousand Years and a Day: Our Time in the Old Testament*. Philadelphia: Fortress, 1962. ix + 280 pp. (third printing, 1982; original Ger, 1957) Amos opposed social injustice. A comparison of ANE law, e.g., Hammurabi's, and biblical law shows the latter with equality. Oppression of the poor violates Israelite law. The Church has ignored the social preaching of the prophets and become the guardian of tradition and conservative power. Amaziah's response to Amos was friendly, in suggesting Amos should go home. Note that Amos is a simple man, speaking simple language, without jargon. The Church must preach for ordinary people. Amos saw his visions while wide awake and sober. Later things changed when prophecy failed and was replaced by visions.

1641. Westermann, Claus. "The Minor Prophets." pp. 102-136 in *Prophetic Oracles of Salvation in the Old Testament*. Louisville, KY: Westminster/John Knox, 1991. 283 pp. Tr, *Prophetische Heilsworte im Alten Testament*. Gottingen: Vandenhoeck & Ruprecht, 1987. A general introduction discusses salvation oracles before the writing prophets. An introduction to the texts of the minor prophets is followed by a study of themes, with selected quotations and commentary. Themes include God's return, restoration and blessing, promise of a king who brings salvation.

1642. Westermann, Claus. "Sexagesimae. Amos 8:11-12." Vol 5:155-160 in *Herr, tue meine Lippen auf: Eine Predigthilfe*, 2nd ed, ed Georg Eichholz. Wuppertal-Barmen: Muller, 1961. Vol 5:viii + 620. (original, 1948). A sermon on the pericope with exegesis and application.

1643. Whitford, John B. "The Vision of Amos." BS (Oberlin) 70, No. 277 (1913), 109-122. Notes the historical background with Samaria soon to fall. Compares other periods in history, the apostolic age, the time of Napoleon, etc. Amos' vision was a new day when every weed would be a flower.

1644. Wicke, Donald W. "Two Perspectives (Amos 5:1-7)." CTM *Currents in Theology and Mission* (Chicago) 13, No. 2 (Ap 86), 89-96. The historical approach (analytical, diachronic, focus on the background) sees a haphazard collection of sayings while a literary approach (synthetic, synchronic, focus on the text) sees a carefully formed unity. Literary themes include the hymn, the name of God, justice, the priestly torah, the lament. Charts show the relationships. The literary approach is more useful for preachers. "One's perspective determines what one looks for and what one hears."

1645. Wielenga, B. *De Leeuw Heeft Debrud: Act Tijdpreeken uit de Profetie van Amos.* Kampen: Kok, 1917. 135 pp. Eight sermons on selected passages, e.g., Amos 3:8.

1646. Wigoder, Geoffrey, et al., eds. "Amos." pp. 56-57 in *The Encyclopedia of Judaism.* NY: Macmillan, 1989. 768 pp. Outlines the book. The election of Israel meant responsibility, not privilege. Amos denounced hypocrisy and urged repentance. An epilogue predicts a future golden age.

1647. Wilbers, H. "Etudes sur trois textes relatifs a l'agriculture: Isaiah 28:27-28; Amos 2:13, 9:9." *Melanges de l'universite Saint-Joseph* (Beirut) 5, No. 1 (1911), 269-282. Amos, pp. 277-282. Reviews methods of interpretation, followed by comparative exegesis.

1648. Williams, A.J. "A Further Suggestion about Amos 4:1-3." VT 29, No. 2 (Ap 79), 206-211. The guilty will be dragged out through the break in the walls. There is also background in the rivalry between Mt Zion and the hills of Bashan, an agriculturally fertile area. The prophets knew ancient mythology and used it for their message.

1649. Williams, Arthur Lukyn (1853-1943). *Joel and Amos.* The Minor Prophets Unfolded. Cambridge: Cambridge University, 1918.

1650. Williams, Donald Leigh. "The Theology of Amos." R&E 63, No. 4 (Fall 66), 393-403. Amos was a preacher, not a systematic theologian. His theology was not new although at the time it sounded new because Israel had prostituted the Mosaic faith. The prophet is brutal in his judgment of the character of worship. He was not, however, advocating the destruction of all formal worship. The Day of Yahweh is the center of his theology but he does not define it. It will be a day of destruction but there is hope. God will destroy the kingdom but not give up his people.

1651. Williams, J.G. "The Alas Oracles of the Eighth-Century Prophets." HUCA 38 (1967), 75-91. A general study of the form, including Amos 5:18-26, Micah 2:1-4. Commentary, analysis, discussion of the *Sitz im Leben*, form criticism.

1652. Williams, J.G. "Irony and Lament: Clues to Prophetic Consciousness." *Semeia* 8 (1977), 51-74. The *hoy* oracles or poetry in Amos, Isaiah and Micah illustrate the concerns. Irony has comedy and incongruity with hidden meanings. The prophets were caught in the middle between God and people, between vision and reality. The prophets all used paronomasia, attribution, exaggeration, juxtaposition, repetition and other elements.

1653. Williams, Walter G. "Amos: Prophet of Moral Responsibility." pp. 151-160 in *The Prophets: Pioneers to Christianity*. NY: Abingdon, 1956. 223 pp. A general introduction to the prophets discusses new sources of knowledge, priest and prophet, professional prophets, moral religion, the Messiah, personal immortality. Gives Amos' personal and historical background and commentary on selected passages. Amos has been called destructive in his criticism. But he not only noted wrong, he said why they were wrong and urged people to turn to God and his moral law to correct the wrong.

1654. Williamson, H.A. "Rendering of Amos 5:25,26." ET 36, No. 9 (1925), 430-431. The term *wns'tm* continues the question of vs 25. It is a challenge to a hollow ceremonialism and the ground of idolatrous practices. Israel has fallen away from the pure worship of the desert when no sacrifice was necessary and they carried the ark.

1655. Williamson, H.G.M. "The Prophet and the Plumb-Line: A Redaction-Critical Study of Amos 7." *OTS* 26 (1990), 101-121 in *In Quest of the Past* ed. A van der Woude (Leiden: Brill, 1990. 123 pp.) The story of Amos' encounter with Amaziah interrupts the series of visions. The Deuteronomists inserted it to show that Amos himself is the plumbline.

1656. Willi-Plein, Ina. "Amosbuch." pp. 15-69 in *Vorformen der Schriftexegese Innerhale des Alten Testaments: Untersuchungen zum literarischen Werden der auf Amos, Hosea und Micha zuruckgehenden Bucher im hebraischen Zwolfprophetenbuch.* BZAW 123, ed Georg Fohrer. Berlin/NY: de Gruyter, 1971. ix + 286 pp. A comparative study relating the MT and LXX, individual parts to the rest of the text. Each book is analyzed and then put together in reconstructed form (Amos, pp. 269-272).

1657. Willmington, Harold. "Glimpses of Greatness: Four Angry Prophets." *Fundamentalist J* 5 (Oct 86), 54. Vignettes on Amos, Obadiah, Hosea and Joel. Amos faced Amaziah with God's judgment but in the end, Israel would be redeemed and restored.

1658. Willoughby, Bruce E. "Amos, Book of." Vol 1:203-212 in *The Anchor Bible Dictionary*, 6 vols, ed David Noel Freedman, et al. NY: Doubleday, 1992. 1:lxxviii + 1232. Reviews the man, history, theological ideas, structure, content, literary and rhetorical features, text and canonicity. Amos was the owner of his sheep (possibly, but doubtful, a temple or court official who tended the temple or royal flocks). He was economically independent, a landed aristocrat. When he finished preaching, he went back to his ranch. People claimed their wealth showed they were righteous. Amos preached against social injustice. The first edition of the Bible dates between 560-540 BCE by the Jews in exile. The book of Amos was part of that.

1659. Wilton, Edward. "The Prophet Amos, and 'the River of the Wilderness'," *J of Sacred Literature and Biblical Record* (London, 1848-1868), 4th ser, 5 (1864), 175-180.

1660. Winckler, Hugo (1863-1913). "Einzelnes." pp. 175-187 in *Alttestamentliche Untersuchungen.* Leipzig: Pfeiffer, 1892. viii +

192 pp. Available on microfiche, 1987-2573. Discusses, pp. 183-185, Am 1:5-6,9; 2:2, 16; 3:9; 7:16; 9:6. Exegesis, translation, comparison of MT and LXX, identification of sites, review of earlier opinions.

1661. Winckler, Hugo. "Zum alten Testament: Amos 8:14." No. 2 (1894), 194-195 in *Altorientalische Forschungen*. First series, No. 1-6 (1893-1897). Leipzig: Pfeiffer, 1897. 573 pp. Exegesis. Compares MT and LXX, the Mesha stele, the god Chemosh and Moab.

1662. Winter, Alexander. "Analyse des Buches Amos." *Theologische Studien und Kritiken* 83 (1910), 323-374.

1663. Winton, George B. *Pleaders for Righteousness: Studies in the Prophecies of Amos and Hosea*. Leadership Training Series 2. Bible Course ed E.B. Chappell. Nashville: Cokesbury, 1928. 225 pp. Each chapter closes with discussion questions. A general introduction notes there is little orderly thought in these books. There is a general review of prophecy from Samuel to Micah. The earlier prophets were called seers and sons of the prophets, a phrase used by Amos. As the two kingdoms grew in prosperity, their national religion became ritualized. National religion was encouraged by religious leaders but Amos, Hosea, Isaiah and Micah brought a new, universal, moral dimension to religion. The six chapters on Amos consider his place, call, personality, the historical background in the northern kingdom, his idea of God (a universal ruler), his silencing (by church and state), and the literary character of the book. Amos is the first of the prophets to record his message, or a summary of it, in a book. It is in three sections. The progress of archaeology continues to throw light on the many obscure passages.

1664. Wisdom, Thurman. "A Funeral Dirge for Living (Amos 5:1-9)." BV 27, No. 2 (Nov 93), 17-22. Herodotus says that in Egypt, at the end of a banquet, a coffin with a corpse was carried around to remind people of their end. The people of Israel were like Christians in America today. Amos lamented (funeral dirge) for them but there is hope if you seek the Lord. Exegetical study and commentary with the doom proclaimed in vss 1-3, and the appeal for hope in vss 4-9. People hide behind a shroud of religious activity but they have a distorted view of God. They should worship God rather than the stars or other pagan symbols.

1665. Witaszek, Gabriel. "Israelite Society in the Light of Social Criticism of the Prophet Amos" (Pol). *Ruch Biblijny* 43 (1990), 105-111.

1666. Witaszek, Gabriel. *The Prophets Amos and Micah Confront Social Injustices* (Pol). Tuchow: Mala Poligrafia. Redmeptorystow, 1992. 222 pp. Abbreviated version of the Gregorian University dissertation with bibliography updated to 1991. Gives the social and historical background, the social message, the similarities and differences of the two. They drew on earlier material but faced distinctive social problems from the shift from a nomadic to settled existence. We face similar challenges today. Rev, OTA 16, No. 2 (June 93), 432 # 1592.

1667. Wittenberg, Gunther H. "Amos and Hosea: A Contribution to the Problem of the 'Profetenschweigen' in the Deuteronomistic History." OTE 6, No. 3 (1993), 295-311. In the final years of Josiah, Amos' radical message of doom and Hosea's rejection of kingship were unacceptable to the deuteronomist so he left them out of his history.

1668. Wittenberg, Gunther H. "Amos 6:1-7: 'They dismiss the day of disaster but you bring near the rule of violence'." *J of Theology for Southern Africa* (Cape Town) 58 (Mar 87), 57-69. Translation, exegesis, commentary. Discusses the text, the *marzech* feast for the dead, the disastrous day of the Lord, editing by the Amos school and the deuteronomic school. Concludes God is a God of justice and modern ideologies are idolatries.

1669. Wittenberg, Gunther H. "A Fresh Look at Amos and Wisdom." OTE ns 4, No. 1 (1991), 7-18. Agrees with Coote on the three layers of Amos. One belongs to Amos; two to the Judean court in the time of Josiah. Wisdom influence is found in "B." However, Wittenberg does not think wisdom and the court were closely connected. The connection of "B" with the "people of the land" and the Deuteronomic movement should be investigated.

1670. Wolfe, Rolland Emerson. "The Editing of the Book of the Twelve."
ZAW 53, No. 1 (1935), 90-129. Finds 13 editors in the Book, some
of whom worked on all 12 books while others worked on shorter
groups. They include the Day of Jahwe editor, the doxologist, etc.
Secondary additions to the text should not be deemed of lesser
value. Much of the material quoted later, e.g., in the NT, 62-74%
of the OT references come from these editors.

1671. Wolfe, Rolland Emerson. "Amos." pp. 3-73 in *Meet Amos and
Hosea: The Prophets of Israel*. NY: Harper & Brothers, 1945. xxx
+ 180 pp. He reviews the historical background, Amos' travel to
Bethel, his call for righteousness in religion, politics and business.
Amos was a great preacher of ethical religion. Wolfe speculates
that Amos may have been martyred but his spirit lived on.

1672. Wolfendale, James. "Homiletic Commentary on Amos." pp. 242-
330 in *Homiletical Commentary on the Minor Prophets*. The
Preacher's Complete Homiletical Commentary on the Old
Testament (on an original plan) with Critical and Explanatory
Notes, Indices, etc. etc. by Various Authors. London: Dickinson,
1879. iii + 742 pp. Reprinted as *The Preacher's Complete
Homiletic Commentary of the Books of the Minor Prophets*. Grand
Rapids: Baker, 1978. The introduction discusses the man, his time,
book and analysis, with an outline. "Its style indicates vigour of
mind and great moral culture." Each chapter has exegetical notes
followed by homiletic suggestions, outlines, illustrations.

1673. Wolff, Hans Walter. "Amos." pp. 87-355 in *Joel and Amos. A
Commentary on the Books of the Prophets Joel and Amos*, ed S.
Dean McBride, Jr. Hermeneia, ed Frank Moore Cross, Jr., et al.
Philadelphia: Fortress, 1977. xxiv + 392 pp. Tr, *Dodekapropheton
2 Joel und Amos*, 2nd ed. Biblischer Kommentar 14, No. 2, ed
Siegfried Herrmann, et al. Neukirchen-Vluyn: Neukirchener, 1975.
3rd ed, 1985 (original, 1969). The introduction discusses the
historical background, the man, his language (commission, free
speech, visions, peculiar language elements, dynamics), message,
the formation of the book. The commentary includes a series of
excursi, e.g., on "Israel," the hymns, the woes, etc. There is a
general bibliography and sections of the text have bibliography,
followed by translation, critical apparatus, discussion (e.g., form,

setting, interpretation, aim). The closing oracles are about fifth century BCE.

1674. Wolff, Hans Walter. *Amos the Prophet: The Man and His Background* ed John Reumann. Philadelphia: Fortress, 1973. xii + 100 pp. Tr *Amos' geistige Heimat.* Wissenschaftliche Monographien zum Alten und Neuen Testament 18, ed Gunther Bornkamm and Gerhard von Rad. Neukirchen-Vluyn: Neukirchener, 1964. Philadelphia, 1973, and, *L'enracinement spirituel d'Amos.* Geneva: Labor et Fides, 1974. 125 pp. The editor introduces Amos, prophecy and Wolff. *Geistige Heimat* might be translated "spiritual home." Wolff discusses the rhetorical forms of Amos (didactic question, "Woe-cry," numerical sequence, exhortation), characteristic themes (Israel and the nations, the "Right" way, justice and judgment, the poor and needy, extravagant life) and peripheral problems (Tekoa, the House of Isaac, Amos and Isaiah, wisdom and the proclamation of judgment). He concludes that Amos lived out of the oral tradition of ancient Israelite clan wisdom. Part of the theory is that in his shepherd wanderings, Amos was in contact with the Edomites and the wisdom of the East. He is the only prophet who speaks of the House of Isaac in parallel with Israel and of the high places of Isaac in parallel to the sanctuaries of Israel and only Amos refers to the sanctuary at Beer-sheba. Isaac was the father of Edomites and Israelites.

1675. Wolff, Hans Walter. *Confrontations.* See "Irresistible" (#1679, #1680).

1676. Wolff, Hans Walter. "Das Ende des Heiligtums in Bethel." pp. 287-298 in *Archaologie und Altes Testament: Festschrift fur Kurt Galling zum 8. Januar 1970* ed Arnulf Kutschke and Ernst Kutsch. Tubingen: Mohr, 1970. vi + 363 pp. A detailed analysis with a review of earlier studies.

1677. Wolff, Hans Walter. "Hunger nach Gerechtigkeit - ungestillt." pp. 29-35 in *Zuwendung und Gerechtigkeit: Heidelberger Predigten III. [Festschrift fur] Claus Westermann zum 60. Geburtstag am 7. Oktober 1969* ed Paul Philippi. Gottingen: Vandenhoeck & Ruprecht, 1969. A sermon.

1678. Wolff, Hans Walter. "The Irresistible Word: Amos and the Well-deserved End." pp. 9-21 in *Confrontations with Prophets: Discovering the Old Testament's New and Contemporary Significance.* Philadelphia: Fortress, 1983. 78 pp. Tr *Prophetische Alternativen: Entdeckungen des Neuen im Alten Testament.* Munich: Kaiser, 1982. Amos resists, pleading for the salvation of his people. But God shows him the people have brought it on themselves; the end is sure.

1679. Wolff, Hans Walter. "The Irresistible Word (Amos)." *Currents in Theology and Mission* 10, No. 1 (Feb 83), 4-13. From *Confrontations with Prophets.* God's call could not be resisted. Wolff discusses this and autobiographical references, God's judgment, the prophet's three essential messages - an end to evil, we have brought it on ourselves, we face the future together as convicts given amnesty in Jesus.

1680. Wolff, Hans Walter. "Predigt uber Amos 5:1-5." EvT 28, No. 1 (1968), 1-8. Gives a translation and a sermon with homiletic suggestions.

1681. Wolff, Hans Walter. "Der Prophet Amos." pp. 105-410 in *Dodekapropheton 2. Joel und Amos.* Biblischer Kommentar Altes Testament xiv, 2. Neukirchen: Neukirchener, 1969. ix + 464 pp. An earlier edition is dated 1967, 2nd ed 1975. Cf Eng tr. Hermeneia series.

1682. Wolff, Hans Walter. *Prophetische Alternativen.* See "Irresistible" (#1679, #1680).

1683. Wolff, Hans Walter. *Die Stunde des Amos: Prophetie und Protest.* Munich: Kaiser, 1969. 215 pp. 3rd ed, 1974. The four parts are on Amos and his proclamation, the exegesis of chs 3-4, preaching from various passages and the translation and classification of the book.

1684. Wolters, Al. "Wordplay and Dialect in Amos 8:1-2." JETS 31, No. 4 (Dec 88), 407-410. Judah's dialect differed from Israel's. Amos was imitating the northern dialect in which both words are pronounced alike. Wolters gives modern analogies in American and British English.

1685. Woude, Adam Simon van der. "Amos 5:4b." pp. 171-173 in *Keus uit twaalf postillen* ed M.H. Bolkestein and Kr. Strijd. 's-Gravenhage: Boekencentrum B.V., 1976. 264 pp. Reprinted from Postille 19 (1967-1968), 164-166. For preaching.

1686. Woude, Adam Simon van der. "Bemerkungen zu einigen umstrittenen Stellen im Zwolfprophetenbuch." pp. 483-499 in *Melanges bibliques et orientaux en l'honneur de M. Henri Cazelles* ed Andre Caquot and Matthias Delcor. Alter Orient und Altes Testament 212. Neukirchen-Vluyn/Kevelaer: Neukirchener/Butzon & Bercker, 1981. xii + 543 pp. Exegesis of selected units. Discusses Amos 5:25-26 (pp. 485-490) with translation, notes on earlier studies, comparison with other texts.

1687. Woude, A.S. van der. "Three Classical Prophets: Amos, Hosea and Micah." pp. 32-57 in *Israel's Prophetic Tradition: Essays in Honour of Peter R. Ackroyd* ed Richard J. Coggins, et al. Cambridge: Cambridge University Press, 1982. xxi + 272 pp. Disagrees with liberal and pietistic Protestantism that the prophets were individualists who rejected the institutions of their day. This is eisegesis. Modern study overstates the prophetic commitment to the traditions at the expense of the personal experience of God. A review of current scholarship of each of the three prophets. Amos (pp. 34-43) studies have become a library.

1688. Wright, John. "Did Amos Inspect Livers?" *Australian Biblical Review* 23 (Oct 75), 3-11. No. Discusses Amos as a cultic official (can't tell for sure), the meaning of *noqed* (not livers but sheep), *boqer* (cowherd) and Amos' probable return to caring for animals.

1689. Wright, Samuel Lee. "O homem de Deus e o homem do rei." *Revista Teologica* (Rio de Janerio, Brazil) 2, No. 3 (June 86), 37-42. Available on microfilm, PTS 3593. Amos 7:10-17 begins with the word of God from Amaziah and ends with it from Amos. Rev, OTA 9 (1986), 305.

1690. Wright, T.J. "Amos and the 'Sycamore Fig'." VT 26, No. 3 (July 76), 362-368. Surveys studies on the term *boles* which suggests Amos was a nipper of sycamores, to help ripen the fruit, but also to pollinate, and also to collect as fodder for his livestock.

1691. Wurthwein, Ernst. "Amos 5:21-27." TLZ 72 (1947), 143-152. Reprinted, pp. 55-67 in *Wort und Existenz: Studien zum Alten Testament* by Wurthwein. Gottingen: Vandenhoeck & Ruprecht, 1970. 319 pp. Discusses the role of the cult in the classical prophets and Amos in particular, with a review of interpretations.

1692. Wurthwein, Ernst. "Amos-Studien." ZAW 62, Nos. 1-2 (1950), 10-52. Reprinted, pp. 68-110 in *Wort und Existenz: Studien zum Alten Testament* by Wurthwein. Gottingen: Vandenhoeck & Ruprecht, 1970. 319 pp. Gives a general review of cult prophets, compares the latter with writing prophets, notes scholarly opinions, and asks if Amos was a prophet? The latter leads to a discussion of Amos 7:10-17, the calling and the office of prophet, Amos' visions, the true and false prophets, the oracles against the nations.

1693. Wyk, W.C. Van. "The Cushites in Amos 9:7" (Afrikaans). *Hervormde Teologiese Studies* 22, No. 4 (1967), 38-45. Notes earlier opinions. The text refers to the Exodus. The Ethiopians, like Israel, were freed from Egyptian control. Rev, IZBG 15 (68-69).

Y.

1694. Yamashita, Tadamori. "Professions." Vol. 2 (1975), 41-68 in *Ras Shamra Parallels: The Texts from Ugarit and the Hebrew Bible* ed Loren R. Fisher. *Analecta Orientalia* 50. Rome: Pontifical Biblical Institute, 1975. xii + 508 pp. No. 28 is "Noqed." 2:63-64. The word means shepherd, the title of a high official, perhaps a temple official. Gives a review of scholarly opinions.

1695. Yates, Kyle M., Jr. *Studies in Amos.* Nashville: Convention Press, 1966. viii + 136 pp. A study for the laity including the nature of prophecy, Amos' character, call, message, relationship with Israel, historical background including the international scene. Each unit of the commentary closes with suggestions for class preparation and advanced study.

1696. Yeivin, S. "The Social, Economic, and Political Situation According to Amos and Hosea" (Heb). pp. 97-111 in *Studies in the Minor Prophets* ed B.Z. Luria. Jerusalem: Kiryat Sepher, 1981.

1697. Yeo, Khiok-Khing. "Amos (4:4-5) and Confucius: The Will (Ming) of God (Thien)." *Asia J of Theology* (Singapore) 4 (1990), 472-488. Notes traditional interpretations. The pericope is satirical poetry with indictments against Israel's injustice. Combined with 5:21-24, the basis of justice is theocentric and human oriented. This is true of Confucius as well. The latter's human centeredness is mandated by heaven. Rulers are to model the mandate of heaven. Morality is more important than religiosity. Love is the basis of a just society.

1698. Yoshida, Hiroshi. "Prophecy and salvation: The case of Amos Kiyo" (Japanese). *The Bulletin of the Christian Research Institute Meiji Gakuin University* 14 (1981), 27-47 (Japanese). God's grace and judgment are both expressions of his free will. Grace comes first. Amos spoke out of personal experience. Rev, OTA 4 (1981), 251.

1699. Young, G.L. "A Short Study in the Book of Amos." *The Bible Student* 8, No. 5 (Nov '03), 295-297. Discusses the man, his message, the evils of the time, his concept of God as universal creator of the universe.

1700. Youngblood, Ronald. "*lqr't* in Amos 4:12." JBL 90, No. 1 (Mar 71), 98. Alters G.W. Ramsey's (JBL 89:187-191) to summon your gods.

Z.

1701. Zalcman, Lawrence. "Astronomical Illusions in Amos." JBL 100, No. 1 (1981), 53-58. Text, p. 53, has "allusions." Notes numerous earlier studies, gives transcription and translation, discusses constellations (God made Pleides and Orion) and translates 5:9 as "Who flashes forth destruction on the strong; As 'Destruction shall come on the fortress'." MT is correct. God overcomes human injustice.

1702. Zalcman, Lawrence. "Piercing the Darkness at *boqer* (Amos 7:14)." VT 30, No. 2 (1980), 252-255. Notes numerous earlier studies. Emends to *doqer*, "piercer," and translates, "I am a piercer of sycamore figs." He also emends 1:1 *noqedim* to *noqerim*, "piercers," based on the LXX.

1703. Zawiszewski, Edward. "Ksiega Amosa: Wstep - Przeklad - Komentarz." Vol 12, Part 1 (1968), 159-260 in *Ksiegi Prorokow Mniejszych: Ozeasza - Joela - Amos - Abdiasza - Jonasza - Micheasza*. Pismo Swiete Starego Testamentu ed Stanislawa Lacha et al. Catholic University of Lublin. Poznan: Pallottinum, 1968. Part 1:424 Extensive bibliography. Discusses the character of Amos, historical background, Amos' religion (cult, morality), literary problems (authorship, style, text). The commentary has the text in Polish with verse by verse explanation.

1704. Zeijdner, H. "Nog iets over den profeet Amos." *Stemmen voor Waarheid en Vrede* 27 (1890), 613-634.

1705. Zenger, Erich. "Die eigentliche Botschft des Amos: Von der Relevanz der politischen Theologie in einer exegetischen Kontroverse." pp. 394-406 in *Mystik und Politik: Theologie im Ringen um Geschichte und Gesellschaft: Johann Baptist Metz zu Ehren* ed Edward Schillebeeckx. Mainz: Matthias-Grunewald,

1988. 413 pp. Exegesis of the vision cycle. Amos' relevance today does not depend on political theology.

1706. Zevit, Ziony. "A Misunderstanding at Bethel - Amos 7:12-17." VT 25, No. 4 (Oct 75), 783-90. The first part of Amos' reply was self-justification while the second part was a judgment speech against Amaziah. Amos claimed to be a *nabi* and not something new. He denied being a prophet with royal patronage.

1707. Zevit, Ziony. "Expressing Denial in Biblical Hebrew and Mishnaic Hebrew, and in Amos." VT 29, No. 4 (Oct 79), 505-509. Amos denied he was a court prophet. Absolute denial is possible in biblical Hebrew while this construction is not used in Mishnaic.

1708. Ziegler, Joseph, ed. "Amos." pp. 480-205 in *Duodecim prophetae*. Septuaginta Vetus Testamentum Graecum, Auctoritate Societatis Literarum Gottingensis editum 13. Gottingen: Vandenhoeck & Ruprecht, 1943. 339 pp. 2nd ed 1967. A critical edition of the Greek text with critical apparatus. The general introduction discusses the Greek text, various manuscripts, relationships to other versions (e.g., Old Latin, Coptic, Syriac, Ethiopian, Arabic, Armenian), the textual families (W, B-S-V), the Alexandrian text, Jerome's hexaplar, the Lucian edition, younger editions, orthography, text and apparatus.

1709. Ziegler, Joseph. "Beitrage zum griechischen Dodekapropheton." pp. 345-412 in *Nachrichten der Akademie der Wissenschaften zu Gottingen*, Philologisch- Historische Klasse, 1943. Septuaginta-Arbeiten 2. Reprinted, pp. 71-138 in *Sylloge: Gesammelte Aufsatze zur Septuagint* by Ziegler. Mitteilungen des Septuaginta-Unternehmens de Akademie der Wissenschaften in Gottingen 10. Gottingen: Vandenhoeck & Ruprecht, 1971. 678 pp. Exegesis, word studies, text criticism, comparison of Greek and Latin, studies in Cyril of Alexandria's text of the 12 prophets.

1710. Ziegler, Joseph. "Beitrage zur koptischen Dodekapropheton-Ubersetzung." Bib 25, No. 2 (May 44), 105-142. Amos, pp. 111-113. Reprinted, pp. 268-305 in *Sylloge: Gesammelte Aufsatze zur Septuagint* by Ziegler. Mitteilungen des Septuaginta-Unternehmens de Akademie der Wissenschaften in Gottingen 10. Gottingen:

Vandenhoeck & Ruprecht, 1971. 678 pp. Exegesis, comparative textual criticism.

1711. Ziegler, Joseph. "Die Einheit der Septuaginta zum Zwolfprophetenbuch." pp. 1-16 in *Verzeichnis der Vorlesungen an der Staatlichen Akademie zu Braunsberg im Wintersemester 1934/35*. Braunsberg: Kirchhain, 1934. Reprinted, pp. 29-42 in *Sylloge: Gesammelte Aufsatze zur Septuagint* by Ziegler. Mitteilungen des Septuaginta-Unternehmens de Akademie der Wissenschaften in Gottingen 10. Gottingen: Vandenhoeck & Ruprecht, 1971. 678 pp. Exegesis, comparative textual criticism.

1712. Ziegler, Joseph. "Der griechische Dodekapropheton-Text der Complutenser Polyglotte." Bib 25, No. 3 (Oct 44), 297-310. Reprinted, pp. 229-242 in *Sylloge: Gesammelte Aufsatze zur Septuagint* by Ziegler. Mitteilungen des Septuaginta-Unternehmens de Akademie der Wissenschaften in Gottingen 10. Gottingen: Vandenhoeck & Ruprecht, 1971. 678 pp. Exegesis, comparative textual criticism.

1713. Ziegler, J. "Die jungeren griechischen Ubersetzungen als Vorlagen der Vulgata in den prophetischen Schriften." pp. 1-92 in *Verzeichnis der Vorlesungen an der Staatlichen Akademie zu Braunsberg im Wintersemester 1943/44*. Braunsberg, Ostpr.: Kirchhain, 1934. Reprinted, pp. 138-228 in *Sylloge: Gesammelte Aufsatze zur Septuagint* by Ziegler. Mitteilungen des Septuaginta-Unternehmens de Akademie der Wissenschaften in Gottingen 10. Gottingen: Vandenhoeck & Ruprecht, 1971. 678 pp. Exegesis, word study, comparative textual criticism including Jerome, Aquila, Symmachus, Theodotion.

1714. Ziegler, Joseph. "Studien zur Verwertung der Septuaginta im Zwolfprophetenbuch." ZAW 60, Nos. 1-3 (1944), 107-131. Reprinted, pp. 243-267 in *Sylloge: Gesammelte Aufsatze zur Septuagint* by Ziegler. Mitteilungen des Septuaginta-Unternehmens de Akademie der Wissenschaften in Gottingen 10. Gottingen: Vandenhoeck & Ruprecht, 1971. 678 pp. Exegesis, comparative textual criticism.

1715. Ziegler, Joseph. "Der Text der Aldina im Dodekapropheton." *Bib* 26, No. 1 (Feb 45), 37-51. Reprinted, pp. 306-320 in *Sylloge: Gesammelte Aufsatze zur Septuagint* by Ziegler. Mitteilungen des Septuaginta-Unternehmens de Akademie der Wissenschaften in Gottingen 10. Gottingen: Vandenhoeck & Ruprecht, 1971. 678 pp. Exegesis, comparative textual criticism.

1716. Ziegler, Joseph. "Zur Dodekapropheton - LXX." *ETL* 38 (1962), 904-906. Reprinted, pp. 587-589 in *Sylloge: Gesammelte Aufsatze zur Septuagint* by Ziegler. Mitteilungen des Septuaginta-Unternehmens de Akademie der Wissenschaften in Gottingen 10. Gottingen: Vandenhoeck & Ruprecht, 1971. 678 pp. A review of available manuscripts with a special note on Hab 3.

1717. Zimmer, Karl, ed. "Amos." pp. 51-76 in *Praparation zu den Kleinen Propheten mit den notigen die Ubersetzung und das Verstandnis des Textes erleicheternden Anmerkungen. 1. Die Propheten Hosea, Joel, Amos, Obadja, Jonah.* Halle: Anton, 1895. iv + 89 pp. A listing of the Hebrew words in order of appearance (chapter and verse), translation into German, critical apparatus in footnotes.

1718. Zimmerli, Walther. "Frucht der Anfechtung des Propheten." pp. 131-46 in *Die Botschaft und die Boten, Festschrift fur Hans Walter Wolff zum 70. Geburtstag* ed Jorg Jeremias and Lothar Perlitt. Neukirchen-Vluyn: Neukirchener, 1981. ix + 426 pp. Tr, Perdue, "The Fruit of the Tribulation of the Prophet." pp. 349-365 in *A Prophet to the Nations: Essays in Jeremiah Studies* ed Leo G. Perdue and Brian W. Kovacs. Winona Lake, IN: Eisenbrauns, 1984. xv + 399 pp. Amos and others were threatened externally. Their inner suffering is the human reflection of the much greater suffering of Yahweh himself. This perception of Yahweh's nature is the fruit of the prophet's tribulation.

1719. Zimmerli, Walther. "Das Gottesrecht bei den Propheten Amos, Hosea and Jesaja." pp. 216-235 in *Werden und Wirken des Alten Testaments: Festschrift fur Claus Westermann zum 70. Geburtstag* ed Rainer Albertz, et al. Gottingen/ Neukirchen-Vluyn: Vandenhoeck & Ruprecht/ Neukirchener, 1980. 481 pp. A survey of interpretations with analysis of selected verses.

1720. Zimmerman, A. "The Ethics of Amos." *Reformed Church Review* (Philadelphia), 4th series, 4, No. 2 (1900), 196-212. Gives historical background, background of his preaching in Moses and tradition, discusses ethical ideas and foreign nations, Judah, Israel, perverted judgment, oppression, greed, luxury, religion. The basis of ethics is a universal God.

1721. Ziv, Judah. "Amos 7:14" (Heb). BM 28 [Issue No. 92], No. 1 (1982/1983), 49-53. Tekoa is too barren for sheep or sycamores so these refer to Amos' character as an ordinary person. Rev, OTA 6 (1983), 284.

1722. Zobel, Hans Jurgen. "Prophet in Israel und Judah. Das Prophetenverstandnis des Hosea und Amos." *Z fur Theologie und Kirche* 82, No. 3 (1985), 281-299. Amos is discussed on pp. 293-297. Reviews interpretations of Amos' status.

1723. Zobel, Konstantin. *Prophetie und Deuteronomium: Die Rezeption prophetischer Theologie durch das Deuteronomium.* BZAW 199, ed Otto Kaiser. Berlin/NY: de Gruyter, 1992. ix + 267 pp. Discusses Yahweh, the God of Israel, and Israel, the people of Yahweh, and compares human and divine love in the prophets, including Amos, though he and Micah also include a word of warning. A second discussion on Israel's estrangement from God includes Amos, pp. 91-95.

1724. Zolli, Eugenio. "Amos 4:2b." *Antonianum* (Rome) 30, No. 2 (Ap 55), 188-189. Exegetical analysis and earlier interpretations.

1725. Zolli, Israele. "Note Esegetiche (Amos 2:7a)." *Rivista degli Studi Orientali* (Rome) 16, No. 2 (1936), 178-183. Gives the Hebrew and transliteration, exegetical commentary including earlier views.

1726. Zollner, W. "Amos." pp. 15-41 in *Amos und Hosea.* Handreichung zur Verliefung Christlicher Erkenntnis 2, ed Jul. Moller and Zollner. Gutersloh: Vertelsmann, 1897. vi + 77 pp. Reviews the home, main themes, the historical background, the golden future, the significance of Amos.

360   The Book of Amos

1727. Zorell, F. "Zu Amos 1:3,6. usw." Bib 6, No. 2 (1925), 171-173. Exegesis, drawing on the MT, LXX, Peshitta, Vulgate.

1728. Zucker, David J. "Amos." pp. 117-123 in *Israel's Prophets: An Introduction for Christians and Jews*. NY: Paulist, 1994. xiv + 208 pp. Describes the political background, biography, structure of the text, message (rulers, relationships and responsibilities), the Christian scriptures, Jewish sources (Amos reduced all the laws to one: Seek me and live), selected texts for study.

1729. Zuylen, W.H. van, J. Overduin, A.S. Timmer. *De profeten Hosea, Joel, Amos, Obadja, Jona, Micha*. Kampen: Kok, 1940. viii + 139 pp.

DISSERTATIONS

Arieti, James Alexander. A Study in the Septuagint of the Book of Amos. Stanford University, 1972. 154 pp. DAI 33, No. 8 (Feb 73), 4373.

Asen, Bernhard Arthur. Amos' Faith: A Structural-Developmental Approach. Diss. St Louis University, 1980. 172 pp. DAI 41, No. 7 (Jan 81), 3149-3150A. Analyzes Amos with James Fowler's faith development ideas. Amos is Stage 5.

Auer, Franz X. Vulgatastudien an Hand der Kleinen Propheten, I: Oseas bis Micha. Diss. Breslau, 1942.

Barstad, Hans M. *The Religious Polemics of Amos: Studies in the Preaching of Am 2:7B-8; 4:1-13; 5:1-27; 6:4-7; 8:14.* VTS 34. Leiden: Brill, 1984. xiv + 244 pp. Diss. Studies in the Religious Polemics... Oslo: Det Teologiske Fakultet, 1982. See main entry.

Bartczek, Gunter. *Prophetie und Vermittlung. Zur literarischen Analyse und theologischen Interpetation der Visionberichte des Amos.* Europaische Hochschulschriften Series 23, Vol 120. Frankfurt am Main/Bern/Cirencester, UK: Lang, 1980. 330 pp. Diss. Die Visionsberichte des Amos. Literische Analyse und theologische Interpretation. Wilhelms University (Munster im Westfalen), 1977. See main entry.

Baumgartner, Walter. "Kennen Amos und Hosea eine Heilseschatologie?" *Schweizer Theologische Z* (Zurich) 30 (1913), No. 1:30-42; No. 2: 95-124; No. 3:152-170. Diss. Zurich, 1913. See main entry.

Beach, Eleanor Ferris. Image and Word: Iconography in the Interpretation of Hebrew Scriptures (Samaria Ivories). Claremont Graduate School,

1991. 372 pp. DAI 52, No. 3 (Sep 91), 949. The symbolism on the ivories is appropriate for funerals, e.g., the marzeach of Amos 6:4-7.

Berg, Werner. *Die sogenannte Hymnenfragmente im Amosbuch.* Europaische Hochschulschriften, Series 23, Theology 45. Bern/Frankfurt am Main: Herbert Lang/Peter Lang, 1974. vii + 356 pp. Diss. Ludwig-Maximilians-Universitat, 1974. See main entry.

Bergler, Siegfried. *Die Hymnischen Passagen und die Mitte des Amosbuches.* Ein Forschungsbericht. Diss. Tubingen, 1979. 249 pp.

Bjorndalen, Anders Jorgen. *Untersuchungen zur allegorischen Rede der Propheten Amos und Jesaja.* BZAW 165, ed Otto Kaiser. Berlin/NY: de Gruyter, 1986. xi + 398 pp. Diss. Oslo, 1982. See main entry.

Blechmann, Malke. *Das Buch Amos im Talmud und Midrasch.* Leipzig, 1937. [[[Wal has Diss. Wurzburg, 1937.

Block, Michael David. Samuel Terrien's *The Elusive Presence* as Reflected in the Day of the Lord in Amos, Joel, and Zephaniah. Southwestern Baptist Theological Seminary, 1990, 234 pp. DAI 52, No. 1 (July 91), 189. *The Elusive Presence: The Heart of Biblical Theology,* San Francisco: Harper & Row, 1978. Discusses Terrien's place in the history of OT theology, analyzes the day of the Lord and the references in Amos, Joel and Zephaniah.

Brown, Henry C., Jr. The Positive Elements in the Preaching of Amos and Hosea. Southwestern Baptist Theological Seminary, 1954. Not available from DAI. See ADD

Bushey, Stanley Lewis. The Theology of Amos. Diss. Bob Jones University, 1979. Not available from UMI. See ADD.

Carroll R.[sic], Mark Daniel. *Contexts for Amos: Prophetic Poetics in Latin American Perspective.* JSOT Supplement 132, ed David J.A. Clines and Philip R. Davies. Sheffield, England: JSOT, 1992. 362 pp. Diss. University of Sheffield, 1990. See main entry.

Christensen, Duane L. "Amos and the Transformation of the War Oracle." pp. 17-73 in *Transformations of the War Oracles in Old Testament*

Prophecy: Studies in the Oracles Against the Nations. Harvard Dissertations in Religion 3, ed Caroline Bynum and George Rupp. Missoula, MT: Scholars Press, 1975. xii + 305 pp. See main entry.

Cleary, F.X. The Interpretation of Suffering According to Amos and Hosea: The Origins of Redemptive Suffering. Diss. Gregorian Pontifical University, Rome, 1978. DAI 40 (1979-80), 158-C.

Crenshaw, James L. *Hymnic Affirmation of Divine Justice: The Doxologies of Amos and Related Texts in the Old Testament.* SBL Dissertation Series 24. Missoula: Scholars Press, 1975. xii + 178 pp. Diss. Jimmy Lee Crenshaw, The Doxologies of Amos: A Form-Critical Study in the History of the Text of Amos. Vanderbilt University, 1964. v + 256 pp. DAI 25, No. 9 (Dec 66), 5415. See main entry.

Crusemann, Frank. *Studien zur Formgeschichte von Hymnus und Danklied in Israel.* Wissenschaftliche Monographien zum Alten und Neuen Testament 32 ed Gunther Bornkamm and Gerhard von Rad, et al. Neukirchen-Vluyn: Neukirchener, 1969. Diss. Johannes Gutenberg-Universitat Mainz, 1968. ix + 348 pp. See main entry.

Curtis, John J. An Application of the Syntax of Hebrew Verbs to the Writings of Amos. Southern Baptist Theological Seminary, 1949. Not available from UMI. See ADD

Dearman, John Andrew. *Property Rights in the Eighth-Century Prophets: The Conflict and Its Background.* SBL Dissertation Series 106 ed J.J.M. Roberts and Charles Talbert. Atlanta, GA: Scholars Press, 1988. x + 171 pp. Emory University, 1981. 312 pp. DAI 42, No. 5 (Nov 81), 2172. See main entry.

Dingermann, F. Massora-Septuaginta der kleinen Propheten. Diss. Wurzburg, University of Wurzburg, 1948.

Doorly, William J. *Prophet of Justice: Understanding the Book of Amos.* NY: Paulist, 1989. iv + 92 pp. Diss. Preaching from the Book of Amos to address problems of economic injustice. Diss. Lancaster Theological Seminary, 1987. 141 pp. DA 48, No. 4 (Oct 87), 948. See main entry.

Ebo, D.J.I.O. "O that Jacob would survive": A study of hope in the book of Amos. Diss. University of Nigeria, 1985. Abstract in *African J of Bible* 1, No. 2 (Oct 86), 186. See main entry.

Ehrlich, Carl Stephen. From Defeat to Conquest: A History of the Philistines in Decline, c. 1000-c 730 BCE (First Millenium BCE). Harvard University, 1991. 381 pp. DAI 52, No. 5 (Nov 91), 1861. The history of the Philistines.

Eubanks, Seaford William. Amos: Artist in Literary Composition. Southern Baptist Theological Seminary, 1943. Not available from UMI. See ADD

Fabian, Norbert. Sozialkritische Ansatze in der alttestamentlichen Prophetie, dargestellt am Propheten Amos. Versuch einer praxisbezogenen Aufarbeitung. Diss. Munster i.W., 1973. See main entry under Fabian, *Protest gegen Ausbeuter*.

Feigon, Gershon J. *Yemenite Targum Manuscript to the Twelve Minor Prophets*. San Diego, CA: Bureau of Jewish Education, 1971. 55 pp. Diss. Yeshiva University, 1946. See main entry.

Fey, Reinhard. *Amos and Jesaja: Abhangigkeit und Eigenstandigkeit des Jesaja*. Wissenschaftliche Monographien zum Alten und Neuen Testament 12 ed Gunther Bornkamm and Gerhard von Rad. Neukirchen-Vluyn: Neukirchener, 1963. 159 pp. Diss. Georg-August-Universitat (Gottingen), 1961. See main entry.

Fleischer, Gunther. *Von Menschenverkaufern, Baschankuhen und Rechtsverkehrern. Die Sozialkritik des Amosbuches in historisch-kritischer, sozialgeschichtlicher und archaologischer Perspektive*. Athenaums Monografien Theologie. Bonner Biblische Beitrage 74 ed. Frank-Lothar Hossfeld and Helmut Merklein. Frankfurt am Main: Athenaum, 1989. xiv + 486 pp. Diss. Bonn: Katholisch Theologischen Fakultat, 1988. See main entry.

Giles, Terry. Amos and the Law. Michigan State, 1989. 263 pp. DAI 50, No. 7 (Jan 90), 2095. Prophetic ethics are drawn from the Torah via the wisdom tradition. Differences are due to the change in mode of production from the tenth to eighth centuries.

Gillis, Paul M. A Sociological Interpretation of the Writings of Amos. University of Pittsburgh, 1934. Not available from UMI. See ADD

Guiterrez, R.C. See Gutierrez Riocerezo, C.L.

Gutierrez Riocerezo, C.L. La Justicia Social en los Profetas del Siglo. VIII: Amos, Oseas, Isaias y Miqueas. Diss. Fribourg (Suisse), 1970.

Harbin, L. Byron. A Study of Amos' Attitude Toward the Cultus. New Orleans Baptist Theological Seminary, 1964. Not available from UMI. See ADD

Hausmann, Jutta. "Amos." pp. 184-187 in *Israels Rest: Studien zum Selbstverstandnis der nachexilischen Gemeinde*. Beitrage zur Wissenschaft vom Alten und Neuen Testament 7, ed Siegfried Herrmann and Karl Heinrich Rengstorf. Stuttgart: Kohlhammer, 1987. ix + 301 pp. Diss. Friedrich-Alexander-Universitat (Erlangen-Nurnberg), 1986/1987. See main entry.

Heyns, M. Amos - Advocate for Freedom and Justice; A Socio-historical Investigation. Diss. Unisa (Pretoria), 1989. OT Essays 2, No. 3 (1989), 108.

Hobbs, A.G.W. The Communication of the Prophetic Message in Pre-Exilic Israel. University of Kent at Canterbury (UK), 1990. 434 pp. DAI 52, No. 6 (Dec 91), 2174. Uses social science techniques including transactional analysis, role theory, etc. to study Amos 7:10-17 and other calls and messages.

Hockenhull, Brenda Rae. The Use of Series in the Book of Amos. Diss. New Orleans Baptist Theological Seminary, 1987. 237 pp. DAI 48, No. 4 (Oct 87), 944. Studies five series, e.g., oracles against the nations, woes, visions. Considers genre, context, intent, etc. Shows the prophet as a literary artist and gives a new outline for the book.

Howard, George Eulan. The LXX Book of Amos. Hebrew Union College - Jewish Institute of Religion (Ohio), 1964. Not available from UMI. See ADD

Hunter, A. Vanlier. *Seek the Lord! A Study of the Meaning and Function*

of the Exhortation in Amos, Hosea, Isaiah, Micah, and Zephaniah.
Baltimore: St. Mary's Seminary & University, 1982. xix + 324 pp. Diss.
Basel: University of Basel, 1981. See main entry.

Igleheart, James Hayden, Jr. Education and Culture in the Book of Amos:
A Re-Evaluation. University of Kentucky, 1964. 147 pp. DAI 30, No. 5
(Nov 69), 1886.

Israel, Richard D. Prophecies of Judgment: A Study of the Protasis-
Apodasis Text Structures in Hosea, Amos and Micah. Claremont
Graduate School, 1989. 429 pp. DAI 50, No. 8 (Feb 90), 2526. The
apodasis is the future conditioned by the protasis. Reviews scholarly
opinions, messenger speech forms, law. Uses a synchronic exegesis.
Yahweh is the guarantor of justice.

Jimenez, C. Relecturas de Amos--Isaias. Diss. Jerusalem: Franciscan
Biblical Institute, 1973. ii + 244 pp.

Johnson, Sherman Elbridge. *The Septuagint Translators of Amos.*
Chicago: University of Chicago Libraries, 1938. ii + 24 pp. Diss.
University of Chicago, 1936. See main entry.

Kida, Kenichi. Die Entstehung der Prophetischen Literatur bei Amos.
Diss. Munich, 1973.

Krause, Martin. Das Verhaltnis von Sozialer Kritik und Kommender
Katastrophe in den Unheilsprophezeiungen des Amos. Diss. University
of Hamburg, 1972. iv + 168 + xiv (bibliography). DAI (1978-79) C 39,
No. 590. See main entry.

Kuntz, Manfes. Ein Element der Alten Theophanieuberlieferung und seine
Rolle in der Prophetie des Amos. Diss. University of Tubingen, 1968. 265
pp. TLZ 94 (1969), 387-389. See main entry.

Kusznitski, S. Joel, Amos, Obadja, Qua aetate et quibus de rebus sint
locuti. Diss. Breslau; Vratislaviae: Jungfer, 1872.

Lee, Adam Chun-Wing. The Concept of Kingship in the Book of the
Twelve. Southern Baptist Theological Seminary, 1986. 274 pp. DAI 47,
No. 8 (Feb 87), 3083. Studies kingship in OT as a whole and then surveys

the minor prophets. Anti-monarchial texts in Hosea and Amos are not anti-kingship as such but oppose malpractice. Hopes for a restored Davidic kingship are for an ideal king, reunion of north and south, reunion with Yahweh, security and prosperity. Yahweh's kingship is universal. He will be recognized as king in the restored nation.

Lehming, Sigo. Offenbarung und Verkundigung. Studien zur Theologiegeschichtlichen bedeutung des Verhaltnis von Berufung und Theologie bei Amos und Hosea. Diss. University of Kiel, 1953.

Lemcke, Gunther. Die Prophetenspruche des Amos und Jesaja metrisch-stilistisch und literar-asthetisch betrachtet. Diss. Breslau: Buchdruckerei H. Fleishmann, 1914.

Lewis, Ralph Loren. "Amos." pp. 14-75 in The Persuasive Style and Appeals of the Minor Prophets Amos, Hosea, and Micah. Diss. Ann Arbor: University of Michigan, 1958. v + 222 pp. DAI 20, No. 4 (Oct 66), 1483. See main entry.

Lyngdoh, Bosetin C. "The Demand of Social Justice in the Prophecy of Amos and its Meaning for Socio-Political Structure of India." Calvin Theological J 20 (Nov 85), 361. Diss. Calvin Theological Seminary (Grand Rapids, MI), 1985. vii + 103 pp. See main entry.

Mahaffey, Edward Lamar. An Investigation of Social Justice as it Relates to the Message of Amos. New Orleans Baptist Theological Seminary, 1993. 182 pp. DAI 55, No. 3 (Sep 94), 606. Studies the violations of justice, the basis of justice (nature of Yahweh), judgment for lack of social justice.

Markert, Ludwig. Struktur und Bezeichnung des Scheltworts. Eine gattungskritische Studie anhand des Amosbuches. BZAW 140, Fohrer. Berlin: de Gruyter, 1977. xii + 330 pp. Diss. Friedrich-Alexander-Universitat (Erlangen-Nurnberg), 1974. See main entry.

Mbele, Philemon. La justice sociale ou l'ultimate possibilite de salut pour Israel selon le prophete Amos. Diss. Montpellier: Faculte de theologie protestante, 1988.

Meinhold, Johannes. Studien zur Israelitischen Religionsgeschichte. Band

1. Der Heilige Rest, Teil 1: Elias, Hosea, Amos, Jesaja. Bonn: Weber, 1903. viii + 160 pp. Diss. Marburg, 1903. Amos, pp. 33-63. See main entry.

Montgomery, Jimmy Jonathan. Analyzing a Local Church Ministry in Terms of Justice as Reflected in the Book of Amos for the Enhancement of Mission and Liberation Using Systems Theory. DMin, Emory University, 1987. Not available from UMI. See ADD

Moore, Dana Charles. Amos' Apologia: A Defense of his Prophetic Ministry. Southwestern Baptist Theological Seminary, 1994. 204 pp. DAI 56, No. 1 (July 95), 230. Amos defended his ministry in several ways. Studies the call. Amos 3:3-8 and 7:10-17 are the core.

Nagele, Sabine. *Laubhutte Davids und Wolkensohn: Eine auslegungsgeschichte Studie zu Amos 9:11 in der judischen und christlichen Exegese.* Arbeiten zur Geschichte des Antiken Judentums und des Urchristentums 24 ed Martin Hengel, et al. Leiden: Brill, 1995. Diss. Eberhard Karls University (Tubingen), 1993. See main entry.

Newell, James Otis. The Means of Maintaining a Right Relationship with Yahweh: An Investigation of Selected Passages from the Hebrew Prophets of the Eighth Century BC. New Orleans Baptist Theological Seminary, 1988. 196 pp. DAI 50, No. 3 (Sep 89), 710. Includes Amos. Gives historical background, what does not maintain a right relationship (injustice, idolatry) and what does (doing good, establishing justice, covenant loyalty, humble submission to YHWH).

Nicholson, Helen S. Un Poeta Montaes: Amos de Escalante. Stanford University, 1935. Not available from UMI. See ADD

Niditch, Susan. *The Symbolic Vision in Biblical Tradition.* Harvard Semitic Monographs 30. Chico, CA: Scholars Press, 1980. xii + 258 pp. Diss. Harvard, 1978. See main entry.

Nishizu, Teruo J. Bethel and the Rebellions of Israel: Redactional Elements in the Book of Amos. Diss. Chicago: Divinity School, 1982.

Nogalski, James. "Amos." pp. 74-122 in *Literary Precursors to the Book of the Twelve.* BZAW 217 ed Otto Kaiser. Berlin: de Gruyter, 1993. ix +

301 pp. Diss (part of), University of Zurich, 1991. See main entry.

Ogden, Daniel Kelly. A Geography of Amos. University of Utah, 1982. 256 pp. DAI 42, No. 11 (May 82), 4850. A study of places, plants, geographical features, etc.

Oliver, Anthony. Salvation as Justice in Amos 5:18-27: Implications for Jamaica. Caribbean Graduate School of Theology, MA, 1991. 200 pp. Discusses the incongruity of religious activism and social injustice.

Olmo Lete, Gregorio del. "La Vocacion de Amos (Amos 7:10-17; 9:1-4)." pp. 179-207 in *La Vocacion del Lider en el Antiguo Israel. Morfologia de las Relatos Biblicos de Vocacion*. Bibliotheca Salmanticensis III, Studia 2. Salamanca: Universidad Pontificia Salamanca, 1973. 467 pp. Diss. Universidad Pontificia Salamanca, 1973. See main entry.

Olyan, Saul M. Problems in the History of the Cult and Priesthood in Ancient Israel. Diss. Harvard University, 1985. 232 pp. DAI 47, No. 1 (July 86), 211. For ch 1, see main entry. Ch 1 is on Amos 8:14 and pilgrimages without social justice. Ch 2 is on Asherah (probably Yahweh's consort) and her cult symbol. Both were a legitimate part of the Yahweh cult in non-deuteronomic circles. Ch 3 is on ben Sira.

O'Neill, Dennis Michael. The Attitudes of Amos, Hosea, Jeremiah, and Deutero-Isaiah concerning the Man/God relationship: A Study in Hebraic Monotheism. Michigan State University, 1979. Ann Arbor, MI: University Microfilms, 1979. viii + 137 pp. Available in microfilm, 1 reel, 35 mm. DAI 40, No. 4 (Oct 79), 2126. See main entry.

Osswald, Eva. Urform und Auslegung im Masoretischen Amostext. Ein Beitrag zur Kritik an der Neueren Traditions geschichtlichen Methode. Diss. Jena, 1951. Reviewed in ThLZ 80, No. 3 (Mar 55), 179. Reviews the history of interpretation of Amos.

Parsons, Robert Thad, Jr. A Commentary by Dr. Francis Brown on the Book of Amos. MA, Baylor University, 1983. 161 pp. MAI 22, No. 1 (Spr 84), 83.

Pleins, J. David. Biblical Ethics and the Poor: The Language and Structures of Poverty in the Writings of the Hebrew Prophets (Oppression,

Exploitation, Justice, Injustice). University of Michigan, 1986. 349 pp. DAI 47, No. 6 (Dec 86), 2201. See main entry.

Pomykala, Kenneth E. *The Davidic Dynasty Tradition in Early Judaism: Its History and Significance for Messianism.* SBL Early Judaism and Its Literature 7 ed William Adler. Atlanta, GA: Scholars Press, 1995. Diss. Claremont Graduate School, 1992. See main entry.

Premnath, Devadasan N. The Process of Latifundization Mirrored in the Oracles Pertaining to 8th Century B.C.E., in The Books of Amos, Hosea, Isaiah and Micah. Diss. Graduate Theological Union (Berkeley), 1984.

Ramirez, Guillermo. The Social Location of the Prophet Amos in Light of a Cultural Anthropological Model. Emory University, 1993. 370 pp. DAI 54, No. 12 (June 94), 4475. Uses the group/grid model to show Amos belonged to a strong group with rigid boundaries while cultural idiosyncrasies give both a high and low grid.

Rillett Wood, Joyce Louise. Amos: Prophecy as a Performing Art and Its Transformation in Book Culture. University of St. Michael's College (Canada), 1993. 572 pp. DAI 54, No. 12 (June 94), 4475. The early prophets were performing poets, using words, music and song.

Routtenberg, Hyman J. *Amos of Tekoa: A Study in Interpretation.* NY: Vantage Press, 1971. 194 pp. Diss. Rabbinic Interpretations of Amos. Boston University, 1943. See main entry.

Said, Dalton H. Longing for Justice: A Study on the Cry and Hope of the Poor in the Old Testament. University of Edinburgh (UK), 1987. 421 pp. DAI 49, No. 3 (Sep 88), 528. Latin American liberation theology. Exegesis of verses with the cry, which is always of injustice so ultimately God has to do something. Justice equals liberation of the poor. Includes Hebrews in Egypt as a continuing "type." Amos' message is hope for the poor and oppressed.

Sanchez, Edesio. God and Gods: Issues in Biblical Theology from a Latin American Perspective. Union Theological Seminary in Virginia, 1987. 212 pp. DAI 48, No. 11 (May 88), 2909. A study of idolatry and social justice. The latter is inseparable from loyalty to Yahweh. This plus the exodus and covenant show the difference between Yahweh and other gods. Discusses Amos, Hosea, Jeremiah, etc.

Scherb, D.-A. Introduction aux Propheties d'Amos. Essai d'Interpretation des Chapitres Vii, Viii et IX. Thesis. Strassbourg, 1869.

Schultz, Arnold C. Amos and the Popular Religion in Israel. ThD. Northern Baptist Theological Seminary, 1945. Not available from UMI. See ADD

Schuurmans Stekhoven, J.Z. *De Alexandrijnsche Vertaling van het Dodekapropheton.* Leiden: Brill, 1887. viii + 137 pp. Diss., State University of Gronigen, 1887. See main entry.

Sebok (Schonberger), Mark. "Amos." pp. 32-41 in *Die syrische Uebersetzung der zwolf kleinen Propheten und ihr Verhaltniss zu dem Massoretischen Text und zu den Alteren Uebersetzungen Namentlich den LXX und dem Targum.* Breslau: Preuss und Junger, 1887. iii + 75 pp. Diss. Leipzig: Leipzig University, 1887. See main entry.

Shelly, Patricia Joyce. Amos and Irony: The Use of Irony in Amos's Prophetic Discourse. Iliff School of Theology and University of Denver, 1992. 184 pp. DAI 53, No. 5 (Nov 92), 1548. Amos made sophisticated use of his literary and theological traditions. This includes the use of irony,

Shoot, Frederick von Buelow, Jr. The Fertility Religions in the Thought of Amos and Micah. University of Southern California, 1951. Not available from UMI. See ADD

Sievi, J. Amos and Muhammad. Diss. Pontificia Studiorum Universits A.S. Thoma Qq. in Urbe. Chur, Selbstverlag des Verf., 1977. 112 pp.

Siew, Tye Yau. The Missionary Message of the Prophets for Missiology in Malaysia. ThM. Fuller Theological Seminary, School of World Mission, 1993. 154 pp. MAI 31, No. 4 (Winter 93), 1513. Christianity is still seen as a foreign religion. The Church may need a more relevant biblical model for missiology. The missionary message of Amos, Jeremiah, et al, is an appropriate model for Malaysia.

Sipos, Istvan. The "Polyglot" Arabic Text of Amos: A Comparative and

Critical Study. Princeton University, 1934. Not available from UMI. See ADD

Steenbergen, N. Van. Motivation in Relation to the Message of Amos. Diss. Los Angeles, 1953.

Stenzel, M. Das Dodekapropheton der lateinischen Septuaginta: Untersuchungen uber die Herkunft und die geschichtliche Entwicklung der lateinischen Textgestalt des nichthieronymianischen Dodekapropheton. Diss. Wurzburg, Wurzburg University, 1949. For part 5, See main entry

Thompson, C.L. The Idealogical Background and an Analysis of Economic Injustice in the Book of Amos. Diss. Southwestern Baptist Theological Seminary. 1956.

Travis, James Leslie. An Investigation of Pesha'im as it Relates to the Nations in the Book of Amos. New Orleans Baptist Theological Seminary, 1960. Not available from UMI. See ADD

Turnham, Timothy John. Wealth and Righteousness: Selected OT Teachings on Material Possessions (Ethics, OT), Job, Leviticus, Amos. Southern Baptist Theological Seminary, 1984. 153 pp. DAI 45, No. 12 (June 85), 3664. Available on microfiche. See main entry.

Tuschen, W. Die historischen Angaben im Buche des Propheten Amos Diss. Freiburg im Breisgau: Universitat Freiburg, 1951.

Vanhorn, William Wayne. An Investigation of *Yom Yahweh* as it Relates to the Message of Amos (Day of the Lord). New Orleans Baptist Theological Seminary, 1987. 207 pp. DAI 49, No. 4 (Oct 88), 854. Compares the Day with the Covenant, people's expectation of victory and Amos' prediction of judgment for the violation of the covenant.

Waller, Herbert S. The Unity of the Book of Amos. Southern Baptist Theological Seminary, 1948. Not available from UMI. See ADD

White, Kenneth O. The Doctrine of God in Amos with Its Implications. Southern Baptist Theological Seminary, 1934. Not available from UMI. See ADD

Whitesides, R.A.D. The Gospel According to Amos. Diss. Princeton, 1952.

Witaszek, Gabriel. I profeti Amos e Micha nella lotta per lagiustizia sociale nell'VIII secola a.C. Diss. Rome: Gregorianae Pontifical University, 1986. No. 3325. 302 pp.

Witaszek, Gabriel. *Prorocy Amos i Micheasz wobec niesprawiedliwosci spolecznej* (The Prophets Amos and Micah Confront Social Injustices). Tuchow: Mala Poligrafia. Redmeptorystow, 1992. 222 pp. Abbreviated version of the Gregorian University dissertation with bibliography updated to 1991.

Woodward, Beverly Floyd. A Study of the Norms of Indictment in Amos. ThD. Union Theological Seminary in Virginia, 1970. Not available from UMI. See ADD

Wyszowadzki, W. The Idea of Justice in the Book of Amos (Polish). Diss. University of Warsaw, 1982. 167 pp.

JOURNALS

Acta Theologica (Bloemfontein) 12, No. 2 (1992), 85-94. - Kloppers

Advent Review and Sabbath Herald = RH 154 (4 Aug 77), 9. - Neufeld

Adventist Review 159 (28 Jan 82), 4-7. - Andreasen

Aegyptus (Milan) 34, No. 1 (Jan-June 54), 35-62. - Rinaldi

Aevum 26 (1949), 316-356. - Rinaldi

Africa Theological J (Makumira, Tanzania) 18, No. 1 (1989), 17-27. -Ebo

AION ns 17 (1967), 331-334. - Liverani

AJSL (Chicago) 12, No. 2 (Ap-July 1896), 267. - Margolis
   17, No. 3 (Ap 01), 170-171. - Margolis
   18, No. 2 (Jan 02), 65-93. - Day
   19, No. 1 (Oct 02), 45-48. - Margolis
   19, No. 2 (Jan 03), 116-117. - Bewer
   49, No. 2 (Jan 33), 102-114. - Irwin

American J of Theology (Chicago, 1897-1920) 1, No. 1 (Jan 1897), 140-145. - Harper

Amsterdamse Cahiers voor exegese en Bijbelse theologie (Kampen)
   6 (1985), 83-90. - van der Wal
   6 (1985), 91-110. - Blok
   6 (1985), 111-143. - Bogaard

The Andover Review (Boston, 1884-1893) 9 (1888), No. 52 (Ap), 426-431; No. 53 (May), 528-547. - Duff

Andrews University Seminary Studies = AUSS (Berrian Springs, MI)

25, No. 1 (Spr 87), 9-26. - Freedman
29, No. 1 (Spr 91), 3-18. - Hasal

Anglican Theological Review (Evanston, IL, 1918) 6, No. 3 (Dec 23), 245-247. - Fischer

Annales Archeologiques Arabes Syriennes (Damascus) 28/30 (1978-1980), 141-143. - Pope, M

Annali della Facolta di Lettere e filosofia dell'Univ (Naples) 28 (1985s), 15-21. - Annecchino Manni

Annual of the Swedish Theological Institute 8 (1970-1971), 123-130. - Sawyer

Antonianum (Rome) 30, No. 2 (Ap 55), 188-189. - Zolli

Archiv fur Religionspsychologie (Tubingen) 14 (1980), 237-245. - Kallstad

Asbury Seminarian (Wilmore, KY) 21, No. 2 (Ap 67), 14-18. - Lewis, Ralph

Ashland Theological J 21 (1989), 8-13. - King, D

Asia J of Theology (Singapore) 4 (1990), 472-488. - Yeo

Assemblees du Seigneur (Bruges)
    46 (1964), 30-35. - Hauret
    56 (1974), 56-61. - Derousseaux
    57 (1974), 68-73. - Buis

Austin Seminary Bulletin 90, No. 6 (Mar 75), 7-34. - March

Australian Biblical Review 23 (Oct 75), 3-11. - Wright, John

Baptist Review of Theology (Gormley, Ontario) 5 (1995), 35-91. - Dempster

BASOR = *Bulletin of the American Schools of Oriental Research*

108 (1947), 5-6. - Speiser
129 (Feb 53), 25-26. - Malamat
198 (Ap 70), 41. - Freedman

Beth Miqra/Mikra = BM

Bib = *Biblica* (Rome)
6, No. 2 (1925), 171-173. - Zorell
8, No. 1 (1927), 87-92. - Power
8, No. 4 (1927), 441-444. - Keimer
17, No. 3 (1936), 359-364. - Junker
25, No. 2 (May 44), 105-142. - Ziegler
25, No. 3 (Oct 44), 297-310. - Ziegler
26, No. 1 (Feb 45), 37-51. - Ziegler
42, No. 3 (1961), 359-366. - Dahood
55 (1974), 15-22. - Howard, G
59, No. 2 (1978), 265-266. - Dahood
59, No. 3 (1979), 339-350. - Waard
62, No. 2 (1981), 169-184. - Foresti
73, No. 3 (1992), 305-330. - Dorsey
76, No. 3 (1995), 343-387. - Weigl

Bibbia e Oriente (Milan)
4 (1962), 83-84. - Rinaldi
10, No. 6 (1968), 253-265. - Sansoni

Bibel und Kirche (Stuttgart)
22, No. 4 (1967), 110-116. - Sievi
22, No.4 (1967), 116-119. - Sasowski
22, No. 4 (1967), 120-122. - Speidel

Bibel und Leben (Dusseldorf)
10 (1969), 157-164. - Haag
10 (1969), 219-221. - Rusche
12 (1971), 215-231. - Botterweck

Bibel und Liturgie (Klosterneuberg)
36 (1962-1963), 84-96, 164-172, 243-255, 295-308. - Praeger/Prager
48 (1975), 256-259. - Schultes

Bible Bhashyam (Kerala) 11 (1985), 215-223. - Kallikuzhuppil

Bible et Terre Sainte (Paris)
47 (May 62), 5-6. - Maigret
No. 164 (Sep-Oct 74), 24. - Decroix
No. 164 (Sep-Oct 74), 24. - Deltombe
No. 165 (Nov 74), 24. - Deltombe

Bible et Vie Chretienne (Paris) = BVC
32 (Mar-Ap 60), 27-36. - Fransen
8 (Dec 54-Feb 55), 61-75. - Florival
17 (Mar-May 57), 17-29. - Feuillet

Bible Review
1, No. 2 (Sum 85), 48-51. - Freedman, D
5, No. 2 (Ap 89), 16-21. - Richardson, H

The Bible Student
4 (July-Dec '01), 148-154. - Day
8 (1903), 295-297. - Young

The Bible Student and Teacher (NYC). Later called Bible Champion ('13-30), then CFL ('31-9)
5, No. 1 (July '06), 17-23. - King, F
5, No. 4 (Oct '06), 267-272. - McKim
28 (1922), 362-363. - Bates

The Bible Today = BT

Bible Translator = BTr
15, No. 1 (Jan 64), 31-34. - Moeller
22, No. 3 (July 71), 116-117. - Grether
26, No. 2 (Ap 75), 201-211. - Smalley
29, No. 1 (Jan 78), 222-224. - Smalley
30, No. 1 (Jan 79), 118-127. - Smalley
31, No. 1 (Jan 80), 119-125. - Smalley
42, No. 2 (Ap 91), 201-205. - Hope

Biblia y Fe 17 (50, 1991), 171-193. - Struik

Biblical Archaeology = BA 56, No. 2 (June 93), 94-104. - Beach

Biblical Archaeology Review 15, No. 4 (July/Aug 88), 34-44. - King

Biblical Interpretation 4, No. 1 (Feb 96), 76-100. - Carroll

Biblical Review 16, No. 4 (Oct '31), 574-578. - Osborn

Biblical Theology Bulletin
   2, No. 3 (Oct 72), 242-261. - Craghan
   23, No. 2 (Sum 93), 54-63. - Berquist

Biblical Viewpoint = BV

Biblical World = BW

Bibliotheca Sacra = BS

Biblische Z = BZ

BIES = *The Bulletin of the Israel Exploration Society* (Jerusalem) 16, Nos. 1/2 (1951), III. - Malamat

Bijdragen 50 (1989), 203-209. - Beentjes

BM = *Beth Miqra/Mikra* (Jerusalem)
   11 [Issue Nos. 25/26], Nos. 1-2 (Nov 65), 103-107. - Ashbel
   12 [Issue No. 30], No. 2 (Mar 67), 6-11. - Luria/e
   12 [Issue No. 30], No. 2 (Mar 67), 12-16. - Braslabi/ Braslavi
   12 [Issue No. 31], No. 3 (July 67), 87-101. - Braslabi
   13 [Issue No. 32], No. 1 (Oct 67), 24-26. - Grintz
   13 [Issue No. 32], No. 1 (Oct 67), 56-64. - Braslabi
   13 [Issue No. 33], No. 2 (Jan 68), 141-144. - Waitz/Weitz
   14 [Issue No. 39], No. 4 (Sep 69), 40-57. - Weisman
   17 [Issue No. 48], No. 1 (Oct-Dec 71), 5-16. - Braslabi
   18 [Issue No. 54], No. 3 (Ap-June 73), 287-301, 421-422. - Luria/e
   18 [Issue No. 54], No. 3 (Ap-June 73), 375-381, 426-427. - Gilead
   21 [Issue No. 66], No. 3 (Ap-June 76), 330-332, 494. - Loewenstamm
   21 [Issue No. 66], No. 3 (Ap-June 76), 333-346, 493. - Halevi

22 [Issue No. 69], No. 2 (Jan-Mar 77), 194-198, 278-279. - Givati
27 [Issues 89-90], Nos. 2-3 (1982), 174-182. - Nagah/Nageh/Nogah
28 [Issue No. 92], No. 1 (1982), 49-53. - Ziv
30 [Issue No. 101], No. 2 (Jan-Mar 85), 259-262. - Luria/e
33 [Issue No. 114], No. 3 (1988), 392-396. - Bachar
34 [Issue No. 118], No. 3 (1989), 250-254. - Ginat
36 [Issue No. 125], No. 2 (Jan-Mar 91), 160-165. - Mishael

BN = *Biblische Notizen* (Munich)
16 (1981), 60-100. - Weimar
31 (1986), 7-10. - Dahmen
32 (1986), 41-53. - Begg
37 (1987), 129-138. - Seidl
41 (1988), 76-101. - Utzschneider
45 (1988), 40-41. - Hirth
48 (1989), 89-104. - Uehlinger

BS = *Bibliotheca Sacra*
59 (1902), 192-197. - Braithwaite
59, No. 234 (1902), 366-374. - Braithwaite
68 (1911), 308-342. - Stibitz
70, No. 277 (1913), 109-122. - Whitford
84, No. 336 (Oct '27), 402-410. - Lineberger
85, No. 337 (Jan '28), 53-63. - Kelso
147, No. 586 (Ap-June 90), 188-197. - Chisholm

BT = *The Bible Today* (Collegeville, MN. 1962)
4 (Feb 63), 224-230. - Stuhlmueller
14, Issue No. 60 (Ap 72), 782-786. - Craghan
19, No. 5 (Sep 81), 295-300. - Peifer
19, No. 5 (Sep 81), 301-305. - Sowada
19, No. 5 (Sep 81), 306-313. - Bailey
19, No. 5 (Sep 81), 314-319. - Miller
20, No. 3 (May 82), 160-165. - Badia
21, No. 6 (Nov 83), 406-408. - Kolbusz
31, No. 5 (Sep 93), 265-271. - Nash
32 (1967), 2221-2228. - Lucal
33, No. 5 (Sep 95), 294-297. - Davis

Bulletin of the American Schools of Oriental Research = BASOR

Bulletin of the American Society of Papyrologists (NY) 16, No. 3 (1979), 201-204. - Kraft, R

The Bulletin of the Christian Research Institute Meiji Gakuin University 14 (1981), 27-47 (Japanese). - Yoshida

The Bulletin of the Israel Exploration Society = BIES

Buried History (Melbourne) 23 (1987), 7-15. - Crocker

BV = *Biblical Viewpoint* (Greenville, SC, 1967)
 14 (Ap 80), 62-67. - Bushey
 27, No. 2 (Nov 93), 3-7. - Bell
 27, No. 2 (Nov 93), 9-16. - Neal
 27, No. 2 (1993), 17-22. - Wisdom
 27, No. 2 (Nov 93), 23-28. - Jaeggli
 27, No. 2 (Nov 93), 29-34. - Steveson
 27, No. 2 (Nov 93), 35-45. - Barrett
 27, No. 2 (Nov 93), 47-54. - Bell

BW = *Biblical World*
 12, Nos. 2-5 (Aug-Nov 1898), 86-89; 179-182; 251-256; 333-338. - Harper
 12, No. 5 (May 1899), 340. - Day
 13, No. 3 (Mar 1899), 196-197. - Paton
 17 (1901), 265-271. - Jordan
 20, No. 5 (Nov '02), 361-369, No. 6 (Dec '02), 457-464. - Betteridge
 24 (1904), 448-462. - Harper
 31, No. 1 (Jan '08), 62-67. - Soares

BZ = *Biblische Z* (Freiburg im Breisgau)
 2, No. 2 (1958), 179-189. - Botterweck
 3 (1905), 355-367. - Happel
 8 (1910), 133-134. - Ciric
 23, No. 1 (1935), 150-157. - Durr
 ns 20, No. 1 (1976), 122-125. - Loretz
 21 (1977), 200-218. - Keel
 30, No. 2 (1986), 250-256. - Schenker

Calvin Theological J 20 (Nov 85), 361. - Lyngdoh

The Canadian J of Religious Thought (Toronto) 8 (1931), 397-406. - King, G

Catalyst 7, No. 11 (Nov 75), 12 min. - Cooper

Catechistes 27 (1956), 267-277. - Mousset

Catholic Biblical Quarterly = CBQ

Catholic Lawyer 35, No. 1 (1993), 97-107. - Enman

CBQ = *Catholic Biblical Quarterly*
   19, No. 2 (Ap 57), 199-212. - Benson
   23, No. 2 (Ap 61), 227-233. - Glanzman
   26, No. 2 (Ap 64), 221-225. - Hillers
   34, No. 1 (Jan 72), 39-53. - Crenshaw
   35, No. 3 (July 73), 346-349. - Limburg
   41, No. 4 (Oct 79), 517-532. - Overholt
   42, No. 3 (July 80), 293-309. - Gitay
   47, No. 3 (July 85), 420-427. - Barre
   53, No. 3 (July 91), 365-387. - Schmitt

Chicago Studies 24, No. 2 (Aug 85), 193-207. - Collins, J

Christentum und Wissenschaft
   7 (1931), 181-289. - Stephany
   9 (1933), 161-176. - Herntrich

Christianisme Social (Paris) 74 (1966), 303-312. - Atger

Collectanea Theologica Universitats Fujen 5, No. 20 (1974), 165-171. - Fang

Collectiones Brugenses 47 (1951), 405-410; 48 (1952), 3-7, 27-31. - Laridon

Concordia J 9, No. 6 (Nov 83), 243. - Graudin

Concordia Theological Monthly = CTM
  10, No. 1 (Feb 83), 4-13. - Wolff
  13, No. 2 (Ap 86), 89-96. - Wicke

Crozer Quarterly (Chester, PA, 1924-52) 4, No. 2 (Ap '27), 204-206. - Pollard

CTM = *Concordia Theological Monthly*

CTQ
  47, No. 2 (Ap 83), 164-165. - Maier
  47, No. 2 (Ap 83), 165-166. - Maier

Cuestiones Teologicas Medellin 27 (1983), 1-14. - Jimenez

Cultura Biblica (Madrid/Segovia) 23, No. 1 (Jan-Feb 66), 36-42. - Alonso Diaz
  25, No. 253 (Nov-Dec 73), 347-352. - Ruiz Gonzales

CurTm 13 (1986), 89-96. - Wilck

Dansk Teologisk Tidsskrift 30, No. 2 (1967), 65-101. - Gottlieb
  52, No. 4 (1989), 243-250. - Nielsen

DBAT (Dielheim)
  4 (1973), 1-12. - Kahlert
  23 (1986), 121-155. - Krech
  24 (1987), 127-145. - Diebner

Dor le Dor (Jerusalem)
  5, No. 3 (Spr 77), 101-110. - Uffenheimer
  10, No. 3 (1982), 183-186. - Lubsczyk, H

  10, No. 3 (1982), 183-186. - Luria/e/ja, Ben Zion
  16 (1987), 213-216. - Katzoff

Drew Gateway 55 (Wint 84-Spr 85), Nos. 2&3, 3-27. - Walzer

Economic Botany (NY Botanical Gardens) 22, No. 2 (Ap 68), 178-190. - Galil

384   Journals

Eretz-Israel = EI

EI = *Eretz-Israel* (Jerusalem)
  3 (1954), 83-83, IV. - Ginsberg
  14 (1978), 69-73, 125*. - WeissHoard, G
  16 (1982), 43*-50*. - Fohrer
  16 (1982), 125-133. - Howard, G
  20 (1989), 98*-106*. - King

Epistemonike Epeteris Thessalonikis 29 (1988), 207-289. - Kaimakis

Estudios Biblicos (Madrid) 19, No. 1 (1960), 91-95. - Diez Macho
  25, Nos. 3-4 (1966), 349-354. - Bartina
  26, No. 3 (1967), 249-274. - Trapiello

Estudios Teologicos (Guatemala) 6, No. 11 (Jan-June 79), 115-180. -
Estalayo-Alonso

Estudos Biblicos (Petropolis, Brazil)
  attached to Revista Eclesiastica Brasileira 45, No. 177 (Mar 85), 1-
  224.
  5 (1985), 26-39. - Schwantes

ET = *Expository Times* (London)
  3, No. 10 (July 1892), 479-480. - Taylor, J
  3, No. 11 (Aug 1892), 520-521. - Taylor, J
  4, No. 1 (Oct 1892), 48. - Taylor, J
  4, No. 3 (Dec 1892), 130-132. - Jordan, J
  9, No. 7 (Ap 1898), 334. - Cheyne
  11, No. 2 (Nov 1899), 83-88. - Smith, John
  11, No. 10 (July 1900), 442-446. - Danson
  12, No. 5 (Feb 01), 235-236. - Box and Oesterley
  12, No. 7 (Ap 01), 318-319. - Taylor, J
  12, No. 8 (May 01), 377-378. - Box
  13, No. 1 (Oct 01), 40-41. - Osterley
  15, No. 2 (Nov 04), 64-65. - Taylor, J
  23, No. 2 (Nov 11), 93. - Hommel
  26, No. 5 (Feb 15), 237. - Daiches
  26, No. 5 (Feb 15), 237. - Maclagan
  26, No. 11 (Aug 15), 521-522. - Daiches

26, No. 12 (Sep 15), 562-563. - Daiches
36, No. 9 (June 25), 430-431. - Williamson
38, No. 1 (Oct 26), 44-45. - Highfield
38, No. 8 (May 27), 377-378. - Burn
53, No. 12 (Sep 42), 367-370. - Jack
55, No. 7 (Ap 44), 191-194. - Riach
60, No. 6 (Mar 49), 159. - Mackenzie
60, No. 9 (June 49), 256-258. - Jellicoe
66, No. 4 (Jan 55), 109-112. - Watts, J
67, No. 3 (Dec 55), 91-92. - Driver, G
67, No. 10 (July 56), 318. - MacCormack
68, No. 3 (Dec 56), 94. - Ackroyd
68, No. 10 (July 57), 301-302. - Vogt
68, No. 10 (July 57), 302. - Driver, G
71, No. 3 (Dec 59), 86-87. - Soper
92, No. 7 (Ap 81), 196-200. - Davies, G
98, No. 11 (Aug 87), 342-344. - Cornick
98 (1987), 363-364. - Coggins
103, No. 12 (Sep 92),364-368. - Mowvley
104, No. 3 (Dec 92) 71-76. - Thompson
105, No. 8 (May 94), 244-245. - Camroux
106, No. 4 (Jan 95), 105-109. - Noble

Eternity 33, No. 11 (Nov 82), 37-38. - Putnam

ETR = *Etudes Theologiques et Religieuses* (Montpellier)
7 (1932), 158-172. - Bruston
41, No. 1 (1966), 13-19. - Martin-Achard
46, No. 2 (1971), 113-124. - Casalis
50, No. 2 (1975), 133-159. - Vischer

Etudes Franciscaines (Paris) 2, No. 4 (Feb 51), 61-83. - Cornet

Etudes Theologiques et Religieuses (Montpellier) = ETR

The Evangelical Quarterly (London) 12, No. 1 (15 Jan 40), 48-59. - Miller, P

Evangelische Theologie (Munich)
10, No. 1 (1950), 26-38. - Robscheit

23, No. 8 (1963), 404-423. - Smend
29 (1969), 169-183. - Kellermann
33, No. 1 (Jan-Feb 73), 32-53. - Fendler
53, No. 2 (1993), 109-123. - Gillingham

Evangelist 83 (1932), 7-10. - Huxoll

Exp = *The Expositor* (London)
2nd ser, 3, No. 5 (May, 1882), 338-352. - Matheson
2nd ser, 8, No. 5 (Nov 1884), 321-338. - Cox, S
3rd ser, 5 (1887), 161-179. - Davidson, A
3rd ser, 6, No. 33 (1887), 161-173. - Davidson, A
4th ser, 8 (1893), 96-109. - Taylor, J
5th ser, 5, No. 1 (Jan 1897), 41-51. - Cheyne
6th ser, 1, No. 6 (June 1900), 460-461. - Burkitt
6th ser 2, No. 6 (Dec 1900), 414-428. - Muss-Arnolt
6th ser, 5, No. 2 (Feb '02), 82-85. - Farrar, F
8th ser, 9 (Mar '15), 272-288. - Moffatt
8th ser, 21 (1921), 1-18. - McFadyen
8th ser, 24, No. 2 (1922), 45-51. - Lofthouse

Expository Times - see ET

Foi et Vie
83, No. 4 (Sep 84), 26-34. - Roemer
83, No. 5 (Sep 84), 35-44. - Waard and Dieterle

Fundamentalist J 5 (Oct 86), 54. - Willmington

The Furrow (Maynooth, Ireland) 38, No. 3 (Mar 87), 151-161. - Kee, A

Gereformeerd Theologisch Tijdschrift 72, No. 1 (1972), 1-18. - Ridderbos

Grace Theological J 8, No. 1 (Spr 87), 141-142. - Schmidt, D

Hagoren
5 (1936), 43-55. - Hayuth
6 (1936), 77-78. - Hayuth

The Hartford Quarterly (Hartford, CT) 4, No. 4 (Sum 64), 65-68. - Radanovsky

Harvard Theological Review
  67, No. 4 (Oct 74), 427-436. - Christensen
  79 (1986), 337-348. - Hauan

Hebraica
  1, No. 4 (Ap 1885), 242-243. - Peters
  2, No. 3 (Ap 1886), 175. - Peters
  5, Nos. 2-3 (Jan-Ap 1889), 131-136. - Carrier

Hebrew Annual Review (Columbus, Ohio)
  7 (1983), 203-220. - Paul, S
  11 (1987), 35-58. - Eslinger
  11 (1987), 223-246. - Landy

Hebrew Studies (Louisville, KY)
  18 (1977), 132-148. - Rosenbaum
  18 (1977), 149-159. - Carny

Henoch 16 (1994), 23-47. - Blum

Hervormde Teologiese Studies (Pretoria, 1943) = HTS
  1, No. 1 (1943), 9-21. - Gemser
  1, No. 2 (1944), 49-58. - Gemser
  22 (1967), 38-45. - Wyk
  47 (Mar 91), 5-25. - Loader

His (Downers Grove, IL)
  30, No. 2 (Nov 69), 7-9. - Breisch
  30, No. 3 (Dec 69), 16-18. - Breisch
  30, No. 4 (Jan 70), 28-30. - Breisch
  30, No. 5 (Feb 70), 15-16, 21. - Breisch

Homiletic Review (NY) = HR

Horizons in Biblical Theology 15, No. 1 (June 93), 56-82. - Noble

HR = *Homiletic Review* (NY) 18, No. 1 (July 1889), 62-65. - Beecher

19, No. 2 (Feb 1890), 157-160. - Beecher
32, No. 1 (July 1896), 24-27. - McCurdy
51, No. 1 (Jan '06), 49-51. - Beecher
108, No. 1 (1934), 61-63. - Bose

HUCA (Cincinnati)
  11 (1936), 19-140. - Morgenstern
  12/13 (1937-1938), 1-53. - Morgenstern
  14 (1939), 1-22. - Eitan
  15 (1940), 59-305. - Morgenstern
  24 (1952-1953), 85-106. - Reider
  25 (1954), 41-83. - Morgenstern
  32 (1961), 175-178. - Cohen, S
  32 (1961), 295-350. - Morgenstern
  36 (1965), 153-160. - Cohen, S
  38 (1967), 75-91. - Williams, J
  43 (1972), 23-27. - Ouellette

IEJ = *Israel Exploration J* (Jerusalem)
  18, No. 4 (1968), 201-207. - Haran
  19, No. 3 (1969), 150-157. - Weiss

Indian J of Spirituality 4, No. 2 (1991), 149. - Aerathedathu

The Indian J of Theology 26 (July-Dec 77), 132-142. - John, E

Interpretation = INT (Richmond, VA)
  3, No. 3 (July 49), 338-348. - Hyatt
  13, No. 3 (July 59), 259-272. - Mays
  13, No. 3 (July 59), 273-285. - Howie
  13, No. 3 (July 59), 286-295. - Vischer
  13, No. 3 (July 59), 296-315. - Barackman
  25, No. 3 (July 71), 355-358. - Bright
  27, No. 4 (Oct 73), 423-434. - Tucker
  32, No. 1 (Jan 78), 31-45. - Tucker

The Interpreter. A Church Monthly Magazine (London) 3, No. 3 (Ap '07), 296-304. - Brown

Irish Theological Quarterly (Maynooth)

22, No. 1 (1955), 68-73. - Leahy
41 (Ap 74), 120-133. - Collins, J

Israel Exploration J = IEJ

JAOS (New Haven)
  59 (1939), 421. - Kraft, C
  61, No. 1 (1941), 63-64. - Meek
  61, No. 3 (1941), 190-191. - Meek

JBL 7, No. 1 (1887), 33-42. - Mitchell
  8, No. 1 (1888), 14-40. - Beecher
  13, Nos. 1&2 (1894), 1-15. - Schmidt, N
  13, No. 1 (1894), 61-63. - Torrey
  13. No. 1 (1894), 80-90. - Paton
  15, Nos. 1&2 (1896), 151-154. - Torrey
  18, Nos. 1&2 (1899), 214-215. - Macdonald
  23, No. 1 (1904), 94-96. - Montgomery
  25, No. 1 (1906), 25-28. - Toy
  25, No. 1 (1906), 51-52. - Montgomery
  27, No. 2 (1908), 99-127. - Barry
  28, No. 2 (1909), 200-202. - Bewer
  30, No. 1 (1911), 61-65. - Bewer
  31, No. 3 (1912), 143. - Montgomery
  35, Nos. 3&4 (1916), 280-287. - Haupt
  35, No. 2 (1916), 288-292. - Haupt
  43, No. 1 (1924), 46-131. - Budde
  44, No. 1 (1925), 63-122. - Budde
  56, No. 1 (1937), ix. - Bailey
  58, No. 1 (1939), vi. - Gehman
  58, No. 4 (1939), 331-347. - Bosshard
  59, No. 1 (1940), vii. - Gordis
  67, No. 1 (Jan 48), vi. - Reider
  67, No. 3 (Sep 48), 245-248. - Reider
  70, No. 1 (1951), xii. - McCullough
  70, No. 1 (1951), xiii. - Crook
  71, No. 1 (Mar 52), 33-38. - Kapelrud
  72, No. 4 (Dec 53), 247-254. - McCullough
  73, No. 3 (Sep 54), 144-151. - Crook
  83, No. 4 (Dec 64), 416-417. - Rahtjen

84, No. 4 (Dec 65), 400-406. - Peiest
85, No. 1 (Mar 66), 89. - Richardson, H
85, No. 3 (S 66), 351-353. - Sinclair
86, No. 4 (Dec 67), 416-423. - Weiss
87, No. 3 (Sep 68), 267-276. - Gevirtz
89, No. 2 (June 76), 187-191. - Ramsey
89, No. 3 (Sep 70), 313-318. - Fishbane
90, No. 1 (Mar 71), 98. - Youngblood
90, No. 2 (June 71), 206-208. - Coote
90, No. 4 (Dec 71), 397-403. - Paul, S
91, No. 3 (Sep 72), 391-393. - Fishbane
92, No. 3 (Sep 73), 375-381. - Richardson, H
93, No. 3 (Sep 74), 329-337. - Everson
93, No. 3 (Sep 74), 338-347. - Arieti
97, No. 1 (Mar 78), 97-99. - Isbell
97, No. 2 (June 78), 183-190. - Paul, S
100, No. 1 (Mar 81), 53-58. - Zalcman
104, No. 1 (Mar 85), 109-110. - Jacobs
104, No. 3 (Sep 85), 385-400. - Good
105, No. 4 (Dec 86), 611-631. - Barre
106, No. 2 (June 87), 217-222. - Limburg
106, No. 2 (June 87), 223-229. - Shaw
107, No. 2 (July 88), 289-291. - Smith, Gary
107, No. 4 (Dec 88), 725-727. - Cooper
111, No. 4 (Wint 92), 683-689. - Steinmann
111, No. 4 (Wint 92), 690-693. - Giles
113, No. 3 (Fall 94), 484-493. - Ceresko
114, No. 2 (Sum 95), 209-226. - Noble

Jeevadhara (Kerala)
19, No. 110 (Mar 89), 118-132. - Walle
68 (1982), 111-128. - Koonthanam

JETS = *J of the Evangelical Theological Society*
13 (1970), 81-89. - Heicksen
20, No. 2 (June 77), 97-111. - Kaiser
27, No. 3 (Sep 84), 275-276. - Garrett
28, No. 4 (Dec 85), 411-420. - Finley
30, No. 2 (June 87), 139-158. - McComiskey
31, No. 4 (Dec 88), 407-410. - Wolters

34, No. 2 (Mar 91), 33-42. - Smith, Gary

J for Semtics/Tydskrif vir Semitistiek 4, No. 2 (1992), 130-150. - Burger

J for the Study of the OT = JSOT

JJS (London) 7, Nos. 1-2 (1956), 91-92. - Wainwright

JNES
  9 (1950), 215-217. - Neuberg
  15, No. 1 (Jan 56), 33-39. - Watts, JDW
  22, No. 2 (Ap 63), 128-132. - Neiman
  24, No. 3 (July 65), 285-296. - Landsberger
  25, No. 2 (Ap 66), 106-112. - Staples
  36, No. 3 (July 77), 213-214. - Isbell

J of Egyptian Archaeology 11 (1925), 241-246. - Bell and Thompson

J of Reform Judaism (NY) 25 (Sum 78), 47-50. - Mehlman

J of Religion (Chicago)
  7 (1931), 136-145. - Thomas
  23, No 3 (July 43), 194-205. - Andrews, M

J of Religious Thought
  25, No. 1 (1968-1969), 79-82. - Churn
  35, No. 1 (Spr-Sum 78), 35-44. - Rice

J of Sacred Literature and Biblical Record (London, 1848-1868), 4th ser, 5 (1864), 175-180. - Wilton

J of Semitic Studies (Manchester, 1956) = JSS 26, No. 1 (Spr 81), 7-9. - Ahlstrom

J of Theological Studies = JTS

Journal of Theology for Southern Africa (Cape Town) 58 (Mar 87), 57-69. - Wittenberg

J of Theology of the American Lutheran Conference (Minneapolis) 7

(1942), 684-694. - Sandrock

JSOT = *J for the Study of the OT* (Sheffield, Eng)
24 (1982), 47-63. - Lang
26 (June 83), 107-113. - van der Wal
51 (Sep 91), 119-121. - Bulkeley
65 (Dec 94), 23-24. - Davies, P

JTS = *J of Theological Studies*
28 (1926-1927), 184-185. - Burrows, E
39, No. 3 (July 38), 260-273. - Driver, G
41, No. 2 (Ap 40), 162-175. - Driver, G
ns 1, No. 2 (Oct 50), 158-168. - Smythe
4, No. 2 (Oct 53), 208-212. - Driver, G
7, No. 1 (Ap 56), 69-70. - Thomas, D
32, No. 2 (Oct 81), 423-429. - Porter

Judaica 23, No. 2 (1967), 68-74. - Schmid, H

Judaism 19 (1907), 15-29. - Shaskolsky

Katechetische Blatter (Munich) 115 (1990), 387-390. - Bechman

Kirche und Kanzel 14 (1931), 1-16. - Schaumberger

Kirisuto-kyo Gaku (Christian Studies) 28 (1986). - Kobayashi

Kwansei Gakuin University Annual Studies (Nishinomiya) 4 (1956),
25-100. - Josaki

Laval Theologique Philosophique 28 (1972), 185-192. - Beaucamp

Learning for Living
2, No. 1 (Sep 62), 6-9. - Ackroyd
2, No. 1 (Sep 62), 9-12. - Handley

Leshonenu 33, No. 1 (1968), 15-17. - Speier

Liber Pontificalis 49, No. 1 (1974), 641-652. - Muntag

Life of the Spirit (London, 1946-1964) 14 (1959-1960), 349-358. - Potter

The Liguorian 55 (Ap 67), 46-50. - Eberhard

The Living Word (Kerala, India) 100 (1994), 182-191. - Manakkatt

London Quarterly H R 178 (Oct 53), 271-274. - Jessop

Lumen Vitor 24 (1975), 385-411. - Hernando

Lutheran Church Review (Philadelphia, 1882-1927) 37, No. 2 (Ap 1918), 111-133. - Benze

The Lutheran Quarterly (Gettysburg, PA) 40, No. 1 (Jan 1910), 34-64. - Hanson

Madregoth 1 (1940), 23-31. - Lattes

Melanges de l'universite Saint Joseph = MUSJ (Beirut)
4 (1910), 30. - Jouon
5 (1911-1912), 269-282. - Wilburs
10 (1925), 1-46. - Jouon

Melita Theologica 3, No. 2 (1950), 75-93; 4, No. 1 (1951), 34-48. - Sant

Mid-America Theological J
19 (1995), 51-55. - Spradlin
19 (1995), 99-113. - Simmons

Ministry 5 (1965), 66-69, 118-120. 6(1966), 21-23, 98-105, 158-162. 7 (1967), 178-183. 8 (1968), 77-82, 185-190. 9 (1969), 22-26. - Bernard

Monatsschrift fur Geschichte und Wissenschaft des Judentums 67 (1923), 137. - Schlesinger

Nanzan Theological Journal 6 (Feb 83), 1-21 (Japanese). - Nishizu

394   Journals

Nederlands Theologisch Tijdschift (Gravenhage)
   41, No. 2 (1987), 89-98, 156. - van der Wal
   48, No. 3 (July 94), 177-190, 230. - Dijkstra
   49, No. 2 (Ap 95), 124-139. - Paas

Ned Geref Teologiese Tydskrif
   33, No. 2 (June 92), 150-156. - Snyman
   36, No. 2 (June 95), 139-150. - Heyns

Neue Kirchlich Z (Erlangen/Leipzig, 1890)
   25, No. 9 (1914), 701-715. - Caspari
   41, No. 12 (1930), 812-824. - Caspari

Neue Z fur Systematische Theologie und Religionsphilosophie 33, No.
   2 (1991), 112-138. - Muller, Hans

New Covenant 23 (S 1993), 34. - Martin, G

Nieuwe Theologische Studien (Wageningen)
   10 (1927), 1-7. - Boehmer
   10 (1927), 82-83. - Boehmer

Norsk Teologisk Tidsskrift
   28 (1927), 1-31. - Mowinckel
   49 (1948), 120-128. - Mowinckel
   59 (1958), 76-79. - Kapelrud
   84, No. 3 (1983), 157-166. - Kapelrud
   84, No. 3 (1983), 167-185. - Otzen
   85, No. 1 (1984), 39-54. - Ulrichsen

Nova et Vera 37, No. 3 (1962), 217-223. - Mamie

Novum Testament
   10, Nos. 2-3 (1968), 234-240. - Treu
   24, No. 1 (1982), 37-53. - Richard, E

The Old and New Testament Student (New Haven, CT, 1889-1892) 12,
No. 1 (Jan 1891), 28-33. - Flocken
Continued by Biblical World

Old Testament Essays (Pretoria) = OTE
2 (1984), 81-97. - Nell
1, No. 2 (1988), 21-30. - Bosman
1, No. 2 (1988), 31-45. - Helberg
2, No. 3 (1989), 108. - Heyns
3, No. 3 (1990), 303-316. - Heyns
4, No. 1 (1991), 7-18. - Wittenberg
6, No. 1 (1992), 72-89. - Heyns
6, No. 3 (1993), 295-311. - Wittenberg

The Old Testament Student (New Haven, CT, 1883-1889)
3, No. 1 (Sep 1883), pp. 2-6. - Chambers
5, No. 1 (Sep 1885), 13-17. - Elliott
5, No. 8 (1886), 335-337. - Denio
6, No. 5 (Jan 1887), 136-139. - Curtis
8, No. 1 (Sep 1888), 10-19. - Chancellor
8, No. 8 (Ap 1889), 284-290. - Atkinson
Continues, The Hebrew Student (1881-1882)

OLZ

17 (1914), 155-156. - Sellin
20 (1917), 296-298. - Humbert

Open Court (Chicago) 9, No. 400 (25 Ap 1895), 4473-4475. - Cornill

Orita (Ibadan, Nigeria) 24, Nos. 1-2 (June-Dec 92), 76-84. - Adamo

Oudtestamentische Studien (Leiden) = OTS
2 (1943), 18-34. - Dijkema/Dykema
5 (1948), 132-141. - Beek
8 (1950), 85-99. - Bentzen
19 (1974), 113-134. - van Leeuwen
21 (1981), 129-154. - Lust
23 (1984), 19-38. - Tromp

Pacific Theological Review (San Anselmo) 8 (Sum 76), 13-19. - Coote

Palastina-Jahrbuch 17 (1921), 31-46. - Sutterlin

Palestine Exploration Fund Quarterly Statement (London, 1869) 44 (1912), 159. - Farmer

Palestra del Clero 13, No. 1 (1934), 449-452. - Priero

Pastoralblatter 106 (1966), 418-434. - Schneider

PG
   66 (1864), cols 241-304. - Theodore
   71 (1859), cols 407-582. - Cyril
   81 (1859), cols 1663-1708. - Theodoret

PL
   21 (1867), cols 1057-1104. - Julian
   21 (1849), cols 1167-1172. - Julian
   25 (1865), cols 1037-1150. - Jerome
   28 (1865), cols 1089-1098. - Jerome

The Plain Truth 60, No. 1 (Jan 95), 20-21. - Earle

Poetics 15 (1986), 89-109. - Hardmeier

The Princeton Seminary Bulletin
   68, No. 2 (Aut 75), 90-93. - Gregoriew
   ns 11, No. 3 (1990), 240-252. - Freedman, D

Proceedings: Eastern Great Lakes and Midwest Biblical Societies 5 (1985), 81-86. - Jackson, J

R&E

   30 (1933), 284-295. - Sampsey
   63, No. 4 (Fall 66), 375-385. - Kelly, P
   63, No. 4 (Fall 66), 387-392. - Watts, JDW
   63, No. 4 (Fall 66), 393-403. - Williams, D
   63, No. 4 (Fall 66), 405-412. - Howington
   63, No. 4 (Fall 66), 413-425. - Francisco
   63, No. 4 (Fall 66), 427-428. - Francisco
   63, No. 4 (Fall 66), 429-440. - Owens
   72, No. 4 (Fall 75), 465-72. - Kelly, P

92, No. 2 (Spr 95), 147-151. - Nogalski
92, No. 2 (Spr 95), 153-167. - Hayes, J
92, No. 2 (Spr 95), 169-174. - Escobar
92, No. 2 (Spr 95), 189-193. - Watts, JDW
92, No. 2 (Spr 95), 195-206. - Loscalzo
92, No. 2 (Spr 95), 207-217. - Richardson, P

RB = *Revue Biblique*
9, No. 4 (1900), 586-594. - Condamin
10 (1901), 352-376. - Condamin
14 (ns 2), No. 2 (Ap '05), 163-187. - Hoonacker
26, Nos. 1&2 (Jan & Ap '17), 218-246. - Desnoyers
71, No. 2 (1964), 215-229. - Prignaud
80, No. 3 (July 73), 321-331. - Ouellette
87, No. 4 (1980), 481-513. - Vesco
93 (1986), 563-580. - Schenker
98, No. 2 (Ap 91), 170-189. - Dempster

Recherches de Science Religieuse (Paris) 20, No. 2 (1930), 298-311. - Condamin

Reformed Church Review 4 (1900), 308-311. - Zimmerman

Reformed Theological Review (Hawthorne, Victoria, Australia) 18, No. 1 (Feb 59), 1-6. - Maclean

Religion och Bibel (Lund) 25 (1966), 57-78. - Carlson

Religious Studies Review 7, No. 2 (Ap 81), 128-132. - Watts, JDW

Restoration Quarterly (Abilene, TX)
8, No. 3 (1965), 175-178. - Roberts
13, No. 1 (1970), 1-16. - Roberts
21, No. 3 (1978), 161-175. - Rector
25, No. 3 (1982), 158-166. - Snyder
29 (Abilene 1987), 193-208. - Moore
34, No. 3 (1992), 170-172. - Daniel, J

Revista Biblica (Buenos Aires)
45, ns 12, No. 4 (1983), 209-301. - Andinach

53, ns 44, No. 4 (1991), 217-229. - Alvarez Valdes

Revista de Interpretacion Biblica Latin-Americana = RIBLA

Revista Eclesiastica Brasileira (Brazil) 45 (1985). - Schwantes

Revista Teologica (Rio de Janeiro, Brazil) 2, No. 3 (June 86), 37-42. - Wright, S

Revue Archeologique (Paris) ns 2 (1971), 215-258. - Dentzer

Revue Biblique = RB

Revue d'histoire et de philosophie religieuses 35 (1955), 95-103. - Vermes

Revue de Sciences Religieuses 51, Nos. 2-3 (Ap-July 77), 169-186. - Coulot

Revue de Theologie et de Philosophie ns 5 (1917), 5-35. - Humbert

Revue des Etudes Juives (Louvain/Paris, 1880) = REJ
  44 (1902), 14ff. - Halevy
  137 (1978), 149-153. - Sperber

Revue Semitique 11 (1903), No. 1:1-31; No. 2:97-121; No. 3:193-209; No. 4:289-300; 12 (1904), No. 1:1-18. - Halevy

RIBLA: *Revista de Interpretacion Biblica Latinoamericana* (San Jose, Costa Rica)
  1 (1988), 87-99. - Schwantes
  11 (1992), 49-63. - Arango
  12 (1992), 69-81. - Reimer

Rivista Biblica (Buenos Aires) 1 (1972), 33-39. - Mallau

Rivista Biblica (Italy)
  9 (1961), 235-242. - Devescovi
  16 (1968), 129-142. - Boschi
  29, No. 2 (Ap-June 81), 147-176. - Spreafico

Rivista degli Studi Orientali (Rome)
16, No. 2 (1936), 178-183. - Zolli
28 (1953), 149-152. - Rinaldi

Rivista del Clero Italiano (Milan) 73 (1992), 590-599. - Maggioni

Roczniki Teologiczno-Kanoniczne: Annales de Theolgie et du Droit Canon (Lublin)
27, No. 1 (1980), 43-51. - Szwarc
35, No. 1 (1988), 5-14. - Szwarc

Ruch Biblijny (Cracow)
36, No. 2 (1983), 122-131. - Szwarc
43 (1990), 105-111. - Witaszek
44 (1991), 18-25. - Witaszek

Sal Terrae 9 (1920), 686-693, 804-811. - Perez

Salesianum 41, No. 3 (July-Sep 79), 425-440. - Loss

Schrift 52 (Aug 77), 132-137. - Janssen

Schweizerische Theologische Umschau 13, No. 5 (Dec '43), 108-115. - Maag

Schweizerische Theologische Z (Zurich)
30 (1913), No. 1:30-42; No. 2: 95-124; No. 3:152-170. - Baumgartner
34 (1917), No. 1:10-21; No. 2:68-79; No. 3:145-157; No. 4:190-208. - Kohler

Science et Esprit
21, No. 3 (1969), 435-441. - Beaucamp
27, No. 1 (Jan-Ap 75), 5-34. - Dion

Scripture (London/Edinburgh, 1946-68) 17, No. 40 (Oct 65), 109-116. - Alger
replaced by Scripture Bulletin

Scripture Bulletin 16, No. 2 (Sum 86), 26-32. - Dines

Der Seelsorger 24 (1954), 229-235, 273-278. - Sauermann

Sefarad (Madrid)
46 (1986), 333-344. - Morag
46 (1986), 381-390. - Orlinsky

Semeia 8 (1977), 51-74. - Williams, J

Semitics (Pretoria)
1 (1970), 27-37. - Crenshaw
3 (1973), 67-84. - Super

Shnaton (Jerusalem) 1 (1975), 129-149, xxiii. - Weisman

Shofar 12, No. 4 (Sum 91), 145-147. - Paul

Sinai 31 (1952), 253-264. - Weiser

Sinhak Sasang (Seoul) 65 (1989), 259-290. - Kim

Society of Biblical Archaeology, Proceedings (London) 23, No. 172 (Jan 1901), 36-38. - Oesterley

South East Asia J Theology (Singapore/Manila, 1959+)
1, No. 3 (Jan 60), 20-33. - Lempp
23, No. 2 (1982), 116-120. - Andrew, M

Southern Methodist Review 22 (1897), 75-92. - Newton

Southwestern Journal of Theology = SWJT

Stemmen voor Waarheid en Vrede
20 (1887), 531-559. - Zeijdner/ Zeydner
27 (1890), 613-634. - Zeijdner

Stimme der Gemeinde 24 (1972), 113-115, 145-146, 193-196, 225-227, 289-292. - Schottroff

Student World 57 [Issue No. 224], No. 2 (1964), 105-109. - Adler

Studien 1 (1875), 122-145. - Valeton

Studien und Mitteilungen aus dem Benedictiner- und Cistercienserorden 28, No. 2 (1907), 413-415. - Doller

Studies in Religion/Sciences Religieuses (Waterloo, Ontario) 11 (1982), 29-33. - Craigie

Studium Biblicum Franciscanum Liber Annuus (Jerusalem)
2 (1951-1952), 5-86. - Randellini
25 (1975), 90-103. - Cox

Svensk Exegetisk Arsbok (Lund) = SEA
16 (1951), 7-20. - Danell
33 (1968), 76-82. - Erlandssen

SWJT = *Southwestern Journal of Theology* (Fort Worth, 1917-1924; ns Oct 58)
5, No. 2 (Ap '21), 59-67. - Copass
9, No. 1 (Fall 66), 21-26. - Watts, JDW
9, No. 1 (Fall 66), 27-35. - Honeycutt
9, No. 1 (Fall 66), 37-48. - Walker
9, No. 1 (Fall 66), 49-56. - Smith, Ralph
9, No. 1 (Fall 66), 57-67. - Huey
9, No. 1 (Fall 66), 69-79. - Strange
38, No. 1 (Fall 95), 4-10. - Byargeon
38, No. 1 (Fall 95), 11-19. - Hall
38, No. 1 (Fall 95), 20-29. - Johnson
38, No. 1 (Fall 95), 29-35. - Pigott
38, No. 1 (Fall 95), 36-42. - Beyer
38, No. 1 (Fall 95), 44-48. -

Tarbiz
34, No. 2 (Jan 65), 107-128. No. 3 (Ap 65), 211-223. No. 4 (July 65), 303-318. Heb with Eng summary, pp. I-II of each issue. - Weiss
34 (July 65), 319-322, ii. - Loewenstamm
35, No. 4 (June 65), 301-303. - Talmon
36, No. 4 (July 67), 307-318. - Weiss

TE = *The Theological Educator* (New Orleans, 1967)
52 (Fall 95), 27-36. - Moore
52 (Fall 95), 37-45. - Mosley
52 (Fall 95), 47-56. - Byargeon
52 (Fall 95), 57-68. - Cole
52 (Fall 95), 69-78. - Brown
52 (Fall 95), 79-85. - Bailey

Teologisk Tidsskrift (Copenhagen) Series 4, Vol 9 (1928), 96-98. -
Boehmer

Theologia Evangelica (Pretoria)
7, No. 1 (Ap 74), 3-21. - Eybers
17, No. 3 (Sep 84), 57-58. - Goliath, A

Theologia y Vida 4 (1963), 23-35. - Moreno

Theologiai Szemle (Budapest)
15 (1972), 215-218. - Szabo
30 (1987), 35-37. - Veraszto

Theologie und Glaube 27 (1935), 686-695. - Junker

Theologisch Praktische Quartalschrift (Linz, Austria) 69, No. 1 (1916),
1-13. - Roesler

Theologisch Tijdschrift (Leiden)
14 (1880), 114-158. - Oort
25 (1891), 121-125. - Oort
25 (1891), 125-126. - Oort
34 (1900), 429-437. - Houtsma

Theologische Blatter 7, No. 7 (July '28), cols 177-182. - Weiser

Theologische Literaturzeitung = TLZ

Theologische Quartalschrift (Munich/Tubingen)
76, No. 4 (1894), 605-642, and, vol 77, No. 2 (1895), 209-229. -
Schulte
81, No. 4 (1899), 512-552. - Vetter

106 (1925), 308-335. - Fischer, J
151, No. 2 (1971), 134-145. - Mittmann

Theologische Rundschau 4, No. 4 (1932), 195-213. - Kohler

Theologische Studien
7 (1889), 222-228. - Schuurmans-Stekhoven
18 (1900), 193-225. - Gunning

Theologische Studien und Kritiken = TSK (Hamburg, 1828-1942)
22, No. 4 (1849), 869-914. - Dusterdieck
76 (1903), 35-47. - Boehmer
78, No. 3 (1905), 323-358. - Rothstein
83 (1910), 323-374. - Winter
100, No. 4 (1927-1928), 437-438. - Bauer, L

Theologische Z = TZ

Theology (London) 19, No. 113 (1929), 266-272. - Burkitt

Tidsskrift for teologi og kirke (Oslo) 2, no. 1 (1931), 111-127. - Seierstad

TLZ = *Theologische Literaturzeitung*
72 (1947), 143-152. - Wurthwein
79 (1954), 81-94. - Kahle
80, No. 3 (Mar 55), 179. - Osswald
94 (1969), 387-389. - Kuntz
96, No. 9 (Sep 71), 653-670. - Wagner

Today's Parish 21 (Oct 89), 27-28. - Craghan

Tradition (NY) 20, No. 4 (Wint 82), 327-331. - Shapiro

Transactions of the Glasgow University Oriental Society 17 (1959), 62-64. - Dobbie

Trierer Theologische Z
59 (1950), 4-13. - Junker
65, No. 6 (1956), 321-328. - Junker

95 (1986), 282-301. - Bohlen

TZ (Basel)
9, No. 2 (Mar/Ap 53), 81-92. - Stenzel
21, No. 4 (July-Aug 65), 318-328. - Amsler
23, No. 1 (Jan-Feb 67), 1-25. - Weiss
35 (1979), 321-341. - Berridge
48, Nos. 3&4 (1992), 315-328. - Dietrich

UF = *Ugarit-Forschungen* (Kevelaer/Neukirchen-Vluyn)
1 (1969), 65-70. - Fenton
6 (1974), 487-488. - Loretz
10 (1978), 434-435. - Dietrich
11 (1979), 371-377. - Herrmann
13 (1981), 127-135. - Loretz
24 (1992), 179-215. - Loretz
24 (1992), 217-248. - Loretz
25 (1993), 319-325. - Paas

Universalist Quarterly and General Review (Boston, 1844-1891), ns 11 (1874), 424-438. - Laurie

Verbum Caro 15 [Issue No. 60], No. 4 (1961), 390-398. - Keller

VD = *Verbum Domini* (Rome, 1-47 [1921-1969])
17 (1937), No. 3 (Mar 37), 82-87; No. 4 (Ap 37), 114-116. - Rinaldi
34 (1956), 202-210. - Bartina
36 (1958), 284-291. - Bouwman
Continued by Biblical Theology Bulletin

La Vie Spirituelle 74 (1946), 834-852; 75 (1946), 424-437. - Dumeste

The Virginia Seminary Magazine 3 (1889-1890), 161-170. - Crawford

Vortrag: Nach dem Gesetz u. Zeugnis 29 (1929-1930), 359-365, 425-435. - Moller

Vox Evangelica 6 (1969), 42-53. - Allen, L

VT
1, No. 4 (Oct 51), 293-296. - Bic
2, No. 2 (1952), 170-171. - Murtonen
3, No. 3 (July 53), 305-310. - Speier
4, No. 3 (1954), 276-295. - Reider
11, No. 2 (Ap 61), 228-231. - Rabinowitz
12, No. 4 (Oct 62), 417-438. - Gese
13, No. 2 (1963), 144-150. - Gluck
15, No. 1 (Jan 65), 1-15. - Brueggemann
16, No. 3 (July 66), 312-324. - Farr
16, No. 4 (Oct 66), 387-395. - Brunet
17, No. 3 (July 67), 266-297. - Haran
17, No. 4 (Oct 67), 430-463. - Gottlieb
19, No. 4 (Oct 69), 385-399. - Brueggemann
20, No. 1 (Jan 70), 108-112. - Howard, G
20, No. 3 (July 70), 287-303. - Mauchline
20, No. 4 (Oct 70), 496-500. - Muraoka
21, No. 3 (July 71), 338-362. - Boyle
22, No. 1 (Jan 72), 107-110. - Holladay
25, No. 2a (May 75), 286-297. - Barstad
25, No. 2a (May 75), 500-524. - Szabo
27, No. 1 (Jan 77), 117-125. - Puech
27, No. 2 (Ap 77), 209-212. - Hoffmann
28, No. 3 (July 78), 358-359. - Paul, S
30, No. 1 (1980), 67-80. - Story
31, No. 4 (1981), 482-488. - Lang
33, No. 3 (July 83), 341-347. - Pfeifer
34, No. 1 (Jan 84), 106-108. - Mulder
34, No. 4 (Oct 84), 476-481. - Pfeifer
34, No. 4 (Oct 84), 481-482. - Segert
35, No. 1 (1985), 98-99. - Bronznick
36, No. 2 (1986), 129-145. - Geyer
36, No. 2 (Ap 86), 246-248. - Smelik
37, No. 1 (Jan 87), 26-38. - Fritz
37, No. 3 (July 87), 327-339. - Pfeifer
38, No. 2 (Ap 88), 230-233. - Pfeifer
38, No. 1 (Jan 88), 22-40. - Gosse
39, No. 1 (Jan 89), 13-22. - Kessler
39, No. 2 (Ap 89), 240-242. - Loretz
39, No. 3 (July 89), 341-354. - Stoebe

39, No. 4 (Oct 89), 497-503. - Pfeifer
41, No. 1 (Jan 91), 123-127. - Pfeifer
41, No. 4 (Oct 91), 475-481. - Pfeifer
43, No. 1 (Jan 93), 88-101. - Rosel
43, No. 3 (July 93), 411-418. - Nogalski
43, No. 4 (Oct 93), 433-441. - Asen
44, No. 3 (July 94), 393-396. - Cathcart
44, No. 4 (Oct 94), 559-562. - Snyman
45, No. 1 (Jan 95), 45-61. - Dell
45, No. 3 (July 95), 307-317. - Levin
46, No. 1 (Jan 96), 56-73. - O'Connell

VTS
15 (1966), 193-206. - Kapelrud
16 (1967), 279-283. - Segert
26 (1974), 55-63. - Schoville
32 (1981). - Gese
34 (1984). - Barstad

Die Welt des Orients 6, No. 2 (1971), 189-204. Amos 1:9-10. - Muller, Hans

Wesleyan Studies in Religion (Buckhannon, WV)
62 (1969-70), 5-11. - Richardson
62 (1969-1970), 13-17. - Sanders

Wort und Dienst (Bielefeld)
5 (1957), 160-181. - Stoebe
10 (1969), 85-103. - Schmid
18 (1985), 49-71. - Hardmeier

Yediot/Yedio's Bahaqirat Eretz-Isael Weatiqoteha (Jerusalem) 30 (1966), 56-69. - Haran

Z fur wissenschaftliche Theologie 44, No. 1 (1901), 11-73. - Hirscht

ZAW (Giessen)
3, No. 1 (1883), 87-126. - Hoffmann
3, No. 2 (1883), 219-272. - Vollers
3, No. 2 (1883), 279-280. - Hoffmann

4, No. 1 (1884), 1-20. - Vollers
5, No. 2 (1885), 179-184. - Buhl
7, No. 2 (1887), 177-202. - Cornill
20, No. 3 (1900), 332. - Riedel
30, No. 1 (1910), 37-41. - Budde
31, No. 1 (1911), 1-43. - Duhm
31, No. 2 (1911), 81-110. - Duhm
31, No. 3 (1911), 161-204. - Duhm
32, No. 2 (1912), 274-277. - Lohmann
33, No. 1 (1913), 78-80. - Baumgartner
33, No. 3 (1913), 265-271. - Albert
34, No. 1 (1914), 42-44. - Praetorius
35, No. 1 (1915), 12-25. - Praetorius
35, No. 1 (1915), 62-63. - Elhorst
38, No. 1 (1919), 105-111. - Volz
39, No. 2 (1921), 218-229. - Budde
46, ns 5, No. 1 (1928), 49-59. - Weiser
47, No. 1 (1929), 17-44. - Baumann
47, No. 1 (1929), 45-54. - Horst
50, ns 9, No. 4 (1932), 221-239. - Krause
52, ns 11, No. 1 (1934), 22-41. - Seierstad
53, No. 1 (1935), 90-129. - Wolfe
60, Nos. 1-3 (1944), 107-131. - Ziegler
62, Nos. 1-2 (1950), 10-52. - Wurthwein
64, ns 23, No. 1 (1952), 62. - Baumann
66, ns 25, No. 3 (1954), 314-315. - Driver, G
68, ns 27, Nos. 1-3 (1956), 1-17. - Hesse
68, ns 27, Nos. 1-3 (1956), 17-24. - Hyatt
69, No. 1 (1957), 55-69. - Gese
75, No. 2 (1963), 155-175. - Fensham
77, No. 2 (1965), 168-193. - Schmidt, W
78, No. 3 (1966), 292-316. - Neubauer
79, No. 1 (1967), 42-52. - Crenshaw
79, No. 1 (1967), 82-83. - Schwantes
80, No. 2 (1968), 203-215. - Crenshaw
81, No. 3 (1969), 384-387. - Hobbs
82, No. 1 (1970), 117-121. - Soggin
82, No. 1 (1970), 121-122. - Hoffmann
82, No. 3 (1970), 341-346. - Hoffmann
85, No. 2 (1973), 226-227. - Rendtorff

86, No. 4 (1974), 393-403. - Bjorndalen
86, No. 3 (1974), 504-537. - Koch
88, No. 1 (1976), 56-71. - Pfeifer
91, No. 3 (1979), 423-435. - Osten-Sacken
92, No. 3 (1980), 397-404. - Brooke
93, No. 1 (1981), 37-50. - Hoffmann
93, No. 3 (1981), 439-443. - Pfeifer
94, No. 3 (1982), 413-415. - Hoffken
96, No. 1 (1984), 112-118. - Pfeifer
97, No. 2 (1985), 233-244. - Bracke
98, No. 3 (1986), 434-435. - Jackson
100, No. 1 (1988), 70-81. - Borger
100, Supplement (1988), 123-138. - Jeremias
100, No. 2 (1988), 269-277. - Pfeifer
100, No. 3 (1988), 413-415. - Rottzoll
101, No. 2 (1989), 286-289. - Loretz
106, No. 3 (1994), 434-445. - Waschke
108, No. 1 (1996), 55-69. - Rupprecht

Z des Deutschen Palastina-Vereins 52 (1929), 141-148. - Sellin

Z fur Althebraistik (Stuttgart)
3, No. 2 (1990), 214-220. - Soden, von
6 (1993), 235-238. - Pfeifer

Z fur die Neutestamentliche Wissenschaft und di Kunde de Alteren
Kirche 82, Nos. 1/2 (1991), 67-87. - Van de Sandt

Z fur Theologie und Kirche
55, No. 2 (1958), 145-169. - Lehming
57, No. 1 (1960), 1-16. - Gunneweg
82, No. 3 (1985), 281-299. - Zobel

AUTHOR/EDITOR INDEX

Persons not listed in alphabetical order of the text: editors, second authors, et al. References are to entry number.

SCRIPTURE INDEX

References are to entry number.

SUBJECT INDEX

Several ubiquitous terms are left out, e.g., exegesis, Israel. References are to entry number.